CONTRACT LAW IN THE SOUTH PACIFIC

CONTRACT LAW IN THE SOUTH PACIFIC

Jennifer Corrin

2nd edition

INTERSENTIA

Intersentia Ltd
8 Wellington Mews
Wellington Street | Cambridge
CB1 1HW | United Kingdom
Tel.: +44 1223 736 170
Email: mail@intersentia.co.uk
www.intersentia.com | www.intersentia.co.uk

Distribution for the UK and Ireland:
NBN International
Airport Business Centre, 10 Thornbury Road
Plymouth, PL6 7PP
United Kingdom
Tel.: +44 1752 202 301 | Fax: +44 1752 202 331
Email: orders@nbninternational.com

Distribution for Europe and all other countries:
Intersentia Publishing nv
Groenstraat 31
2640 Mortsel
Belgium
Tel.: +32 3 680 15 50 | Fax: +32 3 658 71 21
Email: mail@intersentia.be

Distribution for the USA and Canada:
Independent Publishers Group
Order Department
814 North Franklin Street
Chicago, IL 60610
USA
Tel.: +1 800 888 4741 (toll free) | Fax: +1 312 337 5985
Email: orders@ipgbook.com

Contract Law in the South Pacific. 2nd edition

Artwork on cover: Seb Antoniou / sebantoniou.com

ISBN 978-1-78068-786-5
D/2020/7849/10
NUR 822

British Library Cataloguing in Publication Data. A catalogue record for this book is available from the British Library.

FOREWORD

The only criticism I have of this prodigious work is that the author has underplayed its significance. Tchaikovsky was worried sick when he started composing his Sixth Symphony that he had lost his creative flair and that it would be a flop. But it turned out to be one his greatest works. So it is with Jennifer Corrin who prefaces her wonderful second edition of *Contract Law in the South Pacific* with the misleading and slightly self-deprecating statement that it is 'designed primarily for students studying contract law in the South Pacific'. As if practitioners might consider glancing at it on the odd occasion if they have nothing better to do with their time.

No. This is not just a student textbook. It is an essential, invaluable and accessible tool for every lawyer in the South Pacific or any lawyer anywhere dealing with the South Pacific. That includes, especially, magistrates and judges. No one with a legal issue, whether in business, in private practice or in the public sector, or whether they are a bush lawyer in a village considering how to deal with a dispute over an agreement to sell customary land to a neighbour or a foreign enterprise, can gain an understanding of their legal rights and obligations, or those of their clients, or those of government, without an appreciation of the law of contract, as it applies in this region.

They will not find the answers in *Halsbury's Laws of England* or in any conventional contract text. Nor will they find them on the internet, easily. The answers are most likely to be found in this book; or at least there will be signposts to resolution.

The author sets out the basic principles in an agreeable and familiar way. For those of us raised on a diet of offer, acceptance and consideration, chapter headings such as 'Formation of Agreement', 'Acceptance', 'Intention to Create Legal Relations' and 'Privity of Contract' are instantly recognisable. We feel comfortable with the chapter outline, a valuable research tool in itself as it extends for 19 pages. The content of each of the 20 chapters is summarised in a helpful and informative way, providing users (not necessarily readers, as not many of us will have the time to read the book as if we are reading a novel) with the tools necessary to get down to the nitty-gritty of case law and statute law on all manner of contract issues.

We are often reminded by the author that a knowledge of the common law of England and Wales, alone, is only a first step when addressing any contractual issue in the South Pacific. Each jurisdiction has an independent legislature.

Statute law is an important modifier of the common law of contract. Lest we lapse in to a state of ignorant bliss and forget that were dealing with a myriad of disparate, dynamic and evolving cultures, Chapter 2, 'Contract and Customary Laws', has been introduced to edify us, and it does that in a profound and pithy way. While it is a pleasant thought that there is, or we should strive to achieve, a unified body of jurisprudence that can be called the contract law of the South Pacific, it does not exist and it is unlikely ever to exist, so it is not a useful endeavour to pretend otherwise or to strive to bring it into existence.

The five tables in the opening chapters are concise ready-reckoners of critical information essential to appreciating the interplay of common law, statute law and customary law that combine to form the body of contract law for each of the jurisdictions covered by this book.

It is particularly pleasing that Papua New Guinea (PNG) has been brought within the fold of this second edition. PNG is integral to the South Pacific. It is the most populous country in the region and it may well be the most litigious. There is a rich body of contract law, some of it home-grown, already in PNG; and its growth and maturity will be engendered by this work.

While there are separate legal systems in this part of the world, they are connected inextricably and symbiotically by the strength and endurance of their underlying cultures and traditions and the commonality of their historical development. While a significant decision by the Court of Appeal of Fiji on a thorny issue of contract law will not be binding on other courts in the region, it will be potentially of enormous persuasive value, if that issue is raised in another country in the region – and if the Fiji decision is known about.

This book is a terrific feat of scholarship. More than that, it is a work of great practical utility. No advocate in any court in the South Pacific should appear in a contract case ever again without checking this book first.

Justice David Cannings CBE
Judge of the National Court and the Supreme Court
of Papua New Guinea

PREFACE

This book examines the principles of contract law that apply in the island countries of the South Pacific. It identifies the common law and statutes that govern that law within the member countries of the University of the South Pacific, that is, Cook Islands, Fiji, Kiribati, Marshall Islands, Nauru, Niue, Samoa, Solomon Islands, Tokelau, Tonga, Tuvalu, and Vanuatu. This second edition also looks at the relevant law in Papua New Guinea.

Like many other branches of the law, contract law has yet to establish its own identity in the region. There is limited evidence of the emergence of a local jurisprudence, through either national parliaments or the courts. However, there are significant differences between South Pacific contract laws and those of England and Wales. This divergence is partly a result of legislative developments in the law of contract in England and Wales, which do not necessarily apply in the region. It is also the result of regional innovation in the form of legislative changes, particularly in the form of consumer protection legislation. In addition, there is some divergence in the common law, where local courts have, on occasion, departed from English decisions or applied them in the context of local factors. In some cases, the courts have followed the law in other parts of the Commonwealth and, for this reason, the book makes reference to the contract law of countries such as Australia and New Zealand. In a small number of cases, regional courts have begun to develop a unique jurisprudence more suited to local circumstances, and these decisions are highlighted in the text.

The phrase 'South Pacific contract law' is used in this book to distinguish regional law from that of England and Wales, rather than to denote a uniform law of contract in the South Pacific. There are significant differences between the contract laws of individual countries within the region. These differences are partly the result of diverging approaches taken by regional courts, particularly in how far each is prepared to depart from the common law of England and Wales. They are also the result of Pacific countries having disparate legislation in force, both in the form of different statutes introduced from overseas and of legislative innovation by some regional parliaments. These regional laws are compared and their distinguishing features discussed.

Divergence in the law of contract is also a consequence of the prevalence of customary laws, which often impact upon agreements and disputes at the village level. The status and application of customary laws differs from country to country in the region. In countries where customary laws are recognised as a source of state law, they may have effect outside the village setting. In this second edition, this inter-relationship between customary laws and state law and the question of whether there is a customary law of contract are explored in an entirely new chapter.

This book is designed primarily for students studying contract law in the South Pacific. However, it is also intended as a source of reference for courts, lawyers, and individuals interested in exploring contract law as it operates in the South Pacific. Whilst contract law is still rooted in the common law of England and Wales, foreign textbooks on contract law are not adequate to cater for regional law students or lawyers. As mentioned in the preface to the first edition, breaking away from such texts encourages research into South Pacific law and provides a platform for the development of a regional jurisprudence, more in accord with local circumstances and culture. Whilst Pacific island countries 'saved' foreign law on independence, they did so as a transitional measure and did not intend to be bound forever to English law or academic works.

Thanks are due to Intersentia, the publisher of this edition, for the display of confidence in this area of publishing and for the editorial assistance. I should also like to thank my mentor, Professor Tony Angelo, and the Faculty of Law at Victoria University Wellington, where I conducted most of the research for this book. I must also thank those Pacific lawyers who have answered my queries about the law in force, in particular, Mr Nicholas Mirou at the University of Papua New Guinea, and my colleagues at the School of Law at the University of the South Pacific. The School kindly hosted my visit in July this year, during which I worked on the final stages of this book. Finally, I must acknowledge the contribution of my brilliant research assistant, Anna Kretowicz, for all her help in bringing this edition to fruition.

Jennifer Corrin
6 November 2019

CONTENTS

LIST OF CASES

LIST OF LEGISLATION

AUSTRALIA

COOK ISLANDS

EUROPE

FIJI

FRANCE

KIRIBATI

MARSHALL ISLANDS

NAURU

NEW ZEALAND

NIUE

PAPUA NEW GUINEA

SAMOA

SINGAPORE

SOLOMON ISLANDS

TOKELAU

TONGA

TUVALU

UGANDA

UNITED KINGDOM

VANUATU

CHAPTER 1
INTRODUCTION

1. INTRODUCTION

This book deals with the general principles of contract law that apply in the island countries of the South Pacific.[1] Like many other branches of the law, contract law has yet to establish its own identity in the region. It is still based on the law of England,[2] with limited evidence of the emergence of a local jurisprudence, either through national parliaments or courts. However, there are significant differences between English and South Pacific contract laws. Divergence is partly a result of legislative reforms and developments in the common law of contract in England, which do not necessarily apply in the region due to countries having specified different cut-off dates,[3] after which English laws no longer apply. It is also the result of regional innovation in the form of legislative changes and local case law. In some instances, the courts have followed the law in other parts of the Commonwealth and, in a small number of cases, they have begun to develop a unique jurisprudence more suited to local circumstances.[4] In Tonga, it was stated in *Leiola Group Ltd v Moengangongo*,[5] a case relating to an employment contract, that the common law of England was to be applied, 'with such modifications as may be required by these provisions which focus attention on the circumstances prevailing in the Kingdom of Tonga'. Similarly, in *RSI Holdings (Samoa) Ltd v Attorney-General*,[6] the court held that in determining the contractual dispute and considering discretionary remedies, it was for the Samoan courts 'to apply Samoan standards, needs, resources, and the like'.

Divergence is also a consequence of the prevalence of customary laws, which often govern agreements and disputes at the village level. In countries

---

1 The countries included are Cook Islands, Fiji, Kiribati, Marshall Islands, Nauru, Niue, Papua New Guinea, Solomon Islands, Tokelau, Tonga, Tuvalu, Samoa, and Vanuatu.

2 See further J. Corrin and D. Paterson, *Introduction to South Pacific Law*, 4th ed., Intersentia, Cambridge 2017, pp. 24, 32–34.

3 See below for the definition of the term 'cut-off date'. See further J. Corrin and D. Paterson, above n. 2, pp. 22, 39–40.

4 See further J. Corrin and D. Paterson, above n. 2, pp. 6–11.

5 [2010] TOCA 10, [11].

6 [2012] WSSC 130, [77] et seq.

where customary laws are formally recognised as a source of law[7] they may also have effect outside the village setting. Whether there is a customary law of contract is a contentious question, and is discussed more fully in chapter 2.

There are also significant differences between the contract laws in each of the regional countries, and the phrase 'South Pacific contract law' is used in this book to distinguish regional law from that of England and Wales, rather than to denote a uniform law of contract in the South Pacific. These differences are partly the result of diverging approaches taken by regional courts, particularly in how far they are prepared to depart from the common law of England. They are also the result of countries having specified different cut-off dates from each other, and of legislative innovation by some regional parliaments, both in the form of new legislation and amendments to laws introduced from overseas. The status and application of customary laws also differs from country to country.[8]

This book examines the general principles of contract law applying throughout the USP region. It compares the laws of individual countries, highlighting their distinguishing features. It also highlights significant differences between the regional law of contract and the contract law of England. Some reference is also made to the contract laws of Australia and New Zealand, particularly where regional courts have preferred that law to the law of England.

2. DEFINITION OF A CONTRACT AND THE LAW OF CONTRACT

A contract is a legally binding agreement made between two or more people who intend it to have legal effect. It therefore requires two things:

- an agreement; and
- legal enforceability.

Additionally, it is important to consider:

- the terms of the agreement;
- what constitutes a breach; and
- the remedies for a breach.

7 See the comments in *RSI Holdings (Samoa) Ltd v Attorney-General* [2012] WSSC 130, [77]. See further J. Corrin and D. Paterson, above n. 2, chapter 3.

8 See section 3.4.

The law of contract is the law that governs legal enforceability and governs these three considerations. As described by Anson, it is, 'that branch of law which determines the circumstances in which a promise shall be legally binding on the person making it'.[9] But the boundaries and content of the law of contract, and whether there can be said to be one general law governing all contracts, is a matter of dispute.[10]

In addition to the general principles of contract, which are the subject matter of this book, particular rules apply to particular types of contract, such as sale of goods contracts, insurance contracts, employment contracts, shipping contracts and construction contracts. Some of these are referred to or discussed, but the more specialised commercial laws are not covered.

3. SOURCES OF CONTRACT LAW IN THE SOUTH PACIFIC REGION

Having looked at what contract law is, it is important to understand the sources of contract law in the South Pacific. This section seeks to answer the question, 'where does the law of contract come from?'.

3.1. COMMON LAW AND EQUITY

In common law countries, contract is a 'common law' subject.[11] That is, it is derived from judicial decisions, as opposed to Acts of Parliament.[12] Equity also plays an important role in the law of contract. Equity consists of rules originally made by the Lord Chancellor, and then by the English Court of Chancery, to assist in ameliorating the rigidity and harshness of the English common law.

The cases that establish the principles of contract applying in common law countries are mainly English. Most of them are from the nineteenth and twentieth century, having developed to accommodate the growth in commerce and the changes brought about by the industrial revolution in Britain. The common law of contract is continuing to develop through modern cases,

---

9 J. Beatson, A. Burrows and J. Cartwright, *Anson's Law of Contract*, 30th ed., Oxford University Press, Oxford 2016, pp. 1–2.

10 See e.g. M.P. Furmston (ed.), *Cheshire, Fifoot and Furmston's Law of Contract*, 17th ed., Oxford University Press, Oxford 2017, pp. 30–31.

11 See A.L. Diamond, 'Codification of Contract Law' (1968) 31 *Modern Law Review* 361 for a discussion of the merits of codification of contract law.

12 See further M. Arnheim (ed.), *Common Law*, Ashgate, Dartmouth 1994.

not only in England, but also throughout the Commonwealth and in other common law countries. It is therefore important to know whether, and to what extent, the cases that embody modern developments apply in the South Pacific.

Generally, common law and equity apply throughout the region, apart from in Niue, where it has been replaced by the common law of Niue.[13] In most countries it is the English common law (and equity) which has been adopted as part of the law.[14] For example, in Papua New Guinea, the Supreme Court has recently stated in *National Capital District Commission v Yama Security Services Ltd*[15] that 'it is the common law of England, not that of Australia, which forms a constitutionally stipulated foundation of our underlying law'. Similarly, in Tonga it was stated in *Leiola Group Ltd v Moengangongo*[16] that the common law of England was to be applied.

However, in Samoa it has been held that the courts are free to choose from amongst common law principles as developed throughout the Commonwealth.[17] There is frequent reference to New Zealand case law.[18] In *RSI Holdings (Samoa) Ltd v Attorney-General*[19] the court stated that 'Samoan Courts ordinarily refer to New Zealand … extended to the United Kingdom and Australia for determination of common law and equity cases'.

On occasion, the courts in Fiji have also shown an inclination to follow Australian and New Zealand contract precedents in preference to the English law.[20] In *Nair v Public Trustee of Fiji and the Attorney-General of Fiji*,[21] Lyons J said:

> In my opinion the future of the law in Fiji is that it is to develop its own independent route and relevance, taking into account its uniqueness and perhaps looking to Australia and New Zealand for more of its direction. This certainly is the implication when reading s 100(3) of the Constitution[22] which establishes that the customary law of Fiji shall become part of the overall body of law of this country and further, as to the later assertion, this was the sentiment expressed by the Chief Justice when convening the Supreme Court. Thus it is timely that this modern doctrine of equitable

---

13 Interpretation Act 2004 (Niue), s 4(e).
14 See further J. Corrin and D. Paterson, above n. 2, pp. 37–38.
15 [2017] PGSC 34.
16 [2010] TOCA 10, [11].
17 *Olo v Police* [1992] WSSC 1.
18 See e.g. *Keil v Digicel (Samoa)* [2010] WSSC 93; *RSI Holdings (Samoa) Ltd v Attorney-General* [2012] WSSC 130, [77].
19 [2012] WSSC 130, [77] et seq.
20 See e.g. *Attorney-General of Fiji v Pacoil Fiji Ltd* [1996] FJCA 9, 16, where the Court of Appeal cited with approval the Australian case law on estoppel; see also the reference to New Zealand case law, at 20.
21 Unreported, High Court, Fiji, Lyons J, 8 March 1996, 24.
22 This section appears in the Constitution of Fiji 1990, which has since been repealed by the Constitution of the Republic of Fiji Islands 2013, which does not contain a similar section.

> estoppel as formulated and approved by the High Court of Australia and the Court of Appeal of New Zealand be incorporated into the law of Fiji ...[23]

More recently, in *Prasad v Sunrise Corporation Ltd*,[24] the Fiji Court of Appeal referred to the 'Anglo-Australian law' relating to transaction of business in the corporate name prior to incorporation and stated that there was no reason to suppose that the law of Fiji was any different.[25] In *Digicel (Fiji) v Fiji Rugby Union*,[26] the Supreme Court referred to both Australian and English authority and commented that they were, 'two jurisdictions that follow the Common law of England as does Fiji'.[27] It seems, therefore, that English cases are still regarded as highly persuasive, if not binding, and may be the first to be called on in consideration of traditional areas of common law.[28]

New Zealand precedents are often followed in countries which it formerly administered. An example can be found in *Framhein v Tepaki Investments Ltd*,[29] where the High Court of Cook Islands applied the approach of the New Zealand Court of Appeal in holding that contracts could be interpreted by reference to subsequent events. In Marshall Islands, American common law is more relevant.[30] In cases dealt with under French law in Vanuatu, whilst there is no system of binding precedent, jurisprudence may be of persuasive value.[31]

In all countries of the region there are conditions on the application of the common law. Generally, these are that:

- the principles must be consistent with the Constitution and Acts of Parliament; and
- they must be applicable to local circumstances.

Accordingly, principles of common law may be altered or excluded by local statute. They may also be discarded by regional courts, if they are inapplicable

23 The Court of Appeal appeared to agree on this: *Public Trustee of Fiji v Nair* [1997] FJCA 55.
24 [2005] FJCA 23.
25 Ibid., [18]. See also *Ward v Chandra* [2016] FJSC 30.
26 [2016] FJSC 40.
27 Ibid., [78].
28 See e.g. *Mani v Mani* [2017] FJCA 63, where the Court of Appeal referred only to English cases in discussing offer and acceptance.
29 [2007] CKHC 7.
30 Constitution of Marshall Islands 1979, Art. XIII continues in force 1980 1 TTC 103, which applied the American law as expressed in the American Law Institutes Restatement or as generally understood to the Trust Territories. See e.g. *Minaj Holdings Ltd v International Maritime Trading Company Ltd* [2012] MHHC 2.
31 L. Cohen-Tanugi, 'Case Law in a Legal System Without Binding Precedent: The French Example' [2016] *Stanford Law School China Guiding Cases Project Commentary No. 17* <http://cgc.law.stanford.edu/commentaries/17-Laurent-Cohen-Tanugi> accessed 20.02.2019. See also *Pentecost Pacific Ltd and Phillipe Pentecost v Hnaloane* (1980–88) 1 VLR 134 (CA), discussed in section 3.2.

to the circumstances of the country in question.[32] For example, in *Australia and New Zealand Banking Group Ltd v Ale*[33] the Supreme Court, considering the English common law doctrine of unjust enrichment, held that the 'courts of Western Samoa should not be bogged down by academic niceties that have little relevance to real life'.[34] On this basis, the Supreme Court dismissed the argument that civil disputes must fall into either contract or tort, and adopted the United States approach of not distinguishing the form or nature of a gain received. Another example is *Tonolei Development Corporation Ltd v Waka*,[35] where the rules of acceptance were modified to take into account the fact that there was no local postal service in Papua New Guinea.

Regional circumstances may also affect the weight to be given to evidence when a court is applying the common law. For example, in *Maeaniani v Saemala*,[36] Daly CJ said, in the context of a plea of *non est factum*:[37]

> I venture to suggest that a Solomon Islands Court would always approach the evidence as befits this nation rather than as befits a country at a different stage of development.

Theoretically, the ability to reject a principle of common law on the basis that it is inapplicable to local circumstances renders the distinction between English common law and common law developed elsewhere in the Commonwealth largely academic, as a regional court which prefers a Commonwealth authority may justify following it on the grounds that the English common law is inapplicable to local circumstances.[38] In practice, courts rarely consider this question, and tend to assume that common law principles are applicable, and only occasionally draw a distinction between the common law as it has developed in different jurisdictions.[39]

In addition to the general conditions on the application of English common law, in some countries there is a cut-off date after which, theoretically, new

---

32 The Law Reform Commission of Papua New Guinea has expressed the view that the law of contract generally is unsuitable for the circumstances of Papua New Guinea: Law Reform Commission of Papua New Guinea, *Fairness of Transactions*, Report No. 6, December 1977, 5. See further chapter 2.

33 [1980–3] WSLR 468.

34 Ibid., 469.

35 [2002] PNGLR 36. See further D.K. Srivastava, 'Case Note: *Tonolei Development Corporation Ltd. v. Lucas Waka*' (1982) 10 *Melanesian Law Journal* 175.

36 [1982] SILR 70.

37 *Non est factum* is discussed in chapter 14.

38 For Australian and New Zealand examples of circumstances justifying departure from English common law on the basis of inapplicability see *Australian Consolidated Press v Uren* [1969] 1 AC 118 and *Invercargill City Council v Hamlin* [1996] 2 WLR 367.

39 See e.g. *R v Loumia* [1984] SILR 51, where the common law on provocation was applied without consideration of local circumstances. For an example of a case where applicability was considered, see e.g. *Naki v AGC (Pacific) Ltd* [2005] PGNC 163.

English judicial decisions will not form part of the law. In some countries there is no cut-off date and in others the position is unclear. The dates that appear to apply in the countries under discussion can be seen in Table 1.

Table 1. Cut-off dates for judicial decisions

Country	Cut-off Date
Cook Islands	14 January 1840[40]
Fiji	2 January 1875[41]
Kiribati	No cut-off date[42]
Marshall Islands	Not applicable
Nauru	31 January 1968[43]
Niue	English common law no longer applies[44]
Papua New Guinea	16 September 1975[45]
Samoa	Unclear[46]
Solomon Islands	7 July 1978[47]
Tokelau	No cut-off date[48]
Tonga	No cut-off date[49]
Tuvalu	No cut-off date[50]
Vanuatu	30 July 1980[51]

Source: Compiled by the author.

The effect of the legislative provisions imposing a 'cut-off' date is not to render the introduced common law made after the date specified irrelevant. Such decisions are highly persuasive, and in practice the regional courts will nearly always follow such decisions. Further, in Papua New Guinea, it has been held that an English decision made after the cut-off date that corrects an error in the common law is binding, as opposed to a case which develops the common law,

40 Cook Islands Act 1915 (NZ), s 615.
41 Supreme Court Ordinance 1876, s 35.
42 Laws of Kiribati Act 1989, s 6(1).
43 Custom and Adopted Laws Act 1971, s 4. Cf. *Detabene v Ronphos* [2011] NRSC 9.
44 Interpretation Act 2004, s 4.
45 Constitution of Papua New Guinea 1975, Sch. 2.2(1).
46 Constitution of Samoa, Art. 111(1) suggests that there is no cut-off date, but the Supreme Court has held that it is 1 January 1962: *Okesene v Rossi* [2010] WSSC 92.
47 Constitution of Solomon Islands, Sch. 3 para. 4(1).
48 Tokelau Act 1948, s 4B(1). But see *Suveinakama v Council for the Ongoing Government of Tokelau* [2019] TKHC 1 [31], which refers to counsel's argument that there is a cut-off date of 1996.
49 Civil Law Act 1966, s 3; Evidence Act, s 166.
50 Laws of Tuvalu Act Cap 1.06, s 6(1).
51 Constitution of Vanuatu, Art. 93(2).

which is not.[52] Similarly, the Court of Appeal in Solomon Islands has expressly held that English decisions made after the cut-off date will be binding if they are merely declaratory of the pre-existing law.[53] It is only decisions that make new law that do not become part of the law, and this is a rare occurrence. Further, once a superior regional court has followed an English decision it will be binding on lower courts of that country in accordance with the doctrine of precedent, whether it was decided before or after any cut-off date.[54] This also appears to be the approach in Nauru, where, in *Detabene v Ronphos*,[55] the Supreme Court accepted that the English law on unjust enrichment was as declared in *Lipkin v Karpnale Ltd*,[56] a case decided in 1991, well after the 1968 cut-off date.

In Papua New Guinea, as discussed further in chapter 2, common law and equity are subordinate to the underlying law, which derived primarily from customary law. However, as explained by Cannings J in *Naki v AGC (Pacific) Ltd*,[57] '[t]he Courts have, generally, not seen a great need to formulate new rules and develop the underlying law where contractual principles are involved'.

3.2. FOREIGN LEGISLATION

Statute plays an increasing role in regulating contracts, but the law remains predominantly judge-made law. One area where parliaments have intervened is consumer law, where legislation has been passed to protect consumers in their dealings with commercial bodies. There have also been a number of statutes passed to remedy particular defects in the common law.

Just as in the case of the common law and equity, it is important to know whether English Acts regulating the law of contract are binding in South Pacific countries. Generally, English Acts apply throughout the region, apart from in Niue, Marshall Islands, Samoa, Tokelau and Tonga. The statutes introduced in the region are normally specified to be those 'of general application in force in England'. This imposes a threshold condition: if an English Act is not of 'general application' it will not be part of the law. Unfortunately, the term 'general application' is not defined.[58] It has received some judicial attention within the region, but the case law is conflicting. In *Indian Printing and*

---

52 *The State v Pokia* [1980] PNGLR 97; *Waghi Savings and Loans Society Ltd v Bank of South Pacific Ltd* [1980] PGSC 4.

53 *Cheung v Tanda* [1984] SILR 108.

54 For an example of a case where a lower court was reprimanded for not following the doctrine of precedent, see *New Britain Palm Oil Ltd v Sukuramu* [2008] PGSC 29.

55 [2011] NRSC 9.

56 [1991] 2 AC 548.

57 [2005] PGNC 163.

58 See further J. Corrin and D. Paterson, above n. 2, pp. 35–37.

Publishing Co v Police,[59] the Supreme Court of Fiji interpreted the condition as distinguishing between public statutes not necessarily binding upon all the population, for example the Companies Act or the Friendly Societies Act, and public statutes which are binding upon everyone, for example the Offenses against the Person Act.

In *Harrisen v Holloway*,[60] the Court of Appeal appear to have been of the view that to be an Act of general application, the subject matter of the Act must be organised in the same way in Vanuatu as it is in England. In *R v Ngena*,[61] the High Court of Solomon Islands defined a statute of general application as 'one that regulates conduct or conditions which exist among humanity generally and in a way applicable to humanity generally'. They distinguished this from an Act that is 'restricted to regulating conduct or conditions peculiar to or in a way applicable only to persons, activities or institutions in the United Kingdom.'[62] The definition of general application applied in *R v Ngena* was followed by the High Court of Tuvalu in *In the Matter of the Constitution of Tuvalu and of the Laws of Tuvalu Act 1987*.[63] It could be applied equally in other countries of the region and has the advantage that it is less likely to lead to the same Act being interpreted as being of general application in one country, but not in others.[64]

In addition to being of general application, statutes, like common law, are subject to conditions on their application:

- The provisions must be consistent with the Constitution and/or other local Acts of Parliament.
- They must be applicable to local circumstances.

In most countries of the region, there is a 'cut-off' date after which English statutes no longer apply. The dates that appear to apply in the countries under discussion can be seen in Table 2.

59 (1932) 3 FLR 142.

60 (1980–88) 1 VLR 147.

61 [1983] SILR 1.

62 Reference in this case was to the United Kingdom, rather than England, because, as mentioned, it is Acts of the United Kingdom that are continued in force by the Constitution of Solomon Islands. In countries where English Acts are continued in force, no doubt England would be the country of reference.

63 Unreported, High Court, Tuvalu, Donne CJ, 1989.

64 See, for example, the Administration of Estates Act 1925 which was accepted as an Act of general application in Solomon Islands in *Koru v OAUE* [1985/6] SILR 132 but not accepted in Nigeria: *Re Sholu* (1932) 11 NLR 37; the Guardianship of Infants Act 1925, which was accepted as an Act of general application in Solomon Islands in *K v T* [1985/6] SILR 49 but not in Kenya: *Krishnan v Kumari* [1954] 28 KLR 3. See further J. Corrin, 'Transplant Shock: The Hazards of Introducing Statutes of General Application' in V. Breda (ed.), *Legal Transplants in East Asia and Oceania*, Cambridge University Press, Cambridge 2019, p. 34.

Table 2. Cut-off dates for legislation

Country	Cut-off Date
Cook Islands	14 January 1840[65]
Fiji	2 January 1875[66]
Kiribati	1 January 1961[67]
Marshall Islands	[Trust Territory Code] 1 May 1979[68]
Nauru	31 January 1968[69]
Niue	English Acts no longer apply[70]
Papua New Guinea	Specified legislation only[71]
Samoa	No English Acts remain in force[72]
Solomon Islands	7 July 1978[73]
Tokelau	English Acts no longer apply[74]
Tonga	English Acts no longer apply[75]
Tuvalu	1 January 1961[76]
Vanuatu	1 January 1976[77]

Source: Compiled by the author.

In Niue, Tokelau and Tonga, the English statutes of general application no longer apply.[78] In Samoa, English Acts were replaced in a piecemeal fashion, and now there are none still in force. In Papua New Guinea, only a specified

65 Cook Islands Constitution Act 1964 (NZ), Art. 77 read with Cook Islands Act 1915 (NZ), s 615. The English Act must also have been in force in New Zealand at the commencement of the Cook Islands Act in order to apply.

66 Constitution of Fiji Islands 1997 read with Supreme Court Ordinance 1875, ss 35, 37.

67 Constitution of Kiribati 1979, s 5 read with Western Pacific (Courts) Order 1961 (UK), s 15.

68 Constitution of Marshall Islands 1979, Art. XIII.

69 Custom and Adopted Laws Act 1971, s 4.

70 Interpretation Act 2004, s 37(4).

71 Constitution of Papua New Guinea 1975, Sch. 2.6.

72 The Constitution of Samoa 1962 saved English Acts then in force. All except one were abolished by the Reprint of Statutes Act 1972. The remaining Act was repealed in 1975 by the Wills Act (Samoa), s 23. Four New Zealand Acts still apply: Constitution of Samoa 1962, Art. 114; Reprint of Statutes Act 1972 (Samoa).

73 Constitution of Solomon Islands, Sch. 3 para. 1.

74 Repeal of Laws Rules 1997.

75 Civil Law (Amendment) Act 2003.

76 Constitution of Tuvalu Cap 1.02, ss 2(2), 5 read with Western Pacific (Courts) Order 1961 (UK), s 15.

77 Constitution of Vanuatu 1980, Art. 95 read with the High Court of the New Hebrides Regulation 1976, s 3.

78 Interpretation Act 2004, s 37(4) (Niue); Repeal of Laws Rules 1997 (Tokelau); Civil Law (Amendment) Act 2003 (Tonga). See further J. Corrin Care, 'Colonial Legacies?' (1997) 21 *The Journal of Pacific Studies* 34.

list of English and Australian Acts are in force, and these were adopted at independence as Acts of Papua New Guinea's Parliament.[79] In Marshall Islands, English Acts do not apply, but the Trust Territory Code applies subject to a cut-off date of 1 May 1979.[80]

Important English legislation includes:

- Bills of Exchange Act 1882
- Bills of Sale Act 1878
- Contracts (Rights of Third Parties) Act 1999
- Fair Trading Act 1973[81]
- Law of Property Acts 1925 and 1989
- Law Reform (Frustrated Contracts) Act 1943
- Misrepresentation Act 1967
- Sale of Goods Acts 1893[82] and 1979[83]
- Supply of Goods (Implied Terms) Act 1973
- Unfair Contract Terms Act 1977

In Samoa, the Bankruptcy Act 1908 (NZ), the Property Law Act 1952 (NZ) and ss 360 and 362 of the Samoa Act (NZ) continue to apply, as in force at 25 January 2008.[84] In Cook Islands and Niue, the following New Zealand Acts of relevance to contract apply, as in force at the date of independence:[85]

- Bills of Exchange Act 1908[86]
- Mercantile Law Act 1908[87]
- Property Law Act 1952
- Sale of Goods Act 1908[88]

---

79 Constitution of Papua New Guinea 1975, Sch. 2.6(1)(b)–(d), (2).

80 Constitution of Marshall Islands 1979, Art. XIII.

81 This Act has been repealed in the UK by the Restrictive Trade Practices Act 1976, which was in turn repealed by the Competition Act 1998.

82 Applied in Vanuatu in *ANZ v Marchand* [2001] VUCA 2.

83 This Act was applied in Tonga in *Tu'iva v Fifita & JSP Auto Trading Ltd* [1991] Tonga LR 63, but has since been repealed by the Civil Law (Amendment) Act 2003.

84 Revision and Publication of Laws Act 2008, s 11 and Sch.

85 Cook Islands became independent on 4 August 1965. Niue became independent on 19 October 1974.

86 Cook Islands Act 1915 (NZ), s 625 (the Bills of Exchange Amendment Act No. 21 of 1971 (NZ) is also specifically applied by the New Zealand Laws Act 1973 (CI)); Niue Act 1966 (NZ), s 682.

87 Cook Islands Act 1915 (NZ), s 632; Niue Act 1966 (NZ), s 694. The Sale of Goods Act 1908 (NZ) was amended in Cook Islands by Consumer Guarantees Act 2008.

88 Cook Islands Act 1915 (NZ), s 638 (amended by Consumer Guarantees Act No. 21 of 2008 (CI), not yet in force); Niue Act 1966 (NZ), s 701. The Sale of Goods Act applies as at the date of independence, being 4 August 1965 in Cook Islands and 19 October 1974 in Niue.

The Niue Act 1966 (NZ) governs contracts relating to antiquities in Niue,[89] but the equivalent section in the Cook Islands Amendment Act 1950 has been repealed by the Antiquities and Artifacts Act 1994 (CI). The Chattels Transfer Act 1924 (NZ) applies in Niue,[90] but was repealed in Cook Islands by the Personal Property Securities Act 2017.

In Tokelau, subject to the Contract Rules 2004, the New Zealand law 'for the time being in force' applies in relation to mistake, misrepresentation, duress, undue influence, unconscionability and frustration.[91] Accordingly, the Contract and Commercial Law Act 2017 (NZ), which re-enacts the Sale of Goods Act 1908, the Contractual Mistakes Act 1977 and the Frustrated Contracts Act 1944, and the Personal Property Securities Act 1999 (NZ) apply in those areas of law. The Bills of Exchange Act 1908 (NZ) also applies in Tokelau,[92] and the Chattels Transfer Act 1924 (NZ) may be in force where the Personal Property Securities Act 1999 (NZ) does not apply.[93]

In addition to these statutes, English and New Zealand legislation governing interpretation, incapacity, formalities, business mediums and limitation periods may have implications for contract law in some countries of the region. A number of other English and New Zealand Acts are relevant to certain types of contract, such as guarantees, insurance, land and personal property, price control, employment and hire purchase. These Acts will be discussed in the relevant chapters.

In addition to Acts of general application and other laws enacted or made overseas for Pacific Island countries, in some countries, colonial laws, made locally before independence, may still be in force. This legislation is usually in the form of ordinances or regulations.[94] Only a few of these laws are of relevance to the law of contract. One example is the Bills of Sale Regulation Cap 23, which is in force in Vanuatu.

It is important to note that these English and New Zealand legislation and colonial laws can be amended by the legislature of the independent states of the region, and that this has happened on many occasions. As a result of

---

89 Section 647.

90 Niue Act 1966 (NZ), s 684. This Act may also apply in Tokelau in areas other than mistake, misrepresentation, duress, undue influence, unconscionability and frustration: Tokelau (New Zealand Laws) Regulations 1975 (NZ). The Act applies as amended by the Legislation (Correction of Errors and Minor Amendment) Act 2004 (Tokelau), s 16.

91 Contract Rules 2004 (Tokelau), R 19.

92 Application of New Zealand Law Rules 2004 (Tokelau), R 3(1)(i) and (ii). All amendments would appear to apply as the Rules state that 'Acts passed in substitution will apply': R 3(2)(vii).

93 Tokelau (New Zealand Laws) Regulations 1975 (NZ), reg 3, as amended by the Tokelau Amendment Act 1986, s 15. The Act applies as amended by the Legislation (Correction of Errors and Minor Amendment) Act 2004 (Tokelau), s 16.

94 See further J. Corrin and D. Paterson, above n. 2, pp. 16–20.

this and of the cut-off dates, which preclude reforms in the originating country from applying, these statutes may differ considerably from the original version.

In Vanuatu, it is still possible for a civil case to be dealt with under French law, which is contained in the French Civil Code in force in New Caledonia at the date of independence.[95] Thus, for example, in *Jean My v Societe Civile Sarami*[96] the plaintiff's claim for cancellation of the contract and damages was based on Article 184 of the Code. Prior to independence, although certain laws applied to all inhabitants of the Condominium, French law applied in other areas to French citizens and those opting to be dealt with under the French system. Since independence, it is clear that French law will not apply to any question that is governed by local legislation. Thus, in *Pentecost Pacific Ltd and Phillipe Pentecost v Hnaloane*,[97] a dispute regarding an alleged breach of contract of employment was governed by the Employment Act 1983 of Vanuatu.

Where there is no local legislation, the circumstances in which French law will apply, as opposed to English law, are not entirely clear. The right to opt for a system of choice was terminated at independence.[98] The question of applicable law arose for consideration in the case of *Mouton v Selb Pacific Ltd.*[99] This was an action for breach of a contract of employment, drafted in French, and made between a plaintiff of French origin and a Vanuatu company with a French shareholder and managing director. The contract was stated to be subject to Joint Regulation No. 11 of 1969.[100] In fact, that Regulation had been superseded in 1983 by the Employment Act of Vanuatu.[101] That Act set out the general principles and minimum standards for terms of employment. However, provided those minimums were observed, the Act did not prevent parties making their own bargain. Accordingly, Chief Justice d'Imecourt held that it was intended that the provisions of Joint Regulation 11 should, where possible, be incorporated within the contract, including the provisions as to unilateral termination on the grounds of stipulated events of gross misconduct.

The contract also contained a 'tacite reconduction' clause, whereby the contract was to be renewed by tacit 'reconduction' unless a party gave notice in writing, at least three months prior to the expiry of the fixed period of the contract, that the contract was at an end. The Chief Justice regarded Art. 93(2) of the Constitution as making it clear that French law still applied where there was

95 French Civil Code (Overseas Territory) Code, 15 December 1952.

96 [1980–88] 1 VLR 163.

97 (1984) 1 VLR 134.

98 Exchange of Notes, 23 October 1979, para. C.

99 [1995] VUSC 2.

100 For an explanation of Joint Regulations see J. Corrin Care, 'Bedrock and Steel Blues: Finding the Law Applicable in Vanuatu' (1998) 24 *Commonwealth Law Bulletin* 594.

101 Cap 160.

a lacuna in the law.[102] His Lordship proceeded to address the choice of French law over English in the following words:

> The Court has not been referred to any English authorities on the subject, indeed the words to be interpreted are French words. It would not be right to translate them into English and then to give to that translation an interpretation that it would not have had in French or in French law. In that context French law is the law of Vanuatu, just as there are instances when English law is the law of Vanuatu.

His Lordship therefore concluded that the tacite reconduction clause had to be interpreted in accordance with French law. His Lordship also stated, obiter, that, in the absence of Vanuatu laws on point, French laws would apply, inter alia, in contracts involving French nationals or 'optants'.[103] His Lordship was also of the view that French law would automatically apply where a document in French required interpretation.[104]

In *Pentecost Pacific Ltd and Phillipe Pentecost v Hnaloane*,[105] the substantive law was dealt with in local legislation.[106] However, there was no local legislation relating to procedure. The Court of Appeal did not discuss whether there was any right to 'opt'. Rather it appears to have considered that, at least in the circumstances of this case, the choice between English and French law on procedure would be decided according to the nationality of the defendant, who was French. In this case, the Court of Appeal applied the French Procedural Code for employment tribunals of French Overseas Territories.[107] This rendered admissible the 'widest possible selection of types of evidence as to the content and to the existence of a contract of employment'.

It would seem reasonable to expect that if all parties to the contract were French, French law would normally apply. However, this assertion must be viewed in the light of *Banque Privee de Credit Moderne v Jet Service Ltd*,[108] where the plaintiff and the second defendant were French and the agreement in dispute was made in New Caledonia, where French law applied. Notwithstanding, English common law was applied on issues of waiver and illegality. It is not clear whether the loan agreements were in French, but it is to be assumed that they were in English. Normally, it seems fair to assume that, if not all the parties are

102 Presumably His Lordship regarded lack of provision as to the meaning of 'tacite reconduction' as amounting to a lacunae. Equally, it could be argued that as the Employment Act covers the field, the term was not intended to have any special meaning under the law of Vanuatu.

103 But see *Banga v Waiwo* [1996] VUSC 5, where Vaudin d'Imecourt CJ expressed the view that the right to 'opt' had been terminated.

104 See also *Selb Pacific Ltd v Mouton* [1996] VUSC 4, applying the Bankruptcy Act 1914 UK.

105 (1984–88) 1 Van LR 134.

106 Employment Act Cap 160.

107 15 December 1952.

108 See also *Banque Indosuez Vanuatu Ltd v Ferrieux* (1989–94) 2 Van LR 490 where the parties both appear to have been French, yet the English common law was applied.

French, the nationality of the defendant will be an important factor, as will the language of the contract and the legal terms contained in it.

3.3. REGIONAL LEGISLATION

The number of local enactments relating to contract law has steadily risen since independence, but there are still relatively few in force in the region. The most important of these Acts include:

Cook Islands:

- Consumer Guarantees Act 2008
- Carriage of Goods Act 1998
- Fair Trading Act 2008
- Gaming Act 1967
- Hire Purchase Act 1986
- Illegal Contracts Act 1987[109]
- Infants Amendment Act 2009
- Personal Property Securities Act 2017[110]

Fiji:

- Bills of Exchange Act Cap 227
- Bills of Sale Act Cap 225
- Commerce Commission Decree 2010
- Consumer Credit Act 1999
- Sale of Goods Act Cap 230[111]
- Indemnity Guarantee and Bailment Act Cap 232

Kiribati:

- Bills of Sale Ordinance Cap 4
- Consumer Protection Act 2001

Marshall Islands:

- Consumer Protection Act[112]
- Sale of Goods Act 1986[113]
- Unfair Business Practices Act[114]

---

109 Illegal Contracts Act No. 20 2008 (CI) is not yet in force.
110 In force 8 December 2017.
111 See *RC Manubhai & Company v Rafiq* [2017] FJHC 250.
112 20 MIRC Cap 4.
113 23 MIRC Cap 1.
114 20 MIRC Cap 3.

Niue:
- Minors Contracts Act 1969

Papua New Guinea:
- Goods Act 1951
- Fairness of Transactions Act 1993[115]
- Personal Property Securities Act 2011

Samoa:
- Bills of Exchange Act 1976
- Fair Trading Act 1998
- Frustrated Contracts Act 1975
- Infants Act 1961
- Sale of Goods Act 1975

Solomon Islands:
- Bills of Sale Act Cap 174
- Consumer Protection Act Cap 63

Tokelau:
- Contract Rules 2004

Tonga:
- Bills of Exchange Act Cap 108
- Consumer Protection Act 2000
- Contracts Act Cap 26 (this Act was repealed in 1990,[116] but continues to apply to contracts entered into before that date).[117]

Tuvalu:
- Bills of Sale Act Cap 40.04
- Sale of Goods Act Cap 40.60

Vanuatu:
- Bills of Sale Regulation Cap 23
- Law Reform (Contract Law) Act 2009

When introduced in 1992, Fiji's Fair Trading Decree went further than any other South Pacific statute in encroaching on the notion of freedom of contract. It was said to reflect 'a new environment of both competition and

115 This Act came into force on 25 September 1998 (Gazette No. G111/1998).
116 Contracts (Repeal) Act 1990.
117 See *Mangisi v Koloamatangi* [1999] TOCA 9.

consumer protection'.[118] That Act was repealed by the Commerce Commission Decree 2010, which now provides the consumer law in Fiji. In the interim, other Pacific countries have introduced consumer protection legislation, including Kiribati, Marshall Islands, Solomon Islands and Tonga.

In addition to the Pacific Islands' statutes listed above, many countries within the region have legislation governing interpretation, incapacity, formalities, business mediums and limitation periods. Most countries also have legislation governing specific types of contract, such as insurance, property, price control, employment and hire purchase. These Acts will be discussed in the relevant chapters. As mentioned above, since independence many regional countries have passed legislation to modify the foreign statutes as they are to apply locally.

3.4. CUSTOMARY LAW

At independence, many countries within the region recognised customary law as a formal source of law. However, customary transactions do not always fit neatly into the definition of contract developed through the English law. The topic of customary laws and the common law of contract is dealt with in the next chapter.

4. THE RELATIONSHIP BETWEEN CONTRACT LAW AND OTHER AREAS OF LAW

Law, like many other disciplines, is divided into categories, intended to assist in understanding and application. However, it should always be borne in mind that that these categories are interlinked, and often overlap. In practice, factual situations often fall within more than one of the traditional categories of law.[119]

The law of contract is traditionally regarded as part of the law of obligations. The other two divisions within the law of obligations are tort and restitution. Where overlap between these, or other, categories of law results in more than one cause of action arising from the same set of facts, it is known as 'concurrent liability'. For example, a person who takes his or her car to the garage may enter into a binding contract for repairs to be done. The repairs may then be carried out and paid for. If the car is not repaired properly, there will be a right to sue in contract, for breach of the contract to repair. There may also be

118 *Attorney-General of Fiji v Pacoil Fiji Ltd* [1996] FJCA 9.

119 See A.W.B. Simpson, *A History of the Common Law of Contract*, Clarendon Press, Oxford 1975.

a right to sue in tort if the work is carried out negligently. An example from Fiji can be seen in *Lal v Chand*,[120] where the vendor of a house he had built himself was successfully sued in tort and contract by the purchaser for the negligent work done, which he had fraudulently represented in the contract as being soundly constructed.

The question has arisen, particularly in relation to the law of obligations, whether a plaintiff is free to choose from amongst concurrent causes of action.[121] Where the plaintiff has suffered physical damage, the courts have accepted that there is free choice.[122] At one time there was some doubt whether concurrent claims could be made in the case of pure economic loss.[123] However, in the leading case of *Henderson v Merrett Syndicates Ltd*,[124] the House of Lords decided that where concurrent liability arises, the plaintiff is free to sue in either or both contract and tort. This is also the position in other Commonwealth jurisdictions, such as Australia,[125] Canada[126] and New Zealand.[127] The right is subject to the restriction that actions in tort will not be allowed where tortious liability is inconsistent with the contract, that is, where the parties have agreed, either expressly or by implication, that the tortious remedy is limited or excluded.[128]

It has been suggested that the restriction in *Henderson v Merrett Syndicates Ltd* prevents a more onerous standard of performance liability being imposed by tort, as there will normally be an implied term of the contract to that effect.[129] However, in *Holt v Payne Skillington*,[130] the English Court of Appeal held that there was no reason why a duty of care in tort could not be imposed by the general law which was wider in scope than the duty which arose from the contractual relationship between the parties. The contractual duty was limited

---

120 (1983) 29 FLR 71, 74.

121 For a summary of the reasons why a party would want to choose one cause of action arising under the law of obligations as opposed to another, see A. Burrows, *Understanding the Law of Obligations*, Hart Publishing, Oxford 1998, pp. 17–20.

122 *Jackson v Mayfair Window Cleaning Co Ltd* [1952] 1 All ER 215. For a discussion of concurrent liability see A. Taylor, 'Concurrent Liability' (2019) 82 *Modern Law Review* 17.

123 *Tai Hing Cotton Mill Ltd v Liu Chong Hing Bank* [1986] AC 80; *Simms Jones Ltd v Protochem Trading New Zealand Ltd* [1993] 3 NZLR 369, 381. See further J. Swanton, 'Concurrent Liability in Tort and Contract: The Problem of Defining the Limits' (1996) 10 *Journal of Contract Law* 21.

124 [1994] 3 WLR 761.

125 *Bryan v Maloney* (1995) 69 ALJR 375; *Astley v Austrust* (1999) 161 ALR 155; *Brookfield Multiplex Ltd v Owners Corporation Strata Plan 61288* (2014) 254 CLR 185.

126 *Central Trust Co v Rafuse* (1986) 31 DLR (4th) 481.

127 *Riddell v Porteous* [1999] 1 NZLR 1; *Price Waterhouse v Kwan* [2000] 3 NZLR 39; *Allison v KPMG Peat Marwick* [2000] 1 NZLR 560.

128 *Henderson v Merrett Syndicates Ltd* [1994] 3 WLR 761, 788.

129 Burrows, above n. 121, p. 21.

130 [1996] PNLR 179 (CA).

by the factual basis of the contract. In tort, however, provided that the required assumption of responsibility and concomitant reliance were shown, a duty of care was established.[131]

As illustrated by *Lal v Chand*,[132] regional courts have shown a willingness to recognise concurrent liability. In *Australia and New Zealand Banking Group Ltd v Ale*[133] the Supreme Court of Samoa considered it unnecessary to insist on categorisation at all, preferring the American approach of not distinguishing claims on the basis of form or nature. Another example can be seen in *Hunt v Australasian United Steam Navigation Company Ltd*,[134] where the plaintiff delivered a cargo of bananas to the defendant for shipment to Fiji. In spite of the contract of carriage between the parties, the plaintiff was permitted to sue in negligence. Accordingly, the position is now that, subject to tortious liability being consistent with the contract, a party may choose between actions in contract and tort.[135] In practice, where concurrent liability exists, parties usually sue in both contract and tort, although a party may recover only once.[136]

The overlap between contract and tort sometimes leads to difficulties in distinguishing the two. In *Pacific Travel Service v Ali*,[137] the respondent paid the appellant for a concessionary airfare to New Zealand and the appellant agreed to make all the arrangements, including obtaining a travel permit. The permit was refused and no refund for the airfare was available due to the terms attaching to concessionary fares. Judgment was given for the respondent by the magistrate at first instance and by the Supreme Court on appeal. On further appeal to the Court of Appeal it was argued that this was a claim in tort for negligence by the appellant and that as the statement of claim made no mention of this, the claim should fail. The Court of Appeal cited with approval Lord Justice Greer's words in *Jarvis v Moy*:[138]

> The distinction in the modern view, for this purpose, between contract and tort may be put thus: where the breach of duty alleged arises out of a liability independently of the personal obligation undertaken by contract, it is tort and it may be tort even though there may happen to be a contract between the parties, if the duty in fact arises independently of that contract. Breach of contract occurs where that which is complained of is a breach of duty arising out of the obligations undertaken by the contract.

---

131 In this case such a duty was not made out as the plaintiff had not acted to his detriment on advice given.
132 (1983) 29 FLR 71, 74.
133 [1980–3] WSLR 468.
134 [1919] 2 FLR 72.
135 *Henderson v Merrett Syndicates Ltd* [1994] 3 WLR 761, 788.
136 See e.g. *Pentecost Pacific Ltd and Phillipe Pentecost v Hnaloane* (1980–88) 1 VLR 134 (CA).
137 [1974] FJCA 2.
138 [1936] 1 KB 399, 405.

In the present case it was held that there was a definite breach of duty arising out of the contractual obligation on the part of the appellant to obtain a valid travel ticket to New Zealand. It was therefore incorrect to say that the action was founded in tort.

Similar difficulties have arisen regarding the overlap between contract and the third division of the law of obligations, restitution. Restitution is concerned with preventing unjust enrichment and was at one time thought to be part of the law of the contract.[139] Whilst it has been recognised that restitution is a separate area of the law of obligations there is a broad overlap, for example, where one party has taken the benefit of services rendered by the other. In *Australia and New Zealand Banking Group Ltd v Ale*,[140] the Supreme Court of Samoa considered it unnecessary to insist on division of claims in a rigid way, preferring the American approach of not distinguishing claims on the basis of form or nature. He stated that:

> The debate as to whether all civil disputes must fall either into contract or tort or whether quasi-contract is a legitimate category it seems to me must be rather bemusing for the pragmatic bystander in the South Pacific half a world away from the esoteric discussions taking place in the courts of England.[141]

The law of contract also overlaps with other categories of law, such as property law, which governs various types of rights in tangible and intangible property. Whilst property rights may be transferred by a contract, they may be conferred by other means, such as a gift or devolution on death. Further, property rights are generally enforceable against the whole world, rather than being restricted to enforcement against other parties to the transaction conferring present rights. There may also be criminal law repercussions arising from facts surrounding a contractual transaction. For example, where a contract is void for illegality the facts may render one or both of the parties liable to prosecution.[142]

5. CLASSIFICATION OF CONTRACTS

There are several ways of classifying contracts, which are useful when discussing their formation and their consequences. The most important terms are as follows.

---

139 Most of the law of restitution was originally known as 'quasi-contract'.
140 [1980–3] WSLR 468.
141 Ibid., 469.
142 See also *Partridge v Crittenden* [1968] 2 All ER 421, discussed in chapter 3.

5.1. SIMPLE CONTRACTS AND CONTRACTS UNDER SEAL

A simple contract is any binding contract other than a contract under seal. It can be oral, written, or partly oral and partly written. It consists of a promise to do or refrain from doing something, in exchange for something given or promised in return. The parties must intend the agreement to have legal effect.

A contract under seal, more often referred to as a deed, is a promise made by written agreement under seal. The promise will be binding even though no consideration has been given for it. It is usually made by signing in front of a witness. Originally, delivery of the document to the other party was required, and an adhesive seal had to be attached. These requirements have been abolished in some jurisdictions, such as Fiji and England and Wales.[143] Deeds are discussed further in chapter 10.

5.2. BILATERAL AND UNILATERAL CONTRACTS

Where a contract is formed by the exchange of promises it is known as a bilateral contract. Both parties make a promise at the time of the formation of the contract, which they are bound to carry out. One example is a simple contract of sale where goods have to be ordered. The vendor promises to obtain the goods and pass them to the buyer and the buyer promises to pay for them when they arrive.

Where a contract is formed by one party making a promise and indicating that they agree to be bound if and when the offeree does a specified act, this is known as a unilateral contract. There is only one promisor, who is bound to fulfil the promise if the offeree carries out the act. A unilateral contract may also be formed when one person does an act on the understanding that the other party will give a promise in exchange. The most common type of unilateral contract is one that consists of a promise in return for an act. An example is an offer of a reward in exchange for an act, such as the supply of information,[144] the submission of a winning competition entry[145] or the winning of a race.[146] Other examples are the offer to pay the price if goods are delivered[147] and the offer to carry a passenger in return for buying a ticket.[148] Another example is the offer constituted by the supply of goods[149] or services,[150] in a situation where it

---

143 Property Law Act Cap 130 (Fiji), s 4; Law Reform (Miscellaneous Provisions) Act 1989 (UK), s 1.

144 *Williams v Carwardine* (1833) 172 ER 1101.

145 *Vaioleti v Cross* [1990] Tonga LR 108.

146 *Earl Ellesmore v Wallace* [1929] 2 Ch 1.

147 *Fragano v Long* (1825) 4 B&C 219.

148 *Denton v Great Northern Railway Co* (1856) 5 E&B 860.

149 *Weatherby v Banham* (1832) 5 C&P 28.

150 *Rust v Abbey Life Assurance Co Ltd* [1979] 2 Lloyd's Rep 334.

is clear that payment is expected, which is accepted if the other party permits this to go ahead. For example, in *Steven v Bromley & Son*,[151] charterers loaded cargo onto a ship, and this was carried by the shipowners. The act of loading by the charterers was held to constitute an offer to pay a reasonable price, which was accepted by the shipowner's acquiescence. In summary, in a unilateral contract only one party makes a promise, whereas in a bilateral contract both parties do.

The distinction between this type of contract and a bilateral contract is significant in several ways. For instance, in a unilateral contract, the promisee is originally under no obligation to the promisor, so no action can be taken against the promisee until the act is, at least, embarked upon.[152] In *Myers v Bavadra*,[153] Ashton-Lewis J distinguished unilateral and bilateral contracts in the following way:

> If acceptance is by way of counter-promise a bilateral contract comes into being. If acceptance is by way of performing certain acts which are stipulated in the offer, then a unilateral contract comes into being. In a unilateral contract the offeror usually makes a promise stipulating acceptance on the part of the offeree by the performance by the offeree of an act or acts. …
>
> Thus, if the consideration required from the offeree is a promise, the giving of that promise will result in a bilateral contract in which mutual promises are exchanged. If, on the other hand, the requested consideration by the offeror from the offeree, is an act other than a promise, the performance of that act creates a unilateral contract which will bind the offeror.

5.3. EXECUTED AND EXECUTORY CONTRACTS

Executed contracts are contracts where one of the parties has fulfilled his or her side of the bargain, leaving an outstanding liability on one side only. An act or forbearance is given for a promise, such as where a person carries out an action in response to an offer in an advertisement.

Executory contracts are contracts where promises are exchanged. Both parties have yet to do the acts or fulfil the promises that are the subject of the agreement. For example, a contract for services, where the employer promises to pay the contractor and the contractor promises to do the work.

The terms 'executed' and 'executory' are perhaps more accurately used to describe the status of consideration than to describe the contract itself.

151 [1919] 2 KB 722.
152 See later as to whether acceptance takes place on completion of the act or at some prior time.
153 [1993] FJHC 114.

5.4. UNENFORCEABLE, VOID, VOIDABLE AND ILLEGAL CONTRACTS

An unenforceable contract, as the name would suggest, is one that, although valid, cannot be sued on for some legal reason. Many valid contracts cannot be sued on due to a statutory impediment. For example, in some jurisdictions contracts for the sale of land are required to be evidenced in writing.[154] An agreement that does not comply with this requirement will be unenforceable.

A void contract is one that is a nullity (of no effect) due to some fundamental defect. An example is a contract that is contrary to public policy, such as a contract in restraint of trade. Usually, no title passes under a void contract and money paid or property transferred can generally be recovered.[155]

A voidable contract is an otherwise valid contract, where the law gives one party an option whether or not to proceed with the agreement. An example is a contract induced by misrepresentation. The innocent party can choose whether to go ahead with the contract and claim damages in respect of any loss caused by the misrepresentation or may rescind (cancel) the contract.

An illegal contract is one that is contrary to law or contrary to public policy. An obvious example of the former is a contract to commit a crime. No action can be brought on the contract and, generally, property transferred under it cannot be recovered.

A contract that is contrary to a customary law might also be illegal in countries where customary laws are recognised under state law. This is discussed further in the next chapter.

---

[154] E.g. Property Law Act Cap 130 (Fiji); Land and Titles Act Cap 93 (SI); Law of Property Act 1925 (UK). This and other formalities affecting contracts are discussed in chapter 9.

[155] Property may pass to a minor even though the contract is rendered void, *Stocks v Wilson* [1913] 2 KB 235.

CHAPTER 2
CONTRACT AND CUSTOMARY LAWS

1. INTRODUCTION

A complex question of vital importance to the law of contract in the South Pacific is whether there is a customary law of contract. There are differing views on this. Traditional societies have been described as 'status based', as rights and duties of community members tend to be dictated by their place in society, rather than by agreement.[1] This is the context in which Maine proclaimed that 'the movement of progressive societies has hitherto been a movement from Status to Contract'.[2] More specifically, it has been argued that customary transactions are too different from contracts to be equated with them. For example, Scaglion has expressed the view that:

> In customary law, a wide variety of social obligations exist. On the surface, some such obligations appear to be oral contracts: one partly agrees to provide goods and/or services at a later date in exchange for goods or services received. Yet, in custom, such social obligations are not really binding and no real traditional mode of redress other than shame and social pressure exists. The result of habitual defaulting is a bad name and difficulties in enlisting aid. It would be incorrect to apply existing contract legislation to such situations: magistrates should clearly distinguish such practices from contracts in the western sense.[3]

Roebuck, Srivastava and Nonggorr go as far as to say that '[t]raditional transactions are not contracts as understood in the modern common law and no good can come of confusing them'.[4]

One way of approaching this question is to look at each of the rules that underpin the common law and ask whether they apply to customary transactions. Some of the possible, generalised, distinctions between dealings

1 M. Gluckman, *The Ideas in Barotse Jurisprudence*, Manchester University Press, Manchester 1972, n. 171.
2 H.J.S. Maine, *Ancient Law*, John Murray, London 1861, p. 100.
3 R. Scaglion, *Customary Law in Papua New Guinea: A Melanesian View*, Monograph 2, Papua New Guinea Law Reform Commission, 1983, p. ix.
4 D. Roebuck, D.K. Srivastava and J. Nonggor, *The Context of Contract in Papua New Guinea*, University of Papua New Guinea Press, Waigani 1984, p. 44.

in a customary context and commercial contracts are set out in the comparative table below.

Table 3. Customary and commercial transactions compared

Customary Transactions	**Contractual Transactions**
Status based	Rights based
Obligatory	Voluntary
Group focus – benefits and burdens may be imposed on group members	Individual focus – privity of contract applies
Dealings may be between groups or communities with no legal capacity under state law[5]	Contracts must be entered into by legally recognised persons or bodies
Rarely bargain-based and the terms are governed by tradition	Parties bargain and may (within legislative limits) set the terms
Implicit reciprocity	Consideration required
Regulate social relationships	Regulate business relationships
Intention to create a customary transaction	Intention to create (common law) legal relations
Aims are relational	Aim is to maximise benefit
Terms are implicit and flexible	Terms must be expressed with certainty
Binding in honour	Binding in law
Enforceable by the community	(Ultimately) enforceable by the courts
Personal	Impersonal
Self-help may be a recognised sanction	Self-help is not a recognised sanction
No right to damages	Injured party has the right to damages if loss has been suffered
Usually entered into face to face	May be entered into remotely
Ceremonial formalities may be required	Written formalities may be required

Source: Compiled by the author.

It seems obvious from this that dealings in a customary setting do not always fit neatly into the definition of contract developed through the English law of contract. However, these suggested distinctions are generalisations, and assume that all customary transactions are of the same nature. In reality, customary laws do not constitute an homogenous body of uniform laws, but differ from place to place and are very much context dependent. Further, a broader distinction may be drawn in some parts of the Pacific between reciprocal transactions and other customary exchanges. The former are part of 'a complicated shifting network of reciprocal obligations that continues

5 For an example of a case illustrating the difficulties that such dealings involve for a formal court, see *Island Enterprises Limited v Naitoro* [1990] SBHC 53.

over time'.[6] In Melanesia, bride price is a common example of a reciprocal transaction, and in Polynesia the giving of gifts on the death of a relative.[7] The latter are not so bound up with obligation and consist of the exchange of goods or services of the basis of choice, traditionally by way of barter, where one party needs or wants what the other has to offer. Increasingly such exchanges involve cash, which brings them closer to common law contracts. The separation of these two categories puts a new slant on the differences set out in the table above, and many of the distinctions do not apply. This makes the question of when a transaction has 'crossed the border from custom to contract' more difficult to decide.[8] Failure to differentiate between reciprocal transactions and other customary exchanges has led to difficulties, highlighted in some of the cases discussed below.

In any event, there are certainly some commonalities between traditional transactions and contractual dealings. In Papua New Guinea, there is evidence of a range of traditional transactions for the exchange of goods, and support for the view that there is a customary law of contract may be found in the Report of the Law Reform Commission of Papua New Guinea on Fairness of Transactions.[9] This refers to customary transactions of a commercial nature.[10] The legislation[11] resulting from that report defines the term 'transaction' to mean:

> any contract, promise, agreement, dealing or undertaking of an economic or commercial nature, whether supported by consideration or not entered into between parties, and includes –
>
> (a) an informal, complete or incomplete transaction; and
> (b) a transaction governed by customary law ...[12]

Customary transactions are thereby included in a group of agreements bound together by being of an economic or commercial nature.

Roebuck, Srivastava and Nonggorr also acknowledge that:

> It is neither possible nor desirable to deny the conceptual and commercial importance of Papua New Guinea's traditional transactions. They contribute greatly to the

6 N. Seddon, 'Reciprocity, Exchange and Contract' (1974) *Melanesian Law Journal* 49.
7 See e.g. *Po'uhila v Veikune* [1996] Tonga LR 11.
8 *Po'uhila v Veikune* [1996] Tonga LR 11.
9 Report No. 6, December 1977.
10 Ibid., p. 1. See also *Golpak v Malori* [1993] PNGLR 491, which cites the previous Land Act (ss 73, 74) Cap 185 as referring to 'customary contract' (although that phrase does not appear in the version of that Act now repealed which is available on Paclii).
11 Fairness of Transactions Act 1993, s 39(1).
12 Ibid., s 3.

> economic growth of village communities. Some are purely commercial in nature and just like common law contracts.[13]

Support for a common foundation, in the context of Tokelau, can be found in 'Contract Codes, Coral Atolls and the Kiwi Connection',[14] where Professor Angelo points out that whilst there is little in the culture of Tokelau which specifically addresses the notion of contract of Western European culture:

> There is however, a strong indication both within contemporary society and in the folklore of Tokelau that basic tenets of contractual obligations are recognised and honoured in Tokelau culture.

Further, traditional laws should be distinguished from 'living' customary laws, as they are practised in the post-colonial era. Customary laws are not static; they develop over time to respond to the changing needs of the community. As local communities gradually come to engage more with the commercial sector and the state, this no doubt has a profound influence on customary law. The Report of the Law Reform Commission of Papua New Guinea on Fairness of Transactions, for example, refers to customary transactions of a commercial nature.[15]

In any event, drawing distinctions does not answer the question of whether there is a customary law of contract. Just because the common law rules do not apply does not mean that there is no law of contract in custom, but only that the same rules do not apply. Consideration of the differences between the two systems may nevertheless be important for two reasons. First, if a dispute is categorised as customary, it may fall outside the jurisdiction of a state court. Secondly, if it is dealt with by a state court, the fact that it is a customary transaction rather than common law dispute may affect the outcome of the case. For example, if an agreement does not qualify as a contract, the court may refuse to enforce it. On occasion, parties have attempted to rely on a distinction between customary and common law dealings to deny the validity of an agreement under state law. Examples can be found in two cases from Nauru where the existence of a contract was challenged on the basis that the transaction was only customary, with opposing results. *Hiram v Solomon*[16] is an example of a case where a contract was held to exist. In that case, the plaintiff was one of several co-owners of three portions of land. The plaintiff allowed her daughter (B) and son-in-law and their children to move into a

---

13 D. Roebuck, D.K. Srivastava and J. Nonggor, above n. 4, p. 43.

14 A. Angelo, 'Contract Codes, Coral Atolls and the Kiwi Connection' in H.-J. Ahrens (ed), *Festschrift fur Erwin Deutsch*, Carl Heymanns, Germany 1999, p. 877.

15 Above n. 9, p. 1. See also clause 1 of the Fairness of Transactions Bill 1977.

16 [2011] NRSC 25.

house on one of the portions of land with her. The plaintiff said, 'This house I now give to you (the son-in-law) and [B], it now belongs to [B] and the kids'. B and the son-in-law took steps to ensure that all the co-owners agreed to their owning the house, and all but three signed a document, provided by the Lands and Survey Department, to that effect. One of the signatures was the plaintiff's. B eventually lost her job, so she and her husband leased the house out to a third party. After B died, the plaintiff asked her son-in-law for half the rental profits. When he refused, the plaintiff claimed that her signature on the document was a forgery and that B was only living in the house on the basis of a customary/verbal arrangement, revocable at any time. In the alternative, she claimed that the agreement had been revoked by a second document signed by most of the landowners.

The court did not accept that the plaintiff's signature was forged on the original document. As it was validly executed, it passed an interest in the property to B and her husband. The plaintiff could not unilaterally revoke the agreement and had no claim to the rental payments. In this case the written documents created a legally enforceable contract under state law. Had the plaintiff been able to establish that this was merely a customary transaction, then the court would have had to embark on an exploration of the applicable customary laws to ascertain whether revocation was allowed.

In the second case, *Tom v Heinrich*,[17] the plaintiff and defendants were closely related and owned adjoined pieces of land. Their mothers agreed that the defendants' mother could install a petrol bowser on the plaintiff's mother's land close to a jointly owned store. In exchange, the plaintiff's family was entitled to free petrol and to purchase goods on credit from the store under the defendants' mother's name. After the defendants' mother died, the defendants took over the shop and said that the arrangement had ceased. The plaintiff sued for breach of contract. The defence was that 'at its highest there had been a customary, social arrangement between close friends that was never intended to be the subject of action in the courts'. In the alternative, the defence relied on the fact that the breach had occurred outside the six-year limitation period for a contract claim. The court agreed that a claim in contract would have been statute barred, but also held that the terms of the contract were so vague as to be incapable of enforcement. In this case the failure to establish a contract under state law meant that the only possibility was a customary transaction, and this does not appear to have been argued as establishing an enforceable agreement under customary laws. Eames CJ did not explore this possibility, merely stating that this was an 'oral agreement between elders of two families' and that he had no doubt this was a 'longstanding friendly arrangement

17 [2012] NRSC 12.

between the female elders of the two families, which fell far short of a formal contract.'

2. THE ROLE OF CUSTOMARY LAWS IN THE LEGAL SYSTEM

In most countries of the region, customary laws continued to operate throughout the colonial period. Whilst they were given limited, if any, recognition in written laws,[18] they continued to be observed by those persons who felt themselves bound by the customary system, and to whom confirmation or endorsement by any outside authority was unnecessary. Customary laws are still recognised by those whose customs are embodied in those laws, irrespective of what is provided in the written laws of the state on this basis. Where disputes about transactions arise at village level, like other minor local disputes, they are governed by customary laws and determined locally without consideration of whether they should be categorised as 'contractual' in the common law sense.

Whether customary laws are applicable to the determination of contractual disputes by the state, outside the customary sphere is a more difficult question. For example, where a dispute arises in a commercial setting or where one or more parties to the dispute do not recognise customary laws, are those laws relevant? From the state's perspective, the answer requires examination of the three questions:

1. To what extent are customary laws recognised by state courts?
2. If recognised, where do they rank in relation to other laws?
3. To what extent do the answers to questions 1 and 2 accord with the reality?

These questions will now be examined in turn.

2.1. TO WHAT EXTENT ARE CUSTOMARY LAWS RECOGNISED BY STATE COURTS?

At independence, or shortly afterwards, many Pacific countries recognised customary law as a formal source of law. The position regarding recognition can be summarised as per Table 4.

---

[18] For the extent of recognition in individual jurisdictions see further J. Corrin and D. Paterson, *Introduction to South Pacific Law*, 4th ed., Intersentia, Cambridge 2017, chapter 3.

Table 4. Recognition of customary laws

Country	**Custom Expressly Recognised**
Cook Islands	In relation to land only[19]
Fiji	In relation to land only[20]
Kiribati	Yes, in certain matters[21]
Marshall Islands	Yes[22]
Nauru	Yes, in certain matters[23]
Niue	In relation to land only[24]
Papua New Guinea	Yes[25]
Samoa	Yes[26]
Solomon Islands	Yes[27]
Tokelau	Yes[28]
Tonga	No
Tuvalu	Yes, in certain matters[29]
Vanuatu	Yes[30]

Source: Compiled by the author.

In Kiribati, Nauru and Tuvalu, the matters regulated by customary laws are restricted to a specified list. None of these lists specifically mention contract. However, in Nauru, the list in includes 'any matter affecting Nauruans only',[31] and thus may be applied by the courts to customary transactions provided that all parties are Nauruan. In Kiribati and Tuvalu, the lists include 'a transaction that – (i) the parties intended should be; or (ii) justice requires should be,

19 Cook Islands Act 1915 (NZ), s 422.
20 Native Lands Act 1915 Cap 133, s 3. The Constitution Amendment Act 1997 removed customary law as a general source of law and this remains the same under the Constitution of the Republic of Fiji 2013. See formerly Constitution of Fiji 1990, s 100.
21 Laws of Kiribati Act 1989, s 4(2).
22 Constitution of Marshall Islands 1978, Art. X, ss 1, 2.
23 Custom and Adopted Laws Act 1971, s 3.
24 Niue Amendment Act (No. 2) 1968 (NZ), s 23.
25 Constitution of Papua New Guinea 1975, Sch. 1.2.2(1); Underlying Law Act 2000, s 1(1).
26 Constitution of Samoa 1962, Arts. 101(2) and III(1).
27 Constitution of Solomon Islands 1978, ss 75, 76 and Sch. 3 para. 3.
28 Constitution of Tokelau 2006, s 12(4); Tokelau Amendment Act 1996 (NZ), s 9; Custom as a Source of Law Rules 2004, R 2.
29 Laws of Tuvalu Act Cap 1.06, s 4(2).
30 Constitution of Vanuatu 1980, Arts. 47(1), 95(3).
31 Custom and Adopted Laws Act 1971, s 3.

regulated wholly or partly by customary law and not by any other law',[32] which, again, gives scope for customary laws to be applied to customary transactions.

2.2. WHERE DO CUSTOMARY LAWS RANK IN RELATION TO OTHER LAWS?

In those countries where customary laws are expressly recognised as a general source of law, the Constitution is the supreme law, and in most situations, ranks above customary law.[33] Statute is also superior to customary law.[34] However, there is no uniformity regarding the status of customary law in relation to common law, and in many cases their relative position is uncertain.

In Papua New Guinea, the cases in which customary laws will apply to contractual disputes have been laid down by the Underlying Law Act 2000. This legislation provides that the law is derived from the Constitution and legislation, and (next in the hierarchy) from the underlying law.[35] This underlying law consists of, in order of precedence,[36] customary laws and the 'common law in force in England immediately before the 16th September 1975'.[37] In practice, the courts have largely been content to apply the common law. As explained by Cannings J in *Naki v AGC (Pacific) Ltd*,[38] '[t]he Courts have, generally, not seen a great need to formulate new rules and develop the underlying law where contractual principles are involved'.[39]

In Kiribati and Tuvalu, legislation provides that customary laws are to apply to:

> a transaction that –
>
> (i) the parties intended should be; or
> (ii) justice requires should be,
>
> regulated wholly or partly by custom and not by law ...[40]

---

32 Laws of Kiribati Act 1989, Sch. 1 para. 4; Laws of Tuvalu Act Cap 1.06, Sch. 1 para. 4.

33 But see e.g. *Pusi v Leni* [1997] SBHC 100, where Muria CJ stated that it should not automatically be assumed that the Constitution would override customary law, but that it would depend on the circumstances of the case.

34 See e.g. *Pentecost Pacific Ltd and Phillippe Pentecost v Hnaloane* (1980–88) 1 VLR 134, where the Court of Appeal made it clear that customary law was not applicable where there was a relevant statute, particularly where that statute was passed by the Parliament of Vanuatu after independence. However, this may not be the case where the statute is not enacted by the local parliament: see *K v T* [1985/6] SILR 49, where it was held that although local Acts were superior to common law, United Kingdom Acts were not.

35 Constitution of Papua New Guinea, s 9(f).

36 Underlying Law Act 2000 (PNG), s 4.

37 Ibid., s 3(1).

38 [2005] PGNC 163. See also *Harding v Teperoi Timbers* [1988] PNGLR 128.

39 The courts have also marginalised customary laws in contract cases by subjecting them to adjectival laws: see e.g. *John v Siune* [2005] PGDC 35; *Mel v Dupai* [2005] PGDC 88.

40 Laws of Kiribati Act 1989, Sch. 1 para. 4(j); Laws of Tuvalu Act 1989, Sch. 1 para. 4(i).

In Solomon Islands, the Customs Recognition Act makes an identical provision,[41] but that Act has not yet been brought into force.[42] However, courts in countries without this provision may still be inclined to apply customary law in these circumstances, at least in those countries where customary laws are clearly superior to common law. Support for this view can be found in *Success v Premier of Guadalcanal Province*.[43] In this case, which is discussed further in chapter 8, the Court of Appeal of Solomon Islands held that the doctrine of privity does not apply to agreements relating to customary land and timber rights, stating that, given the concept of group ownership that applies to customary land, '[t]he common law concept of privity of contract does not and cannot apply'.[44]

The position can be summarised as per Table 5.

Table 5. Ranking of customary laws

Country	Customary Laws Ranked above the Common Law
Cook Islands	In customary land cases[45]
Kiribati	In certain matters[46]
Marshall Islands	Uncertain
Nauru	Yes[47]
Niue	In customary land cases[48]
Papua New Guinea	Yes[49]
Samoa	Uncertain
Solomon Islands	Yes[50]
Tokelau	In certain circumstances[51]

(continued)

41 Customs Recognition Act 2000, s 8(g).
42 This Act is based on the Customs Recognition Act 1963 (PNG), s 5(g), which was repealed by the Underlying Law Act 2000.
43 [2011] SBCA 19.
44 Ibid., [9].
45 Cook Islands Act 1915, s 422.
46 Laws of Kiribati Act 1989, s 6(3)(b).
47 Customs and Adopted Laws Act 1971, s 4.
48 Niue Act 1966, s 23.
49 Underlying Law Act 2000, s 23. See *Naki v AGC (Pacific) Ltd* [2005] PGNC 163, where Cannings J expressly required the principles relating to formation of contracts to be consistent with customary laws.
50 Constitution of Solomon Islands, Sch. 3 para. 3(2).
51 Where the General Fono is requested by the court to give information on a Tokelau custom and does so, 'the Court shall determine issues concerning the matter of custom by reference to that information'. See Custom as a Source of Law Rules 2004, R 2(4).

Table 5 *continued*

Country	**Customary Laws Ranked above the Common Law**
Tuvalu	In certain matters[52]
Vanuatu	Uncertain[53]

Source: Compiled by the author.

Whatever the ranking of customary laws in the hierarchy of state laws in relation to common law and equity, in most jurisdictions, the latter does not apply if it is inapplicable to the circumstances of the country.[54] This limitation offers an opportunity for the courts to adapt the common law to take account of prevailing customs and culture.

2.3. TO WHAT EXTENT DO THE ANSWERS TO THESE QUESTIONS ACCORD WITH THE REALITY?

In spite of the theoretical hierarchy, even in countries where customary laws are stated to be superior to the common law and equity, the courts tend to follow the common law. There do not appear to be any reported examples of non-domestic contract cases within the region which have been decided in accordance with customary law.[55] Neither have courts in Pacific countries used inapplicability as an avenue for rejecting or adapting the common law on the basis that it does not accord with customary laws. This may be due to one or more of a number of reasons. For example, the type of contractual dispute to which customary law might apply is more likely to be decided outside the formal court system. Further, judges and counsel in the formal system may have no knowledge or training in customary law. Customary laws are rarely pleaded or argued by counsel.[56] The fact that legislative schemes have been put in place to govern commercial use of customary land and other resources, such as the Forest Resources and Timber Utilisation Act[57] in Solomon Islands, may also be relevant. Other factors are relevant, such as the requirement by

52 Laws of Tuvalu Act Cap 1.06, s 6(3)(b).

53 Constitution of Vanuatu 1980, ss 45(1), 93(3). See *Banga v Waiwo* [1996] VUSC 5, where it was held that customary law should only be applied if there is no other applicable law. This decision has been the subject of some criticism.

54 See e.g. Constitution of Solomon Islands 1978, Sch. 3 para. 2(1)(b).

55 There are examples of disputes involving bride price, but these are regarded as domestic. See e.g. *To'ofilu v Oimae* [1997] SBHC 33.

56 See e.g. *Keboki Business Group (Inc) v State* [1984] PNGLR 281 where the court commented on the failure of counsel to respond to an invitation to call evidence or make submissions in relation to customary law.

57 Cap 40.

the courts that customary law be proved by evidence before it can be applied[58] and the difficulty inherent in transferring fundamentally different concepts from one legal system into another.[59]

Customary law may also be viewed as inapplicable to commercial transactions and/or to cases where expatriate parties are concerned. An example of this is the case of *Semens v Continental Air Lines*.[60] The plaintiff claimed damages for personal injuries suffered by him at Pohnpei Airport when he was employed by a sub-contractor to unload cargo from a Continental Air Lines plane. To decide the claim, interpretation of a clause of the contract was required. The court had to consider which source of law was applicable. It was held that the Constitution was the supreme law, but that it had no application to the facts. The next source of law in the hierarchy was customary law. No such law having been put before him by the parties, the Chief Justice held that he would only be under an obligation to search for an applicable custom or tradition if the nature of the dispute and surrounding facts indicated that this was likely. His Lordship felt that this was not such a case, as the business activities which gave rise to the suit were not of a local or traditional nature. Although goods handling and moving might take place in a traditional setting, baggage and freight handling at an airport was of an international, non-local nature. The Chief Justice gave as a further reason for his decision the fact that three of the four defendants were not Micronesians. Lastly, he relied on the fact that the contract revealed no intention of the parties to be governed by customary law. Accordingly, the common law of the United States was applied. This case was decided by the Supreme Court of the Federated States of Micronesia, and may be distinguished on the grounds that customary laws are expressly stated to be subject only to the Constitution. However, the case is still a good illustration of the issues that arise in deciding whether customary laws are applicable in contract cases.

2.4. INTERSTITIAL RECOGNITION

Whether or not customary laws are recognised by the state, there is room for interstitial recognition by a court in the interpretation of the law or in the exercise of its discretion. This was recognised by the High Court of Fiji in *Naqa v Fiji Electricity Authority*.[61] In that case, the defendant acquired some of the plaintiffs' customary land for a hydro project. The plaintiffs

58 See e.g. *Sukutaona v Houanihou* [1982] SILR 12 and *Sasango v Beliga* [1987] SILR 91.

59 The temptation to oversimplify the process was judicially recognised in *Lilo v Ghomo* [1980–81] SILR 229.

60 [1985] FMSC 3.

61 [2005] FLR 264.

were permitted by the defendant to continue to use the land for traditional purposes, agriculture, grazing and logging, and to use the waters for the village supply. A dispute arose as to the use of waters in the catchment area on the land and the right to compensation. After a takeover of the power station by certain the landowners, attempts were made to settle the dispute, culminating in a 'Joint Statement of Understanding' pursuant to which the defendant was to pay $52.8m to the plaintiff. However, the defendant later disputed that this was a binding agreement on the basis that its agents had no authority to settle and that there was no intention to be bound. In concluding that there was a binding agreement, the court commented on the fact that the parties had subsequently participated in a traditional Fijian ceremony to denote resolution of their grievances. Whilst the court recognised that this did not have any substantive effect, it considered that it was relevant in ascertaining objectively the intention of the parties to be bound, stating that:

> The defendant points to that ceremony and submits that it is irrelevant as the case falls to be determined by conventional legal principles and not by reference to traditional ceremonies. This is not an occasion on which I need to explore the significant cultural impact of ceremonies on domestic law and the importance of making agreements in Fiji in a traditional way ... however ... such ceremonies are an every day experience in the lives of our citizens and have real meaning. I accept the evidence ... that these ceremonies set the seal on agreements with Fijians by having both parties embrace the arrangements by the sharing of 'yaqona' the presentation of 'tabua' and the offering of respect to the agreement, ancestry and parties involved by eloquent rhetoric. Parliament has the power under the Constitution to make provision for the application of customary laws and for dispute resolution in accordance with traditional Fijian processes (Section 86 of the Constitution). The fact that Parliament has that power doesn't yet elevate these ceremonies into a legal significance but it does underscore their importance in the objective assessment of whether or not Fijians intend to be bound to an agreement at any point in time. I accept the sincerity and respect given by the parties to the agreement under this ceremony. I find it objectively points to an immediate intention to be bound. An objective bystander would be taken to be informed of their importance in signifying an intention to be bound.

Customary laws may also influence a court in the interpretation of a contract. An example can be found in *Leahy v Otri*,[62] which was a dispute over whether there was a valid contract for certain customary land to be transferred to the plaintiff. The defendant claimed that there were oral terms included in the contract and that the plaintiff had repudiated the contract by not complying with those terms. The plaintiff denied that those terms were part of the agreement.

62 [2009] PGNC 314.

The court held that these 'extra' terms were not included in the contract because 'logic and commonsense as well as custom and usage in contract negotiations between two parties would also require and dictate that if anything, all the terms and conditions of a contract of sale of land would be publicly spelt out'. The court's decision was influenced by the fact that they were 'dealing with a group of customary landowners and as far as they [were concerned], the contract of sale was entered in public and concluded with a feast at Kenta village in 1995'.[63] The defendant stated in his affidavit that the terms he wanted to include '[were] not meant for the whole village or public to hear'.

It is clear that the common law of contract continues to dominate the courts' approach to agreements in Pacific Island countries. Little attention is paid to customary laws surrounding reciprocal arrangements or customary exchanges; in fact, the difference between these types of transactions is not even acknowledged. Even in Papua New Guinea, where the Underlying Law Act gives scope for the development of an underlying law of contract based on customary laws, the common law continues to prevail. Common lawyers continue to test the facts against rules that are often ill fitting. It is arguable that regional constitutions have given state courts a mandate to search for a more prominent role for customary laws in contract cases, at least where there is a customary context. This is particularly so in those countries of the region where customary laws have not only been given formal recognition as a general source of law but have also been emphasised in the preamble to the constitution and in specific provisions relating to customary land.[64] Notwithstanding, it is important to keep in mind the potential for customary laws to apply. This possibility, as it relates to particular areas of the common law of contract, is discussed in the following chapters.

63 Ibid., [40].

64 See e.g. Constitution of Vanuatu 1980, Art. 73: 'All land in the Republic of Vanuatu belongs to the indigenous custom owners and their descendants'; Art. 74: 'the rules of custom shall form the basis of ownership and use of land in the Republic of Vanuatu'.

CHAPTER 3
FORMATION OF AN AGREEMENT

1. INTRODUCTION

The courts have developed rules to assist in determining whether a legally binding agreement has been reached by the parties. These rules are useful tools to use when trying to analyse facts. However, some courts have expressed the view that the rules are too restrictive, and that it is more important to look at the circumstances as a whole to see whether there is a contract, rather than to analyse the facts to establish separate legal elements of an agreement.[1] The artificiality which may result from adherence to the rules in complex cases was pointed out in *New Zealand Shipping Co Ltd v A M Satterthwaite & Co Ltd*,[2] where Lord Wilberforce said:

> English Law, having committed itself to a rather technical and schematic doctrine of contract, in application takes a practical approach, often at the cost of forcing the facts to fit uneasily into the marked slots of offer, acceptance, and consideration.

There may be cases where the courts are prepared to find that the essence of contract is present, even though it is difficult to analyse the transaction in terms of the rules discussed in this chapter.[3] Further, if a party has been led to assume that a contract exists or will be made, the courts may be prepared to treat the situation as contractual on the basis of estoppel. This is discussed further in chapter 7.

In the Pacific region, courts often take the traditional rules as a starting point in determining whether an agreement has been formed.[4] In *Naqa v Fiji*

---

1 See e.g. *Estate Management Services Ltd v Lakshman* [2017] FJHC 183, [34], citing the view of Denning LJ in *Butler Machine Tool Co Ltd v Ex-Cell-O Corporation (England) Ltd* [1979] 1 WLR 401. See also *Gibson v Manchester City Council* [1978] 1 WLR 520 and *Trentham Ltd v Archital Luxfer* [1993] 1 Lloyd's Rep 25.

2 [1975] AC 154, 167.

3 See e.g. *Soakai v Kingdom of Tonga* [1998] TOSC 5.

4 In *Gibson v Manchester City Council* [1979] 1 WLR 294 the House of Lords rejected the more flexible approach, preferring the rigidity of offer and acceptance to the alternative of uncertainty. For regional examples of reliance on the traditional approach see e.g. *Media Enterprises Pty Ltd v Fiji Broadcasting Commission* [1999] FJHC 80; *Peseta v Siliato* [2016]

Electricity Authority,[5] the Fiji High Court cited *Fletcher Challenge Energy Ltd v Electricity Corporation of New Zealand Ltd*[6] where the New Zealand Court of Appeal held that the prerequisites to formation of a contract are:

a. An intention to be immediately bound (at the point where the bargain is said to have been agreed); and
b. An agreement, express or found by implication, or the means of achieving an agreement, (eg an arbitration clause) on every term which:
   i. was legally essential to the formation of such a bargain; or
   ii. was regarded by the parties themselves as essential to their particular bargain.

The New Zealand case was also cited with approval by the Supreme Court of Samoa in *Poulos v Samoa Rugby Union Incorporated*.[7]

In basic terms, the prerequisites require the following elements to be present in order for a contract to be formed:

- intention to create legal relations;
- agreement (offer and acceptance);[8] and
- certainty of the terms.

This chapter is concerned with the second requirement, that is agreement.[9] The other elements are discussed in later chapters.

In Tokelau, the formation of contracts is governed by the Contract Rules 2004, based on the principles of the United Nations Convention on Contracts for the International Sale of Goods 1980.

2. AGREEMENT

An agreement requires at least two parties.[10] They are commonly referred to as the 'promisor' and 'promisee'. In the case of a unilateral contract there is

---

WSDC 53, [5]; *Piokole v Logona* [2017] PGNC 79; see further A. Kretowicz, 'Collective Bargaining in Papua New Guinea' (2019) 25 *Comparative Law Journal of the Pacific* 117; *Naki v AGC (Pacific) Ltd* [2005] PGNC 163; *Veltro Ltd v Steven Liu Huang* [2006] PGNC 197; *Strickland Brothers v Attorney-General* [2014] WSSC 15; *Bluesky Communications Ltd v Attorney-General* [2007] WSSC 58; *Transol Shipping Company Ltd v Laore* [2013] SBHC 182; *Venter v National Bank of Vanuatu* [2018] VUCA 6.

5 [2005] FLR 264.

6 [2002] 2 NZLR 433, 444.

7 [2011] WSSC 86, [76].

8 See e.g. *FR8 Logistics Ltd v Eagan* [2016] VUSC 152.

9 See e.g. *Ram v Native Lands Trust Board* [2011] FJHC 404.

10 *Prasad v Sunrise Corporation Ltd* [2005] FJCA 23.

only one promisor and the promisee may accept the unilateral offer by taking the requisite action, but is not required to give a promise in return. In the case of a bilateral contract, which consists of the mutual exchange of promises, both parties will be 'promisors' and 'promisees'. Which party is being referred to depends on the context in which the words are being used. If the context does not make it clear, alternative terms, referring to the capacity of the parties in the contract, such as 'vendor' and 'purchaser' or 'employer' and 'employee', may be more helpful.

The parties must be of the same mind in order for an enforceable agreement to arise.[11] As stated by the Fiji Court of Appeal, '[e]ntering into an agreement (contract) is meeting of minds (consensus ad idem) which means both parties to an agreement have the same understanding of its terms and conditions'.[12] Similarly, in *Wewela v Commodities Export Marketing Authority*,[13] in deciding whether the parties had reached agreement for the sale of a property, the High Court said that there had to be a meeting of the minds before a contract could be formed. In deciding whether or not there has been a meeting of the minds, the courts adopt an objective approach.[14] Accordingly, the courts look at the circumstances surrounding the alleged agreement, and in particular what the parties have said and done, and ask themselves whether a reasonable person would conclude from that evidence that agreement has been reached. As stated by the Kiribati Court of Appeal in *Kiribati Shipping Services Ltd v Waysang Kum Kee*:[15]

> The starting point is that for the purpose of the law of contract, offer and acceptance are to be assessed objectively. If a purchaser outwardly conducts itself in a way which makes it reasonable for a vendor to conclude that the purchaser is accepting the vendor's offer, it is immaterial whether the purchaser privately had other intentions. Nor is the vendor concerned to inquire into the factors which may or may not have motivated the purchaser to communicate an acceptance. All that is necessary is that, to a reasonable person in the position of the vendor, the purchaser appears to be accepting the vendor's offer.

This is as opposed to a subjective approach, which attempts to find out what was present in the minds of the parties, seeking to establish whether the parties actually intended to agree.

The main reason for this approach is that it is impossible to obtain reliable and adequate evidence to prove a particular person's actual intention or state

11 *Compass Rose v Taomati Iuta* (Unreported, High Court, Kiribati, 14 May 1982); *Wewela v Commodities Export Marketing Authority* [2018] SBHC 45.
12 *Mani v Mani* [2017] FJCA 63, [16]; *Reweru v Agigo* [2015] NRSC 4, [9].
13 [2018] SBHC 45, citing *Solomon Islands Broadcasting Corporation v Bisili* [2000] SBHC 5.
14 See e.g. *Kiribati Shipping Services Ltd v Waysang Kum Kee* [2009] KICA 15.
15 [2009] KICA 15, [18].

of mind. Further, the law considers that if a party acted or spoke in a certain way then the other party is entitled to interpret those actions or words in a reasonable manner and rely on that interpretation. It is not open to parties to allege that their words or actions were intended to have a different effect from that which a reasonable person would interpret them as having. Consequently, if a party's words or actions would cause a reasonable person to believe that a specific promise or agreement exists, those actions will be binding regardless of the party's subjective intention. For example, if a party signs a written document containing contractual terms, that party will usually be taken to have agreed to those terms.[16]

In the Pacific, the question arises whether the objective test should be applied against the background of local circumstances, rather than using standards applicable in England, where the test was developed through the common law. There is some indication in regional decisions on contract that courts are prepared to judge what is reasonable through the eyes of a Pacific Islander.[17] For example, in *Compass Rose v Taomati Iuta*,[18] in considering whether there had been a meeting of the minds, the court took into account the fact that shaking hands was not a Kiribati custom and had no significance. However, case law in other fields of law has indicated that the courts do not always assess reasonableness by reference to local culture and practices.[19] Support for applying the objective test in the Pacific context can be found in the recognition provisions discussed in chapter 1, according to which common law and equity only apply if they are applicable to local circumstances. This might be taken to suggest that the proper approach to the objective test is to consider reasonableness from the standpoint of a local person.

Unless a statute requires a contract to be in a particular form, either as a condition of existence or of enforceability, the agreement need not be in writing.[20] It may be oral or arise from the conduct of the parties.[21] If it is in writing, it need not be in a single document. For example, it may be contained in an exchange of letters[22] or emails. The occasions when the agreement must be in writing are discussed further in chapter 10.

---

16 *L'Estrange v F Graucob Ltd* [1934] 2 KB 394.

17 See e.g. *Maeaniani v Saemala* [1982] SILR 70.

18 Unreported, High Court, Kiribati, 14 May 1982.

19 See e.g. *R v Loumia* [1984] SILR 51. See further J. Corrin Care, 'Cultures in Conflict: The Role of the Common Law in the South Pacific' (2002) 6 *Journal of South Pacific Law* 1.

20 See e.g. *CP Homes Ltd v Ali* [1995] SBHC 115; *Media Enterprises Pty Ltd v Fiji Broadcasting Commission* [1999] FJHC 80; *RC Manubhai & Company v Rafiq* [2017] FJHC 250; *GMR Muhammed & Sons v Wati* [2014] FJMC 161.

21 See e.g. *Pupu v Tourism Development Corporation* [2002] PNGLR 36. N.B. in Papua New Guinea, the formation of sale of goods contracts is governed by the Goods Act 1951, s 5(1).

22 *Mudaliar v Gibson* [1987] 33 FLR 56.

Agreement normally consists of two parts – the offer and the acceptance[23] – and different rules apply to each. However, as mentioned above, the modern approach to offer and acceptance acknowledges that it is necessary to consider the circumstances of the case as a whole in order to ascertain whether there has been an offer and an acceptance.[24] In some cases it is difficult to analyse an agreement, particularly if the negotiations are oral and protracted. This was the case in *Framhein v Tepaki Investments Ltd*,[25] where the Cook Islands High Court held that the employment contract in question was formed when the plaintiffs actually started working for the defendant. Where the contract is in writing, it may be unnecessary to inquire whether there has been an offer and an acceptance.[26]

3. THE OFFER

3.1. DEFINITION

An offer has been described as 'a definite promise to be bound provided that certain specified terms are accepted'.[27] It has also been described in more detail as:

> an intimation, by words or conduct, of a willingness to enter into a legally binding contract, ... which in its terms expressly or impliedly indicates that it is to become binding on the offeror as soon as it has been accepted by an act, forbearance, or return promise on the part of the person to whom it is addressed.[28]

An offer may be express or implied. An express offer may be written, oral or partly written and partly oral. As explained by the Court of Appeal of Fiji in *Mani v St Fort Investment Ltd*,[29] an implied offer may arise from a course of dealings. This would be the case if it clear from what the parties said, the way they reacted to or conducted themselves towards each other, that each had a common, though unspoken, understanding that a promise had been made.

---

23 *Mani v Mani* [2017] FJCA 63, [14].

24 See e.g. *Estate Management Services Ltd v Lakshman* [2017] FJHC 183, [34], citing *Butler Machine Tool Co Ltd v Ex-Cell-O Corporation (England) Ltd* [1979] 1 All ER 965.

25 [2007] CKHC 7, [40].

26 *Ralulu v iTaukei Land Trust Board* [2016] FJHC 535, citing *L'Estrange v F Graucob* (1934) 3 KB 394.

27 M.P. Furmston, *Cheshire, Fifoot and Furmston's Law of Contract*, 17th ed., Oxford University Press, Oxford 2017, p. 44.

28 J. Beatson, A. Burrows and J. Cartwright, *Anson's Law of Contract*, 30th ed., Oxford University Press, Oxford 2017, p. 35.

29 (1985) 31 FLR 136.

The person who makes the offer is referred to as the offeror. The person to whom the offer is made is referred to as the offeree. As mentioned above, a person who makes a promise is known as the 'promisor'. If the promise constitutes an offer, the person making it will also be the offeror. The offeror's role in the formation of the contract must be completed by a final declaration of readiness to undertake an obligation on certain conditions, leaving the offeree the choice of acceptance or refusal. The offeror must be prepared to implement the promise, if called upon to do so by the offeree.

3.2. DISTINCTION BETWEEN AN OFFER AND OTHER DEALINGS

In whatever form it is made, the offer must be made with the intention that the offeror will be bound if it is accepted.[30] A distinction must be drawn between offers and other dealings which may resemble offers but do not go so far in committing the person making them.

3.2.1. Invitation to Treat

An invitation to treat is a statement of intention of willingness to do business.[31] It does not indicate a willingness by the person who makes it to enter into a contractual relationship.[32] It may indicate a willingness to receive offers.

Whether or not a particular statement or act amounts to an offer or an invitation to treat depends upon the intention of the person making the statement or doing the act. The question is whether, judged objectively, that person intended to make a binding offer or not.

There are some well recognised categories of invitations to treat, which will now be discussed.

3.2.1.1. Advertisements

Generally, advertisements are not regarded as offers, but as invitations to treat. For example, in *Grainger v Gough*,[33] a wine merchant sent out a circular catalogue, listing his wines and the prices. It was held not to amount to an offer to supply an unlimited amount of that wine. Similarly, in *Partridge v Crittenden*,[34]

---

30 *Bexter v Glengrow (SI) Co Ltd* [2018] SBHC 59.

31 See e.g. *Ram v Native Lands Trust Board* [2011] FJHC 404; *Qaranivalu v Native Land Trust Board* [2013] FJHC 12.

32 *Bexter v Glengrow (SI) Co Ltd* [2018] SBHC 59.

33 [1896] AC 325.

34 [1968] 2 All ER 421.

an advertisement for 'Bramblefinch cocks, Bramblefinch hens 25s each' in a periodical was held to be an invitation to treat rather than an offer. The offence of offering for sale a wild bird contrary to s 6(1) of the Protection of Birds Act 1954 (UK) was therefore not established.

A regional example can be found in *Police v Tapuolo*,[35] a criminal case, where it was relevant to establish whether a contract had been formed. The defendant made known to the public that he was operating a game called 'ponesi', which was a game of chance or lottery. The court held that this constituted an invitation to treat. When a member of the public placed a bet with the defendant, that was an offer, and when he accepted the money and recorded the bet, that was acceptance and created a 'contract of chance'.

The courts' approach to advertisements operates well in practice as advertisers would otherwise be obliged to sell to every person who accepted the offer contained in the advertisement. It is still open to the court to hold that the advertiser has gone further than making an invitation to treat if the language used indicates a willingness to be bound by the terms contained in the advertisement. This was the case in *Carlill v Carbolic Smoke Ball Company*.[36] In that case the defendant advertised that it would pay £100 to anyone who purchased and used its smoke ball in the specified manner and subsequently contracted flu. The defendant stated that £1,000 had been placed in a bank account to pay claimants. The plaintiff used the smoke ball but still caught flu. The defendant refused to pay her claim for £100, arguing that the advertisement was only an invitation to treat. The Court of Appeal held that the defendant's statement that it had deposited the money indicated a willingness to be bound by the terms of the advertisement. The defendant was therefore bound by its offer when the plaintiff accepted it by using the product.

Advertisements may also contain 'mere puff', that is, extravagant claims which are clearly not intended to be binding. Mere puff falls short of an invitation to treat, as it is so farfetched that no reasonable person would believe it. Although it is made to attract attention to the subject matter of the advertisement, and in that sense is designed to assist in the eventual formation of a contract, the claim does not form a term of the contract or amount to a representation regarding those terms.[37] In *Carlill v Carbolic Smoke Ball Company*,[38] the defendant argued that the advertisement was mere puff,

---

35 [2015] WSSC 6.

36 *Carlill v Carbolic Smoke Ball Company* [1893] 1 QB 256, approved in *Police v Tapuolo* [2015] WSSC 6.

37 For an explanation of what is meant by 'representation', see chapter 8.

38 [1893] 1 QB 256.

but the court did not accept this, as the language used indicated a serious intention.

3.2.1.2. Goods Displayed in Shops

The display of goods for sale at marked prices is generally regarded as an invitation to treat. This point was of relevance in *Pharmaceutical Society of GB v Boots Cash Chemists*,[39] where the defendant was accused of contravening a statute that required certain drugs to be sold under the supervision of a qualified pharmacist. The defendant sold drugs in its supermarket on a self-service basis; the pharmacist was at the checkout. If the contract was made when the item was selected, the statute would have been contravened. The Court of Appeal held that the display of goods was not an offer, but an invitation to treat. The contract was concluded when the cashier told the customer the total price and the money was paid. As no offer was made at the display stage, selecting an item from the shelves was not acceptance and no contract had been concluded. Accordingly, the statute had not been breached.

The same approach has been applied to the display of goods in a shop window.[40] However, it has been suggested that vending machines and automatic ticket machines represent an offer, which can be accepted by a person choosing to insert money.[41]

3.2.1.3. Auctions

An auctioneer's request for bids is usually an invitation to treat. Thus, in *Payne v Cave*[42] the defendant bid £40 for goods being auctioned, but before they were knocked down to him he purported to withdraw his bid. It was held that a bid is merely an offer and can be withdrawn at any time prior to acceptance. Acceptance occurs on the fall of the hammer, and as the defendant had withdrawn his bid before that happened, his offer had terminated and the auctioneer could not accept.[43]

Payne v Cave should be compared with *Warlow v Harrison*,[44] where it was made clear that auctions 'without reserve' may amount to an offer to sell to the highest bona fide bidder.

---

39 [1953] 1 QB 401. Approved in *Police v Tapuolo* [2015] WSSC 6.

40 See *Fisher v Bell* [1961] 1 QB 394, where the display of a flick knife with a price tag in a shop window did not amount to the offence of offering such a knife for sale.

41 *Thornton v Shoe Lane Parking* [1971] 2 QB 163.

42 (1789) 100 ER 502. See also *Harris v Nickerson* (1873) LR 8 QB 286, where it was held that notice that an auction would be held was not an offer but a statement of intention.

43 See now Sale of Goods Act 1979 (UK), s 57(2).

44 (1859) 120 ER 920. See also *Hordern House v Arnold* [1989] VR 402.

3.2.1.4. Tenders

An invitation to submit tenders is normally construed as an invitation to treat[45] unless the wording of the invitation indicates that tenders of a particular type, for example, 'the lowest, will be accepted'. In *Spencer v Harding*[46] the defendant sent out a circular reading, 'we are instructed to offer for sale by tender the stock in trade of Messrs G Eilbeck & Co … which will be sold at a discount in one lot … The tenders will be received and opened at our offices.' The plaintiff submitted the highest tender, but the defendant refused to sell to him. It was held that an announcement calling for tenders was not a firm promise to sell to the person submitting the highest tender. It only indicated a willingness to receive offers to buy. As stated by the High Court of Fiji:

> [T]here are particularly complex tender situations … where the acceptance of a tender will simply result in a preliminary contract which is subject to conditions to be finalised later … However, the less formal the tender process, the less scope there is for a finding that the acceptance of a tender gave rise only to a preliminary process.[47]

Normally the tender submitted in response to the invitation will be the offer, which the offeree may accept or reject. It is common practice for negotiations to take place after the submission of a tender and in this case either party may make a counter-offer or fresh offer during the negotiations.

This point is illustrated by *Sivans Transport Ltd v Nadi Town Council.*[48] In that case, the plaintiff submitted a tender to the defendant for refuse collection, but said that the tender figure was open to negotiation. The defendant's Health Committee resolved that the plaintiff's tender be recommended for approval by the whole Council, subject to further negotiation with the plaintiff by a sub-committee with a view to reducing the figure. The sub-committee met with the plaintiff's representative and persuaded him to submit a lower figure. This lower figure was referred to the full Council, which rejected it. The Court of Appeal held that the discussions which the sub-committee had with the defendant did not indicate an acceptance by the sub-committee of the original tender, and in any event it had no authority to accept. Rather, the discussions constituted an effort by the sub-committee to persuade the defendant to submit a reduced offer. There was accordingly no breach of contract.

Another case in which negotiations took place after the close of tenders is *Beti v Aufiu.*[49] The plaintiff submitted a tender of $70,000 for a house in response

45 *Sonalisali Island Resort Ltd v Fortune 8 Ltd* [2017] FJHC 275.
46 (1870) LR 5 CP 561. See also *Gibson v Manchester City Council* [1979] 1 WLR 294.
47 *Sonalisali Island Resort Ltd v Fortune 8 Ltd* [2017] FJHC 275, [20]–[23].
48 (1981) 27 FLR 192.
49 [1991] SBHC 45.

to an advertisement. He subsequently received a letter from the defendant informing him that the highest tenderer had failed to complete and giving him 20 days to confirm his tender bid. The plaintiff telephoned the defendant and informed him that the tender still stood. The defendant later sold the property to a third party. It was held that there was an agreement to sell the property for $70,000 based on the defendant's offer by letter and the plaintiff's acceptance by telephone. As a third party had acquired rights in the property, the plaintiff was awarded damages.

In certain circumstances, an invitation to submit a tender may amount to a contract to consider the tender submitted. In *Blackpool & Fylde Aero Club v Blackpool Borough Council*,[50] the defendant invited tenders to operate pleasure flights from their airport. The plaintiff, the existing concession holder, submitted a tender in the form requested and within the time limit prescribed. However, the defendant did not clear its letterbox on the day tenders closed and did not receive the plaintiff's tender. It was recorded as received later and not considered. It was held that in certain circumstances an invitation to tender could give rise to a binding obligation to consider tenders that conform to the conditions of tender. In this case, the fact that the tenders had been solicited from known parties and since invitation prescribed a clear, orderly and familiar procedure, it was implied that a contractual relationship was intended.[51]

To avoid any doubt about whether an invitation to submit tenders is an offer, words may be placed in the advertisement making the position clear. In *Auspacific Construction Co Pty Ltd v Attorney-General of Kiribati*,[52] the document was headed, 'This Expression of Intention and any Expression of Interest … will become binding only on a bidder and the Government after a formal Memorandum of Agreement has been agreed and executed by both the successful bidder and the Government'. This was held to preclude the possibility of the invitation to submit tenders constituting an offer.

Tenders can be contrasted with quotations, where the quote normally forms the offer and the contract is formed on acceptance.[53]

3.2.1.5. Transport Arrangements

The distinction between an offer and an invitation to treat has proved particularly difficult to make in the case of public transport contracts and other

---

50 [1990] 1 WLR 1195.

51 See *Feroz Khan Transport Ltd v Fiji Sugar Corporation* [2008] FJHC 284, where the court stated that it 'is only a matter of time before the developments in this area of law, as has happened in other common law jurisdictions are applied in Fiji'.

52 [1997] KICA 6.

53 *Rarotonga Glass and Aluminium Ltd v Castaway Beach Villas Ltd* [2006] CKHC 6, [8].

travel arrangements. In the case of travel by bus, for example, it is uncertain whether a passenger who boards a bus is accepting an offer of carriage or whether the passenger is making an offer in response to an invitation to treat by the bus company. Much will depend on the facts and the practice prevailing in the country where the bus operates. In Fiji, buses run to a timetable and along an established route. Passengers wait at the designated bus stop and the bus automatically stops to let passengers board and alight. This is similar to the situation in Britain, where the timing of the offer was considered in *Wilkie v London Passenger Board*.[54] In that case, the plaintiff was not an ordinary passenger, but an employee of the defendant and had a bus pass. Greene MR suggested, obiter, that the presentation of a bus for people to board is an offer, which is accepted when a person gets properly on board the platform or inside the bus.

By way of contrast, in some countries, such as Vanuatu, buses do not operate on a particular route or to a timetable. The intending passenger waves the bus down and asks the driver whether the bus is going to a particular destination. If the answer is in the affirmative, the passenger boards the bus, but the fare is only paid after the passenger arrives at the destination. In this situation, it would appear that the contract is made prior to entry in the bus and that the passenger makes the offer, when he or she asks if the bus is going to the required destination, and that this is accepted when the bus driver replies that it is.

Airline travel is another problematic situation. The Australian High Court held in *MacRobertson Miller Airline Services v Commissioner of State Taxation WA*[55] that the issue of a ticket to a prospective airline passenger was either a receipt for the payment of a fare (per Barwick CJ) or an offer (per Stephenson and Jacobs J). It was not an acceptance, and therefore no contract was made at that stage. The court held that acceptance was usually made by a passenger, either orally or by conduct.

Travel by sea also gives rise to uncertainties. In *Oceanic Sun Line Shipping Co v Fay*,[56] which concerned carriage on a vessel. It was held that a contract was effected by the issue of an 'exchange order', which bound the carrier to issue a ticket. However, in *Baltic Shipping Co v Dillon*[57] the contract was held to have been made when the receipt for the tickets was issued by the respondent, following payment and the issue of a booking acknowledgement form.

With regard to travel by train, in *Denton v Great Northern Railway Co*,[58] it was held that a statement in a railway timetable that a certain train would run at a certain time was an offer capable of acceptance.

---

54 [1947] 1 All ER 258.
55 (1975) 133 CLR 125.
56 [1988] 165 CLR 197.
57 (1991) 22 NSWLR 1.
58 (1856) 5 E&B 860.

The categories of invitation to treat are not closed.[59] However, some of the cases concerning the distinction between an offer and an invitation to treat are conflicting, and appear to have been decided on an individual basis, rather than on general principles. This makes it difficult to predict the type of situation that might amount to an invitation to treat. In doubtful cases, the following questions will be relevant:

1. Was the statement specific and clear, and capable of immediate acceptance; and
2. was it made with the intention of being bound by an acceptance?

If the answer to both questions is yes, then an offer was made.

3.2.2. Mere Supply of Information

An offer must also be distinguished from a mere supply of information. In *Harvey v Facey*,[60] the plaintiff telegraphed the defendant asking, 'will you sell us Bumper Hall Pen? Telegraph lowest cash price'. The defendant replied by telegraph, 'Lowest Price for Bumper Hall Pen £900'. The plaintiffs telegraphed, 'We agree to buy BHP for £900 asked by you. Please send us your title deed'. The Privy Council held that there was no contract. The second telegram was not an offer but merely an indication of the price the defendants would want if they eventually decided to sell.

3.3. COMMUNICATION OF THE OFFER

An offer cannot be accepted unless the acceptor is aware of both its existence and its terms. Therefore, offers are only effective after they have been communicated. In *Taylor v Laird*[61] the plaintiff was engaged to command the defendant's ship and to take certain explorers on an expedition up the River Niger. The plaintiff gave up his command in the course of the expedition, but helped to work the ship home, without the defendant's knowledge. His claim for remuneration failed.

3.3.1. Cross-Offers

As an offer must be communicated before it can be accepted, cross-offers cannot constitute a binding agreement. 'Cross-offers' occur when parties forward offers

59 See e.g. *Gibson v Manchester City Council* [1979] 1 WLR 294, where the defendant's letter stating 'the Corporation may be prepared to sell the house to you' was held to be, at most, an invitation to treat.
60 [1893] AC 552.
61 (1856) 25 LJ Ex 329.

to each other at the same time and in substantially the same terms. In such cases there are two offers but no acceptance.

This was the case in *Tinn v Hoffman & Co*,[62] where the parties wrote to each other on the same day, the plaintiff offering to buy 800 tons of iron at 69 shillings per ton, and the defendant offering to sell the same quantity for the same price. The plaintiff was unable to enforce the defendant's offer as it had not been validly accepted; an exchange of offers does not amount to offer and acceptance.

3.3.2. *To Whom May an Offer be Made?*

An offer can be made to:

- a named person or persons;
- a class of people; or
- the whole world.

The question of whether an offer may be made to the whole world arose in *Carlill v Carbolic Smoke Ball Company*,[63] where it was confirmed that there was nothing to prevent such an offer being made.

3.4. PRESCRIPTION OF THE MODE OF ACCEPTANCE

The offeror may prescribe the method of acceptance either expressly or by implication. Failure to adopt that method is at the offeree's risk. However, in an appropriate case an equally expeditious method of communication may be acceptable.

An offeror may also waive the need for communication of acceptance. As the requirement of notification is for the benefit of the offeror, he or she has the option of dispensing with this requirement. In order to show that the need for communication of acceptance has been waived and that an agreement has subsequently arisen, it must be proved that:

1. there is an express or implied intimation from the offeror that a particular mode of acceptance will suffice, and that the particular mode does not involve communication; and
2. there was some overt act or conduct on the part of the offeree which demonstrates an intention to accept and which conforms to the mode of acceptance indicated by the offeror.

---

62 (1873) 29 LT 271.

63 [1893] 1 QB 256, approved in *Police v Tapuolo* [2015] WSSC 6.

In *Carlill v Carbolic Smoke Ball Co*[64] the defendant argued that there could not be a binding agreement as the plaintiff had not communicated acceptance. It was held that the nature of the transaction indicated that the offeror had waived the normal requirement of communication of acceptance.

Waiver will normally be implied in the case of a unilateral contract, particularly in 'reward' cases, that is, where there is an offer of a promise to pay a reward for performance of an act specified in the advertisement, such as the return of a lost dog. In these cases, performance of the act is an adequate indication of assent, provided the person who performs the act is aware of the offer.

3.5. TERMINATION OF THE OFFER

The rules governing termination of an offer can be summarised as follows:

- An offer can be terminated at any time before it has been accepted.[65]
- Once an offer has been accepted, it becomes irrevocable.

The second rule is illustrated by *Great Northern Railway Co v Witham*.[66] In that case, the plaintiff advertised for tenders for the supply of such iron articles as they might require between 1 November 1871 and 31 October 1872. The defendant submitted a tender to supply the articles required on certain terms and in such quantities as the company 'might order from time to time'. The plaintiff accepted the tender. Orders were given and executed for some time on the terms of the tender, but finally the defendant was given an order which he refused to execute. The plaintiff sued for breach of contract based on the defendant's failure to perform the order. It was held that when the tender was accepted a binding agreement arose and the defendant was liable for breach of contract. This did not mean that the defendant had to go on supplying forever. If an invitation to treat relates to such goods of a certain type as may be ordered from time to time, a tender is a standing offer that is accepted on each occasion an order is given. The acceptance of the tender was not a blanket acceptance but intimated that the plaintiff would accept from time to time, as they required goods. Thus, each time they placed an order it was an acceptance, restricted to the quantity of goods in the order. The defendant could revoke at any time before an order was placed, but had to fulfil existing orders once made.

An offer can be terminated in a number of ways, as explained in the following sections.

64 [1893] 1 QB 256.
65 *Alai v Kakai* [2009] SBHC 1.
66 (1873) LR 9 CP 16.

3.5.1. Revocation of the Offer

An offer can be freely revoked at any time prior to acceptance. In *Alai v Kakai*,[67] the defendant's representative applied to the Commissioner of Lands to buy a piece of land. The Commissioner offered a 50-year fixed term estate with the relevant fees and the purchase price to be paid within 30 days of the offer. The defendant moved onto the land but did not pay. Sixteen months later, the Commissioner wrote to him revoking the offer on the grounds of non-payment. The land was then sold to someone else. The defendant refused to vacate, arguing that the Commissioner was not able to revoke his offer. It was held that the Commissioner had the power to revoke the offer, pursuant to the Land and Titles Act.[68] The offer had specified as the requirement for acceptance payment of the fees and the purchase price within a prescribed period of time. As the defendant failed to pay within the time specified, the offer lapsed through time and it was validly revoked.

Once accepted, an offer becomes irrevocable. Revocation occurs when the offeror formally withdraws the offer. This point is illustrated by *Payne v Cave*,[69] where it was held that a bid at auction is merely an offer and can be withdrawn at any time prior to acceptance. Acceptance occurs on the fall of the hammer, and as the defendant had withdrawn his bid before that happened his offer had been revoked and the auctioneer could not accept it.

3.5.1.1. Options

A promise to keep an offer open for a certain period of time will be binding if it is supported by consideration or if it is contained in a deed.[70] Such a promise is called an option. Options are particularly important in relation to contracts for the sale of land, as it is a common commercial procedure for a prospective purchaser of land to take out an option over the land while he considers whether or not to proceed with the purchase. The effect of the option is to prevent the offeror from selling the land to a third party during the period of the option.

A promise by the offeror to keep the offer open for a fixed period will not create an option. In *Myers v Bavadra*,[71] the defendants wrote to the plaintiff offering to sell him some shares and stated that the offer was valid for 90 days. During the course of the 90 days, the defendants replaced their original offer with different terms, including a condition precedent that the plaintiff must have other shares in the company transferred to him before he could buy theirs.

---

[67] [2009] SBHC 1.
[68] Cap 133, s 5.
[69] 100 ER 502.
[70] *Mountford v Scott* [1975] 1 All ER 198.
[71] [1993] FJHC 114.

On the 90th day after the original offer was made, the plaintiff purported to accept it. It was held that the bare promise to keep the original offer open was not binding on the defendants.[72] This was the case even though the offeree had paid out money during the negotiation of the agreement. The court held that this would not create an option unless this was specifically agreed between the parties. Ashton-Lewis J commented that:[73]

> To create such an open offer for a certain time requires agreement or intention between the parties in that regard, and separate consideration from the offeree flowing to the offeror to keep his offer open on those terms exclusively for the agreed period of time. In the case at hand, I am satisfied that all the defendants did was to make a bare promise to keep their offer open ... and the expense[s] incurred by the plaintiff was not the price agreed to between the parities to do so.

3.5.1.2. Communication of Revocation

Revocation of an offer is ineffective until communicated to and received by the offeree. For example, in *Byrne v Van Tienhoven*,[74] the defendant wrote to the plaintiff on 1 October offering to sell him a quantity of tinplate and suggesting a reply by cable. When the plaintiff had not replied by 8 October, the defendant wrote revoking their offer. The plaintiff, who had cabled acceptance on 11 October, did not receive that letter until 20 October. It was held that the revocation was ineffective. Whilst an offer can be revoked at any time before acceptance, a revocation is not effective until it has been communicated to the offeree. Here the revocation was not effective until 20 October, by which time the defendant's offer had been validly accepted. Accordingly, an enforceable contract had arisen on 11 October.

The law does not specify how the revocation should be communicated. All that is required is that the offeree actually becomes aware of it. Thus, an offeree cannot accept it in the knowledge that it has been revoked, even if this knowledge was obtained from a third party rather than the offeror. For example, in *Dickinson v Dodds*,[75] the defendant offered to sell the plaintiff some houses for £800 on Wednesday, stating that the offer was 'to be left over until Friday 9am'. Despite this, the defendant sold the houses to a third party on Thursday. The plaintiff heard of the sale through his agent on Thursday evening, and attempted to accept the defendant's offer by handing him a formal acceptance before 9am on Friday morning. It was held that no one can accept an offer which they know to have been withdrawn.

---

[72] See also *Routledge v Grant* (1828) 130 ER 920.
[73] *Myers v Bavadra* [1993] FJHC 114, [24].
[74] (1880) 5 CPD 344.
[75] (1876) 2 Ch D 463.

Dickinson v Dodds[76] also illustrates the point that revocation may be communicated by conduct rather than words. The defendant's conduct in agreeing to sell the property to a third party was held by the court to be as good as saying, 'I withdraw the offer'.

3.5.1.3. Revocation of a Unilateral Offer

As explained above, an offer can be revoked at any time before acceptance. This raises a problem where the contract is unilateral. Where a unilateral contract consists of an act done in return for a promise, the acceptance takes the form of performance of the act specified in the offer. The traditional view is that acceptance is the complete performance of the act. However, it could be unjust to insist on this as it would mean that the offeror can withdraw the offer at any time before completion of the act, even if the offeree has commenced to do the act. For example, if a firm of food manufacturers offers a prize to anyone who eats one ton of its noodles within two months, they would be able to revoke after six weeks, in spite of the fact that someone is only a few pounds short. Accordingly, it is now accepted that in some cases the offer contemplates that unequivocal commencement of performance amounts to acceptance, after which there can be no withdrawal.

In *Errington v Errington*,[77] a father promised his son and daughter-in-law that his house, in which they were living, would belong to them as soon as they had paid off the instalments of a mortgage on the premises. They commenced to pay with his knowledge. Denning LJ considered that this promise could not be revoked:

> The father's promise was a unilateral contract – a promise of the house in return for their act of paying the instalments. It could not be revoked by him once the couple entered on performance of the act, but it would cease to bind him if they left it incomplete and unperformed.

However, in *Luxor (Eastbourne) Ltd v Cooper*,[78] the offer specifically stated that an agent's commission would only be paid on completion of a sale. The House of Lords refused to imply a promise by the offeror not to revoke the offer prior to completion.

3.5.2. Rejection of the Offer

An offer will terminate if it is rejected by the offeree. Normally rejection must be communicated. However, the rejection need not be express, but may take the

---

76 Ibid.

77 [1952] 1 KB 290. See also *Daulia v Four Mill Bank Nominees Ltd* [1978] 2 All ER 557.

78 [1941] AC 108.

form of conduct which justifies the offeror in concluding that the offeree does not intend to accept the offer.

A counter-offer is deemed to be a rejection of the offer.[79] Counter-offers are discussed in section 4 below.

3.5.3. *Lapse of Time*

An offer must be accepted within the prescribed time, or if no time is specified, within a reasonable time. What is reasonable is a question of fact and will depend on all the circumstances of the case. Relevant factors may be:

- the subject matter of the contract; for example, it is likely to be much shorter in the case of perishable goods;
- the means used to communicate the offer; for example, an offer communicated by email may indicate urgency;
- the consideration involved;
- the complexity of contract documents; and
- whether the value of the subject matter fluctuates.

In *Ramsgate Victoria Hotel Co v Montefiore*,[80] the defendant wrote to the plaintiff on 8 June, offering to purchase shares in the plaintiff company. He did not receive any answer until 23 November, when he was informed the shares had been allotted to him. He refused to accept them. It was held that the defendant's offer had lapsed by reason of the delay by the plaintiff in notifying acceptance.

3.5.4. *Failure of a Condition Subject to which the Offer was Made*

An offer which is made subject to a condition, such as 'subject to finance from National Bank', will terminate when it becomes clear that the condition cannot be fulfilled, for example if the bank refuses to grant the loan.

This will also be the case where the condition to which the offer is subject is implied, for example a condition that the goods are in existence or that they are of merchantable quality. In *Financings Ltd v Stimson*,[81] the defendant offered to buy a car on hire-purchase terms from the plaintiff. Before the plaintiff indicated its acceptance the vehicle was stolen and damaged. It was held that the plaintiff could not validly accept after this event as the offer had lapsed.

---

79 *Hyde v Wrench* (1840) 49 ER 132.
80 (1866) LR 1 Ex 109.
81 [1962] 1 WLR 1184.

3.5.5. *Death*

In general, an offer appears to continue after the death of the offeror, up until the time that the offeree receives notice of the death.[82] Once such notice has been received, it is too late to accept.[83] The exception to this is that an offer which is personal to the offeror, for example an offer by an artist to carry out a commission, comes to an end on the death of the offeror, whether or not the offeree has received notice.

An offer is determined by the death of the offeree. Personal representatives are not bound by a subsequent acceptance.[84]

4. ACCEPTANCE

4.1. DEFINITION

In *Myers v Bavadra*[85] acceptance was defined as:

> an unequivocal communication to the offeror by the offeree of agreement to both the terms of the offer, and that the offeree commits himself to the contract.

Acceptance has also been defined as:

> the expression, by words or conduct, of assent to the terms of the offer in the manner prescribed or indicated by the offeror.[86]

4.1.1. *The Form of Acceptance*

The phrase 'words or conduct' makes it clear that acceptance may be express or implied from conduct. The words may be written or spoken. A regional example of an agreement arising from conduct can be found in *Pupu v Tourism Development Corporation*,[87] where it was held that an agreement for the defendant to purchase artefacts from the plaintiff arose from the conduct of the parties in allowing the goods to be transferred to the defendant's premises and selling some of the goods to third parties.

---

82 But see *Dickinson v Dodds* (1876) 2 Ch D 290.
83 *Coulthart v Clementson* (1879) 5 QBD 42.
84 *Foley v Classique Coaches Ltd* [1934] 2 KB 1.
85 [1993] FJHC 114.
86 J. Beatson, A. Burrows and J. Cartwright, above n. 28, p. 42.
87 [2002] PNGLR 36.

4.1.2. *Unilateral and Bilateral Contracts*

The distinction between unilateral and bilateral contracts, discussed in chapter 1, can be important when considering if and when a contract is made. If the terms of the offer require the offeree to make a promise in return, there will be outstanding obligations on both sides on acceptance, and therefore a bilateral contract. For example, if the offeror offers a job to a prospective employee and requires a contract of employment to be signed to indicate acceptance, both parties will be making promises to the other. Each party is both a promisor and promisee. Both sides have future obligations.

In the case of a unilateral contract, where the offeror alone gives a promise, the offer is accepted by complying with the terms of the offer, for example by giving information for which a reward is offered.[88]

4.2. WHO CAN ACCEPT AN OFFER?

Generally, an offer can only be accepted by the person to whom it is made. If an offer is made to more than one person, any of the offerees may accept, so it is up to the offeror to ensure that he or she is not faced with more than one acceptance. In reward cases, the tendency has been to construe offers as capable of acceptance only by the first person to accept.[89]

A person cannot accept an offer of which he or she is unaware. Thus, if an act is done which fulfils the terms of a unilateral offer, but the actor is unaware of the offer, there is no acceptance.[90] For this reason, cross-offers cannot amount to acceptance.[91]

Not only must the acceptor be aware of the offer, but also he must not forget about it. For example, in *R v Clarke*[92] the Government of Western Australia offered a reward for information leading to arrest and conviction of the murderer of two police officers. The defendant saw the proclamation in May. On June 6 he gave false information to protect the murderers. On June 10 he gave information which led to the conviction of two of the murderers. The defendant admitted that in providing the information his only motive had been to clear

[88] A unilateral contract can also consist of an act done in return for a promise, e.g. where a person carries out work or supplies goods in circumstances where it is clear that payment is required. The act constitutes the offer and the acquiescence in the carrying out of the act is the acceptance. See e.g. *Steven v Bromley & Son* [1919] 2 KB 722.

[89] *Lancaster v Walsh* (1838) 150 ER 1327.

[90] There is no regional or British authority directly on point, but *Fitch v Snedaker* (1868) 38 NY 248 is in accord with academic principle. See to the contrary *Gibbons v Proctor* (1891) 64 LT 594.

[91] See *Tinn v Hoffman & Co* (1873) 29 LT 27, discussed above.

[92] (1927) 40 CLR 227; [1928] ALR 227.

his own name, and that at that time the reward had passed out of his mind. His claim for the reward failed as the High Court held that he had not acted in reliance on or pursuant to the offer.

Provided the offer is present in the offeree's mind when the act is carried out, the fact that there is another motive for the act is irrelevant. For example, in *Williams v Carwardine*[93] a reward was offered for information leading to discovery of identity of a particular murderer. The plaintiff gave information, knowing about the reward, but with the motive of easing her conscience. It was held that motive was irrelevant, provided that the acceptor knew of the reward.

4.3. FACT OF ACCEPTANCE

An acceptance must be unqualified, and must correspond with the terms of the offer. Accordingly, certain responses will not amount to an acceptance even though they may resemble one.

4.3.1. A Counter-Offer is not an Acceptance

A counter-offer brings the original offer to an end. Neither offer can be accepted unless it is renewed. In *Hyde v Wrench*,[94] the defendant wrote to the plaintiff on 6 June offering to sell his farm for £1,000. The plaintiff immediately made an offer of £950. On 27 June the defendant rejected the offer of £950. On 29 June the plaintiff purported to accept the offer of 6 June. The plaintiff sued for specific performance. It was held that there was no contract. The counter-offer was a rejection of the offer by the defendant, which could not subsequently be accepted.

This is a straightforward case, but more complex interactions may occur. For example, an acceptance may be accompanied by further details of the terms agreed. Whether or not these details add to the terms of the offer to such an extent as to constitute a counter-offer is a question of fact. In *Industrial (SP) Ltd v Mathieson*,[95] the court held that a letter of acceptance drawing the offeror's attention to certain assumptions on the part of the offeree and dealing with some finer details of the offer was not a counter-offer.

Where a person goes further than this, and purports to accept an offer, but introduces new terms not in the offer, no contract is made. The offeree is in effect refusing the offer and making a counter-offer of his/her own. In *Butler Machine*

93 (1833) 172 ER 1101.
94 (1840) 49 ER 132.
95 [1977] FJCA 15.

Tool Co Ltd v Ex-Cell-O Corporation (England) Ltd,[96] the plaintiffs offered to sell a machine to the defendants on 23 May 1969. The terms included a condition that all orders were accepted on the sellers' terms, which were to prevail over any terms and conditions in the buyer's order. The terms also included a term that the specified price would be varied if it differed from the sellers' prices prevailing on the date of delivery. On 27 May the defendants submitted an order on different terms and conditions, not including a price variation clause. The order had a tear-off acceptance slip for signature and return, which said that the order was accepted on the terms and conditions stated therein. On 5 June the sellers signed and returned the tear-off slip. The buyers could not accept delivery until a few months later than agreed. The price variation clause was invoked, but the buyers refused to pay. It was held on appeal that the buyer was not liable as their form of 27 May was a counter-offer, which was accepted by the seller.

The law relating to counter-offers has assumed greater importance now that the use of pre-printed forms has become everyday business practice. Firms have pre-printed purchase order forms (known in some countries of the region as 'LPOs'), pre-printed sales order forms, pre-printed delivery dockets, bills of lading, etc. Where there is a difference between the two forms, which terms are to prevail? This problem is known as 'the battle of the forms' and put simply, the last set of terms delivered and accepted will prevail.[97] However, once the offer is accepted, no further terms may be introduced.[98] The difficulties that this involves is illustrated by *Butler Machine Tool Co Ltd v Ex-Cell-O Corporation (England) Ltd*,[99] discussed above.

4.3.2. A Mere Inquiry does not Amount to Acceptance

A mere inquiry does not amount to an acceptance, but neither will it terminate the offer. It must be distinguished from a reply which introduces new terms and amounts to a counter-offer. In *Stevenson v McLean*[100] it was held that the offeree could still accept an offer of a certain quantity of iron at 40 shillings net cash per ton, even though he had telegraphed requesting information as to possible terms of credit.

The test to determine whether a reply amounts to a counter-offer or mere inquiry is whether a reasonable person in the position of the offeror would

---

96 [1979] 1 WLR 401; [1979] 1 All ER 965.
97 See further E.H. Hondius and C. Mahé, 'The Battle of the Forms: Towards a Uniform Contract Solution' (1998) 12 *Journal of Contract Law* 268.
98 *Jayaar Impex Ltd v Toaken Group Ltd* [1996] 2 Lloyd's Rep 437.
99 [1979] 1 WLR 401; [1979] 1 All ER 965.
100 (1880) 5 QBD 346.

regard the purported acceptance 'as introducing a new term into the bargain and not as a clear acceptance of the offer'.[101]

4.3.3. *A Conditional Assent does not Amount to Acceptance*

Where an offer is accepted on certain conditions, it will not amount to an acceptance. For example, where a purported acceptance is made 'subject to the preparation of a formal contract', there is no binding contract until the formal contract is executed. In *Winn v Bull*[102] the defendant agreed to lease of a house from the plaintiff for a certain term at a certain rent, 'subject to the preparation and approval of a formal contract'. No other contract was entered into between the parties. The plaintiff sued for specific performance. It was held that there was no binding contract.

This case should be contrasted with the situation where the parties intend to make an immediately binding contract, which is later to be merged into a formal contract. In *Branca v Cobarro*[103] the vendor agreed to sell the lease and goodwill of a mushroom farm on the terms of a written document which was declared to be a 'provisional agreement until a fully legalised agreement, drawn up by a solicitor and embodying all the conditions herewith stated, is signed'. It was held that the use of the word 'provisional' showed an intention to be bound from the outset.

4.4. COMMUNICATION OF ACCEPTANCE

The general rule is that an acceptance has no effect until it has been communicated to the offeror. The offeree must do more than mentally assent to the offer. There will be no acceptance if 'the words of acceptance are drowned by an aircraft flying overhead; or if they are spoken into a telephone line after the line has gone dead or become so indistinct that the offeror does not hear them'.[104]

4.4.1. *Acceptance Must be Communicated by the Offeree*

Acceptance must be communicated by the offeree or an authorised agent of the offeree. An acceptance communicated by a third party will not be valid. For example, in *Powell v Lee*[105] the plaintiff was a candidate for headmastership

---

101 *Global Tankers Inc v Amercoat Europa NV* [1975] 1 Lloyd's Rep 666.

102 (1877) 7 Ch D 29.

103 [1947] KB 854.

104 *Entores v Miles Far East Corporation* [1955] 2 QB 327, 332 (per Denning MR), approved in *Arinako v Minipe* [1994] PNGLR 450.

105 (1908) 99 LT 284.

of a school, and the board of managers, with whom the appointment lay, passed a resolution selecting him for the post. One of the managers, acting in his individual capacity, informed the plaintiff of what had occurred, but he received no other intimation. Subsequently the resolution was rescinded and the plaintiff was not appointed to the post. It was held that there had been no valid acceptance, as there was no authorised communication to the plaintiff.

4.4.2. Silence is not Acceptance

An offeror cannot impose contractual liability on the offeree merely by proclaiming that silence shall be deemed to be consent. The offeror cannot make the offeree choose between expressly declining the offer or becoming a party to the contract through failure to reply. So, although the offeror can impose conditions on the method and time of acceptance or waive the need to communicate acceptance altogether,[106] the offeror cannot specify that silence will amount to acceptance.

In *Felthouse v Bindley*,[107] the plaintiff offered by letter to buy his nephew's horse for £3.15s and added, 'If I hear no more about him I consider the horse mine at £3.15'. No answer was received, but the nephew decided to accept and told Bindley, the auctioneer who was selling the nephew's farm stock, not to sell the horse, as it was already sold. Bindley sold the horse by mistake, and the plaintiff sued him for conversion. It was held that as acceptance had not been communicated there was no contract of sale.

This principle is also be reflected in the rule that sending or delivering unordered goods, accompanied by a demand that they be paid for if they are not returned within a certain time does not bind the recipient to pay. However, laypeople may not be aware of this rule and may be intimidated into paying. Accordingly, this is one of the areas where statute has intervened in the area of contract. The Unsolicited Goods and Services Act 1971 (UK) provides that in certain circumstances unsolicited goods may be treated as a gift, and threats and demands may render the supplier guilty of a criminal offence. This Act may apply in Vanuatu, although there is no reported example of its application.

In Fiji, the position is governed by the Commerce Commission Decree 2010. Sections 93–94 deal with unsolicited goods and services and make similar provision to the English Act. The other countries of the region do not have any legislation on this point.

---

106 See below, sections 4.4.3 and 4.4.4.

107 (1862) 142 ER 1037.

4.4.3. *The Need to Communicate Acceptance may be Waived*

Whilst the offeror cannot impose on the offeree the choice of repudiation or liability, the offeror may waive the need to communicate acceptance, as was done in *Carlill v Carbolic Smoke Ball Company*.[108] If the offeror has waived the need to communicate acceptance and the offeree relies on that waiver, intending to accept, a contract will be formed. In the case of a unilateral contract, the need to communicate acceptance is normally presumed to be waived.[109]

4.4.4. *Method of Communication*

As mentioned above, the offeror may prescribe the method of communicating acceptance, either expressly or by implication. If the offeror stipulates that the prescribed mode is the only means of accepting the offeree must accept in that way in order for the acceptance to be valid,[110] although the offeror may waive strict compliance if the offeree is not adversely affected by this.[111] If, however, the offeror is merely suggesting the mode of acceptance, an equally expeditious method may be acceptable. However, offerees who fail to adopt the suggested method of communication do so at their own risk. On the other hand, if the offeree follows the prescribed method of communication, then the risk of any delay will be borne by the offeror.

In the case of unilateral contracts, the need to communicate acceptance is usually regarded as having been waived. However, another way of looking at this is to regard the offeror as having stipulated that the method of acceptance is by performance of an act.[112] This was the approach taken in *Myers v Bavadra*,[113] where Ashton-Lewis J said:

> In a unilateral contract the offeror usually makes a promise stipulating acceptance on the part of the offeree by the performance of an act or acts.

Where no particular method is prescribed, the method to be adopted will depend upon the nature of the offer and the method of communication used to make the offer. The court will look at the surrounding circumstances to determine what is a reasonable method. In *Tonolei Development Corp v Waka*,[114] the offeree's

---

108 See above, section 3.4.

109 *Carlill v Carbolic Smoke Ball Company* [1893] 1 QB 256.

110 *Eliason v Henshaw* (1819) 4 Wheaton 225 (USA).

111 *Manchester Diocesan Council for Education v Commercial and General Investments Ltd* [1970] 1 WLR 241, 246.

112 *Carlill v Carbolic Smoke Ball Co* [1893] 1 QB 256.

113 [1993] FJHC 114.

114 [1983] PGNC 2. See further D.K. Srivastava, 'Case Note: *Tonolei Development Corporation Ltd. v. Lucas Waka*' (1982) 10 *Melanesian Law Journal* 175.

agent collected a written offer from the offeror. Acceptance was delivered to the desk of the offeror's personal secretary. The offeror did not read it and purported to withdraw the offer. It was held that delivery of the acceptance onto the secretary's desk was deemed to be personal delivery to the offeror. The fact that the offer was collected by an agent of the offeree implied that the offeror was inviting acceptance in the same manner.[115]

In *Arinako v Minipe*,[116] the court had to decide whether an offer and acceptance for the sale and purchase of a motor vehicle made by telephone constituted a binding contract. It was held that, there being no rule of law in Papua New Guinea as to whether an offer and acceptance concluded by telephone constituted a binding contract, Schedule 2.3 of the Constitution should be applied to formulate an appropriate rule.[117] As no particular method of acceptance was prescribed, the form of communication depended on the nature of the offer and the circumstances in which it is made. In the circumstances of this case, it was held that the contract was complete when the seller heard the buyer accept by telephone.

Provided that the offeror does not stipulate otherwise, acceptance may be by conduct.[118] For example, an offer to purchase goods may be accepted by supplying them.[119]

4.4.5. The Postal Rule

The postal rule is an important exception to the rule that acceptance must be communicated before it can take effect. According to this rule, acceptance by letter is complete when the letter is posted.[120] It is immaterial that the letter is in fact lost in the post or delayed. The rule also applies to acceptance by telegram, which is complete when the telegram is handed in.[121] However, the proviso is that it must be reasonable for the offeree to notify acceptance by mail or telegram. It will be reasonable for the offeree to respond by mail if the offeror has prescribed post or telegram as the method of acceptance, or if it was within the contemplation of the parties.[122]

The leading case is *Adams v Lindsell*,[123] where the plaintiffs were wool manufacturers in Bromsgrove and the defendants were wool dealers in St Ives.

---

115 D.K. Srivastava, above n. 114, 175.
116 [1994] PNGLR 450.
117 See the discussion of Sch. 2.3 and the Underlying Law Act 2000 (PNG) in chapter 1.
118 *Myers v Bavadra* [1993] FJHC 114.
119 *Harvey v Johnston* (1848) 136 ER 1265.
120 *Kumar v Fiji Post & Telecommunication* [2002] FJCA 10. Delivery to a postman outside the post office will not suffice: *Re London and Northern Bank* [1900] 1 Ch 220.
121 *Bruner v Moore* [1904] 1 Ch 305.
122 *Henthorn v Fraser* [1892] 2 Ch 27, 33.
123 (1818) 106 ER 250.

On 2 September 1817, the defendants wrote to the plaintiffs offering to sell them a quantity of wool and requiring an answer 'in the course of post'. The letter was misdirected and it did not reach the plaintiffs until the evening of 5 September. That same night they posted their acceptance and it was delivered on 9 September. If the original offer had been properly addressed, a reply would have been received by 7 September, and because they had not received a reply by then the defendants sold the wool to third parties on 8 September. The plaintiffs sued for breach of contract. It was held that the defendants were liable for breach of contract. Post was actually specified as the manner of acceptance; therefore acceptance was complete when the letter was posted on 5 September, and a contract was formed on that date.

If the defendants in *Adams v Lindsell*[124] had not prescribed acceptance by mail the contract would only have been complete on posting of the letter if acceptance by post was in the contemplation of the parties. One case where the courts have been prepared to hold that acceptance by post is contemplated is where the offer is itself made by post.[125] The postal rule will not be taken to have been within the contemplation of the parties if its application would produce an absurd result.[126]

This rule has been said to be based on the balance of business convenience.[127] It prevents the offer being revoked whilst acceptance is in transit. It has also been supported by reference to certainty as to the time of formation of the contract as it is easier to prove the date and time of posting from the postmark than to prove when it was delivered or when it was brought to the attention of the offeror. Further, if the offeror has stipulated that acceptance should be by post it is arguable that he or she should bear the risk of the letter getting lost of being delayed.

An offeror who does not want to bear such a risk can exclude the postal rule. Exclusion may be effected by either:

- prescribing a method of communication other than post; or
- requiring actual notification before acceptance is complete.

Actual notification may be required either expressly or by implication. A case example of such stipulation arising by implication is *Holywell Securities Ltd v Hughes*,[128] where acceptance was required to be by 'notice in writing to the ... vendor'. The postal rule was held to be excluded, as the use of the words

124 Ibid.
125 *Household Fire and Carriage Accident Insurance v Grant* (1879) 4 Ex D 216.
126 *Holywell Securities Ltd v Hughes* [1974] 1 All ER 161.
127 *Re Imperial Land Co of Marseilles* (1872) LR 7 Ch App 587, 594.
128 [1974] 1 All ER 161.

'notice in writing' meant that actual communication was required. The postal rule does not apply to notice requirements imposed by statute.[129]

The postal rule applies only to acceptances sent by mail or telegram. Attempts to widen its scope to other means of communication, such as telex, have been unsuccessful.[130] The courts have consistently held that acceptances made by methods of communication which are virtually instantaneous are not complete until communication is received. Accordingly, the postal rule does not apply to acceptance by telephone or fax.

There is no direct authority as to whether the postal rule apples to communication of acceptance by e-mail, but it appears unlikely that the rule will be extended to this medium.[131]

4.4.6. Communication of Acceptance and Jurisdiction

In the case of cross-border contracts, the place where a contract is made is a significant factor in determining jurisdiction and the governing law of contract.[132] As the contract is formed when the acceptance is complete, the time of communication of acceptance is obviously important. Accordingly, the mode of communication and the possible application of the postal rule become relevant to determining jurisdiction and governing law. For example, in *Entores v Miles Far East Corporation*,[133] an offer accepted by a telex sent from Holland to England was held to constitute a contract made in England. Had the acceptance been by letter, the contract would probably have been made in Holland. Similarly, in *Brinkibon Ltd v Stahag Stahl und Stahlwarenhandelsgesellschaft mbH*,[134] the respondents in Vienna sent the appellants in London a telexed counter-offer. This was accepted by telex sent from London to Vienna. It was held that the contract was made in Vienna where the telex was received. However, the court stated that it was not possible to lay down a universal rule. They noted that telex messages may not be instantaneous; for example, they may be sent outside office hours.

It was acknowledged in *Brinkibon Ltd v Stahag Stahl und Stahlwarenhandelsgesellschaft mbH*[135] that no universal rule can cover all cases

---

129 *Attorney-General of Fiji v Kumari* [2015] FJCA 139.

130 *Entores v Miles Far East Corporation* [1955] 2 QB 327 (CA).

131 See K. O'Shea and K. Skeahan, 'Acceptance of Postal Offers by email. How Far Should the Postal Rule Extend?' (1997) 13 *QUT Law Journal* 247; S.W.B. Hill, 'Email Contracts – When is the Contract Formed?' (2001) 12(1) *Journal of Law, Information and Science* 46.

132 See e.g. High Court (Civil Procedure) Rules 1964 (UK), O11 R 1, which applies in Kiribati and Tuvalu; High Court Rules 1988 (Fiji), O11 R 1(1); and Supreme Court Rules 2007 (Tonga), O12 R 1, which all permit service of a writ outside the jurisdiction with leave where a claim is brought on a contract which was made within the jurisdiction.

133 [1955] 2 QB 327, approved in *Arinako v Minipe* [1994] PNGLR 450.

134 [1983] AC 34.

135 Ibid. per Wilberforce LJ.

of acceptance which does not take place face-to-face. Complex cases must be resolved by reference to:

- the intention of the parties;
- sound business practice; and
- judgement as to where the risk should lie.

Where the contract is contained in a signed document, the place of signature may be relevant but will not necessarily be conclusive. In *Banque Privee de Credit Moderne v Jet Service Ltd*,[136] the place of signature was held to be of little relevance in determining where the agreement was made, as the agreement was stated to be subject to approval by the plaintiff in Noumea, New Caledonia.

4.5. REVOCATION OF ACCEPTANCE

The general rule is that an acceptance can be revoked at any time before it is communicated to the offeror. This rule follows from the preceding rule, that acceptance is not complete until communicated.

When the postal rule applies, it is not certain whether a letter or telegram of acceptance can be withdrawn after posting. In theory, it should not be possible to withdraw acceptance because the contract is complete once the letter of acceptance is posted, even though the offeror is unaware of the acceptance until it is received. There is no English authority on point. However, in *Household Fire Insurance Co v Grant*[137] Bramwell LJ suggested, obiter, that the acceptance could be revoked.[138] The New Zealand case of *Wenckhem v Arndt*[139] is sometimes cited as authority in support of the proposition that attempted withdrawal of a postal acceptance is ineffective, but the case was decided on other grounds.[140] This case may be followed in those countries of the region that tend to follow New Zealand courts' decisions, such as Cook Islands, Fiji, Niue and Samoa.[141]

---

136 [1989–1994] 2 Van LR 535.

137 (1879) 4 Ex D 216.

138 This view is supported by A.H. Hudson, 'Retraction of Letters of Acceptance' (1966) *Law Quarterly Review* 169. See also *Dunmore (Countess) v Alexander* (1830) 9 Sh (Ct of Sessions) 190, which involved the simultaneous receipt of two letters.

139 (1873) 1 JR 73.

140 See also the South African case of *A to Z Bazaars (Pty) Ltd v Minister of Agriculture* (1974) (4) SA 392(C).

141 See further chapter 1.

CHAPTER 4
UNCERTAIN AND INCOMPLETE AGREEMENTS

1. INTRODUCTION

In interpreting the terms of a contract, the courts will adopt the meaning which the document would convey to a reasonable person having all the relevant background.[1] Where terms are clear and unambiguous when viewed objectively in the context of the contract as a whole, the courts need go no further.[2] However, although parties may have reached an agreement, in the sense that there has been an offer and an acceptance, its precise terms may be uncertain or the agreement may be incomplete. Uncertainty may occur where the terms of the agreement are indefinite, that is, they are vague or ambiguous. Incompleteness may occur where some terms of the agreement are still being negotiated.

An uncertain or incomplete agreement is not legally enforceable. For a contract to be binding, it must be possible to ascertain what the parties agreed. Whether the parties have reached complete agreement in certain terms is determined objectively.

2. VAGUE OR AMBIGUOUS AGREEMENTS

2.1. THE COURTS' APPROACH

The law requires the parties to make their own contract; and a court will not construct a contract for the parties if clauses are indefinite or unsettled.[3]

1 *Investors Compensation Scheme Ltd v West Bromwich Building Society* [1998] 1 WLR 896, applied in *Unikannara v Catholic Beterin Ambo* [2007] KICA 9; *Dalgro Solomon Islands Ltd v KK Real Estate Proprietor Ltd* [2008] SBHC 90.

2 *Unikannara v Catholic Beterin Ambo* [2007] KICA 9; *Nauru Security Services Inc v Nauru Rehabilitation Corporation* [2012] NRSC 15.

3 *Scammell & Nephew Ltd v Ouston* [1941] AC 251; *SMM Solomon Ltd v Attorney-General* [2014] SBHC 91; *Patterson v National Capital District Commission* [2001] PGNC 71.

A regional example of this is *Sherani v Jagroop.*[4] In that case, the third defendant, who was the executor of the deceased's will and legatee of one undivided half share of the residuary estate, granted the plaintiff an option to purchase his one undivided half share of all land comprised in a particular certificate of title. The court refused to grant specific performance, inter alia on the grounds that it was unenforceable for lack of certainty, as it was impossible to ascertain and identify the area and nature of the land that the third defendant had purported to sell.[5]

However, where it is clear that parties intended to make a contract and thought they had done so, it has been said that it is 'the duty of the Court to construe such documents fairly and broadly, without being too astute or subtle in finding defects'.[6] The courts are particularly anxious to uphold commercial contracts[7] and contracts that have been partly performed.[8] In *Tian Chen Ltd v The Tower Ltd (No. 2)*,[9] the facts of which are set out below, the disputed agreement was commercial and had been partly performed and this was influential in the National Court's decision to uphold the contract.

It is a maxim of law that 'the court will make certain that which it is able to be made certain', so that the mere fact that an agreement is capable of more than one meaning does not make it void or uncertain. The true meaning of the words is a matter for the court to construe. The modern approach to this task was set down in *Investors Compensation Scheme Ltd v West Bromwich Building Society*,[10] where it was held that 'the old intellectual baggage of "legal" interpretation has been discarded' in favour of 'the common sense principles by which any serious utterance would be interpreted in ordinary life'. The principles set out in that case have been adopted in Fiji in *Kumar v National Insurance Company of Fiji*,[11] and dictate that the court must ascertain the meaning which the document would convey to a reasonable person having regard to the 'matrix of fact', that is, all the background knowledge which would have been available to the parties at the time of the contract. The meaning of the document is not the same thing as the meaning of its words, which may be located in a dictionary. Rather, it is what the parties using those words against the relevant background would reasonably have been understood to mean.[12]

As long as the terms of the agreement are capable of bearing some meaning, they will ultimately bear the meaning that the courts or an arbitrator decides

---

4 (1973) 19 FLR 85.
5 See also *Tom v Heinrich* [2012] NRSC 12, discussed in chapter 5.
6 *Hillas (WN) and Co Ltd v Arcos Ltd* (1932) 147 LT 503.
7 *Piokole v Logona* [2017] PGNC 79, [7]–[9].
8 *Teboni v Sawane* [1993] SBHC 37.
9 [2003] PGNC 151.
10 [1998] 1 All ER 98, 114.
11 [2012] FJSC 10, following *Din v Westpac Banking Corporation* [2004] FLR 534, 538.
12 *Investors Compensation Scheme Ltd v West Bromwich Building Society* [1998] 1 All ER 98, 114.

is the proper construction. The courts will look at extrinsic evidence to assist them in construing an ambiguous phrase. In *Lang & Co v R*,[13] the court took into account correspondence, oral statements and the conduct of the parties in interpreting a phrase of the contract that was capable of having three meanings.

An example of an agreement that was too vague to be enforced can be found in *Raffles v Wichelhaus*.[14] In that case, the plaintiff promised to sell and deliver to the defendant 125 bales of cotton at a given price 'to arrive ex Peerless from Bombay'. Unknown to the parties, there were two ships called *Peerless*; one left Bombay in October, whilst the other left in December. The plaintiff's cotton was on the latter ship, while the defendant intended to buy cotton from the former. It was held that the agreement could not be enforced as there was an ambiguity in the terms of the contract, which did not specify which of the ships was meant.

In the English case of *Lambert (Rae) v HTV Cymru (Wales) Ltd*,[15] the plaintiff was the owner of copyright in certain cartoon characters. He assigned to the defendant all existing and further copyrights. One assignment provided for the defendant to use all reasonable endeavours to obtain for the plaintiff rights of first negotiation for book publishing from any assignee. The defendant sold the rights to a third party without obtaining for the plaintiff rights of first negotiation. The Court of Appeal held that the obligation to use all reasonable endeavours enabled a party to know what it was to do and was not so uncertain that it could not found a claim in contract.

2.2. SEVERANCE OF A MEANINGLESS CLAUSE

Vague and ambiguous clauses should be distinguished from meaningless clauses. Provided the rest of the contract forms a concluded agreement, a meaningless clause can often be ignored. In *Nicolene Ltd v Simmonds*,[16] the contractual documentation contained the statement, 'we are in agreement that the usual conditions of acceptance apply'. Since there were no 'usual conditions', it was held that this was a meaningless phrase, which could be ignored. There was still a finalised agreement, which could be enforced.[17]

If the parties do not specify a time within which an obligation is to be fulfilled by implication of law, performance must be within a reasonable time.

---

13 [1930–49] WSLR 52. See also *LG Schuler AG v Wickman Machine Tool Sales Ltd* [1974] AC 235, 261.

14 (1864) 2 Hurl & C 906.

15 [1998] EMLR 629, digested in (1998) 1 CLYB 847.

16 [1953] 1 QB 543.

17 See also *Auspacific Construction Co Pty Ltd v Attorney-General* [1997] KICA 6.

What is reasonable will depend on all the circumstances.[18] In *Tian Chen Ltd v The Tower Ltd (No. 2)*,[19] the parties signed a lease in November 2001 which left the date of possession blank. The defendant argued that the date of possession was an essential term of the lease and, because it could not be ascertained by reference to the written document at the time of execution, the contract was void for uncertainty. In upholding the contract, the National Court ignored the inclusion of the word '2001', which had been referred to in one clause of the contract, regarding it as 'meaningless'. The evidence established that the date of possession was something that the parties had agreed would be decided once the details of the fit out and other similar details had been finalised.

3. INCOMPLETE AGREEMENTS

Generally, if there is a gap in the contract, the court will not fill it in. The parties must have agreed on all essential matters. What are 'essential' matters will differ depending on the subject matter of the contract. For example, in *Motibhai & Co Ltd v The Civil Aviation Authority of Fiji*,[20] Sadal J held that the essential terms of a lease were:

- the identity of the lessor and the lessee;[21]
- the description of the premises;
- the commencement date and the term of the lease; and
- the amount of the rent or details of the other consideration to be paid.

What are 'essential' matters may also differ depending on the parties to the contract, at least where one of the parties usually contracts on the basis of certain variations of a selection of terms. For example, in *Pacific Architects Ltd v Commissioner of Lands*,[22] it was held that an agreement for the sale of land to the plaintiff by the Commissioner of Lands was unenforceable. It failed to specify the boundaries of the land, the price or which of the other usual terms on which the Commissioner usually transferred land applied.

The courts are particularly anxious to uphold agreements that have already been acted upon by the parties.[23] In commercial transactions a court may be able to ascertain the missing terms of the contract from the custom of a

[18] *Singh v Letama Trading Company* (1987) 33 FLR 158.
[19] [2003] PGNC 151.
[20] Unreported, High Court, Fiji, Sadal J, 3 December 1993. Affirmed on appeal in *Civil Aviation Authority of Fiji v Motibhai & Company Ltd* [1995] 41 FLR 31.
[21] See also *Spirit Haus Ltd v Marshall* [2004] PGNC 166.
[22] [1997] SBHC 10.
[23] See e.g. *Latchman Buses Ltd v Prasad and Others* (1960) 7 FLR 90.

particular trade or from a previous course of dealing between the parties. In *Rarotonga Glass and Aluminium Ltd v Castaway Beach Villas Ltd*,[24] the plaintiff claimed payment for the supply for aluminium doors and windows. The main issue was whether there was a contract of supply. The court held that it was common for contracts to be made up partly of documents, partly of oral communications, and 'supplemented as needed by custom and practice'.[25]

In *Hillas (WN) and Co Ltd v Arcos Ltd*,[26] the plaintiff agreed to buy from the defendant '22,000 standards of softwood goods of fair specification over the season 1930'. The written agreement contained an option to buy 100,000 standards in 1931, but without particulars as to the kind or size of timber or the manner of shipment. No difficulties arose on the original purchase for 1930, but when the buyers sought to enforce the option for 1931 the sellers alleged that the failure to define these various particulars showed that the clause was not intended to bind either party. Rather, it was to provide a basis for future agreement. The House of Lords held that the language used, interpreted in the light of the previous course of dealing between the parties, showed a sufficient intention to be bound.

Similarly, in *CP Homes Ltd v Ali*,[27] Palmer J considered that the hire fee for a bulldozer could be carried forward from a previous agreement between the parties. The court may also have regard to a previous course of dealing to determine the manner of performance of a contract, where this has not been specified.[28] This approach has also been taken in Tonga. In *Procorp Ltd v Nuku*[29] the defendant was one of the plaintiff's registered squash growers. According to the plaintiff, the defendant gave verbal instructions for his land to be ploughed and for the plaintiff to supply seeds, fertilisers and chemicals on credit to be repaid from the proceeds of sale of the squash. The defendant claimed that there was never any contract, and even if there was, it was so uncertain as to be unenforceable. The court upheld the contract on the basis that there were prior dealings between the parties, stating that 'what the parties agreed to for the 1998 season was simply a continuation of the arrangement that had been in place for the 1997 season'.

An example of a term implied from prevailing practice can be seen in *Castaway Resorts (Fiji) Ltd v Travelodge Fiji Ltd*.[30] The contract for the sale of land was silent as to who should pay the stamp duty on the transfer.

24 [2006] CKHC 6.
25 Ibid., [36].
26 [1932] All ER Rep 494.
27 [1995] SBHC 23.
28 *Pacific Forum Line v Big Save Timber Ltd* [1994] WSSC 5.
29 [2001] TOSC 50.
30 [1984] FJHC 29.

Kearsley LJ held that the usage of payment of stamp duty by purchasers could be implied into the contract.

The approach of supplying missing terms from a previous course of dealing or by reference to prevailing practice is also likely to be followed in Marshall Islands. It is certainly the approach followed by the Federated States of Micronesia. In *Ponape Transfer & Storage, Inc v Wade*,[31] a prior course of dealing and surrounding circumstances made it apparent that the parties' intention was that employees should be paid for unused holiday time. Accordingly, the court implied a term that the former employee was entitled to be paid for unused holiday time minus the applicable taxes.

3.1. MISSING TERMS AS TO PRICE

A question that arises is whether an agreement to sell at 'a reasonable price' or 'a fair price' is too vague to be enforced. By analogy with sale of goods legislation, which is discussed below, and on the authority of *Sudbrooke Trading Estate Ltd v Eggleton*,[32] it would appear that it is not. There is no clear authority as to whether a range of prices can be regarded as a sufficiently certain statement of price. However, in *Solomon Islands Housing Authority v Onio*,[33] the Court of Appeal of Solomon Islands suggested that such an agreement might be regarded as an agreement to sell at a maximum price of that indicated as the top of the range.

Incomplete contracts may also be validated if a statute provides a formula for inserting the missing term. However, missing terms cannot be supplied by reference to legislation if the contract deals with price in vague terms, rather than remaining altogether silent.[34]

Such legislation exists in relation to sale of goods contracts. It provides that if the missing term is as to the price of goods, the contract will be interpreted as if the buyer were to pay a reasonable price. Examples of such provisions operating within the region are s 8 Sale of Goods Act 1979 (UK) (which substantially reproduces the terms of the Sale of Goods Act 1893 (UK)); s 10 Sale of Goods Act Cap 230 (Fiji); s 9(2) Sale of Goods Act 1975 (Samoa); and s 10 Sale of Goods Act 1986 (Marshall Islands).[35]

---

31 5 FSM Intrm 354 (Pon 1992).

32 [1982] 3 All ER 1. See also *Ifunaoa v Howell Enterprises Ltd* (unreported, High Court, Solomon Islands, 26 September 1984).

33 [1989] SBCA 1.

34 See e.g. *Sudbrooke Trading Estate Ltd v Eggleton* [1982] 3 All ER 1; *Solomon Islands Housing Authority v Onio* [1989] SBCA 1.

35 23 MIRC Cap 1.

This legislation will only assist in contracts for the sale of goods. It will not apply in other spheres, for example contracts for the sale of land. In *Lee v Mitlal*,[36] Mitlal agreed to sell some land to Ram Kissun and to 'give the purchaser [the] right to first refusal' of some adjoining land. Later, however, Mitlal agreed to sell the adjoining land to the plaintiff, Fong Lee. Ram Kissun objected to this and consequently the sale by Mitlal to the plaintiff was delayed. The plaintiff sued for specific performance. The majority of the Court of Appeal held that the clause giving the purchaser the right to first refusal was void as the price at which Ram Kissun could purchase the property was not stated. Neither had any means for ascertaining the price been provided, nor could such a term be implied. There was therefore no concluded agreement to sell the land to Ram Kissun and judgment was given for the plaintiff. Marsack VP said:[37]

> I am fully aware of the desirability of giving effect to a contract where the terms of that contract are clear from the express wording of the contract or necessary inference from the words used. In the present case I feel that it would be possible to place several interpretations upon the clause considered as a whole. As the clause is drawn it is obscure and lacking in the essentials of a clear and ascertainable contract. ... The only method of making ... a binding contract between the parties would, in my opinion, be for the Court itself to supply the missing terms, by choosing among the available possibilities. But that is not the function of the Court. It is not a question of what would be reasonable. It is a matter of deciding by the express terms of the contract, or necessary inference therefrom, exactly what was agreed, and what it is that the Court is asked to enforce.

The Court of Appeal of Fiji has more recently affirmed that price is an essential element of a sale of land, without which the agreement will be void for uncertainty.[38]

This requirement does not always apply in agreements other than for the sale of land, particularly where there has been part performance. In *Fly River Provincial Government v Pioneer Health Services Ltd*,[39] the parties entered into a written contract for the supply of mobile medical and consultancy services. Payment was to be an annual fee of K3,000,000 'plus any variations or extensions to the Contract at commercial rates as agreed to by the [parties]' plus reimbursement 'at commercial rates' for disbursements. The appellant paid for some services, but then fell into arrears and eventually

---

36 (1966) 12 FLR 4. Compare *Brown v Gould* [1971] 3 WLR 334, where an option to renew at a rent 'to be fixed' was held to be valid on the basis that, as the parties had provided no machinery for fixing the rent, the court could make its own valuation.

37 *Fong Lee v Mitlal and Ram Kissun* (1966) 12 FLR 4, 21.

38 *Chand v Kumar* [2011] FJCA 54, [20].

39 [2003] PGSC 4. See also *Spirit Haus Ltd v Marshall* [2004] PGNC 166.

suspended further performance. The appellant argued that the contract was void for uncertainty. Citing *Hillas (WN) and Co Ltd v Arcos Ltd*,[40] the Supreme Court upheld the contract on the basis that

> not all contracts can be precise. That does not necessarily mean that they are bad for uncertainty. ... The law has developed in this way to accommodate the commercial realities. In so doing, they have shown a readiness to uphold a contract where it has been part performed. They have therefore shown a readiness to adopt a wider interpretation of the words used by the parties to a contract.[41]

3.2. AN AGREEMENT TO AGREE IN THE FUTURE

Traditionally, an agreement to agree has not been accepted by the courts as constituting a binding contract. Thus, in *Courtney & Fairbairn Ltd v Tolaini Bros*[42] it was held that an agreement to negotiate was too uncertain. In *Curran v Rankin*[43] a draft agreement for sale and purchase was agreed between the parties. On the evidence it was found that it was not their intention to be bound until a formal contract had been executed. As such an agreement had never been signed, an order for specific performance was refused.

An agreement has also been treated as incomplete if terms have been left out to be determined in a future agreement between the parties. In *May & Butcher Ltd v R*,[44] an agreement had been made for the sale of surplus war equipment to the plaintiffs, the price being left to be agreed between the parties. The parties were unable to agree, and the plaintiffs sought to enforce at a reasonable price, to be determined by the Court. It was held that no contract had been concluded. It should be noted that, as the contract provided its own mechanism for fixing the price of the goods, the Sale of Goods Act could not be used to imply a term that a reasonable price was payable. However, doubt has been cast on the principle expressed in this case by the decision in *Naqa v Fiji Electricity Authority*,[45] where the High Court of Fiji cited and adopted the following words from the Court of Appeal of New Zealand:[46]

> I doubt *May and Butcher v The King* [1934] 2 KB 17, long regarded as one of the leading cases in this area, would be decided the same way today. An agreement to

40 (1932) 147 LT 503.
41 Compare *Patterson v National Capital District Commission* [2001] PGNC 71.
42 [1975] 1 WLR 297.
43 [1964] 10 FLR 212.
44 [1934] 2 KB 17.
45 [2005] FLR 264.
46 *Fletcher Challenge Energy Ltd v Electricity Corporation of New Zealand Ltd* [2002] 2 NZLR 433.

> agree will not be held void for uncertainty if the parties have provided a workable formula or objective standard or machinery such as arbitration or indeed if the Court is able to determine any matter that has been left open.[47]

As mentioned above, where a contract has been wholly or partially performed, the court may be more inclined to imply a term.[48] For example, in *Foley v Classique Coaches*,[49] it was held that an agreement whereby the parties agreed that petrol should be purchased 'at a price to be agreed between the parties from time to time' was valid. Because the parties believed that they had a contract and acted for three years as if they had, a term was implied that the price had to be reasonable. Similarly, if there is a pre-existing agreement between the parties, this may save what would otherwise be an agreement to agree.[50]

This case also illustrates the point that an agreement will not fail for uncertainty, even though a necessary term is left to be agreed in the future, if the contract provides a formula for deciding the matter. It was held that the arbitration clause provided in the agreement applied in the event of a failure to agree on price.[51] In *Naqa v Fiji Electricity Authority*,[52] the court went even further. In determining whether a Joint Statement of Understanding was capable of being a binding agreement, it held that as the agreement was always going to be subject to court oversight, the court had a residual discretion to determine outstanding matters.

Examples of 'agreements to agree' are agreements made 'subject to contract', which are discussed further below, 'letters of intent' and 'memoranda of understanding'. These types of agreement are commonly used to record heads or even terms of agreement, in accordance with which the parties are likely to contract in the future, but which they have not yet committed themselves to.

3.2.1. 'Subject to Contract' Agreements

As discussed in chapter 3, where an offer is accepted conditionally, an agreement is not concluded. Wording such as 'subject to' may be used to indicate an intention not to be finally bound, as where an offer is accepted 'subject to the preparation of a formal contract', in which case there is no binding contract until the formal contract is executed.[53] The words 'subject to contract' may also be used to indicate that the parties are still in the course of negotiation.

---

47 Cf. D.W. McLauchlan, 'Rethinking Agreements to Agree' (1998) 18 *New Zealand Universities Law Review* 77.

48 See e.g. *Hillas (WN) and Co Ltd* [1932] All ER Rep 494.

49 [1934] 2 KB 1 (CA).

50 *Seafright v Bishop Shipping Services* (1976) PNGLR 22.

51 *Foley v Classique Coaches* [1934] 2 KB 1.

52 [2005] FLR 264.

53 See the comparison of *Winn v Bull* (1877) 7 Ch D 29 with *Branca v Cobarro* [1947] KB 854.

If the words 'subject to contract' indicate that terms have yet to be settled by a future agreement between the parties, this is an agreement to agree. Because some of the terms have yet to be decided there is no final assent and the agreement is incomplete. This was the case in *Prasad v Hussein*,[54] where Hammett J held that the parties had been in negotiation and had reached agreement on some terms as to the sale and purchase of the plaintiff's property to the defendant. One term of the agreement was that the parties would enter into a formal contract. However, there were other necessary terms that had not been agreed upon at all, such as the date for completion of the sale and the date for possession of the property, which would also be dealt with in the formal contract. Accordingly, judgment was given for the defendant.

Agreements may be held to be subject to execution of a formal contract by implication from the facts, even though the parties have not expressly stated this. In *Curran v Rankin*,[55] a draft agreement for sale and purchase of land was put in writing by the parties. On the evidence it was found that it was not their intention to be bound until a formal contract had been executed. As it never had been, an order for specific performance was refused.

The implication that the parties do not intend to be bound, arising from the words 'subject to contract' may be displaced by words or conduct of the parties suggesting the contrary. In *Masters v Cameron*,[56] the High Court of Australia stated that 'subject to contract' agreements fall into three classes:

- the parties have reached agreement, intend to be bound immediately, but intend to have their agreement put into a formal document which may be fuller or more precise but no different in effect;
- the parties have reached agreement on all terms, but nevertheless intend performance of one or more terms to be conditional upon entry into a formal agreement; or
- the parties do not intend to finalise their agreement until they execute a formal agreement.

The High Court stated that in the first two cases there was a binding contract, whereas in the last case there was not. In *Jixing Industries Ltd v Aitape Metropolitan Forest Investment Ltd*,[57] the parties entered into a memorandum of understanding, which was held to fall into the third category as set out in *Masters v Cameron*, and therefore it was unenforceable.

---

54 (1967) 13 FLR 98.

55 (1964) FLR 212. See also *Auspacific Construction Co Pty Ltd v Attorney-General* [1997] KICA 6, discussed later in this section.

56 (1954) 91 CLR 353.

57 [2013] PGSC 52.

In *Sami v Veitogavi*,[58] the plaintiff was the manager of a school built on native land, which was held on trust by the Native Land Trust Board. The plaintiff applied to the Board for a new lease and paid the application fee. The Board issued a letter marked 'subject to agreement', offering a lease of 50 years and requiring payment. The plaintiff failed to pay on time, but entered into negotiations with the Board for payment of the balance. The Board accepted the monies and granted the lease. The defendant claimed ownership of the land and disputed the validity of the lease. The court referred to *Masters v Cameron*, but held that 'subject to agreement' in this case did not take its usual meaning and no other contract was required to be executed to obtain the lease. The Board had affirmed the agreement by conduct in attending a meeting to negotiate payment of the balance due, and by accepting the money and granting the lease.

Courts in the South Pacific continue to demonstrate reluctance to enforce an agreement prior to execution of a formal written document if there is any indication that this was the parties' intention. In *Prasad v Hussein*,[59] discussed above, Hammett J expressed the view that the three categories set out in *Masters v Cameron*[60] were not exhaustive and he emphasised that, if the parties were still negotiating any of the necessary terms of their bargain there would be no enforceable contract. In *Auspacific Construction Co Pty Ltd v Attorney-General*,[61] the Court of Appeal of Kiribati concluded that the disputed agreement fell within the third category of case outlined in *Masters v Cameron*.[62] Whilst the words 'subject to contract' were not expressly used, the delivery of a formal document which made provision for signature by both parties was regarded as indicating that the execution of that document by both parties was necessary to constitute a binding contract. Similarly, in *Curran v Rankin*,[63] Mills-Owens CJ appeared to suggest that Fiji will follow the English common law approach of regarding a 'subject to contract' agreement as unenforceable unless there is cogent evidence of a contrary intention.[64]

3.2.2. *Other Types of 'Subject to' Agreements*

Where the words 'subject to', or a similar phrase, are used, the courts have held that they are capable of several meanings depending on the context in

58 [2008] FJHC 391.

59 (1967) 13 FLR 98, 101.

60 (1954) 91 CLR 353.

61 [1997] KICA 6. See also *Pacific Architects Ltd v Commissioner of Lands* [1997] SBHC 10, distinguishing *Storer v Manchester City Council* [1974] 1 WLR 1403.

62 (1954) 91 CLR 353.

63 (1964) FLR 212, 217–219.

64 See further Law Commission of England and Wales, *'Subject to Contract' Agreements*, Report No. 65, 1975 and Working Paper No. 51, July 1973.

which they are used. In addition to agreements which are 'subject to contract', agreements may be subject to other events. They may, for example, be 'subject to finance' or 'subject to the grant of approval'. Such words will not prevent a contract arising if the clause, taken in context, indicates an intention to be bound from the outset and gives sufficient indication of when the condition is satisfied. One example is where the words 'subject to' are used to refer to known and existing criteria, like particulars marked on an existing plan. Another example can be found in *Branco v Cobarro*,[65] where the parties were bound but expressed an intention to set out the agreed terms in a formal document.

Another possible use of the words 'subject to' is to indicate that the parties intend to be bound, but that the binding contract is subject to a condition precedent. For example, a final agreement may be 'subject to planning permission',[66] or 'subject to survey'.[67] In this case, the parties may have reached final agreement, but either the whole agreement or one or more of the parties rights and/or obligations under it are suspended pending the fulfilment of some condition.[68] An example of this can be seen in the case of *Sun Islands Inc v Fewtrell*,[69] where an employment agreement was entered into to commence 'upon final paperworks needed with the lease on the island of Makaha'a'. It was held that as the lease had never been obtained the agreement had never commenced. This is the approach that has been taken by some regional courts to agreements that are subject to consent required by statute. In *DB Waite (Overseas) Ltd v Wallath*,[70] for example, an agreement to transfer a native lease, which required the consent of the Native Land Trust Board under a statute, was held to be valid but inchoate or inoperative pending the grant of consent. This topic is discussed in more detail in chapter 15.

3.2.3. *An Agreement whereby Terms are to be Determined by a Third Person or One of the Parties to the Contract*

It is well established that the parties to a contract may leave terms to be determined by a third party.[71] The only stipulation is that it must be clear that

---

65 [1947] KB 854. See chapter 3, section 4.3.3.

66 *Batten v White* (1960) 12 P & CR 66; *Hargreaves Transport Ltd v Lynch* [1969] 1 WLR 215.

67 *Ee v Kakar* (1979) 40 P & CR 223, but see contra *Marks v Board* (1930) 46 TLR 424.

68 See further R. Brownsword, *Smith & Thomas: A Casebook on Contract*, 13th ed., Sweet & Maxwell, London 2015, pp. 185–91 for a discussion of the problem which arises when the condition gives one party a complete discretion whether to proceed or not. The case law is conflicting.

69 [1991] Tonga LR 8.

70 (1972) 18 FLR 141.

71 *Smallman v Smallman* [1972] Fam 25; *Brauer & Co (Great Britain) Ltd v James Clark (Brush Materials) Ltd* [1952] 2 TLR 349; *AV Pound & Co Ltd v MW Hardy & Co Inc* [1956] 588; *Marten v Whale* [1917] 2 KB 480; *Campbell v Edwards* [1976] 1 WLR 403. This must be

both parties have agreed to be bound by the third party's determination. It is undecided whether an agreement that empowers one of the parties to insert further terms in the contract is valid or not. The answer seems to be that it is.[72] For example, in *Smith v Morgan*,[73] an agreement not to sell land adjoining the defendant's property without first offering it to the defendant at a 'price to be agreed upon' was held not to be an agreement to agree. Rather, it imposed an obligation on the plaintiff to offer the land to the defendant at the price at which she was prepared to sell. This meant that the obligation to name the price of the land was on the vendor only.

4. THE PRESENT POSITION

The present position may be summarised as follows:

- The courts will not write a contract or insert missing terms for the parties.
- The courts will preserve the contract wherever possible by determining the 'true' construction of otherwise ambiguous terms.
- An agreement will not be held void for uncertainty if matters left open can be determined by reference to a formula or objective standard or machinery provided by the parties, or can be determined by the court.
- Sources from which the court may obtain assistance in clarifying an otherwise vague or incomplete agreement include:
  - a trade custom or usage;
  - a previous course of dealing;
  - legislation.[74]
- The courts are particularly anxious to uphold commercial agreements and agreements that have been partly performed.

distinguished from the case where the parties do not intend to be bound until a third party approves the agreement: *Pym v Campbell* (1856) 6 E&B 370.

72 *Lombard Tricity Finance v Paton* [1989] 1 All ER 916.

73 [1971] 1 WLR 803.

74 These three sources are discussed further in chapter 9.

CHAPTER 5

INTENTION TO CREATE LEGAL RELATIONS

1. INTRODUCTION

An agreement will not constitute a binding contract unless it is one that can reasonably be regarded as having been made in contemplation of legal consequences.[1] This is reflected in the definition of a contract as a legally binding agreement between two or more people who intend it to have legal effect. As noted in *Suva Central Ltd v Zaha Ltd*,[2] the continued application of this principle was confirmed in the United Kingdom in *Baird Textiles Holdings Ltd v Marks & Spencer plc*.[3]

Intention to create legal relations, sometimes referred to as 'intention to be bound', must be distinguished from 'willingness to be bound'. 'Willingness to be bound' is the element in the offer that distinguishes it from an invitation to treat. It indicates that the offeror is willing to perform the promise if the offer is accepted. 'Intention to be bound' or 'intention to contract' means the readiness of a party to accept the legal consequences of having entered into a contract, particularly if they do not perform their part of the bargain.

In Tokelau, the Contract Rules 2004 expressly provides that an agreement will not constitute a contract if 'any person making the agreement does not intend to be legally bound'.[4]

2. ASCERTAINING THE PARTIES' INTENTION

The parties may expressly state that the agreement is not to affect their legal relations. If they do not, the court will have to decide from the surrounding

1 *Suva Central Ltd v Zaha Ltd* [2012] FJHC 1272, [30]–[37].
2 [2012] FJHC 1272.
3 [2001] EWCA Civ 274.
4 Contract Rules 2004, R 4(2).

circumstances whether there is an intention to be bound. In *Naqa v Fiji Electricity Authority*,[5] the High Court of Fiji adopted the guidance provided by the New Zealand Court of Appeal in *Fletcher Challenge Energy Ltd v Electricity Corporation of New Zealand Ltd*[6] on how an intention to be immediately bound can be adjudicated. This may be summarised as follows:

- The intention of the parties is to be assessed objectively.
- In determining whether there is an intention to be bound in preliminary negotiations, surrounding circumstances and subsequent conduct are relevant.
- The matrix of fact, including printed and spoken words or actions of the parties in the course of their negotiations, may be considered.
- It is important to bear in mind the dynamics of the negotiation process and the internal inter-relationship of the terms of the bargain.
- The court adopts a neutral approach when determining the parties' intention.
- An agreement to agree is no longer necessarily unenforceable. Once an intention to be bound is found, the court can be proactive in assigning meaning to the terms to be agreed.
- If a court is satisfied that the parties intended a contract, it will do everything within its power to give meaning to the terms or to operate the contract without them.

In relation to the first guideline, the objective test of intention to create legal relations was stressed by the Supreme Court of Samoa in *Keil v Digicel (Samoa)*,[7] which commented that '[a]greement is not a mental state but an act and, as an act, is a matter of inference from conduct'.

The objective test was also referred to in Vanuatu in *Ellis v Attorney-General*.[8] Cooke CJ cited with approval the following words from Halsbury's Laws:

> In many instances there can be no doubt that a legal relationship was intended, and in others it will be equally clear that it was not; but there will also be cases where the matter remains in doubt, and the court is then faced with the task of determining the intention of the parties. Ordinarily the test will be the objective one of whether a reasonable man would regard the offer made to him as one which was intended to create legal relations ...[9]

---

5 [2005] FLR 264, discussed further in chapter 2.
6 [2002] 2 NZLR 433. This case was also applied in *Wolfgramm v Robertson* [2006] Tonga LR 34.
7 [2010] WSSC 93, [18].
8 [1980–88] 1 Van LR 190, 204.
9 Lord Hailsham of Marylebone (ed.), *Halsbury's Laws of England*, 4th ed., vol. 9, Butterworths, United Kingdom 1989, para. 300.

Objective assessment of the parties' intention involves asking what meaning the document would convey to a fair-minded, informed, reasonable and neutral bystander, founded on a fair understanding of all the available circumstances.[10] In conducting this exercise, it is important to take into account local culture and to make the assessment in the light of the prevailing culture. The significance of local culture is illustrated by the case of *Compass Rose v Taomati Iuta*,[11] where the issue was whether a contract had been concluded between the plaintiff's director and the Minister of Trade, Industry and Labour. The relevant discussion occurred at an informal gathering where the parties had been drinking. The Minister eventually said, 'Well if you want to buy [it] you can have it'. The plaintiff said he accepted, made out a cheque and, according to the plaintiff, the two shook hands. When they met the next day, the Minister denied that there was a contract and said that it was all a joke. The court found that although the plaintiff thought that he was entering into a genuine contract, that was the 'subjective position. ... Objectively [the Minister's] position was that he was engaging in a semi-serious but nevertheless light-hearted discussion'. The Minister gave evidence that he had no recollection of shaking hands, but the court held that, 'in any case it is not a Kiribati custom and would have no significance'. The court also referred to the Minister's evidence that 'in Kiribati custom to mix business with pleasure in this way would be considered very bad "form"'. The court concluded that, objectively, there was no legally enforceable contract.

3. DOMESTIC AND SOCIAL AGREEMENTS

The presumption is that domestic and social agreements are not intended to have legal force. The existence of the presumption is important as it affects the balance of proof. If there is a presumption that the agreement is not intended to have legal force, the onus of proof is on the person alleging that there is a binding agreement. As stated in *Suva Central Ltd v Zaha Ltd*,[12] '[t]he onus of proving the absence of legal intention is on the party asserting it ... and the test is an objective one'. However, the presumption is easily rebutted.

Domestic and social agreements can be broken down into:

1. agreements between husband and wife; and
2. other domestic and social agreements.

---

10 *Fletcher Challenge Energy Ltd v Electricity Corporation of New Zealand Ltd* [2002] 2 NZLR 433.

11 Unreported, High Court of Kiribati, 14 May 1982.

12 [2012] FJHC 1272.

In the Pacific region there is possibly a third category, which is customary agreements.

An example of the application of the presumption to an agreement in the first category can be found in *Balfour v Balfour.*[13] The parties were married in 1900 and spent the first 15 years of their marriage in Ceylon, where the husband was employed. In 1915 they went to England on leave. When the husband returned to Ceylon his wife was too ill to accompany him. He agreed to pay her maintenance of £30 a month until she could rejoin him on her promise that she would support herself on that without asking for more. She did not ever go back to Ceylon and the husband ceased payment. She sued for £30 a month. It was held their agreement was not a contract but an ordinary domestic arrangement. As there was no intention to create legal relations, no action lay.

However, in *Merritt v Merritt*,[14] it was held that where a husband and wife are discussing matters such as separation and maintenance, the presumption does not apply as such discussions do not fall within the area of domestic agreements.

An agreement to marry also appears to fall outside the category of cases in which it is presumed that there is no intention to create legal relations. Breach of promise to marry has been specifically recognised by the common law as founding an action for breach of contract. The action has been abolished in England by the Law Reform (Miscellaneous Provisions) Act 1970 (UK), s 1(1), but still exists in some parts of the Pacific region.[15] However, doubts have been expressed about the value of this branch of law. For example, in *Kairun v Bidesi*[16] the court upheld a claim for breach of promise to marry, but Tuivaga J added that:

> This kind of claim is now rather rare which is no doubt a symptom of the increasing independence and self-sufficiency of the fair sex. In England this branch of the law has been abolished as it is thought there was no longer, if there ever was, any legal justification for its existence.

With regard to other domestic and social agreements, examples are agreements for pleasure, such as an invitation to dinner, or to play in a social soccer match. In *Coward v Motor Insurer's Bureau*,[17] an agreement to share the cost of petrol used on a journey was held not to give rise to a legal relationship.

---

13 [1919] 2 KB 571.
14 [1970] 1 WLR 1211.
15 See further O. Jessep, 'Compensation for Breach of Promise to Marry in Papua New Guinea' [1997] *Melanesian Law Journal* 1.
16 Unreported, Supreme Court, Fiji, Tuivaga J, 5 October 1979, 6.
17 [1963] 1 QB 259.

The presumption was rebutted in *Wakeling v Ripley.*[18] In that case, the defendant, who lived in alone in Sydney, wrote to his sister and her husband in England and asked them to come to live with him in return for all his property on death. After considerable correspondence, the sister's husband resigned his lectureship and the couple sold their house and moved to Sydney. Just over a year later, they quarrelled, and the defendant reneged on his promise and sold the house. They sued and were awarded damages at first instance. The defendant's appeal, which included the ground that the agreement was purely social, failed. The extent of the correspondence negotiating the agreement and the seriousness of the consequences of the move showed an intention to be bound.

This case suggests that an important factor in determining whether the necessary intention exists is the gravity of the foreseeable detriment to the promisee. More generally, intention depends on whether a reasonable person would regard the agreement as intended to be binding.

Regional examples in this category include *Dorsamy v Commissioner of Estate and Gift Duty.*[19] The testator sold his farm and distributed the proceeds amongst his seven sons. After his death, his executors contended that these were not gifts but payments for work done, and therefore not subject to duty. It was held that the contractual relationship had to be proved by sufficient evidence. As there was no such evidence, the claim failed.

This case may be contrasted with *Wolfgramm v Robertson*,[20] where the plaintiffs were husband and wife, residing in Tonga and operating a hydroponic farming business. They purchased a solar power system from the defendant, their son in law, who resided in Queensland. The price was AUD$3,300 and it was agreed that the defendant would bring the equipment to Tonga and install it himself. The equipment arrived at the wharf in Tonga, but by then the relationship between the parties had deteriorated and the defendant refused to allow the plaintiffs to collect the equipment. In an action by the plaintiffs for release of the equipment to them, the court noted that this was 'essentially a family dispute', but neither party relied on the presumption that there was no intention to create legal relations and the contract was upheld.

With regard to the suggested third category, in the Pacific region there may be situations where parties reach an agreement which is only intended to be binding in custom, as opposed to under state law. This finds some support in *Tom v Heinrich*,[21] where the parties' mothers, who were closely related, owned adjoining pieces of land. It had been agreed that the defendant's mother could install a petrol bowser on the plaintiff's mother's land in exchange for free goods from the defendant's mother's store. When the defendant's mother died,

18 (1951) SR (NSW) 183.
19 (1976) 22 FLR 70.
20 [2006] Tonga LR 349.
21 [2012] NRSC 12.

the defendant took over the store and he terminated the arrangement for free goods, and the plaintiff sued for breach of contract. The defendant contended that 'at its highest there had been a customary social arrangement between close friends that was never intended to be the subject of action in the courts'. The claim was dismissed on the basis that it was statute barred.[22] However, the court went on to say that there was 'no doubt that there was a longstanding friendly arrangement between the female elders of the two families, which fell far short of a formal contract'. The court appeared to regard this as a customary arrangement, which could not be enforced as a contract.

However, a claim that an agreement was only binding in custom was unsuccessful in the case of *Hiram v Solomon*.[23] The plaintiff was co-owner of land in Nauru. Her daughter moved into a house on part of the land with her husband, the defendant, and children. The plaintiff said, 'This house I now give to you [the defendant] and Blueneldi [the daughter], it now belongs to Blueneldi and the kids'. The plaintiff and all but three of the co-owners confirmed the position by signing a document to that effect. When the daughter lost her job, she and her husband leased the house to a third party. After the daughter died, the plaintiff approached the husband and suggested that the rental profits be split between them. She claimed that the arrangement allowing her daughter and family to live in the house was only a customary arrangement, revocable at any time, or that it was revoked by a document that she had signed by most of the landowners. The court held that the document constituted a valid agreement, passing an interest in the property to the daughter and her husband. The plaintiff therefore had no claim to the rental payments from the husband and could not revoke the agreement. Whilst the defence that the agreement was only a customary one was unsuccessful here, that cannot be taken to rule out such a finding in different circumstances.

4. COMMERCIAL AGREEMENTS

Parties to commercial agreements are presumed to intend to create legal relations. As stated in *Compass Rose v Taomati Iuta*,[24] citing *Edwards v Skyways*,[25] that the onus is 'on the party asserting that a transaction was not intended to have legal effect, and it is a heavy one'. In *Edwards v Skyways Ltd*, the plaintiff was employed as an aircraft pilot and was a member of the defendant company's contributory pension fund. The fund gave a choice of two options when

22 Limitation Act 1939 (UK). See further chapter 20.

23 [2011] NRSC 25.

24 Unreported, High Court of Kiribati, 14 May 1982. The facts of this case are set out in section 2 above.

25 [1964] 1 WLR 349.

a member left employment before reaching retirement age: to withdraw their contributions immediately, or to wait and take a pension payable at the retirement age of 50. On 8 February 1962, the company decided to make some employees redundant and declared that pilots made redundant would be given an ex gratia payment equivalent to the company's contributions. This declaration was published in the pilots' association's newsletter in March. On 1 May the plaintiff accepted redundancy and elected to withdraw his contributions and take the ex gratia payment. His own contributions were repaid, but the company rescinded its decision to make ex gratia payments equivalent to the company's contributions. The plaintiff sued. The company defended the claim on the basis that there was no contractual entitlement because the words 'ex gratia' excluded any intention to be bound. Judgment was entered for the plaintiff on the grounds that this was a commercial agreement and therefore the presumption of intention to be bound arose. The onus of rebutting the presumption by establishing that there was no intention was on the company. The company had failed to discharge this burden. The words 'ex gratia' were insufficient to do this in the context in which they were used.

A similar defence was raised in *Carlill v Carbolic Smoke Ball Company*,[26] where the defendant argued that its advertisement was mere puff. This argument failed.

The lack of a formal contract will not rebut the presumption. In *Keil v Digicel (Samoa)*[27] the court dismissed a claim that there was no agreement due to lack of intention to create legal relations, commenting that:

> The court bears in mind the lack of formality in the preparation of the agreement. Although not in a form of a deed or agreement, there is nothing unusual or surprising in the use of a letter rather than a form of agreement if the intention was to create legal obligation ...[28]

It is sometimes difficult to categorise agreements as 'domestic', 'social' or 'commercial'. This difficulty is illustrated by *Esso Petroleum Ltd v Commissioner of Customs and Excise*,[29] where members of the House of Lords failed to agree on this point, even though the majority reached the same conclusion on whether a contract existed. The appellant was giving away a World Cup coin with every four gallons of petrol purchased. The House of Lords held that this was not a contract of sale for income tax purposes (Fraser LJ dissenting). Viscount Dilhorne and Russell LJ thought the gift of a free coin was not a business matter.

---

26 [1893] 1 QB 296.
27 [2010] WSSC 93.
28 Ibid., [21].
29 [1976] 1 WLR 1.

Simon of Glaisdale and Wilberforce LJJ thought that this was a commercial transaction.

Some promises made by commercial enterprises (especially banks) as to the financial viability of a business are not regarded as legally binding promises but merely statements of intention giving no more than a moral responsibility on the part of a bank or a parent company. These are called 'letters of comfort'. In *Kleinwort Benson v Malaysia Mining Corp*,[30] a letter of comfort was held not to impose liability on the writer. The Court of Appeal stated that their decision was not based on lack of intention to create legal relations, but on the fact that the particular words used only implied a present intention, not an ongoing promise. The judgment in this case indicates that you cannot assume that a 'letter of comfort' will not have any legal effect, as this will depend on the intention of the parties, to be gleaned from the wording of the letter. However, the heading of a document as a 'letter of comfort' will usually be enough to reverse the onus of proof and a person seeking to enforce the promise in the letter will be required to prove that there was an intention to be bound.[31]

5. REBUTTING THE PRESUMPTIONS

As illustrated by *Compass Rose v Taomati Iuta*,[32] *Wakeling v Ripley*[33] and *Merritt v Merritt*,[34] the presumptions relating to intention to create legal relations may be rebutted. The rules governing rebuttal may be summarised as follows:

- The onus of proving contrary intention rests with the party seeking to rebut.
- That party must establish the fact of contrary intention by reference to:
  - the express terms of the agreement; and/or
  - the circumstances surrounding the agreement.

One means of establishing contrary intention is to point to an honour clause. If the parties to an agreement expressly declare that it is to be binding in honour only, there will be no enforceable contract. For example, in *Jones v Vernons*

30 [1989] 1 All ER 785.

31 This decision has been criticised: M.P. Furmston, *Cheshire, Fifoot and Furmston's Law of Contract*, 17th ed., Oxford University Press, Oxford 2017, p. 101, and T.A. Downes, *Textbook on Contract*, 5th ed., Blackstone Press Ltd, London 1997, p. 100.

32 Unreported, High Court of Kiribati, 14 May 1982.

33 (1951) SR (NSW) 183.

34 [1970] 1 WLR 1211.

Pools Ltd[35] the plaintiff sued on a football pools coupon, which he alleged he had posted and the defendants had lost. The defendants relied on the following clause:

> [I]t is intended and agreed that … the pools … and any (associated) agreement or transaction … shall not … give rise to any legal relationship … or be legally enforceable … but all such arrangements, agreements and transactions are binding in honour only.

It was held that the insertion of the honour clause indicated that the agreement was not intended to give rise to a legally binding agreement. Consequently, the plaintiff had no cause of action. Atkinson J commented that '[the plaintiff] has got to trust [the defendants], and, if something goes wrong, it is his funeral and not theirs'.

Whilst some gaming contracts are illegal, as they contravene legislation,[36] in the absence of an honour clause, contracts for legal gaming and lotteries will be upheld. For example, in *Vaioleti v Cross*[37] there was no honour clause and the employer was bound by the agreement to hold a lottery.

Honour clauses are not restricted to competition forms, although these are documents in which they are frequently included. They may be inserted in any business agreement and, if clearly drafted, the courts will take note of them and refuse to enforce the agreement. For example, in *Rose & Frank v Crompton Ltd*,[38] the plaintiffs were the defendant's agents in the United States for the sale of a certain kind of paper. The document setting out the agency agreement contained an honour clause. It purported to provide that the agreement was to be viewed as a definite expression of intention, but not as a formal or legal agreement subject to the jurisdiction of the courts. Under this agreement the plaintiffs made a number of specific orders, which were met by plaintiffs. The defendants suddenly announced that they would fulfil no more orders, and the plaintiffs sued for specific performance of the agreement. It was held that the honour clause indicated that there was no intention to create legal relations and the agreement was unenforceable.

Honour clauses do not have to expressly state that the agreement is binding in honour only. For example, in *Ellis v Attorney-General*[39] the use of the words

---

35 [1938] 2 All ER 626.
36 See e.g. Gaming Act Cap 273 (Fiji).
37 [1990] Tonga LR 108.
38 [1926] AC 445.
39 [1980–88] 1 Van LR 190, 204.

'the government is in no way financially responsible for the project' were held to have made it clear that no contract was intended.

Agreements where the parties expressly deny an intention to create legal relations must be distinguished from those where the parties purport to exclude an agreement from the jurisdiction of the court. Such an exclusion clause is contrary to public policy and void at common law.[40]

[40] *Baker v Jones* [1954] 2 All ER 553. See further chapter 15.

CHAPTER 6
CONSIDERATION

1. INTRODUCTION

Assuming that the parties have reached an agreement that is sufficiently certain and was made with the intention of being legally bound, there may be a further requirement before an enforceable agreement will arise. It is a principle of common law that only those agreements that are supported by consideration or made under seal will be enforced by the courts.[1] As stated in *Valette v Republic of Vanuatu*,[2] consideration 'is an essential part of the cause of action'. Generally speaking, this means that simple contracts require something to be given in exchange for a party's promise.[3]

Consideration will not be an essential element of contracts governed by French law in Vanuatu, as civil law does not require this.[4] Nor would it appear to be required under the law of Tokelau.[5]

2. DEFINITION OF CONSIDERATION

There is no universally accepted definition of consideration. A short explanation of its general nature is, 'the price for which the promise of the other is bought'.[6]

---

1 See e.g. *Peseta v Siliato* [2016] WSDC 53; *Felix v Boblang* [2013] VUSC 98, [93]. It should be noted that if an agreement vests property or an interest in property in a party, then the issue of whether consideration was given for that property is immaterial: *Kulamma v Manadan* (1964) 10 FLR 252, 257.

2 [2010] VUSC 104.

3 *Spirit Haus Ltd v Marshall* [2004] PGNC 166.

4 French civil law does, however require a 'cause'. See further M.S. Mason, 'The Utility of Consideration – A Comparative View' (1941) 41(5) *Columbia Law Review* 825.

5 Contract Rules 2004 (Tokelau). One of the purposes of the Rules is 'to establish the principles of the United Nations Convention on Contracts for the International Sale of Goods 1980 [CISG] as the foundation for the contract law of Tokelau'. The Rules are supplemented by the law of New Zealand 'where necessary' (R 2(v)), so the common law may still apply in certain cases. In particular it will apply in relation to 'factors denying agreement': R 19.

6 Sir F. Pollock, *Pollock's Principles of Contract*, 13th ed., Stevens & Sons, London 1950, p. 133.

In *Dunlop Pneumatic Tyre Co v Selfridge & Co*,[7] Lord Dunedin gave a more detailed definition:

> An act or forbearance of the one party or the promise thereof is the price for which the promise is brought and the promise thus given is enforceable.

This definition emphasises that consideration must be given in exchange for the other party's promise. However, it does not make clear the following requirements for acceptable consideration:

- The detriment must be suffered by the promisee. This is commonly expressed in the principle that 'consideration must move from the promisee'.
- Detriment to the promisee is more important than benefit to the promisor. Consideration must move from the promisee, but it is not necessary that it move to the promisor. It will be sufficient that it moves to a third party.
- Consideration may be either executory (a counter-promise) or executed (an act). However, it must not be past.
- Consideration must be bargained for, that is, the detriment must be suffered with the agreement of the promisor and as the price of the promise.
- Consideration must be something of value in the eyes of the law.[8] This is often expressed by saying consideration must be sufficient, but need not be adequate.

These requirements will now be examined in more detail.

3. PRINCIPLES OF CONSIDERATION

3.1. CONSIDERATION MUST MOVE FROM THE PROMISEE

3.1.1. The General Rule

Parties who wish to sue on a simple contract must show that they have provided consideration for the promise they seek to enforce. Basically this means that a promisee seeking to enforce a promise must have given something in exchange for it. This requirement is expressed in the rule that consideration must move from the promisee.[9]

7 [1915] AC 847, 855. See also the definition in *Currie v Misa* (1875) LR 10 Ex 153, 162.
8 *Patterson v National Capital District Commission* [2001] PGNC 71; *Valette v Republic of Vanuatu* [2010] VUSC 104.
9 *National Housing Commission v Queensland Insurance (PNG) Ltd* [1988–89] PNGLR 474.

The rule that consideration must move from the promisee prevented the plaintiff succeeding in *Dunlop Pneumatic Tyre Co Ltd v Selfridge & Co Ltd*.[10] In that case, the plaintiff company sold some tyres to Dew & Co. The sale was on condition that Dew & Co would not resell the tyres below certain prices and that when Dew & Co came to resell the tyres they would extract a similar promise from the purchaser. Dew & Co sold to the defendant, who agreed to observe the restrictions and to pay to the plaintiff the sum of £5 for each tyre sold in breach of the agreement. The defendant sold some of the tyres below the fixed price and the plaintiff sued. It was held that the plaintiff could not succeed as no consideration had moved from it to the defendant. Lord Chancellor Haldane said:

> [I]n the law of England certain principles are fundamental ... if a person with whom a contract not under seal has been made is to be able to enforce it, consideration must have been given by him to the promisor or to some other person at the promisor's request.

A regional case example is *Qalovaki v WR Carpenter (South Pacific) Ltd*,[11] where the plaintiff sued the defendant for damages incurred as a result of the defendant's failure to repair his vehicle within two weeks, as allegedly promised. The court found that the contract of repair was made between the defendant and the insurer of the vehicle. The alleged promise was unenforceable as the plaintiff had given no consideration to the defendant.

A further regional example is *Mani v St Fort Investment Ltd*.[12] The plaintiff, an estate agent, was contacted by a third party on behalf of an overseas investor and asked to find hotel premises for sale in Fiji. The plaintiff contacted the defendants, who were shareholders in a company, which owned a hotel that was for sale. During the final stage of negotiations the plaintiff raised the question of his commission. The purchaser said that he was not going to pay anything. Fearing a breakdown in communications, the third defendant said that he would pay the commission. He later refused to pay. It was held that the agreement by the purchaser to buy the shares could not amount to consideration for the promise to pay the plaintiff, as it had not passed from the defendant, but from the purchaser.

The rule that consideration must move from the promisee must be distinguished from the doctrine of privity of contract. According to the doctrine of privity, which is discussed in chapter 8, only a party to a contract may sue or be sued on it. The doctrine of privity and the rule that consideration must move from the promisee overlap, and both may apply to the same set of facts. In such

10 [1915] AC 847, 855.
11 Unreported, Supreme Court, Fiji, Tuivaga J, 5 October 1979.
12 (1985) 31 FLR 136, 142.

cases, a claim may fail both on the grounds that the plaintiff did not provide consideration and was not a party to the contract. That was the case in *Dunlop Pneumatic Tyre Co Ltd v Selfridge & Co Ltd*[13] and *Qalovaki v WR Carpenter (South Pacific) Ltd.*[14] However, the rules are not always coincident. For example, a party to a written contract may clearly comply with the doctrine of privity, but may nevertheless be unable to sue on the contract because s/he failed to provide consideration.

Where a promise is made to joint promisees, that is, two or more persons collectively, it is unclear whether consideration must move from each of them. It may be enough if one gives the consideration, provided it is done on behalf of them all.[15]

3.1.2. Exception to the General Rule

An exception to the rule that consideration must move from the promisee can be found in the case of negotiable instruments. A negotiable instrument is a document containing a promise of payment that, when transferred, passes all right to payment to the transferee, for example a cheque. The Bills of Exchange Act of Fiji[16] provides that a person seeking to enforce a negotiable instrument need not have provided consideration directly, so long as consideration has been given at some time. Where value has at any time been given for a bill, the holder is deemed to be a holder for value as regards the acceptor and all parties to the bill who became parties prior to such time.

The Bills of Exchange Acts of Tonga[17] and Samoa[18] make similar provision. There is also a similar provision in the Bills of Exchange Acts of United Kingdom[19] and New Zealand.[20] The former applies in Kiribati, Solomon Islands, Tuvalu and Vanuatu.[21] The New Zealand Act applies in Cook Islands,[22] Niue[23] and Tokelau.[24]

---

13 [1915] AC 847.

14 Unreported, Supreme Court, Fiji, Tuivaga J, 5 October 1979.

15 *Coulls v Bagot's Executor & Trustee Co Ltd* (1967) 199 CLR 460. See also *McEvoy v Belfast Banking Co Ltd* [1935] AC 24. See further B. Coote, 'Consideration and the Joint Promisee' (1978) 37 *The Cambridge Law Journal* 301.

16 Cap 227, s 27(2).

17 Cap 108, s 27(2).

18 1976, s 27(2).

19 1882 (UK).

20 1908, s 27(2).

21 See Personal Property Securities Act 2008 (Van), s 2, which incorporates the definition of 'bill of exchange' or 'promissory note' from the Bills of Exchange Act 1882 (UK).

22 Cook Islands Act 1915 (NZ), s 625.

23 Niue Act 1966 (NZ), s 682.

24 Application of New Zealand Law Rules 2004 (Tokelau), R 3(1)(i) and (ii). All amendments would appear to apply as the Rules state that 'Acts passed in substitution will apply': R 3(2)(vii).

3.2. CONSIDERATION NEED NOT MOVE TO THE PROMISOR

As mentioned above, detriment to the promisee is more important than benefit to the promisor. Whilst consideration must move from the promisee, it is not essential that it moves to the promisor. The promisee may provide the consideration to a third party if directed to do so by the promisor.

3.3. CONSIDERATION MUST NOT BE PAST CONSIDERATION

Where the act or promise relied upon as consideration is done or given before the promisor's promise is made and independent of it, it is known as past consideration. As stated in *Samoa Commercial Bank Ltd v Palm Island Traders*,[25] '[i]t is a well-established principle of contract law that past consideration is no consideration'.

The reason why past consideration is not acceptable in law is reflected in the definition of consideration in *Dunlop Pneumatic Tyre Co v Selfridge & Co*, set out in section 2 above.[26] Consideration is the price of the promisor's promise. If the promise is made after the act or promise relied on, it cannot be said to be the price of that promise. Rather, it is gratuitous.

The principle is illustrated by *Roscorla v Thomas*,[27] where the plaintiff purchased a horse from the defendant, who afterwards warranted that the horse was sound and free from vice. It was in fact a vicious horse. It was held that, as there was no warranty at the time of the original sale, the sale could not be consideration for the subsequent promise as it had already taken place. Accordingly, the warranty could not be enforced.

It is important to distinguish past consideration from executed consideration. In the case of executed consideration, the act relied on as consideration is done in return for the promise. They are both parts of the same transaction.

The fact that part of the consideration is past is irrelevant, provided that there is also present consideration. In *Kulamma v Manadan*,[28] the plaintiff inherited a farm from her late husband which was subject to a 'share-farming' agreement with her husband's brother, under which the brother was to cultivate the farm and share all proceeds equally. After her husband's death the parties continued to act on the agreement. In November 1960, when money was owing to the defendant under the agreement, the plaintiff and her children went to live with the defendant and assigned to him all crops growing on the farm and all receipts

25 [2009] WSSC 4, [38].
26 [1915] AC 847, 855.
27 (1842) 3 QB 234.
28 *Kulamma v Manadan* (1964) 10 FLR 252, 256–57.

from those crops. After a dispute arose, the plaintiff sought to set aside the assignment on the grounds that it was made for past consideration. It was held that this contention failed both on the facts and the law. It was found that the assignment was given as a security of the money owed at that time and for future expenditure that the defendant would incur in maintaining the plaintiff and her children when they joined the defendant's household. Present consideration was constituted by the defendant's promise to maintain the plaintiff and her family, and probably also in his consenting to continue to cultivate the farm.

If a promise made in exchange for past consideration is performed, no action lies merely because the consideration was past.[29]

The following exceptions apply to the rule.

3.3.1. Request of the Promisor

An act done at the promisor's request may result in a legally enforceable agreement, even if the amount of the payment to be made in exchange is fixed subsequently. In *Lampleigh v Braithwait*,[30] the defendant requested the plaintiff to obtain a free pardon for him from the King. The plaintiff incurred certain expenses as a result of his efforts to do this, and the defendant subsequently promised to pay him £100 for his trouble. The defendant did not pay and the plaintiff sued. It was held that the defendant's request and subsequent promise could be regarded as part of the same transaction, and therefore that there was good consideration.

It is arguable that this is not really an exception, but that the request should be viewed as an implied promise to pay a reasonable sum and the subsequent express promise as merely fixing the amount.

The principle has been developed in more recent cases, and in *Pao On v Lau Yiu Long*,[31] it was held that three conditions must be satisfied before the exception applies:

- the act must have been done at the promisor's request;
- it must have been understood that payment would be made; and
- the payment, if it had been promised in advance, must have been legally recoverable.[32]

In *Mani v St Fort Investment Ltd*,[33] the facts of which are set out in section 3.1.1 above, the plaintiff failed to establish that past acts of the plaintiff in facilitating

[29] Ibid., 257.
[30] (1615) 80 ER 255.
[31] [1980] AC 614.
[32] Approved in *Samoa Commercial Bank Ltd v Palm Island Traders* [2009] WSSC 4.
[33] (1985) 31 FLR 136, 141–42.

a sale of shares could amount to good consideration as they preceded the promise to pay. They did not fall within the exception to the rule as they had not been done at the request of the promisor (the third defendant) and there was no understanding that payment would be made.

3.3.2. Negotiable Instruments

The Bills of Exchange Act of Fiji[34] provides that valuable consideration for a bill may be constituted by:

- any consideration sufficient to support a simple contract; or
- an antecedent debt or liability.

Similar legislation is in force in Tonga[35] and Samoa.[36]

As mentioned above, the Bills of Exchange Act 1882 (UK) applies in Kiribati, Solomon Islands, Tuvalu and Vanuatu. The Bills of Exchange Act 1908 (NZ) applies in Cook Islands, Niue and Tokelau.[37] Both Acts contain similar provisions to the regional Acts.[38]

3.4. CONSIDERATION MUST BE BARGAINED FOR

The act or forbearance must be done by the promisee with the agreement or assent of the promisor, that is, as part of the agreement or bargain between the parties. This is another way of stating the rule that there can be no valid acceptance unless it is made in response to the offer.[39]

In *Combe v Combe*,[40] a husband on divorce promised his wife a permanent allowance of £100 per annum. The Court of Appeal refused to hold that a subsequent forbearance on the part of the wife to sue for maintenance amounted to consideration. The husband had not requested her to forbear, and her action could not be said to be in return for the promise to pay.

In *Valette v Republic of Vanuatu*,[41] the plaintiff claimed in respect of damage caused during riots that had taken place in 1998, but the claims were discontinued

---

34 Cap 227, s 27(1).
35 Bills of Exchange Act Cap 108, s 27(1).
36 Bills of Exchange Act 1976, s 27(1).
37 Applying by virtue of Cook Islands Act 1915 (NZ), s 625; Niue Act 1966 (NZ), s 682; and Application of New Zealand Law Rules 2004 (Tokelau), R 3(1)(i) and (ii), respectively. See further section 3.1.2 above.
38 Bills of Exchange Act 1882 (UK), s 27(1); Bills of Exchange Act 1908 (NZ), s 27(1).
39 *R v Clarke* (1927) 40 CLR 227. See further chapter 3.
40 [1951] 2 KB 215.
41 [2010] VUSC 104.

after settlement. When payment was not made, the plaintiff took further action to enforce the alleged settlement agreement, claiming that consideration existed in the form of forbearance from proceeding with the former actions. The court held that, although the plaintiffs 'did, in fact, forbear', there was no acceptance or consideration for this passing from the defendants.

3.5. CONSIDERATION NEED NOT BE ADEQUATE, BUT MUST BE SUFFICIENT

In *Valette v Republic of Vanuatu*, it was held that, '[c]onsideration must be not merely "something of value", but "something of value in the eye of the law"'.

3.5.1. Adequacy

Assuming the type of consideration in question is recognised as legally sufficient, the courts will not enquire into the adequacy or value of the consideration.[42] A promisor cannot complain if what was agreed to be taken in return for the promise is not as valuable as the promise. A promise may be made for nominal consideration.

In *Azam v Azam*,[43] the defendant agreed to transfer his interest in the matrimonial home to his wife for £100 and her agreement to look after their four children as he wanted to leave the country to be with his mistress. The court accepted that this was sufficient consideration in law. Hammett J noted that:

> the defendant appears to be seeking to be released from this agreement because of what he submits is the in adequacy of the consideration moving to him from the plaintiff. It is well established that the courts will not inquire into the adequacy of consideration.

An interesting example of the practical significance of this principle is *Chappell & Co v Nestle Ltd*.[44] In that case, the plaintiff owned the copyright in a dance tune called 'Rockin' Shoes'. The defendant purchased copies of records of the tune for 4d each and offered them to the public for 1s 6d each, plus three wrappers from their bars of chocolate. When they received the wrappers they threw them away. Their main objective was to promote sales of their chocolate, but they also made a profit on the sale of the records. The plaintiff sued the defendant for infringement of copyright and liability turned on whether the defendant could

---

42 *Felix v Boblang* [2013] VUSC 98, [93].

43 (1967) 13 FLR 115.

44 [1960] AC 87. See also *Thomas v Thomas* (1842) 114 ER 482.

rely on s 8 of the Copyright Act (UK). That section required a percentage of the sale price to be paid to the copyright owner, and the defendant was offering to pay that, but only 1s 6d. The plaintiff refused this on the grounds that 1s 6d was only part of the selling price, that is, that the three wrappers were part of the consideration.

The majority of the House of Lords agreed that the wrappers were part of the consideration. The fact that the wrappers were of no value to the defendant and were thrown away was irrelevant. The court made it clear that a party can stipulate the consideration, and the fact that it is not valuable is irrelevant.

Another practical consequence of the rule is that forbearance to sue or an agreement to discontinue litigation is good consideration for a promise given in return, even if the plaintiff would have failed in the original claim. However, this is subject to the following:

- the claim must be reasonable, and not vexatious or frivolous;
- the plaintiff must honestly believe, on reasonable grounds, in the claim's chances of success;[45] and
- the plaintiff must not have concealed from the defendant any fact which the plaintiff knows to be relevant to the validity of the claim.[46]

In *Morris Hedstrom Ltd v Ram*,[47] the Supreme Court held that if the court is satisfied that a cheque is supported by valuable consideration, the adequacy of such consideration is irrelevant and cannot be made the subject of an enquiry.

The only instance where the courts will embark on an investigation into the adequacy of consideration is where they are obliged to do so by statute. For example, in *Dorsamy v Commissioner of Estate & Gift Duty*[48] the court held that the Estate & Gift Duties Ordinance[49] obliged them to investigate the adequacy of consideration.

3.5.2. Sufficiency

Although consideration need not be adequate, in the sense of equal value, there are certain acts and promises which the law regards as being insufficient to amount to consideration. Whilst consideration may be tenuous, it must comprise some element which can be regarded as the price.[50]

45 *Valette v Republic of Vanuatu* [2010] VUSC 104.

46 *Callisher v Bischoffsheim* (1870) LR 5QB 449; *Hercules Motors Pty Ltd v Schubert* (1953) SR (NSW) 301.

47 (1973) 19 FLR 62.

48 (1976) 22 FLR 70.

49 Cap 178, s 2. See now Estate and Gift Duties Act Cap 203 (Fiji).

50 *Patterson v National Capital District Commission* [2001] PGNC 71.

The following categories do not amount to valuable consideration in the eyes of the law.

3.5.2.1. Moral Obligations

A moral obligation to perform a promise does not constitute consideration. This principle is demonstrated by the case of *Eastwood v Kenyon.*[51] On the death of John Sutcliffe, his infant daughter was left as his sole heiress. The plaintiff, the girl's guardian, spent money on her education and for the benefit of the estate, and the girl, when she came of age, promised to reimburse her. The daughter then married the defendant, who also promised to reimburse the plaintiff. The plaintiff sued the defendant on this promise. It was held that there was no valid consideration, as a pre-existing moral duty was not good consideration.

3.5.2.2. Worthy Motives

A promise is not binding because it was actuated by a worthy motive. This principle is illustrated by *Thomas v Thomas.*[52] In that case the plaintiff's husband had expressed the wish that if his wife survived him she should have the use of his house. After his death, his executor agreed to allow her to occupy the house: (a) because of the husband's wishes, and (b) on the payment of £1 per year. It was held that respect for the husband's wishes did not constitute consideration, but £1 per year did.

3.5.2.3. Illegal or Immoral Consideration

Another feature of sufficiency is that the consideration must not be immoral or illegal.[53] In *Lyden v Folau,*[54] the plaintiff and defendant had been living together and had a child. The plaintiff promised the defendant that he would marry her as soon as he got a divorce. He brought various items of furniture to their joint home. Subsequently the defendant married another man. The plaintiff sued to recover his furniture, alleging that they were given on condition that the defendant married him. The defendant alleged that the furniture was an absolute gift. On appeal from the magistrate's finding in favour of the plaintiff, Thompson CJ held that even if there was a conditional agreement, it was based on an immoral consideration and therefore could not be enforced.

---

51 (1840) 113 ER 482.
52 (1842) 114 ER 482.
53 See further chapter 15.
54 [1908–59] Tonga LR 39.

3.5.2.4. Performance of an Existing Public Duty

A promise to perform or the actual performance of an existing public duty imposed by law does not amount to consideration. This is because there is no detriment to the promisee or benefit to the promisor over and above their existing rights and duties.

In *Collins v Godefroy*,[55] the plaintiff received a subpoena to appear at a trial as a witness on behalf of the defendant. The defendant promised him a sum of money for his trouble. It was held that this promise was unenforceable, as a person who receives a subpoena is bound to attend at court and give evidence. There was therefore no consideration for the promise, the plaintiff being under a public duty to attend.

If the promisee acts or undertakes to act in excess of his or her duty, this may be sufficient consideration, even though the act is of the same kind as that which the promisee is legally bound to perform. For example, in *Glasbrook Bros v Glamorgan County Council*,[56] a police authority sued for the sum of £2,200 promised to them by the defendant colliery company, for whose mine they had provided a stronger guard during a strike than was in their opinion necessary. It was held that they had provided good consideration by acting in excess of the duty they owed to the public, which was to provide such policing as they considered necessary.

3.5.2.5. Part Payment of an Existing Debt

Part payment of a liquidated debt in consideration for a simple promise to forego the balance is insufficient in the eyes of the law. This is known as the rule in *Pinnel's Case*.[57] In that case, the plaintiff brought an action in debt against Cole for payment of £8 10s on 11 November 1600. Cole's defence was that the plaintiff had agreed to accept £5 2s 2d on 1 October in full satisfaction of the debt. The court held that payment of a lesser sum on an earlier date could be good consideration, but payment of a lesser sum on the due date could not.

The principle was reaffirmed by the House of Lords in *Foakes v Beer*.[58] The defendant was indebted to the plaintiff on a judgment for the sum of £2,090. It was agreed by the plaintiff that if the defendant paid her £500 in cash and the balance of £1,590 in instalments she would not take any proceedings on the judgment. The defendant paid the money exactly as required, but the plaintiff proceeded to claim an additional £360 as interest on the judgment debt. The

---

55 (1831) B & Ad 950.

56 [1925] AC 270.

57 (1602) 77 ER 237.

58 (1884) 9 App Cas 605. See also *Ferguson v Davies* [1997] 1 All ER 315 (CA).

defendant refused to pay and when sued pleaded that his duty to pay interest had been discharged by the plaintiff's promise not to sue. On appeal from judgment in favour of the plaintiff, the House of Lords held that the defendant was bound to pay, as there was no consideration for that promise. The defendant had paid no more than he was obliged to do. More recently, the rule in *Pinnel's Case* was affirmed by the House of Lords in *Re Selectmove*.[59]

A regional example can be found in *Raniga v Sony (South Pacific) Ltd*,[60] where the defendants owed the plaintiffs $10,103.03. They forwarded a cheque for $8,064.29, listing a number of deductions and stating that if the respondents did not agree with the deductions, they should return the cheque. The plaintiffs banked the cheque and sued for the balance. The defendants alleged on appeal that the letter accompanying the cheque was an offer to settle the account in full and that the offer had been accepted when the cheque was banked. The Supreme Court held that the alleged contract was unenforceable due to lack of consideration.

There are exceptions to the rule:

- *Introduction of a new element in the performance of the existing duty to pay*
  If the creditor agrees to accept something different from that to which s/he is entitled, for example goods instead of cash, this may amount to sufficient consideration. Similarly, if payment is made at an earlier date, this may confer an advantage on the payee and therefore it will amount to sufficient consideration. *Pinnel's Case* is an example of earlier payment, and it was also said in that case that if the debtor had given a horse, hawk or robe this would have been good consideration.

  If the change is made merely for the debtor's convenience, this will not come within the exception. For example, in *Van Burgen v St Edmonds Properties*,[61] payment was made at a different place for the defendant's convenience. The rule in *Pinnel's Case* applied.

- *Composition with creditors*
  This is a process whereby the creditors make an arrangement with the debtor that each will accept a certain percentage of the amount owed to them in full satisfaction of the debt. Such agreements are enforceable even though there is no apparent consideration to supports the promises of the creditors.[62]

---

59 [1995] 2 All ER 531.
60 Unreported, Supreme Court, Fiji, Kermode J, 1979.
61 [1933] 2 KB 223.
62 *Wood v Roberts* (1818) 1271 ER 691.

- *Payment from a third party*
  A creditor who has accepted part payment from a third party in full satisfaction of a debt cannot later sue the debtor for the balance, as to do so would be a fraud on the third party.[63]

The rule that part payment of a liquidated debt is insufficient consideration for a promise was, until fairly recently, part of a wider rule that performance of an existing contractual duty was insufficient consideration to support a further promise made by the promisor. An example of this old rule can be seen in *Stilk v Myrick*.[64] In the course of a return voyage from London to the Baltic, two seamen deserted and the captain, being unable to fill their places, offered extra payment to those remaining if they would work the ship home. On arrival the captain refused to pay, and the promise was held not to be binding. Desertion of crewmen was an emergency of the voyage, and there was already a duty to work the ship home in such a case.

The old rule did not apply if uncontemplated risks had arisen or if the existing contract had been terminated and a new one substituted at a higher rate of pay. This was the case in *Hartley v Ponsonby*,[65] where a ship left England with a crew of 36, but as a result of desertions only 19 remained. Of them, only four or five were able seamen. The plaintiff, an able seaman, successfully sued the Master on a promise to pay him £40 if he would assist in taking the ship from Port Phillip to Bombay with a crew of 19 hands. It was held that the crew was so reduced that it was a danger to life to sail. The contract had come to an end (through frustration) and a new contract had been entered into.

The rule that performance of an existing contractual duty is insufficient consideration to support a further promise made by the promisor must now be seen in the light of the decision in *Williams v Roffey Bros & Nicholls (Contractors) Ltd*.[66] In that case, the defendants were main contractors on a contract for the building of flats. They realised that the plaintiffs, who were the subcontracting carpenters on the job, were in financial difficulty, and that there was a risk that they would not complete the work. The defendants were liable to pay damages under the main contract if the job was not finished on time. To avoid this happening, they offered the plaintiffs an extra payment for each flat they completed. The defendants did not pay the extra money and said there was no consideration for the promise to pay it. It was held by the Court of Appeal that the promise was enforceable.

---

63 *Hirachand Punamchand v Temple* [1911] 2 KB 330.
64 (1809) 170 ER 1168.
65 (1857) 119 ER 1471.
66 [1991] 1 QB 1.

This case has left the law in an uncertain state, as there is no clear ratio, and the Court distinguished *Stilk v Myrick* rather than overruled it. It would appear that the avoidance of disadvantage by the promisor may be consideration for the promise of extra payments for work already agreed to be done. In *Williams v Roffey Bros & Nicholls (Contractors) Ltd*, the defendants' avoidance of the risk of having to pay liquidated damages in the main contract seems to have been regarded as consideration for their promise. However, in *Simantob v Shavleyan (t/a Yacob's Gallery)*,[67] whilst refusing to be drawn on whether *Williams v Roffey Bros & Nicholls (Contractors) Ltd* was wrongly decided, the court held that 'the law presently is that an offer to pay less than an amount already due must, in the absence of consideration, be ineffective'. Further, the court held that the notion of a 'cultural benefit' was not sufficient to amount to consideration.

The rule that performance of an existing contractual duty was insufficient consideration to support a further promise made by the promisor did not extend to performance of an existing duty to a third party. Where the promisee is bound by an existing contractual duty owed to a third party, performance or promise of the performance of that duty has always been regarded as sufficient consideration for the promisor's promise. An example is *Scotson v Pegg*,[68] where the plaintiff entered into a contract with a third party to deliver coal to the defendant. The defendant then made an agreement with the plaintiff that if the plaintiff delivered the coal to him he would unload it at a fixed rate per day. The defendant failed to keep his promise, and when sued pleaded lack of consideration, as the plaintiff was already bound to deliver the coal to him. It was held that performance of an existing contractual promise can be consideration for a separate promise made by a third party.

The decision was confirmed in *New Zealand Shipping Co Ltd v Satterthwaite & Co Ltd*,[69] where the unloading by stevedores of goods from a ship (which they were already bound to a third party to unload) was held to be sufficient consideration for a promise to relieve them from liability for damaging the goods.[70]

---

67 [2018] EWHC 2005. See also *Rock Advertising Ltd (Respondent) v MWB Business Exchange Centres Ltd* [2018] UKSC 24, where the Supreme Court refused to resolve the confusion caused by *Williams v Roffey Bros & Nicholls (Contractors) Ltd* [1991] 1 QB 1.

68 (1861) 158 ER 121.

69 [1975] AC 154.

70 See also *Pao On v Lao Yiu Long* [1980] AC 614.

3.6. ESTOPPEL

The doctrine of equitable estoppel may, in some cases, apply to save an agreement that would otherwise fail for lack of consideration. According to this doctrine, if a person makes a statement of fact and another person acts on it, the maker will be prevented (estopped) from denying the truth of the statement in subsequent litigation. This is discussed further in chapter 7.

CHAPTER 7
PROMISSORY ESTOPPEL

1. INTRODUCTION

The equitable principle of promissory estoppel may, in some cases, apply to save an agreement that would otherwise fail for lack of consideration. By virtue of this principle, if a person makes a statement of fact and another person acts on it, the maker will be prevented (estopped) from denying the truth of the statement in subsequent litigation. Estoppel is related to the notion of waiver,[1] which is also discussed in chapter 17.

Promissory estoppel forms part of the principles of equity introduced into the law of the countries of the region during the colonial era and retained at independence.[2] For example, in *Mariango v Nalau*,[3] the Court of Appeal of Vanuatu said:

> [t]he equitable principles that have application to this case including … estoppel are incorporated into the law of Vanuatu … These equitable principles were known to the common law of England before the relevant date in the constitution of 30 July 1980.[4]

Whilst this chapter is concerned primarily with promissory estoppel, it should be noted that promissory estoppel is only one form of estoppel. Equity recognises other types of estoppel within the broader principle of estoppel, which may be relevant to contractual disputes. These include proprietary estoppel and estoppel by convention. The former may provide relief where agreements relating to land or property fail to comply with statutory requirements. The cases of *Paul v Tuanai*[5] and *Meredith v Pa'u*[6] provide examples of how this principle has been applied within the region.[7] The latter applies when the parties have acted in

1 See e.g. *Patel v Patel* [1992] FJCA 22.
2 See further chapter 1.
3 [2007] VUCA 15, [16].
4 See further Constitution of Vanuatu 1980, Art. 95(2).
5 [1994] WSSC 15.
6 [1994] WSSC 7.
7 See *Pelenato v Vaitusi* [1994] WSSC 38 for an example of tenancy by estoppel.

their dealings on the basis of a mistaken assumption and departure from that assumption by one party would result in a detriment to the other.[8]

A third form of estoppel is contractual estoppel. This was developed in recent years in the context of contracts that attempt to exclude liability for misrepresentation. The courts have held that even though such exclusions are contradicted by the facts, they will be binding on the basis of contractual estoppel.[9] This form of estoppel has been subject to criticism[10] and there is no evidence that it is being applied in the region.

2. DEFINITION

The principle of promissory estoppel can be loosely defined as a rule that applies, in certain circumstances, to keep a party to a promise made in relation to an existing contract. In *Gonewai v William Associates Ltd*,[11] it was stated as a principle which 'prevents a party from unjust departure from what they have agreed'. In *Central London Property Trust v High Trees House*,[12] Lord Denning explained the basis of the principle:

> A promise intended to be binding, intended to be acted upon, and in fact acted on, is binding so far as its terms properly apply.

The promise must have been made by the person against whom estoppel is being alleged or an authorised agent.[13]

In Tokelau, the principle of estoppel has been given statutory form. Rule 173 of the Crimes, Procedure and Evidence Rules 2003 states:

> A person who has by declaration, act or omission intentionally caused or permitted another to believe a thing to be true and to act on that belief in a way which that other person would not have acted but for that belief, shall not be permitted either personally or representative in any proceeding between person or his representative to deny the truth of that thing.

---

8 See R. Hughes and P. MacFarlane, 'The Application of Custom in South Pacific Contract Law and as a Basis for an Estoppel' (2004) 20 *Journal of Contract Law* 1, 11–12. Estoppel by convention is not confined to contractual situations: *Downderry Constructions Ltd v Secretary of State for Transport Local Government and the Regions* [2002] EWHC 2.

9 *Peekay Intermark Ltd v Australia and New Zealand Banking Group Ltd* [2006] EWCA Civ 386; *Springwell Navigation Corp v JP Morgan Chase* [2010] EWCA Civ 1221.

10 See e.g. G. McMeel, 'Documentary Fundamentalism in the Senior Courts: the Myth of Contractual Estoppel' (2011) 2 *Lloyd's Maritime and Commercial Law Quarterly* 185.

11 [2012] FJSC 21.

12 [1947] KB 130.

13 *Attorney-General of Fiji v Pacoil Fiji Ltd* [1996] FJCA 9, 16.

3. THE DEVELOPMENT OF THE PRINCIPLE OF ESTOPPEL

Central London Property Trust v High Trees House[14] is the foundation stone of the modern law of estoppel. In that case, Denning LJ developed the equitable waiver principle into a more extensive principle of law. His main authority for doing this was *Hughes v Metropolitan Railway Co.*[15] In that case the defendant held a lease of certain houses from the plaintiff. The lease contained a covenant of repair within six months of being given notice. The plaintiff gave notice to repair. The defendant then suggested that a sale might be arranged, and said that they would defer carrying out any repairs until this had been discussed. Some negotiations took place, but no agreement was reached. The plaintiff then served notice to quit on the basis of the defendant's failure to comply with the notice to repair. It was held that the plaintiff was not entitled to do this. The notice had been suspended while the negotiations for sale were taking place. Lord Cairns said:

> [I]t is the first principle on which all Courts of Equity proceed, that if parties who have entered in to definite and distinct terms involving certain legal results – certain penalties or legal forfeiture – afterwards by their own act or with their own consent enter upon a course of negotiation which has the effect of leading one of the parties to suppose that the strict rights arising under the contract will not be enforced, or will be kept in suspense, or held in abeyance, the person who otherwise might have enforced those rights will not be allowed to enforce them where it would be inequitable having regard to the dealings which have thus taken place between the parties.

In *Central London Property Trust v High Trees House*,[16] Lord Denning restated this principle, which could be classified as an example of waiver, and developed it into a wider doctrine, which became known as promissory estoppel. The plaintiffs in this case were the owners of a block of flats in London, which they rented to the defendants at a rent of £2,500 per annum. Following the outbreak of the Second World War in 1939, the defendants were unable to find suitable tenants to sub-lease the flats. As a result, the plaintiffs reduced the rent to £1,250 per annum. This arrangement continued until after the war ended in 1945, when the flats became much easier to let. The plaintiffs then sought to return to the original terms of the lease and also queried whether the other half

---

14 [1947] KB 130.

15 (1877) 2 App Cas 439. For regional examples of the application of the principle of waiver see *Bishop of Melanesia v Maile* (1973) 19 FLR 49 and *Vanualevu Hardware (Fiji) Ltd v Sun Insurance Company Ltd* [2013] FJHC 213.

16 [1947] KB 130.

of the rent for the war years was recoverable, as the promise to accept a lower rent was not supported by consideration. It was held that the plaintiffs could recover full rent from the time that the war ended. Although the claim to recover the balance of the rent for the war years was not pursued, Denning LJ took the opportunity to clarify the position. He stated, obiter, that the balance could not be recovered, because the plaintiffs had made a promise not to enforce their right to the balance of the rent and the defendants had acted on this promise. His Lordship regarded this as the logical extension of the principle in *Hughes v Metropolitan Railway Co.*[17]

In *Nair v Public Trustee of Fiji*,[18] Lyons J considered the principle of promissory estoppel as stated by Lord Denning in *Central London Property Trust v High Trees House* and classified it as a 'hybrid' of waiver and estoppel. Lyons J summarised the law as follows:

> The modern doctrine of equit[t]able estoppel requires as its essential element, 'unconscionable conduct', which equity would move to prevent.

However, estoppel is a separate principle from unconscionability, which is discussed in chapter 13.

4. OBJECTIONS TO THE PRINCIPLE OF ESTOPPEL

Lord Denning's extension of the waiver principle in *Central London Property Trust v High Trees House*[19] has caused controversy. Objection to his Lordship's approach has been taken on the basis that:

- it runs counter to the doctrine of consideration; and
- it is contrary to the rule in *Pinell's Case* and the decision of the House of Lords in *Foakes v Beer.*[20]

These objections can be dispensed with by reference to the fact that the equitable principle provides a remedy where none is available under the common law, rather than replacing the common law rules. However, there may still be a conflict in relation to enforceability. Nevertheless, promissory estoppel is a well-established principle in common law countries.

---

17 (1877) 2 App Cas 439.

18 Unreported, High Court, Fiji, Lyons J, 8 March 1996. This case was partly overturned on appeal, but not on this point: *Public Trustee of Fiji v Nair* [1997] FJCA 55.

19 [1947] KB 130.

20 (1884) 9 App Cas 605.

4.1. PROMISSORY ESTOPPEL AND CONSIDERATION

As stated above, Lord Denning's original expression of the principle was objected to on the basis that it undermined the doctrine of consideration. However, the principle has been narrowed down by subsequent decisions.[21] The principle is now limited by the following requirements.

4.1.1. There Must have been a Reliance

Entry into a contract results from the exchange of promises or, in the case of a unilateral contract,[22] the exchange of a promise for an act. Provided that the other elements of a binding agreement are present, there is no need for either party to have relied on the promise in order for it to be enforceable. In the case of promissory estoppel, however, the promise relied on as founding the estoppel cannot be enforced unless the promisee has taken some action in reliance on it.[23] For example, in *Central London Property Trust v High Trees House*[24] the promisee continued with the lease and paid a lower rent in reliance on the promise to forego the balance.

Another example of reliance is where a bank over-credits a customer's account. In *Australia and New Zealand Banking Group Ltd v East*,[25] Tuivaga CJ made it clear that if a customer alters his or her position in ignorance of the mistake, and in reliance on the bank's statement of the amount in the account, the bank is estopped from obtaining a refund.

4.1.2. Estoppel cannot be Used as a 'Sword'

Under English law, the principle of estoppel cannot be used to found a course of action (a 'sword'), but only as a defence (a 'shield'). This is illustrated by *Combe v Combe*,[26] where the husband promised his wife a permanent allowance of £100 per annum on their divorce. At first instance, Byrne J held that the wife could recover on the basis of estoppel, even though she had not given any consideration. The Court of Appeal reversed this decision. The argument that the wife had refrained from suing for maintenance on the strength of the promise and that this amounted to consideration was not accepted. The husband

[21] *RSI Holdings (Samoa) Ltd v Attorney-General* [2012] WSSC 130, [169].
[22] See chapter 1 for a discussion of the meaning of a unilateral contract.
[23] *Burgess v Prasad* (1974) 20 FLR 49, 52; *Moehau v Westpac Bank of Tonga* [2013] TOCA 9.
[24] [1947] KB 130.
[25] [1977] FJSC 47.
[26] [1951] 2 KB 215.

had not requested her to refrain from suing and this forbearance could not be said to be in return for the promise to pay. The Court of Appeal, which included Lord Denning, held that estoppel could not be used as a cause of action but, generally, only as a defence.[27]

This decision makes it clear that, under the English common law, consideration is still required except in the in the case of variation or discharge of an existing contractual[28] relationship. It did not allow the creation of a contract, as consideration was still necessary there. This approach has been repeated in more recent decisions, including *Baird Textile Holdings Ltd v Marks & Spencers plc.*[29]

This restriction does not apply in Australia, where the common law has developed a more extensive role for estoppel. In *Waltons Stores (Interstate) Ltd v Maher,*[30] the principle was used to create new rights.[31] This case supports a wide, general principle of estoppel preventing unconscionable conduct. Brennan J laid down six criteria for the use of equitable estoppel to found an action,[32] which can be summarised as follows:

1. There must be an assumption or expectation on the part of the plaintiff that a particular legal relationship existed or would exist between the parties.
2. The defendant must have induced that assumption or expectation.
3. The plaintiff must have acted or refrained from acting on the basis of the assumption or expectation.
4. The defendant must have known of or intended this.
5. The defendant's action or inaction must be the cause of detriment to the plaintiff.[33]
6. The defendant must have failed to act to avoid the detriment, whether by fulfilling the assumption or expectation or otherwise.

The fifth criterion referred to in *Waltons*[34] is well illustrated by *Nubono v Attorney-General.*[35] The plaintiff sued for the balance of a daily allowance which had been agreed to be paid while he was on Kiritimati Island waiting to be called as a prosecution witness. The allowance was stated in a letter from the police prosecution to be $150 per day, payable until the plaintiff was aboard a ship to

---

27 Compare with the approach of Denning MR in *Amalgamated Investment and Property Co Ltd v Texas Commerce International Bank Ltd* [1947] KB 130, 134.
28 A statutory relationship may suffice. See above n. 15.
29 [2001] EWCA Civ 274.
30 (1984) 164 CLR 387.
31 See also *Commonwealth of Australia v Verwayen* (1990) 170 CLR 394.
32 (1984) 164 CLR 387, 428.
33 *Speakman v Speakman* [2013] FJHC 710.
34 (1984) 164 CLR 387, 428.
35 [2006] KIHC 16.

return home. The High Court of Kiribati applied *Waltons*, but refused to grant relief on the basis that that the plaintiff did not act to his detriment as he had no alternative but to remain on Kiritimati until the ship came; he had already been paid generously and was working while he was away.[36]

The courts in Pacific countries have not been unanimous in their response to this Australian development. In Solomon Islands, the English approach still appears to apply. In *Isabel Timber Company Ltd v Huhurangi Enterprises*,[37] the High Court, citing *Cross on Evidence*, held that the 'doctrine of estoppel cannot be used as a sword, only a shield. It also cannot be used to found an action'.

The courts in Cook Islands,[38] Fiji,[39] Kiribati,[40] PNG[41] and Samoa,[42] have all followed the Australian law as developed in *Waltons Stores (Interstate) Ltd v Maher*. In Samoa, Sapolu CJ cited *Waltons* in *Eteuati v The Pacific Forum Line*[43] and explicitly stated that 'the present trend in the modern development of the principle of estoppel is to set it free from its traditional restriction to a representation or assumption of existing fact'.

In *Nair v Public Trustee of Fiji*,[44] the first defendant, the Public Trustee, advertised land for sale even though there was litigation pending concerning the land and he did not have clear title. It was a condition of the sale, stated in the advertisement, that the Director of Lands' consent be obtained prior to the sale. Due to the pending litigation there was in fact no prospect of this. The first defendant accepted the plaintiff's tender, but later repudiated the agreement on the basis of the court proceedings. Notwithstanding the repudiation, the first defendant represented that a clear title would eventually be available. In an action by the plaintiff for damages the defence alleged that the plaintiff had failed to comply with the condition that the Director's consent be obtained to the sale and raised s 13(i) of the Crown Lands Act, which made such consent a statutory requirement for the sale of land of this type. It was held that the

---

36 *Toloke v Tu'imana* [2012] TOSC 38; *Veamatahau v Tulikifanga* [2015] TOSC 3. Cf. *Kinetisys Inc v Mafi* [2012] TOLC 1; *Hafoka v Mokofisi;* [2000] TOLC 1; *Salvation Army (Tonga) Trust v Nau* [2001] TOLC 2.

37 [2001] SBHC 115.

38 *Rongo v Bank of the Cook Islands Holdings Corporation* [2010] CKHC 60.

39 *Public Trustee of Fiji v Nair* [1997] FJCA 55.

40 *Nubono v Attorney-General* [2006] KIHC 16.

41 *Misima Mines Ltd v Collector of Customs, Internal Revenue Commission* [2007] PGNC 91; *Paradise Farms Ltd v Bank South Pacific Ltd* [2010] PGNC 191.

42 *Liuvae v Samoa Credit Union League* [1997] WSSC 13; *Eteuati v The Pacific Forum Line* [1998] WSSC 29; *Toleafoa v Ben* [2008] WSSC 62; *Liaga v Taleni* [2010] WSSC 166; *RSI Holdings (Samoa) Ltd v Attorney-General* [2012] WSSC 130, [161].

43 [1998] WSSC 29.

44 *Nair v Public Trustee of Fiji* (unreported, High Court, Fiji, Lyons J, 8 March 1996), upheld on appeal on this point: *Public Trustee of Fiji v Nair* [1997] FJCA 55. Cf. *Jamnadas Sports (Fiji) Ltd v Stinson Pearce Ltd* [1994] FJCA 20.

defendant was estopped from raising this defence. Lyons J pointed out that equity is capable of 'outflanking'[45] a statute.

Lyons J considered the restrictions that had been put on the principle of estoppel by English courts and preferred the wider principle, 'free from the fetters of the English Court's insistence on the analogy which waiver and estoppel imposed on it'. His Lordship said that it was 'timely that this modern doctrine of equitable estoppel as formulated and approved by the High Court of Australia and the Court of Appeal of New Zealand[46] be incorporated into the law of Fiji'. As Lyons J went on to point out in *Nair v Public Trustee of Fiji*:[47]

> There must be, to establish an equitable estoppel, those 6 criteria set down by Brennan J as referred to above but the application of the doctrine should be constrained by the necessity to always retain 'a proportionality between the remedy and the detriment which is its purpose to avoid'.

Waltons was also followed in Fiji in the *Attorney-General of Fiji v Pacoil Fiji Ltd.*[48] In that case, the Court of Appeal held that the conduct of the Fiji Trade and Investment Board amounted to a promise that the respondent would receive adequate protection for the establishment of its oil-blending project. *Attorney-General of Fiji v Pacoil Fiji Ltd*[49] was followed in *South Pacific Academy of Beauty Therapy v Coral Surf Resort Ltd.*[50]

In Tonga, the use of estoppel as a sword may conflict with the Evidence Act, which puts the principle in statutory form.[51] The provision is framed in the following terms, which seems to suggest that estoppel is a defence, rather than a cause of action:

1. If a person by his words or conduct wilfully endeavours to cause another to believe in a state of things which the first knows to be false, and if the second believes in that state of things and acts upon his belief, he who knowingly made the first statement is estopped from averring afterwards that such a state of things did not in fact exist.

---

45 The term 'outflank' was borrowed by Lyons J from Deane J in *Waltons Stores (Interstate) Ltd v Maher* (1984) 164 CLR 387, 446.

46 The New Zealand courts take a similar approach to that of the High Court in *Waltons Stores (Interstate) Ltd v Maher* (1984) 164 CLR 387. See e.g. *Burbery Mortgage Finance & Savings Ltd v Hindsbank Holdings Ltd* [1989] 1 NZLR 356, where it was made clear that there need not be a pre-existing contractual relationship: *Gold Star Insurance Co Ltd v Gaunt* (1991) 3 NZBLC 102, where it was made clear that estoppel is no longer just a shield.

47 *Nair v Public Trustee of Fiji* (unreported, High Court, Fiji, Lyons J, 8 March 1996), upheld on appeal on this point: *Public Trustee of Fiji v Nair* [1997] FJCA 55.

48 [1996] FJCA 9.

49 Ibid.

50 [2005] FJHC 359.

51 Evidence Act Cap 15, s 103. See e.g. *Mahe v Mafi* [2012] TOLC 3.

2. If a person, either in express terms or by conduct, makes a representation to another of the existence of a certain state of facts which he intends to be acted upon in a certain way, and it is acted upon in that way in the belief of the existence of such a state of facts to the damage of him who so believes and acts, the first is estopped from denying the existence of such a state of facts.
3. If a person, whatever his real meaning may be, so conducts himself that a reasonable man would take his conduct to mean a certain representation of facts, and that it was a true representation, and that the latter was intended to act upon it in a particular way, and he with such belief does act in that way to his damage, the first is estopped from denying that the facts were as represented.
4. If during the course of a transaction which has resulted in litigation, one person has led another to believe in a certain state of facts by conduct of culpable negligence calculated to have that result, and that culpable negligence has been the real cause of leading and has led the other to act in the transaction by mistake founded on that belief and to his prejudice, the first person cannot be allowed in the litigation as against the second to show that the state of acts referred to did not exist.

In earlier cases, the Tonga courts interpreted this section as meaning that estoppel may only operate as a defence.[52] More recently, the Supreme Court of Tonga has been prepared to follow *Waltons*,[53] in spite of the fact that there may be a conflict with the Act.

The courts in other countries of the region do not appear to have considered whether or not to follow *Waltons*. Assuming that, like Solomon Islands, they chose not to, promissory estoppel will only arise where there is an existing legal relationship between the parties.[54] Normally this will be a contractual relationship, but it may be that a statutory relationship will suffice.[55]

The restriction that estoppel may only be used as a shield and not a sword does not apply to proprietary estoppel.[56]

52 *Fie'eike v Ilavalu* [1995] Tonga LR 190; *Salvation Army (Tonga) Trust v Manase Nau* [2001] Tonga LR 66.

53 *Toloke v Tu'imana* [2012] TOSC 38; *Veamatahau v Tulikifanga* [2015] TOSC 3. Cf. *Kinetisys Inc v Mafi* [2012] TOLC 1; *Hafoka v Mokofisi* [2000] TOLC 1; *Salvation Army (Tonga) Trust v Nau* [2001] TOLC 2.

54 *Combe v Combe* [1951] 2 KB 215; *Jamnadas Sports (Fiji) Ltd v Stinson Pearce Ltd* [1994] FJCA 20.

55 *Durham Fancy Goods Ltd v Michael Jackson* [1968] 2 QB 839 (although this has been implicitly doubted: see *Brikom Investments Ltd v Carr* [1979] 2 All ER 753).

56 *Meredith v Pa'u* [1994] WSSC 7. See section 1 for a discussion of proprietary estoppel.

4.1.3. *It Must be Inequitable for the Promisor to Go Back on the Promise*

It must be inequitable for the promisor to renege on the promise. This is well illustrated by the case of *Maharaj v Chand*.[57] In that case, the appellant was appealing to the Privy Council from a decision of the Court of Appeal of Fiji in an action where the respondent, her former de facto husband, had obtained an order that she give him vacant possession of the matrimonial home. This house had been built on 'native' land, and by statute[58] the respondent was prohibited from granting any interest in it. The appellant had made indirect contributions to instalments on house. The Court allowed the appeal on the basis that, although the statute prevented her gaining an equitable interest, the respondent was estopped from evicting her as she had left her flat to live with him on the understanding she could always stay in the house, and that the respondent was providing a home for her and her children.

The other side of the coin is that, as promissory estoppel is an equitable principle, its application is discretionary, and relief will not be granted if it is inequitable. It may be inequitable because the person seeking to rely on estoppel is guilty of misconduct. For example, in *Nubono v Attorney-General*,[59] the court held that it would not exercise its discretion because the plaintiff did not come to the court with clean hands. In *Raniga v Sony (South Pacific) Ltd*,[60] the appellant gave an ultimatum to the respondent to accept its cheque for a lesser sum or return it. The respondent's acceptance of the cheque did not amount to a promise to accept a lesser sum.[61] Although there was a promise that might raise an estoppel, the element of intimidation in the ultimatum issued by the appellant meant that it was not inequitable for the promise to be withdrawn. It may also be inequitable to grant relief if there is no hardship caused to the promisee by the withdrawal of the promise.

4.1.4. *Estoppel may be Only Suspensory in Effect*

It has never been conclusively determined whether the principle applies to extinguish rights permanently, or whether rights are merely suspended until such time as it is equitable for the promisor to insist on enforcing those rights. For example, in the case of a promise to forego the right to the balance of a debt, is the right to that balance lost forever or merely suspended? Can the right be revived if the circumstances that led to the promise being made come to an end or if there is some other change in circumstances?

---

57 [1986] 32 FLR 119.

58 Native Land Trust Act Cap 134, s 12.

59 [2006] KIHC 16.

60 Unreported, Supreme Court, Fiji, Kermode J, 1979.

61 Following *D&C Builders v Rees* [1966] 2 QB 617. See also *Re Selectmove* [1995] 2 All ER 531.

In some cases, it is clearly only suspensory. For example, in *Hughes v Metropolitan Railway Co*,[62] the obligation to repair was put on hold. In the case of continuing obligations, as for example, the obligation to pay rent, the effect can be both suspensory and extinguishing. In *Central London Property Trust v High Trees House*[63] the right to the instalments of rent falling due during the war were extinguished, but the right to claim the full rent for the future was only suspended. Similarly, in *Tool Metal Manufacturing Co v Tungsten Electric Co*,[64] the owner of royalties on patents promised not to enforce the right to periodic payment. It was held that the owner could withdraw the promise by giving reasonable notice, from which point the original terms of the agreement would come back into operation.

In all these cases, the obligations arising during the operation of the promise were destroyed and the right to insist on performance was lost for that period. But for the future, the original terms were treated as only having been suspended. This suggests that the answer to whether estoppel is suspensory depends on whether the promise relates to a continuing obligation or not. If it does, it would appear that estoppel only suspends the promisor's rights, which can be revived by withdrawal of the promise. On the other hand, a single obligation, such as a 'one-off' payment, can be extinguished by a promise that raises an estoppel.[65]

4.2. PROMISSORY ESTOPPEL AND THE RULE IN *PINNEL'S CASE*

As discussed in chapter 6, according to the rule in *Pinnel's Case*,[66] payment of part of a liquidated debt will not be sufficient consideration for a simple promise to forego the balance. However, if the creditor agrees to accept something different from the original contractual entitlement, for example payment at an earlier date or payment in kind, this may be good consideration.

The rule in *Pinnel's Case* was reaffirmed by the House of Lords in *Foakes v Beer*.[67] *Hughes v Metropolitan Railway Co*[68] was not referred to in *Foakes v Beer*. It must be assumed that the principle of promissory estoppel was not considered relevant to the case of part payment of debts. Notwithstanding, in *Central London Property Trust v High Trees House*,[69] Denning LJ applied promissory

62 (1877) 2 App Cas 439.
63 [1947] KB 130.
64 [1955] 2 All ER 657.
65 *D&C Builders v Rees* [1966] 2 QB 617.
66 (1602) 77 ER 305.
67 (1884) 9 App Cas 605.
68 (1877) 2 App Cas 439.
69 [1947] KB 130.

estoppel to part payment of rent, which is, in essence, the same as part payment of a debt. In *Re Selectmove*,[70] the House of Lords confirmed the continuing application of the rule in *Pinnel's Case*. It now appears to be generally accepted that promissory estoppel will only 'outflank' the rule in *Pinnel's Case* if all the conditions discussed in this chapter are met and, in particular, there has been a meaningful reliance.[71]

5. ESTOPPEL AND STATUTORY DISCRETION

In the case of a discretion conferred by an Act of Parliament, there is a statutory duty to exercise that discretion in accordance with the power conferred. Estoppel cannot be used to restrict that discretion.[72] This applies equally to prevent restriction of discretion conferred by statutory regulations.[73] However, it does not prevent a plea of estoppel succeeding against executive government if this does not significantly hinder the exercise of the relevant discretion in the public interest.[74]

6. CAN A CUSTOMARY SETTLEMENT CREATE AN ESTOPPEL?

If a defendant has settled a claim in accordance with customary law, will this create an estoppel, preventing a common law action in respect of the same claim from succeeding? This question arose for consideration in relation to a claim in tort in *Lemalu v Jessop*.[75] In that case the plaintiff suffered personal injuries due to the negligent driving of the defendant's employee. After the issue of proceedings but before the hearing, the plaintiff accepted an *ifoga* in accordance with Samoan custom and it was argued that this estopped him from succeeding in his claim for common law damages. The evidence established that the *ifoga* had been accepted by the chiefs and orators of the plaintiff's family with the specific reservation that the common law claim would not be withdrawn. Accordingly, Spring CJ found himself 'relieved from the necessity of deciding

70 [1995] 2 All ER 531.

71 *Collier v Wright (Holdings) Ltd* [2007] EWCA Civ 1329, [42], [45]–[47].

72 *Attorney-General (NSW) v Quinn* (1990) 170 CLR 1, 17; *Minister for Immigration v Kurtovic* (1990) 92 ALR 93, 111, both cited with approval in *Attorney-General of Fiji v Pacoil Fiji Ltd* [1996] FJCA 9, 16.

73 *Attorney-General of Fiji v Pacoil Fiji Ltd* [1996] FJCA 9, 16.

74 *Attorney-General (NSW) v Quinn* (1990) 170 CLR 1; *Attorney-General of Fiji v Pacoil Fiji Ltd* [1996] FJCA 9, 16–17.

75 [1969] WSLR 214.

whether such an *ifoga* in the *fa'a-Samoa* would be a valid defence in law to a claim such as the instant one'. Whilst estoppel was not merited on the facts, it appears that the court would have been prepared to entertain such a claim if no reservation had been present.

According to *Combe v Combe*,[76] an estoppel cannot arise in this type of situation, as there is no pre-existing contractual relationship between the parties.[77] Accordingly, unless regional courts are prepared to extend the principle beyond a contractual relationship to a customary or perhaps a tortious relationship,[78] the donor of a customary gift will be left with the difficult task of establishing that this amounted to an enforceable contract.[79] An alternative may be to claim the value of the customary gift as a deduction from the damages awardable.[80]

7. CONCLUSION

It is clear that the doctrine of promissory estoppel is part of the law in the South Pacific. Apart from in Solomon Islands, the courts appear to be prepared to allow estoppel to be used to found an action, rather than only as a defence. Estoppel may also be an avenue for giving increased recognition to customary law and cultural practices in the Pacific.

76 [1951] 2 KB 215.

77 See text above at nn. 54 and 55.

78 In *Durham Fancy Goods Ltd v Michael Jackson* [1968] 2 QB 839 it was held that a statutory relationship would suffice, but this has been doubted in *Brikom Investments Ltd v Carr* [1979] 2 All ER 753.

79 In the case of a gift, the parties do not make a bargain. See *Combe v Combe* [1951] 2 KB 215.

80 By analogy with deductions allowed from damages awarded in tort.

CHAPTER 8
PRIVITY OF CONTRACT

1. INTRODUCTION

Privity of contract is the basic notion that a contractual agreement only binds the parties to the agreement.[1] As stated in *Transol Shipping Company Ltd v Laore*,[2] '[t]he essence of the doctrine of privity of contract is the idea that only those who are parties to the contract can have the rights or liabilities under it, including the right to enforce it or to be sued under it'. Similarly, in *Maoko v Ling*,[3] the court cited *PNGBC v Barra Amevo and Bari Investments*,[4] where it was said that the 'doctrine of privity of contract is that, as a general rule, a contract cannot confer rights or impose obligations arising under it on any person except the parties to it. The scope of the doctrine means only that a person cannot acquire rights, or be subjected to liabilities, arising under a contract to which he is not a party'.

As is discussed further below, it is arguable that the doctrine is not well suited to the circumstances prevailing in the South Pacific. Notwithstanding, the common law on point has been applied by regional courts in most countries and has thus been incorporated into local law.[5]

2. THE CONSEQUENCES OF THE DOCTRINE

The doctrine has two consequences:

- only a party to a contract can be sued on it; and
- only a party to a contract can claim a benefit under it.

These consequences require separate consideration.

---

1 See e.g. *Dunlop Pneumatic Tyre Co Ltd v Selfridge & Co Ltd* [1915] AC 847.
2 [2013] SBHC 182, [26].
3 [2008] PGNC 19, [6].
4 [1998] PNGLR 240.
5 See further chapter 1.

2.1. PREVENTION OF RECOVERY FROM A NON-PARTY

The doctrine of privity has the advantage of protecting third parties from the imposition of liability without their consent. However, this may cause hardship to a party who is trying to enforce a contract, in circumstances where the precise identity of the other contracting party is obscured, for example by internal structuring of a company.[6] A claim against an arm of a legal entity that transpires not to have been the contracting party is liable to be struck out.[7]

Amongst the many regional examples confirming the application of the doctrine of privity in this situation are two cases from Fiji. In *Carpenters Fiji v Samujh*,[8] the respondent delivered his taxi to Suva Motors for repair. Suva Motors subsequently went into liquidation. The appellant took over the business. The respondent sued the appellant for breach of contract, alleging they had failed to repair the vehicle. It was held that the contract was clearly between the respondent and Suva Motors. In response to the respondent's claim that the appellant was Suva Motors' 'successor', the court held that if that was taken to mean that it was a major shareholder that had no bearing as a company was distinct from its shareholders. It was accepted that assignment of the liability could have occurred by novation, either express or implied but, as there no evidence of either, the claim was dismissed.

In *Qalovaki v WR Carpenter (South Pacific) Ltd*,[9] the plaintiff sued the defendant for damages incurred as a result of the defendant's failure to repair his vehicle within two weeks as allegedly promised. The court found that the contract of repair was made between the defendant and the insurer of the vehicle and therefore he could not sue on the alleged promise. The alleged promise was also unenforceable due to lack of consideration moving from the plaintiff to the defendant.

More recently, in *Transol Shipping Company Ltd v Laore*,[10] the High Court of Solomon Islands was called on to decide whether a contract existed between the defendant, a candidate in a by-election who wanted to transport his supporters to an island for the election, and the plaintiff shipping company. The defendant hired the plaintiff, TSC, to charter a boat but did not have sufficient funds. Eventually an agreement was signed between the plaintiff and Solomon Islands' Marine Division for the defendant to obtain a subsidised charter, but

6 See e.g. *Amosa v The Board of Trustees of the Congregational Christian Church in Samoa (Inc) and Leuluai* [1994] WSSC 2, where a claim against the Board of Trustees of a church was dismissed with costs on the ground that the education committee of the church had made the contract.

7 Ibid.

8 Unreported, Supreme Court, Fiji, Civ App 5/1981.

9 Unreported, Supreme Court, Fiji, Tuivaga J, 5 October 1979.

10 [2013] SBHC 182, [26].

the defendant did not sign himself. The trip took longer than expected and the plaintiff sued to recovered for the additional time. The court held that initial discussions were inconclusive and merely exploring the possibility of entering into a charter arrangement. Although the signed charter benefited the defendant, he was not a party and therefore he was not liable.

In *Minaj Holdings Ltd v International Maritime Trading Company Ltd*,[11] the doctrine of privity was held to be well settled in Marshall Islands. In that case, the plaintiff had paid a Chinese corporation to deliver a cargo of cement to Nigeria on a vessel owned by the defendant. The cargo was never delivered, having been offloaded in Cameroon. The plaintiff sued the defendant for breach of contract. The court held that the plaintiff had no cause of action against the defendant because they were not in a contractual relationship. American case law was cited in support, where it was stated, '[i]t is well-settled that a subcontractor may not recover for breach of contract from an owner, rather than a general contractor, absent a contract or privity between it and the owner'.[12]

In *Maoko v Ling*,[13] Cannings J held that this doctrine has been adopted as part of the underlying law of Papua New Guinea. A good example of the difficulties that arise is the case of *Elisara v Attorney-General*,[14] where the question arose whether there was a binding agreement for the payment of compensation for acquisition of customary land. The matter rested on whether the written agreement, signed by the Government representatives and the 'Tu'ua' (senior spokesman for the '*alii* and *faipule*' (chiefs)) was binding on the chiefs and orators of the village, who contended that the Tu'ua did not have authority. The court found that 'traditionally' the Tu'ua was the main spokesperson for the *alii* and *faipule*, but '[w]hether or in what circumstances he has authority in Samoan culture or customs or in some agreed way to bind them by contract is another matter'. It was concluded that the evidence was insufficient to support the trial judge's conclusion that the agreement was authorised by the *alii* and *faipule*.

2.2. PREVENTION OF RECOVERY BY A NON-PARTY

As mentioned, the second consequence of the doctrine operates to prevent a third party from claiming a benefit under a contract, even where this is the clear intention of the contracting parties. Where the doctrine operates in this way, it may result in injustice. As discussed below, there is some legislation which

---

11 [2012] MIHC 2.

12 *Omni Contracting Co Inc v City of New York* No. 603811/08 2010 WL 3951833 (N.Y. Sept. 27, 2010).

13 [2008] PGNC 19, [6].

14 [2004] WSCA 4.

allows a non-party to claim a benefit and also the courts have developed means by which the harsh results of the privity doctrine may be avoided.[15]

In Vanuatu, the position has been altered by statute. As discussed below, the Law Reform (Contract Law) Act 2009 provides that where an agreement expressly purports to confer a benefit on a person who is not a party to it, that benefit may be enforced by that person.[16]

3. PRIVITY AND CONSIDERATION

The doctrine of privity is distinct from the rule that consideration must move from the promisee, although historically they were regarded as branches of the same principle.[17] Both rules will often apply to the same fact situation and may both operate to prevent a third party claiming on a contract. An example is *Tweddle v Atkinson*,[18] where an agreement was made between Guy and Tweddle by which each promised to pay a sum of money to Tweddle's son, William Tweddle, who was engaged to marry, and later did marry, Guy's daughter. The money was to provide for them after marriage. Guy died without having paid and William Tweddle sued Guy's executor. His action failed as William had not provided any consideration. In fact, the plaintiff would have failed even if he had provided consideration because he was not a party to the contract in question.

However, the doctrine of privity and the rule that consideration must move from the promisee are not always coincident. For example, if A, B, and C enter into an agreement whereby A will give B $100 if she types C's assignment, C cannot enforce the agreement as he did not provide any consideration. The doctrine of privity is not a bar to action as they are all parties to the agreement. Conversely, in a building contract, where the employer contracts directly with the principal contractor and the contractor employs the sub-contractor, there is no privity of contract between the employer and the sub-contractor, even if the employer has nominated the sub-contractor. However, the sub-contractor provides services for the employer, which satisfies the requirement of consideration.

4. LIMITS AND EXCEPTIONS

The doctrine of privity does not prohibit assignment. Assignment is a transfer of rights or liabilities such as those that arise under an instrument, chose in

---

15 Contracts (Rights of Third Parties) Act 1999 (UK).
16 Section 4(1).
17 *Price v Easton* (1833) 4 B & D 433.
18 (1861) 121 ER 762.

action or debt.[19] Under certain circumstances, a person who is entitled to the benefit of a contract may assign the benefit of that contract to a third party. Rights will be assigned automatically on death, except where the contract is of a personal nature, such as a contract of employment.[20]

Another practical context in which the doctrine may be limited is in building or renovation contracts. The employer or the architect (as the employer's agent) contracts directly with the principal contractor and, even though they often nominate the sub-contractor, initially there is no privity of contract between them. However, once the employer or architect orders the sub-contractor to do work, a direct relationship has been held to arise.[21]

There are also exceptions to the rule, which fall into two categories:

- exceptions which allow a third party to take a benefit; and
- exceptions which allow liability to be placed on a third party.

4.1. EXCEPTIONS WHICH ALLOW A THIRD PARTY TO TAKE A BENEFIT

Because of the unjust results demonstrated by *Tweddle v Atkinson*,[22] the courts have developed exceptions to the doctrine of privity, which permit third parties to take benefits that were intended for them in certain circumstances.

4.1.1. Trusts

Where a person holds property or rights on behalf of another, or is bound to exercise rights on behalf of another or to accomplish some particular purpose, that person is said to hold the property or rights in trust.[23] The person holding the property or rights is called the 'trustee' and the person on whose behalf the rights are held or must be exercised is called the 'beneficiary'. A trust is an equitable obligation. It is a relationship or association based on confidence, under which one party holds property or rights as trustee for another. Where a trust is created, beneficiaries may sue to enforce rights created in their favour, even if they were not a party to the original agreement. This is a useful device where, for example, the donor wants several people to benefit from his property, but does

---

19 See e.g. *Patel v Badal & Another* (1943) 3 FLR 322.

20 See further M.P. Furmston, *Cheshire, Fifoot and Furmston's Law of Contract*, 17th ed., Oxford University Press, Oxford 2017, chapter 16.

21 *Pioneer Supplies Ltd v Kewal Investment Ltd* [1998] FJHC 12, 16.

22 (1861) 121 ER 762.

23 For a further explanation of the meaning of 'trust' see Lord Hailsham of Marylebone (ed.), *Halsbury's Laws of England*, 4th ed., Vol. 9, para. 501.

not want to divide it up. In the context of the law of contract, and in particular the doctrine of privity, a trust may be employed by one party (the donor) to transfer contractual rights to another party (the trustee) to hold on behalf of a third party (the beneficiary). Such a trust may be established either at the instigation of the promisor or the promisee. In *Dunlop Pneumatic Tyre Co v Selfridge & Co*,[24] Lord Haldane mentioned that a third party could acquire a right under a contract by means of a trust. Beneficiaries may ask the trustee to sue on their behalf to enforce rights conferred by the trust, and if the trustee refuses the beneficiary may sue in person and join the trustee as a co-defendant. However, it should be noted that the beneficiary is not suing on the contract, but on the trust in equity.

An early example of the use of the trust concept to modify the strict requirements of the doctrine of privity is *Gregory v Williams*.[25] In that case, Parker owed money to Gregory and to Williams. Parker agreed with Williams to assign to him the whole of his property, if Williams would pay the debt due from Parker to Gregory. The property was duly assigned, but Williams failed to implement his promise. Parker and Gregory sued, and it was held that Parker was trustee for Gregory, and that Gregory had an equitable right to recovery.

This device appears to create a fertile avenue for evasion of the common law rule. However, the courts have proved reluctant to infer a trust. Clear evidence of the intention to create a trust is required. For example, in *Re Schebsman*[26] the deceased was employed by two companies and agreed with one of them that they would give £5,500 to his widow and daughters. It was held that there was insufficient evidence that the contract created a trust. Clear language was required to prove the existence of a trust.

The case law is conflicting and this area of the law is in need of reform, as the cases where the courts will allow the doctrine of privity to be evaded by using a trust are uncertain.

4.1.2. Agency

Agency denotes a situation where a person (the 'agent') represents or acts on behalf of another (the 'principal'). The doctrine of privity does not prevent a binding agreement arising where a party is represented by an agent.[27] Where an agent contracts on behalf of a principal, the principal is bound even though he or she was not privy to the contract and even where the agency relationship has

---

24 [1915] AC 847, 853.

25 (1817) 3 Mer 582.

26 [1944] Ch 83.

27 See e.g. *Lin Maolin v Wang Qiang* [2006] TOSC 33.

not been disclosed.[28] However, the agent must have authority to act, actual or ostensible, in order to bind the principal.[29]

The agency principle has been developed to allow third parties to take advantage of an exclusion clause in a contract to which they were not party. This device was first used in England during the nineteenth century to allow exemption clauses in railway tickets to be relied on by railway companies in the country's network, even though they did not issue the ticket. Relying on the device, many enterprises put exemption clauses in their contracts, designed to protect not only the main contractor, but also employees and sub-contractors.

In *Scruttons v Midland Silicones Ltd*,[30] a contract was made between a shipping company and the plaintiff, a chemical manufacturer, for the transport of drums of chemicals. Liability in the event of damage by the shipping company was limited to £500. The defendants, a stevedoring company, damaged the drums and the plaintiffs sued them for damages in excess of £500. The defendant pleaded the limitation clause in their defence. It was held that the defendant was a stranger to the contract and had no right to rely on its protection. Lord Reid made it clear that strangers to a contract might take the benefit of an exemption clause if the following four conditions were met:

1. the contract makes it clear that the stranger is intended to be protected by the exclusion clause;
2. the contract makes it clear that the principal is contracting for himself as well as the agent;[31]
3. the principal has authority to act for the agent (later ratification may suffice);[32] and
4. the third party has supplied consideration.

In the present case, the relevant clause did not seek to exempt third parties from liability and therefore the conditions were not met. *Scruttons* was cited with approval in *Dalgro Solomon Islands Ltd v KK Real Estate Proprietor Ltd.*[33]

---

28 See further on agency, M.P. Furmston, *Cheshire, Fifoot and Furmston's Law of Contract*, 17th ed., Oxford University Press, Oxford 2017, chapter 15.

29 *Eastern Marketing Distributors v Attorney-General* [2017] SBHC 133; *Melanesian Rentals Ltd v Evergreen Ltd* [2010] VUSC 211; *No Frills Car Rental Ltd v Government of the Republic of Vanuatu (Vanuatu Police and Mobile Force)* [2004] VUMC 4. A master of a ship has authority to contract for the carriage of goods in the course of the business of the vessel: *International Watersport Management Ltd v Pearl Creations Co Ltd* [2002] TOCA 7.

30 [1962] AC 446.

31 An agent cannot escape personal liability if the agency relationship is not disclosed: *Rarotonga Realty Ltd v Korlender* [2008] CKHC 45.

32 See contra, *Southern Water Authority v Carey* [1985] 2 All ER 1077.

33 [2008] SBHC 90.

In *New Zealand Shipping Co Ltd v Satterthwaite & Co Ltd*[34] (*'The Eurymedon'*), a case with similar facts to *Scruttons*, the stevedore was allowed to rely on the exemption clause in the contract between the cargo owner and the carrier. The exemption clause used in this case was a standard clause specifically developed to protect third parties (known as a 'Himalaya' clause). Lord Wilberforce stated that:

> [T]he bill of lading brought into existence a bargain initially unilateral but capable of becoming mutual between the shipper and the [stevedoring company], made through the carrier as an agent. This became a full contract when the [stevedoring company] performed services by discharging the goods. The performance of these services for the benefit of the shipper was the consideration for the agreement by the shipper that the [stevedoring company] should have the benefit of the exemptions and limitations contained in the bill of lading.[35]

In *Southern Water Authority v Carey*,[36] sub-contractors were not permitted to rely on a limitation clause in the head contract as they failed to meet the third condition laid down in *Scruttons*. It was held that they were not entitled to the benefit of this clause in the absence of evidence that the main contractor had authority from the sub-contractors at the time of the making of the contract.

New Zealand Shipping Co Ltd v Satterthwaite & Co Ltd[37] was followed in *Port Jackson Stevedoring PTA Ltd v Salmon & Spraggon (Australia) PTA Ltd.*[38]

In the Pacific, the principles set out in *Scruttons v Midland Silicones Ltd*[39] have been cited with approval by regional courts, including the National Court of Papua New Guinea in *Rabaul Stevedores Ltd v Seta*,[40] the Fiji High Court in *Feng v Bomani*[41] and the Supreme Court of Tonga in *Cable & Wireless plc v Mataele*.[42]

Whilst many of the cases where the agency principle has been extended to allow a third party to take advantage of an exclusion clause involve marine transport, the principle applies equally to other contracts provided the four conditions are fulfilled. For example, in *Cable & Wireless plc v Mataele*,[43] the contract was for a telephone service. An Australian example is *Lifesavers (A/asia) Ltd v Frigmobile Pty Ltd*,[44] where the benefit of an exclusion clause was extended to apply in a case involving carriage of goods by land.

34 [1975] AC 154.
35 Ibid., 167–68.
36 [1985] 2 All ER 1077.
37 [1975] AC 154.
38 [1981] 1 WLR 138 (PC).
39 [1962] AC 446.
40 [1985] LRC (Comm) 383.
41 [1995] FJHC 97.
42 [1989] Tonga LR 79.
43 Ibid.
44 [1983] 1 NSWLR 431.

4.1.3. Statutory Provisions

In addition to the encroachment of the common law on the doctrine of privity, there are some statutory exceptions to the rule that only a party may take a benefit under a contract. Some of the most important statutory provisions are discussed below.

4.1.3.1. Bills of Exchange

Bills of Exchange Acts in force within the region govern contractual obligations created by the drawing up of a negotiable instrument. A negotiable instrument is a document containing a promise of payment which, when transferred, passes the right to payment to the transferee. The most common example of a negotiable instrument is an uncrossed cheque. The advantage of a negotiable instrument in commercial dealings is that the benefit of the promise to pay is freely transferable. The holder may sue on the instrument in spite of not being a party to the original agreement.

The application of the doctrine of privity to negotiable instruments would create difficulties in many of today's complex commercial dealings. The exemption from the rule is therefore enshrined in statutes governing negotiable instruments and other bills of exchange. Section 38 of the following regional Acts provides that holders in due course may sue on a bill in their own name:

- Bills of Exchange Act Cap 227 (Fiji)
- Bills of Exchange Act Cap 108 (Tonga)
- Bills of Exchange Act 1976 (Samoa)

Section 38(1) Bills of Exchange Act 1882 (UK) makes similar provision. This Act applies in Kiribati, Solomon Islands, Tuvalu and Vanuatu, which do not have locally enacted bills of exchange legislation. Section 38 of the Bills of Exchange Act 1908 (NZ) also allows a holder in due course to sue on a bill, and applies in Cook Islands,[45] Niue[46] and Tokelau.[47]

---

[45] Applying by virtue of Cook Islands Act 1915 (NZ), s 625. The Bills of Exchange Amendment Act 1971 also applies in Cook Islands (NZ Laws Act (No. 2) 1973 (CI)).

[46] Applying by virtue of Niue Act 1966 (NZ), s 682. The 1908 Act applies in Niue as amended by the Legislation (Correction of Errors and Minor Amendment) Act 2004 (Niue), s 10.

[47] Applying by virtue of the Tokelau (Application of New Zealand Laws) Rules 2004, R 3(1)(i) and (ii). All amendments in New Zealand would appear to apply, as the Rules state that 'Acts passed in substitution will apply': R 3(2)(vii).

4.1.3.2. Contracts of Insurance

Certain contracts of insurance are enforceable by third parties even though they are not parties to the contract by virtue of legislation. One example of this is motor vehicle insurance policies. Legislation often provides for action regarding death or personal injury to be taken against the insurer, even though the deceased or injured person was not a party to the insurance contract.[48] Relevant regional Acts include the Motor Vehicle (Third Party) Insurance Act 1972 of Solomon Islands, which provides that the deceased's estate or the injured person may sue the insurer directly, if the owner of the vehicle is dead or cannot be served. The Motor Vehicle (Third Party) Insurance Act of Fiji makes similar provision.[49]

Another example is marine insurance. Marine insurance policies may be taken out to benefit third parties, provided that the third party has an interest in the subject matter of the policy.[50] One example is s 15(2) of the Marine Insurance Act (Fiji).[51]

Life insurance can also be taken out for the benefit of a spouse and children. For example, s 13(2) Married Woman's Property Act of Fiji.[52]

In *Trident General Insurance Co Ltd v McNiece Bros Pty Ltd*,[53] part of the majority of the High Court of Australia thought that the doctrine of privity should be abandoned in relation to insurance contracts.

4.1.3.3. Land Law Legislation

A provision which spans both land law and insurance law is s 47(1) of the Law of Property Act 1925 (UK). This provides that, in sales of land, if a vendor contracts to sell land, and the property on the land is damaged or destroyed prior to completion of the sale, any insurance moneys received by the vendor are held by him in trust for the purchaser.

The Law of Property Act 1925 also allows a third party to claim a benefit under an agreement relating to property. Section 56 provides:

> A person may take an interest in land or other property or the benefits concerning land or other property although he may not be named a party to the conveyance or other instrument.

---

48 See also the Road Traffic Act 1972 (UK). Section 148(4) provides that the insurer is liable to pay any person to whom their insured becomes liable, if that liability is covered by the policy.

49 Cap 177, ss 12–14.

50 Note also that legislation governing marine carriage of goods provides that the holder for the time being of a bill of lading has full contractual rights.

51 Cap 218. See also Marine Insurance Act 1975 (Samoa); Marine Insurance Act Cap 144 (Tonga); Marine Insurance Act 1908 (NZ) (Cook Islands, Niue, Tokelau); Marine Insurance Act 1906 (UK), s 14(2).

52 Cap 37. See also Married Women's Property Act 1882 (UK), s 11.

53 (1988) 165 CLR 107.

In *Beswick v Beswick*[54] Lord Denning held that this provision destroyed the doctrine of privity in relation to all contracts governing any type of property, not just those relating to land. His Lordship was also of the view that any person who might gain an advantage from the instrument could rely on the section to found an action, not just those to whom the instrument in question purported to bestow a benefit on. Taken literally, the words 'other property' are wide enough to have this effect. However, on appeal, the House of Lords rejected this broad interpretation that was taken in *Beswick v Beswick*.[55] Their Lordships held unanimously that s 56 should not be taken outside its context, despite the breadth of its wording.

The Law of Property Act (UK) has been held to apply in a number of regional countries, including Solomon Islands.[56] *Beswick v Beswick* was cited with approval in *Dalgro Solomon Islands Ltd v KK Real Estate Proprietor Ltd*.[57]

4.2. EXCEPTIONS WHICH ALLOW LIABILITY TO BE PLACED ON A THIRD PARTY

The rule of privity is less open to objection where it operates to prevent the imposition of liability on a stranger to a contract. It would be surprising if a contract could impose burdens or obligations on third parties without their agreement. The established exceptions arise in equity, and are part of the law of property and relate only to contracts concerning land.

4.2.1. Covenants in a Lease

A covenant is a promise contained in a deed. The obligations under a lease which 'touch and concern' the land are binding in equity not only on the original covenantor, but also on a successor in title.[58] The basis for this exception is 'privity of estate', which is the relationship which exists between, for example, lessor and lessee or lessor and assignee.

In *Lineen v MacQuarrie*,[59] the Cook Islands High Court had to decide whether a covenant to pay rent was implied by the Property Law Act 1952[60] in the original deed of lease between the parties and, if so, whether it was enforceable against

54 [1966] Ch 538. See also *Smith and Snipes Hall Farms Ltd v River Douglas Catchment Board* [1949] 2 KB 500; *Drive Yourself Hire Co Ltd v Strutt* [1954] 1 QB 250.

55 [1968] AC 58.

56 *Harry v Kalena Timber Co Ltd* [2001] 3 LRC 24.

57 [2008] SBHC 90.

58 *Spencer's Case* (1583) 5 Co Rep 16a.

59 [2008] CKHC 47.

60 Section 106A.

assignees or sublessees. The court held that the term could not be implied, as the lease predated the amendment to the Act that provided for such a term to be implied. However, the Act did empower the court to vary the lease to include this term, which it did. As no copies had been adduced in evidence, the court was unable to determine whether the subsequent agreements were assignments, in which case the covenant would bind the assignee, because a covenant to pay rent runs with the land,[61] or subleases, which do not bind the sublessee to the term of the covenant.[62] Accordingly, no further order was made.

4.2.2. Restrictive Covenants

A restrictive covenant is one that places restrictions on how land may be used. In certain circumstances, restrictive covenants will 'run' with the land and bind not only the original covenantor, but also subsequent purchasers of that land to observe the covenants in favour of owners of adjoining land. Such covenants will only bind subsequent purchasers if they have notice of the covenant, and provided that the covenantee or a successor in title retains land for the benefit of which the covenant was entered into.[63]

This rule is known as the rule in *Tulk v Moxhay*.[64] The facts of that case were that the plaintiff owned several houses in Leicester Square in London. He sold the garden in the centre to a person called Elms. Elms covenanted to keep it as a garden. After a number of subsequent sales, the land was purchased by the defendant, who had notice of the covenant. The defendant proposed to build on the land. The plaintiff, who still owned several adjacent houses, sought an injunction to prohibit this. It was held that the covenant was enforceable in equity against all purchasers subsequent to the original covenantor, provided they had notice.

The rule is now bolstered by statute. For example, s 79 of the Law of Property Act 1925 (UK) applies in a number of countries in the region.[65] The Act raises a presumption that a restrictive covenant relating to land is intended to benefit successors in title. However, this presumption will be rebutted if it is contrary to the purpose of the instrument creating the covenant. In *Morrells of Oxford Ltd v Oxford United Football Club Ltd*,[66] the Court of Appeal held that the presumption created by s 79 was rebutted where it was inconsistent with the words of the instrument, read in their commercial context.

---

61 [2008] CKHC 47, [45].
62 Ibid., [52].
63 *London County Council v Allen* [1914] 3 KB 642.
64 (1848) 41 ER 1143.
65 See further chapter 1.
66 [2001] Ch 459.

In some countries of the region, restrictive covenants are not binding on subsequent purchasers unless they are registered.[67]

4.2.3. Charter of Ships

Generally, the courts have resisted attempts to extend the rule in *Tulk v Moxhay* beyond the realm of land law. However, in *Lord Strathcona SS Co v Dominion Coal Co*,[68] it was applied by the Privy Council to the charter of a ship. The Judicial Committee, on an appeal from Nova Scotia, held that a person who buys a ship with notice that she is subject to a charter agreement is bound by that agreement even though not a party to it.

This decision has been criticised as there can be no direct analogy with this aspect of land law, which depends on privity of estate and requires the plaintiff to have kept an interest in adjoining land.[69] The point has never arisen for direct consideration by regional courts, but it is unlikely to be followed.

5. THE POSITION BETWEEN THE ORIGINAL PROMISOR AND PROMISEE

Both at common law and in equity, the original promisee can sue on the agreement which has been made. Accordingly, if the promisor fails to confer an agreed benefit on a third party, the original promisee can sue on his or her behalf.

However, this does not always solve the third parties' enforcement problems. Apart from the fact that the original promisee may have died and the executor may not wish to be involved in the action, there may be difficulties in the recovery of damages. If the promisee has suffered personal loss, the promisee can recover substantial damages. For example, in *Gregory v Williams*,[70] discussed in section 4.1.1 above, the fact that Williams did not pay the third party meant that Parker still owed a debt to the third party. However, it may be that the promisee suffers no personal damage. For example, in *Tweddle v Atkinson*,[71] the facts of which are set out in section 3 above, the original promisee did not suffer loss when the promisor failed to pay William Tweddle. In such cases it is the third party who has suffered the loss; the promisee is not permitted to recover on the third party's behalf, but is restricted to nominal damages. Similarly, in *Panatown*

---

67 See e.g. Land and Titles Act Cap 133 (SI), s 192(1).

68 [1926] AC 108.

69 *Port Line v Ben Steamers Ltd* [1958] 2 QB 146; *Bendall v McWhirter* [1952] 2 QB 466.

70 (1817) 3 Mer 582.

71 (1861) 121 ER 762.

Ltd v Alfred McAlpine Construction Ltd,[72] it was held that where a contractor was in breach of a contract with the employer to construct a building for a third party, the employer could not recover substantial damages on behalf of the third party. It was confirmed that the only exception to this rule was where it was within the contemplation of the contracting parties that breach by one was likely to cause loss to an identified or identifiable stranger to the contract, rather than to the other contracting party.

However, even though the promisee cannot recover more than nominal damages in a case when the loss is suffered by the third party, the promisee may be able to obtain specific performance or an injunction. This principle is well illustrated by *Beswick v Beswick*.[73] In that case, Peter Beswick had a small coal merchants business. When he retired, he transferred the business to his nephew, the defendant, in return for a promise by the defendant to employ him as a 'consultant' during his lifetime, and after his death to pay an annuity of £5 per week to his widow. On Peter Beswick's death, the defendant failed to pay the widow. She brought an action against him in her personal capacity as the person entitled to benefit under the contract and also in her capacity as administratrix of her deceased husband's estate. It was held that the plaintiff could not succeed in her own right, as she was not a party to the contract, but she could succeed as administratrix. The estate could not recover substantial damages as it was the widow who had suffered loss, not the estate. However, the estate was entitled to specific performance of the contract, as damages were an inadequate remedy.

The question of recovery of loss sustained by a third party was reopened in *Jackson v Horizon Holidays*.[74] In that case, the plaintiff entered into a contract with a travel agent for a holiday for himself and his family. The holiday failed to comply with the brochure description. At first instance the plaintiff was awarded damages for mental distress. The Court of Appeal upheld this award. Lord Denning accepted as an established rule of law that if a person makes a contract for the benefit of a third party that person may sue on the contract for any loss suffered by the third party. Accordingly, the plaintiff could recover damages for himself and for his family.

Lord Denning's approach to the law was rejected by the House of Lords in *Woodar Investment Development v Wimpey Construction*.[75] In that case, the defendants contracted to buy land from the plaintiffs. The purchase price was £850,000. At completion, £150,000 was to be paid to a third party. The plaintiffs sued for breach. It was held the defendants were not in breach, but even if they had been, the court considered that the plaintiffs would not have been entitled to recover the £150,000, either on their own behalf or on behalf of the third party.

72 [2000] 4 All ER 97.
73 [1968] AC 58.
74 [1975] 3 All ER 92.
75 [1980] 1 WLR 277.

6. STATUTORY EROSION OF THE DOCTRINE OF PRIVITY

The doctrine only applies to prevent an action in contract. It does not exclude an action in tort.[76] However, where the only basis for a claim is in contract, and the doctrine of privity prevents enforcement of an agreement by a third party who was intended to benefit, this may be unfair. The fact that the rule has been eroded by statute in certain areas, such as parts of insurance law,[77] merely serves to highlight the unfairness in situations not covered by legislation.

The doctrine of privity of contract has been criticised by academics and the judiciary for over 60 years.[78] In England, criticism led to reform in 1999, when the Contracts (Rights of Third Parties) Act 1999 (UK) was passed.[79] The Act implements, with some amendments, the recommendations of the Law Commission (England and Wales).[80] Section 1 provides that a third party is entitled to sue to enforce a right under an agreement to which he or she is not a party if either:

(a) the contract itself expressly so provides; or
(b) the contract purports and is intended to confer a benefit and a right to enforce it on the third party; and,

in both cases, the third party must be expressly identified in the contract by name, class or description, but need not be in existence when the contract is made.[81]

Where a third party has a right to sue, the contracting parties may not rescind or vary those rights without the third party's consent, unless this right is expressly conferred on the contracting parties by the contract.[82] The court or tribunal may dispense with the third party's consent, for example where it cannot be obtained because his whereabouts are unknown.

---

76 See e.g. *Rookes v Barnard* [1964] AC 1129; *Junior Books v Veitchi* [1983] AC 520.

77 See e.g. Third Parties' (Rights Against Insurers) Acts 1930 and 2010 (UK). See further, *Redman v Zurich Insurance plc* [2017] EWHC 1919.

78 See e.g. *Beswick v Beswick* [1968] AC 58, 72; M.P. Furmston, 'Return to Dunlop v Selfridge?' (1960) 23 *Modern Law Review* 373.

79 For the background to the Act, see the UK Law Commission's report: Law Commission, *Privity of Contract: Contracts for the Benefit of Third Parties*, Report No. 242, July 1996; S. Degeling, 'A Consideration of the UK Law Reform Commission's Consultation Paper "Privity of Contract"' (1993) 6(2) *Journal of Contract Law* 177. Third parties had already been permitted to sue on contracts by statutes passed in other Commonwealth jurisdictions. See e.g. Contracts (Privity) Act 1982 (NZ).

80 Law Commission, above n. 79.

81 This allows contracting parties to confer enforceable rights on, for example, an unborn child.

82 Contracts (Rights of Third Parties) Act 1999 (UK), ss 2(1), (3).

The parties may limit or impose conditions on the third party's right of enforcement in the original contract, such as insisting on enforcement by arbitration rather than litigation.[83] The same remedies are available to a third party claiming pursuant to the Act as are available to an original party to the contract.[84] The same legal prerequisites to recovery also apply, such as causation, remoteness and the duty to mitigate loss.[85]

In addition to the enforcement of 'positive' rights, the Act allows a third party to take advantage of an exclusion or limitation clause in the contract.[86] On the other hand, the third party will be bound by any exclusion or limitation which operates in favour of the promisor.[87] The Act also provides some protection for the promisor, who may rely on any defence or set-off arising out of the contract which would have been available to him against the promisee or would have been available if the third party been a party to the contract.[88] The Limitation Act also applies to an action by a third party.[89]

The third party's right to sue is additional to any right the promisee has in relation to the enforcement of a contract term which benefits a third party.[90] The promisor is protected from double liability by a provision that damages will be reduced to the extent that the promisee has already recovered.[91]

The Act does not affect the existing law regarding negotiable instruments, which is discussed in section 3.1.3.1 above.[92] Restrictions also apply to covenants in the memorandum and articles of association of a company and to employment contracts and contracts for the carriage of goods by sea, rail and air.[93] The Act also prevents a third party from contesting terms limiting the promisor's liability to the third party for negligence (other than negligence causing personal injury or death).[94] The legislation is particularly relevant to commercial contracts that automatically have repercussions for third parties, such as contracts containing an indemnity clause in favour of a third party.

The only two countries in the region to follow Britain's lead are Tokelau and Vanuatu. The Contract Rules 2004 (Tokelau) and the Law Reform (Contract Law) Act 2009 (Vanuatu) provide that where an agreement expressly purports to

83 Ibid., s 1(4).
84 Ibid., s 1(5).
85 Ibid., s 1(5).
86 Ibid., s 1(6).
87 Ibid., s 3(6).
88 Ibid., s 3.
89 Ibid., s 7(3).
90 Ibid., s 4.
91 Ibid., s 5.
92 Ibid., s 6.
93 Ibid., s 6.
94 Ibid., s 7(2).

confer a benefit on a person who is not a party to it, that benefit may be enforced by that person.[95]

Other Commonwealth jurisdictions have also enacted laws permitting third parties to sue on contracts. For example, the Contracts (Privity) Act was passed in New Zealand as long ago as 1982.[96]

In Canada[97] and Australia, the courts have expressed dissatisfaction with the doctrine. In *Trident General Insurance Co Ltd v McNiece Bros Pty Ltd*,[98] part of the majority of the High Court of Australia thought that the principle should be abandoned, at least in relation to insurance contracts.

Apart from Vanuatu, the countries of the region are all generally bound by the doctrine of privity. However, there is one example of a court excluding its application to a customary land agreement. In *Success v Premier of Guadalcanal Province, Rima, Attorney-General*,[99] the Solomon Islands Court of Appeal had to consider timber agreements entered into by the plaintiffs with the trustees of a number of landowners, identified under a statutory scheme. Pursuant to the scheme, a timber-felling licence was issued to the plaintiffs, which was renewed in 2010. However, between the expiry of the first licence and the renewal, a different company, Takolu Timber, entered into a timber agreement with the trustees, covering substantially the same areas and arranged for Rima Timber to carry out felling operations. The plaintiff sought an injunction against Takolu Timber and Rima Timber, which was defended on the grounds that the plaintiff was in breach of its contract with the trustees. The court held that the doctrine of privity does not apply to customary land and timber rights agreements.[100]

This conclusion justified rejecting the argument that those who terminated the agreement did not have the necessary authority, as they were not the original signatories present at the time in 1993. Those who signed the agreement in 1993 did so as representatives or trustees for all landowners; they did not sign as individual legal persons because that is not the nature of customary land 'ownership'. The Court of Appeal expressed this in the following way:

> The whole concept of group ownership of customary land gives each landowner equal rights over the whole of his clan's or tribe's land. Procedures have been established to ascertain the wishes of the members of the land owning group and to identify trustees from their number to sign the timber rights agreement on their behalf. Numerous cases have established the representative nature of those trustees' duties.[101]

95 Contract Rules 2004 (Tokelau), R 23; Law Reform (Contract Law) Act 2009 (Vanuatu), s 4(1).
96 This Act was repealed and re-enacted by the Contract and Commercial Law Act 2017 (NZ).
97 *London Drugs Ltd v Kuchene & Nagel International Ltd* [1992] 3 SCR 299.
98 (1988) 165 CLR 107.
99 [2011] SBCA 19.
100 Ibid., [8].
101 Ibid., [9].

In other regional countries where customary law has been recognised as a superior source of law to common law, this decision would be persuasive, and the possibility certainly exists of raising customary law in reply to a defence of privity of contract. Until this issue has been adjudicated upon, the doctrine of privity must be taken to apply outside Solomon Islands, Tokelau and Vanuatu. Within the common law system there is some scope for accommodating customary relationships by classifying them as a type of trust or agency. Perverting customary concepts by 'converting' them into the closest common law concept, in this instance a trust, is in itself an objectionable process,[102] but in reality this may be the only path available.

[102] See further, *Lilo v Ghomo* [1980-81] SILR 229.

CHAPTER 9
TERMS

1. INTRODUCTION

This chapter is concerned with the problems that arise in determining the binding terms of an agreement. Where terms are in dispute, the courts must look at all the circumstances to determine what was agreed. As stated by the Supreme Court of Tonga, this must be determined on an objective basis:[1]

> The intention of the parties is, as a general rule, to be construed objectively. The language used by one party, whatever his real intention may be, is to be construed in the sense in which it would be reasonably understood by the other, or at least in the sense in which a reasonable person would construe it.

The court will examine any written documents and, in some circumstances, at what the parties said and did. From this evidence the court will determine the terms which are legally binding on the parties.

In *Samoa Commercial Bank Ltd v Palm Island Traders*,[2] it was stated that the modern approach to be applied to the interpretation of contractual documents was to be found in two decisions of the House of Lords, *Mannai Investment Co Ltd v Eagle Star Life Assurance Co Ltd*[3] and *Antaios Compania Naviera SA v Salen Rederierna AB*.[4] According to this approach, sometimes called purposive construction, 'if a detailed semantic and syntactical analysis of a word in a commercial contract is going to lead to a conclusion that flouts business common sense, it must be made to yield to business common sense'.[5]

This chapter examines 'promissory terms'. These terms set out the parties' undertaking to perform their part of the bargain and the details surrounding that undertaking, such as how performance will take place. Promissory terms

1 *Sun Islands Inc v Fewtrell* [1991] Tonga LR 8, 9. See also *International Watersports Management Ltd v Pearl Creations Co Ltd* [2002] TOCA 7; *Misima Mines Ltd v Collector of Customs, Internal Revenue Commission* [2007] PGNC 91.

2 [2009] WSSC 4, [44].

3 [1997] AC 749, 770–71.

4 [1985] AC 191.

5 Ibid., 201.

may be either express or implied. Express terms may be either oral or written or may even be based on conduct of a party. Implied terms may arise from oral or written statements or from the conduct of the parties. As discussed later in this chapter, implied terms may also arise from extrinsic sources.

2. EXPRESS TERMS

2.1. TERMS OR REPRESENTATIONS

Subject to statutory provisions, discussed in chapter 10, promissory terms need not be written. The contract may be partly oral and partly in writing or may arise wholly or in part from conduct.

Some statements made in the course of negotiations do not form part of the contract. Such statements are often oral but may also be in written form. These statements may be representations or, as discussed in the context of the offer, they may be mere puff.[6] A representation is a statement made during the course of negotiations that induced the other party to enter into the contract, but which the parties did not intend to become a term of the contract.

The dividing line between terms and representations is not always clear. The courts have laid down some principles to assist in determining whether a statement is a mere representation or a term. The overriding approach is to determine the matter in accordance with the intention of the parties, determined objectively. In *Oscar Chess v Williams*,[7] Denning LJ put this in the following way:

> The question whether a [term] was intended depends on the conduct of the parties, on their words and behaviour, rather than on their thoughts. If an intelligent bystander would reasonably infer that a warranty was intended, that will suffice.

Similarly, in *Rutherford v Secretary for Justice*,[8] Thompson CJ said:

> [T]he test for ascertaining the intention of parties when entering into a contract is not subjective but objective. The court must decide what a reasonable person looking on would have considered their intentions to be (see eg *Smith v Hughes* (1871) LR 6 QB 597).

6 See chapter 3.
7 [1957] 1 WLR 370, 375. See further chapter 11.
8 [1982] NLR 209. In that case, a letter, which accompanied a formal offer of appointment with an annexed schedule of terms, was admitted as evidence of a missing term, although the point was not taken or argued in this case.

To ascertain the objective intention of the parties, the courts have developed the following principles:

1. If there is a long interval between the making of a statement and the conclusion of the contract, it is probably not a term of the contract.

   What will amount to a long interval depends on the context, and in some cases a few days will suffice. For example, in *Routledge v McKay*,[9] the plaintiff and defendant were discussing the possible sale and purchase of the defendant's motorbike. Both parties were private individuals. On 23 October, the defendant, taking the information from the registration book stated that the motorcycle was a 1942 model. On 30 October, a written contract of sale was made which did not refer to the date of the model. The actual date was later found to be 1930. The buyer's claim for damages failed.
2. If the statement is made orally and it is not included when the contract is reduced to writing, it is probably not a term. This subsidiary rule is really only an illustration of the point that the courts will presume, unless there is evidence to the contrary, that a written document is complete and contains all the terms agreed upon between the parties.
3. If the party who made the statement is in a better position than the other party to ascertain the accuracy of the statement, it is probably a term.
4. If the statement was important in the minds of the parties, it is probably a term.

The importance of the third principle is illustrated by *Oscar Chess v Williams*.[10] In that case, the plaintiffs were car dealers and the defendant wished to obtain a new Hillman Minx in part exchange for a second-hand Morris car. The trade-in price depended on the age of the Morris. The registration book said it was 1948 and the defendant confirmed this in good faith. The plaintiffs took the defendant's word for this and orally agreed to a trade-in with an allowance of £290. Eight months after the trade-in, the plaintiffs found that the date of the Morris was 1939 and that the trade-in price should have been £175. The plaintiffs sued for the difference. The Court of Appeal held that the statement as to the Morris's age was not a term of the contract.

This can be compared with *Dick Bentley Productions v Harold Smith (Motors)*.[11] In that case, a statement made by a motor dealer to a private purchaser, based on a reading of the mileometer, that a car had done only 20,000 miles, whereas in fact it had done 100,000, was held to be a contractual term. *Oscar Chess v Williams*[12] was distinguished on the basis that the private vendor in that case

9 [1954] 1 WLR 615.
10 [1957] 1 All ER 325.
11 [1965] 1 WLR 623 (CA).
12 [1957] 1 All ER 325.

honestly believed, on reasonable grounds, that the statement was true. In this case, the motor dealer was in a position to have known the true mileage.

In *Dick Bentley Productions v Harold Smith (Motors)*,[13] Lord Denning said that if a representation is made in the course of dealing for a contract for the purpose of inducing the other party to act upon it and it does induce that party to enter into the contract, that is prima facie a ground for inferring that it was intended as a term. The maker of a representation may rebut the inference by showing that he was innocent of fault in making it and that it would be unreasonable in the circumstances for him to be bound by it. However, the ratio of the case does not go as far as Lord Denning's statement.

As representations do not form part of the contract, an action for breach is not available if they are untrue. The remedy for misrepresentation is rescission, that is, setting aside of the contract in equity. If fraud or negligence can be proved, damages may also be recoverable. Misrepresentation is considered in chapter 12.

2.2. COLLATERAL CONTRACTS

Even if an oral statement is not a term of the main contract, the courts may be willing to find a collateral contract. Collateral means 'related to' or 'additional to'. A collateral contract is one that exists alongside and is connected to the subject matter of the main contract. The most common type of collateral contract is one where the consideration given for the promise is the making of another contract.

This device has been used by the courts to avoid the dilemma of whether a statement is a term or a representation. It is a way of dealing with a statement that was obviously intended to have some contractual significance, but for some reason has not been included in the terms of the contract. The most common instance of this is where the parol evidence rule applies. According to this rule, which is discussed in section 2.3, oral evidence may not be used to contradict a written contract.

Where a collateral contract is entered into solely to vary or add to a written contract, it is viewed with suspicion by the courts, as the more natural way of dealing with an additional promise would be to vary the main contract to include it. In *Ammar v Deoki*,[14] Spring, JA, citing the words of Lord Moulton in *Heilbut Symons v Buckleton*,[15] made it clear that strict proof of collateral contracts of this kind was required.

In spite of Lord Moulton's words, the courts have since shown themselves more willing to employ this device. One example of this is *City and Westminster*

13 [1965] 1 WLR 623 (CA).
14 (1969) 15 FLR 29, 34.
15 [1913] AC 30.

Properties (1934) Ltd v Mudd.[16] In that case, an oral assurance that a landlord would not enforce a covenant against residing on the premises was held to have given rise to a collateral contract.

A further example of the use of the collateral contract device is *De Lassalle v Guildford.*[17] In that case, the parties negotiated the lease of a house. The terms of the lease were finally agreed to, but the tenant refused to conclude the deal unless the landlord assured him that the drains were in good order. The defendant said that the drains were in order, but it turned out that this was not so, and the plaintiff sued. The defendant defended the action on the grounds that the assurance was not included in the written lease, and thus could not be a term of the contract. It was held that the plaintiff was entitled to succeed, but not because the assurance was a term of the contract. Rather the court held that the promise set up a collateral contract, the consideration for which was entry by the plaintiff into the main contract. The remedy was therefore for breach of this collateral contract.

Similarly, in *Esso Petroleum v Mardon,*[18] an oral estimate of how much petrol would be sold by a new petrol station, which induced the defendant to enter into a lease of the station, was held to be a collateral warranty.

There are two requirements for a collateral contract to be established:

- the person making the oral statement must have intended the statement to be relied upon (that is, it must have been intended to be legally binding); and
- the person to whom the statement was made must have entered into the main contract in reliance upon it.

The courts will not allow evidence of a collateral contract if the main contract contains an entire agreement clause.[19] A party alleging a collateral contract should expressly plead this.[20]

2.3. PAROL EVIDENCE RULE

The parol evidence rule dictates that extrinsic evidence may not be admitted to add, delete or vary the terms of a contract which has been put into writing. 'Parol' literally means oral evidence, but this rule would exclude any extrinsic material, such as a memorandum.

---

16 [1959] Ch 129.

17 [1901] 2 KB 215 (CA).

18 [1976] QB 801.

19 The entire agreement clause will not merely render evidence of a collateral contract inadmissible, it will render the collateral warranty void: *Inntrepreneur Pub Company Ltd v East Crown Ltd* [2000] 2 Lloyd's Rep 611.

20 *Naidu v Singh* (unreported, Court of Appeal, Fiji, Speight P, Mishra and Barker JJA, 27 July 1984).

The rationale for the parol evidence rule was stated in *Bank of South Pacific v Zoloveke*,[21] to be 'that where parties reduced their contract into writing they have decided that whatever is important is included in the contract and whatever is not important is left out'. However, the parol evidence rule does not mean that the court has to examine the written contract in a vacuum. It is now clear that it does not prevent the court from considering extrinsic evidence of background and surrounding circumstances to ascertain the 'matrix of fact' involved.[22] In *Bohn v Vanuatu Maritime Authority*,[23] Lunabek CJ adopted the words of Lord Wilberforce in *Reardon Smith Line Ltd v Yngvar Hansen Tangen*,[24] where he explained that, notwithstanding the parol evidence rule, when constructing a contract, the court must 'place itself in thought in the same factual matrix as that in which the parties were when the contract was made'.

Under French law as applied in Vanuatu, this rule does not apply to employment contracts, where the Code of 15 December 1952 for the French Overseas Territories allowed such evidence to be admitted.[25] However, the rule does apply to contracts governed by the common law in Vanuatu.[26] In Tonga, the rule has been given statutory force. The Evidence Act[27] states that:

> where any transaction has been reduced to the form of a document, no evidence of any oral agreement or statement shall be admitted as between the parties to such document or their representatives in interest for the purpose of contradicting, varying, adding to or subtracting from its terms.

However, the Act also contains exceptions, summarised below, which allow evidence to be given as to:[28]

(a) Any fraud, duress, illegality, want of due execution, in capacity, failure of consideration, error in date, mistake of fact or any other factor invalidating the document or entitling a person to relief relating to it.

The Act gives the following example:

> A sends to B a written application for repayment of his debt and encloses a receipt for the amount. B keeps the receipt but does not send the money,

21 [2014] SBHC 137.
22 *Samoa Commercial Bank Ltd v Palm Island Traders* [2009] WSSC 4, [47]; *Investors Compensation Scheme Ltd v West Bromwich Building Society* [1998] 1 A11 ER 98; *Boat Park Ltd v Hutchinson* [1999] 2 NZLR 74.
23 [2003] VUSC 137.
24 [1976] 1 WLR 989.
25 *Pentecost Pacific Ltd and Phillippe Pentecost v Hnaloane* (1980–88) 1 VLR 134 (CA).
26 *Furet v Rene Ah Pow* [2014] VUSC 5.
27 Cap 15, s 79.
28 Evidence Act Cap 15 (Tonga), s 79(a)–(f).

and when sued for the amount says he has paid it and produces the receipt as evidence. A may prove under (a) the circumstances under which B got possession of the receipt.

(b) A separate oral agreement which is not inconsistent with the terms of the contract, if the court infers that the parties did not intend the document to be a statement of the whole of the transaction between them.

The Act gives the following example:

> A sells B a horse and verbally warrants him sound. A gives B a paper in these words "Bought of A a horse for $20". If the horse proves unsound B may sue for damages and prove under (b) the verbal warranty.

(c) An oral agreement constituting a condition precedent to the attaching of any obligation under a document.

The Act gives the following example:

> A sues B for non-fulfilment of a written agreement. Evidence is admissible under (c) that B signed the document on the understanding between himself and A that it was not to operate as an agreement unless a certain condition was performed.

(d) A distinct subsequent oral agreement to rescind or modify the terms of a document provided that the transactions set out in the document are not required by law to be put in the form of a document.

The Act gives the following example:

> A sues B for the price of goods sold to B under a Tohi Aleabau.[29] Oral evidence that after the Tohi Aleabau had been executed it was agreed verbally between A and B that B should not be called on to pay for the goods for a period which is still unexpired is not admissible because the transaction set out in the Tohi Aleabau is one which is required by section 3 of the Contract Act to be in writing.

(e) Any usage or custom by which any incident not expressly mentioned in the contract is implied into contracts of that type unless that would be inconsistent with the express terms of the contract.

The Act gives the following example:

> A employs B as a labourer and gives him a paper in these words 'Wages $1 per week', evidence that it is a customary incident of contracts with labourers in Tonga that the employer provides their food is admissible.

(f) A fact which shows how the language of a document relates to existing facts.

No example is given of this exception, but it presumably refers to a situation where the extrinsic facts assist to make sense of language of the document.

---

29 Literally translated this means 'contract agreement'.

This provision in the Evidence Act was discussed in *Moehau v Westpac Bank of Tonga*,[30] where it was said that:

> The Act puts into a statutory, and therefore mandatory, form the well-known parol evidence rule of the common law whose rationale is the preservation of finality in written instruments which are intended to reflect the bargain reached by the parties.

In this case, the defendant bank granted a loan to the plaintiff. He repaid some of it, but had difficulties with the balance, so the defendant agreed to restructure it as a new advance and guarantee. The plaintiff fell into arrears again and the defendant sued to recover the debt. The plaintiff appealed from the grant of summary judgment. Applying s 79 of the Evidence Act, the court refused to admit oral evidence that the guarantee was limited to contradict the terms of the written agreement.

The parol evidence rule appears to apply in all countries of the region.[31] In *Pentecost Pacific Ltd and Phillippe Pentecost v Hnaloane*,[32] counsel for the respondent tried to persuade the court that the parol evidence rule was contrary to customary law. It was argued that the Melanesian way of life accorded greater importance to verbal undertakings. The court held that Art 45(1) of the Constitution of Vanuatu 1980 only allowed customary law to be applied if there was no other law applicable to a matter before it.[33] The Employment Act 1983 (Vanuatu) covered all substantive aspects of the dispute. On this basis the court refused to apply customary law. Further, even though there were no local rules of procedure in force, the French Civil Code of 15 December 1952, in force in New Caledonia at the date of independence, governed the admission of evidence in the case of a French defendant. In fact, the parol evidence was admitted in this case by virtue of the 1952 Code, which applied to employment contracts only. In the case of other contracts, parol evidence is inadmissible under the French Civil Code.[34]

The court must apply the plain meaning of the words in the contract rather than interpreting them in the light of extrinsic evidence.[35] In Fiji, the rule was

30 [2013] TOCA 9, [19].

31 See e.g. *Pora v Poliamba Ltd* [2008] PGNC 217; *Samoa Commercial Bank Ltd v Palm Island Traders* [2009] WSSC 4, [47].

32 [1980–88] 1 VLR 134 (CA).

33 For criticism of this approach, see J. Corrin Care, 'Bedrock and Steel Blues: Finding the Law Applicable in Vanuatu' (1998) 24 *Commonwealth Law Bulletin* 594.

34 Art. 1347.

35 *Misima Mines Ltd v Collector of Customs, Internal Revenue Commission* [2007] PGNC 91, citing *Codelfa Construction Pty Ltd v State Rail Authority (NSW)* (1982) 149 CLR 337.

summarised in *HP Kasabia Brothers Ltd v Reddy Construction Co Ltd*,[36] in the following words:

> the express words of the contract must first be construed in the surrounding circumstances but not on the basis of what the parties may have said was their intention at the time. Nor can any prior or subsequent conduct determine the meaning of their written contract unless there is more than one way in which the contract can be construed, that is, unless there is an ambiguity in the way in which the terms are recorded in that event subsequent conduct may be looked at. The paramount task of a court is to consider the express words used, considering them, of course in the context of the whole of the provisions in the writing and the relevant background. It is beside the point that the parties may consider their obligations to be different from the express terms of the recording instrument. That can only be a matter for rectification or estoppel. If the written words are capable of being given a meaning then that is the intention and obligation in accordance with the writing.

In *Sebastian v Air Pacific Ltd*,[37] the Supreme Court of Fiji held that the plaintiff was unable to rely on evidence of an oral undertaking that his employment would be for at least six years to contradict a written contract of employment.[38] In *Macdonald and Co Ltd v Union Steam Ship Co of New Zealand Ltd*,[39] the Supreme Court of Samoa held inadmissible parol evidence adduced to contradict the contents of signed receipts for delivery of goods.

In *Curtain Brothers (Queensland) Pty Ltd v The State*,[40] the parties entered into a written contract for the design and construction of a road. The defendant cancelled the contract, and the plaintiffs commenced proceedings but discontinued them on the basis of a negotiated, written settlement. The plaintiffs sued for enforcement of the settlement agreement. The defendant sought to introduce evidence of the content of the negotiations. In rejecting this evidence and granting the claim the appeal court said:

> Where parties have embodied the terms of the contract in a document, the general rule is that 'verbal evidence is not to be allowed to be given ... so as to add or subtract from, or in any manner to vary or qualify the written contract'.[41]

36 (1977) 23 FLR 235, 255. See also *Fiji Development Bank v Raqona* (1984) 30 FLR 151. For an English case on point, see *Scottish Power plc v Britoil (Exploration Ltd)* [1997] EWCA Civ 2752.

37 *Sebastian v Air Pacific Ltd* [1985] FJSC 41.

38 See also *Henderson v Arthur* [1907] 1 KB 10.

39 [1950–59] WSLR 131.

40 [1993] PNGLR 285.

41 Citing *Bank of Australia v Palmer* [1897] AC 540, 545; *Reliance Marine Insurance v Duder* [1913] 1 KB 265, 273; *Tsang Chuen v Li Po Kwai* [1932] AC 715, 727; *O'Connor v Hume* [1954] 1 WLR 824, 830.

> It is also not permissible to adduce evidence to show that subjective intentions of the parties were not in accord with the written instrument. It is settled law that, where a contract is contained in a document, it is to the document that the courts will look for terms of the agreement.[42]

The rule only applies when the contract is wholly in writing, not when it is partly oral and partly in writing. For example, in *Sun Islands Inc v Fewtrell*,[43] the plaintiff entered into a contract with the defendant whereby the defendant was to assist the plaintiff in setting up a motor scooter hire business. The defendant was then to manage the business. The plaintiff sued the defendant for an account of hire money received and for damages for loss of the use of the goods. The defendant counterclaimed for a fee of $5,000 claimed to be owed for establishing the business and for arrears for salary. The parties had a written employment agreement contained in a faxed letter, but the court admitted extrinsic evidence on the basis that this did not contain the entire agreement but was rather in the nature of an informal memo of their previous agreement. Webster J said:

> Here there are several reasons why extrinsic evidence can be considered under the exceptions to the parol evidence rule. Both parties said in evidence that exhibit 13 [a faxed letter of appointment] did not contain the entire agreement … It was not intended to express the entire agreement … and was perhaps just informal memo of their previous agreement …

However, the parol evidence rule may apply where a distinct part of the contract is in writing. Whether or not a contract, or a distinct part of it, is wholly in writing may itself be a question of dispute. There is a presumption that a document signed by the parties as a contract is a 'whole' contract. However, unless the document expressly states that it contains the entire contract, the court may look at extrinsic evidence to determine the point. In *AM Macdonald and Co Ltd v Union Steam Ship Co of New Zealand Ltd*,[44] the Supreme Court of Samoa accepted oral evidence of a practice of refusing delivery or requiring a qualified receipt when damage to cargo was detected. This supported the court's acceptance of a delivery receipt as a complete agreement incapable of contradiction by parol evidence.[45]

Further, the local context may be one factor to be considered in deciding whether to allow evidence of additional terms. In *Leahy v Otri*,[46] a contract for the sale of land was partly oral and partly in writing. The National Court of

42 Citing *Chitty on Contracts*, 25th ed., Sweet & Maxwell, London 1983, para. 802; *Preston v Luck* (1884) 27 Ch 497, 506 (Cotton LJ); *Life Insurance Co of Australia Ltd v Phillips* (1925) 36 CLR 60, 77 (Isaacs J).

43 [1991] Tonga LR 8.

44 [1950–59] WSLR 131, 133.

45 Ibid., 132.

46 [2009] PGNC 314.

Papua New Guinea refused to accept evidence of additional terms. This decision was influenced by the fact that the contract of sale was entered into in public and concluded with a village feast. In this customary setting, the court considered it most unlikely that additional terms would have been agreed to in secret.[47]

There are two situations where the parol evidence rule may be relevant:

- in deciding on the content of a contract, that is, answering the question 'what are the terms of the contract'; and
- in the interpretation of a contract, that is, answering the question 'what do those terms mean'.[48]

These two situations will now be considered in turn.

2.3.1. Parol Evidence as to Terms

The essence of the parol evidence rule, in the context of determining terms of a contract, is that if the parties intended the contract to be wholly in writing, the written terms may not be altered by reference to parol evidence.

There are a number of exceptions to this aspect of the rule. Parol evidence may be admitted in the following cases.

- *Evidence that the written contract has not yet come into operation*
  Where it is sought to adduce parol evidence to show that the contract is subject to a condition precedent, this may be admissible. In *Pym v Campbell*,[49] the parties entered into a written agreement for the sale and purchase of an invention on the express oral understanding that it should not bind them until a third party approved the invention. In the circumstances, oral evidence was allowed, not to contradict the written document, but to show that the written agreement did not have any force until the condition was fulfilled.

- *Evidence of trade usage or custom*
  Where a well-known trade usage or custom relates to the subject matter of the contract, the parol evidence rule cannot be relied upon to exclude evidence of this.[50]

- *Evidence of a collateral contract*
  Where evidence relates to the terms of a collateral contract, rather than the main agreement, it will be admissible. An example is provided by

47 Ibid., [40].
48 See *Richard Lang & Co v R* [1930–49] WSLR 52.
49 (1815) 119 ER 903.
50 *Hutton v Warren* (1836) 150 ER 517.

De Lassalle v Guildford,[51] the facts of which are set out above in section 2.2. In Fiji, this exception was discussed in *Ammar v Deoki*.[52] In that case, the deceased transferred a lease of land to her daughter by deed, which stated the consideration to be £1,200. The deed acknowledged receipt of the sum. The plaintiff, the deceased's husband, brought an action against the daughter as administrator of his wife's estate for £700 being part of the £1,200, which was said to be outstanding. The defendant admitted paying only £500, but said that this was the oral consideration agreed. The trial judge found in favour of the defendant. The plaintiff appealed on the grounds that the respondent should not have been allowed to give parol evidence that the consideration was only £500, as this contradicts the transfer deed. The Court of Appeal of Fiji held that the general rule that parol evidence is inadmissible when it would have the effect of varying or contradicting a written deed or document is subject to the exceptions, including where the evidence is relates to a collateral contract. In this case, the plaintiff's claim was based not on a deed, but on an alleged collateral agreement that the balance of £700 was to be repayable on demand. Although the plaintiff did not call evidence to establish such a collateral agreement such evidence could have been received. Given the allegation, the defendant was equally entitled to call evidence in denial and to establish that the true consideration was £500.

- *Evidence as to consideration*
  In *Ammar v Deoki*,[53] it was also stated that parol evidence could be adduced to show the absence or existence of consideration, the true consideration, or additional consideration, even where this contradicted a written contract, a deed or a receipt. It was also stated, obiter, that this exception would allow parol evidence to be adduced to show that the consideration was less than that stated in the written document.

- *To show the nature of the transaction or the true relationship between the parties*
  In *Ammar v Deoki*,[54] it was also stated that parol evidence could be adduced to show the nature of the transaction or the true relationship between the parties.

- *Invalidity*
  Evidence may be adduced to show that the contract is invalid, for example evidence of a common mistake in the reduction of the oral agreement to

---

51 [1901] 2 KB 215.
52 (1969) 15 FLR 29.
53 Ibid. See also *Frith v Frith* [1906] AC 254.
54 Ibid.

writing. In *Joscelyne v Nissen*,[55] a father and daughter reached agreement that the father would live on the ground floor of the daughter's house free of rent and all outgoings, and that she would pay gas, electricity, coal bills and the cost of home help to tend her afflicted mother. In fact, the agreement which was put into writing did not expressly say that she was to pay the bills. It was held that oral evidence was admissible to show that the written contract was invalid, due to the mistake of the parties in not properly recording what had been agreed.

Other matters which may be proved by oral evidence are fraud, immorality, illegality, incapacity, duress, undue influence and frustration.[56]

The English Law Reform Commission has considered the rule and recommended its retention.[57] The Commission felt that the exceptions to the rule were wide enough to prevent it being used to unjustly exclude evidence.

2.4. PAROL EVIDENCE AS TO INTERPRETATION

As a general rule, the meaning of a written contract must be found from the document itself.[58] The document should be construed as a whole, the objective being, as far as possible, to find consistent meaning throughout.[59] However, parol evidence is admissible to aid in interpretation of contract terms if:

- it is clearly necessary in order to avoid absurdity or inconsistency;[60] or
- the context in which the word or phrase appears renders its meaning doubtful.[61]

As mentioned above, the modern approach to the parol evidence rule is influenced by the decision in *Investors Compensation Scheme Ltd v West Bromwich Building Society*,[62] where it was held that, in order to ascertain the meaning of a contract, reference should be made to the 'matrix of fact', that is, the background knowledge available to the parties at the time of the contract. However, this is subject to the requirement that this information should have been reasonably available to the parties and the law excludes from the admissible background the previous negotiations of the parties and their declarations

---

55 [1970] 2 QB 86.

56 *Ammar v Deoki* (1969) 15 FLR 29.

57 Law Commission, *Law of Contract: The Parol Evidence Rule*, Working Paper No. 70, 1976.

58 *Jacobs v Batavia and General Plantations Trust* [1924] 1 Ch 287, 295.

59 *Hume v Rundell* (1824) 57 ER 311, 312; *Darin Nominees Pty Ltd v Franklin's Selfserve Pty Ltd* [1999] NSWCA 209; see 'Recent Cases' (2000) 74 ALJ 285.

60 *Fitzgerald v Masters* (1956) 95 CLR 420, 426–27.

61 *Reardon Smith Line v Hansen-Tangen* [1976] 1 WLR 989, 995–96.

62 [1998] 1 All ER 98, 114. See also *LG Schuler AG v Wickman Machine Tools* [1974] AC 235, 261.

of subjective intent. It was conceded by the court that the boundaries of this exception are in some respects unclear. The principles set out in that case appear to have been adopted by the courts in most Pacific Island countries. For example, in Fiji, they were approved by the Supreme Court in *Kumar v National Insurance Company of Fiji*.[63] In Samoa they have been relied on by the Supreme Court in *Samoa Commercial Bank Ltd v Palm Island Traders*[64] and *Samoa National Provident Fund Board v Progressive Insurance Co Ltd*.[65] In Solomon Islands the case was approved, obiter, by the Court of Appeal in *Shiyao v Austree Enterprises Pty Ltd*.[66]

Evidence of refusal to include a particular provision may be adduced to negate an inference otherwise sought to be drawn from surrounding circumstances.[67] This is particularly the case if the fact that the parties have directed their minds to such a provision and have rejected it appears on the face of the contract.[68]

In *Richard Lang & Co v R*,[69] the agreement provided for the purchase of banana case shooks from the plaintiff 'as required by' the defendant's manager. The court held that this might mean one of a number of things. In view of this ambiguity, the court felt able to consider extrinsic evidence, including oral evidence.[70]

However, where the meaning of the contract is clear, extrinsic evidence will not be allowed to contradict it. This aspect of the rule received detailed consideration in Fiji in *Charitra v Marlows Ltd*,[71] where it was pointed out that:

> The paramount task of the court is to consider the express words used in considering them of course in the context of the whole of the provisions of the contract and the relevant background. It is beside the point that the parties may consider their obligations to be different from the express words of the contract. That can only be a matter of rectification or perhaps estoppel. If the written words are capable of being given a meaning then that is the intention and obligation in accordance with the contract.

Under English common law, the parol evidence rule applies not only to exclude evidence from the period before the written contract was entered into, but also to subsequent events.[72] However, the Cook Islands High Court has followed the

---

63 [2012] FJSC 10, following *Din v Westpac Banking Corporation* [2004] FLR 534, 538. See also *Deo Construction Development Company Ltd v Reddy* [2016] FJHC 179; *Korodrau v Training Productivity Authority of Fiji* [2012] FJHC 1425.

64 [2009] WSSC 4, [47].

65 [2011] WSSC 93.

66 [2018] SBCA 13.

67 *Codelfa Construction Pty Ltd v State Rail Authority (NSW)* (1982) 149 CLR 337, 352–53.

68 Ibid.

69 [1930–49] WSLR 52.

70 See also *LG Schuler AG v Wickman Machine Tool Sales Ltd* [1974] AC 235, 261.

71 Unreported, Court of Appeal, Fiji, Spring JA, 2 April 1982.

72 *Charitra v Marlows Ltd* (unreported, Court of Appeal, Fiji, Spring JA, 2 April 1982); *LG Schuler AG v Wickman Machine Tool Sales Ltd* [1974] AC 235, 261, approved in *Secret Hotels2 Ltd v HMRC* [2014] 2 All ER 685.

approach of the New Zealand Court of Appeal and has held that 'it is appropriate to interpret a contract by reference to subsequent events'.[73]

2.5. CLASSIFICATION OF EXPRESS TERMS

Once it has been established that a statement forms a term of the contract, it is necessary to consider what its precise importance and effect is. There are three categories of terms:

- conditions;
- warranties; and
- intermediate or innominate terms

These categories are important as the remedy available for breach of contract depends on the type of term which has been breached.

2.5.1. Conditions

A condition is a vital term, going to the root of a contract, failure to perform which renders performance of the rest of the contract different in substance from that contracted for. To put it another way, if a term is so important that non-performance of it may fairly be considered as a substantial performance to perform the contract at all, it is a condition.

The word 'condition' can be used in different contexts.[74] This chapter is concerned with 'promissory conditions', that is, those terms of the contract which are vital, and which a party has promised to fulfil. Promissory conditions should not be confused with the following uses of the word 'condition':

- *The common meaning*: any stipulation or term of a contract. For example, a purchaser who enquires as to the conditions of sale is normally asking what the terms are.
- *Condition precedent*: conditions which suspend the operation of the contract, for example the term 'subject to finance'. In *Pym v Campbell*,[75] the parties entered into a written agreement for the sale and purchase of an invention subject to the approval of a third party. The written agreement did not have any force until the condition was fulfilled.[76]

---

73 *Framhein v Tepaki Investments Ltd* [2007] CKHC 7.

74 See S.J. Stoljar, 'The Contractual Concept of Condition' (1953) 69 *Law Quarterly Review* 485, where 12 meanings are discerned.

75 (1815) 119 ER 903.

76 See also *Vanualevu Hardware (Fiji) Ltd v Sun Insurance Company Ltd* [2013] FJHC 213, where the condition precedent was waived by the subsequent conduct of the defendant.

- *Condition subsequent*: conditions providing for the determination of the contract, for example a contract of marine insurance subject to the ship remaining within specified waters. In this case, there is a binding agreement until the event occurs. A case example is *The Good Luck*,[77] where the condition subsequent provided that the ship was not to be taken into a particular part of the Persian Gulf. When this condition was contravened, the insurer's obligations automatically ceased.

Whether a term amounts to a condition depends on the intention of the parties, ascertained objectively, at the time when the contract was made. The fact that the contract describes a term as a condition is not conclusive.[78] This principle has been given statutory force in relation to sale of goods contracts. For example, s 13(2) of the Sale of Goods Act of Fiji[79] and s 12(2) of the Sale of Goods Act 1975 of Samoa[80] both provide that 'a stipulation may be a condition though called a warranty in the contract'. The English Sale of Goods Act makes similar provision.[81]

Whether a term is a condition or a warranty is not always easy to ascertain. This is well illustrated by comparing *Bettini v Gye*[82] with *Poussard v Spiers*.[83] In *Bettini v Gye*, the plaintiff was an opera singer who was engaged for performances over three months. He undertook to attend for rehearsals at least six days before the first performance. He arrived four days late and the employer terminated his contract on the basis that this was breach of a condition. It was held that missing four days of rehearsals was not breach of a condition, particularly having regard to the lengthy contract and the nature of the performances.

Poussard v Spiers also involved a plaintiff who was a singer. She was taken ill five days before the first performance, and did not arrive until seven days into the performances. There, the court held that the singer's obligation to appear on the first night was a condition, and the employer had been justified in terminating the contract and taking on a substitute.

Breach of a condition normally amounts to repudiation of the contract and discharges the innocent party from further performance.[84] The innocent party is entitled to sue for damages as well as treating the contract as discharged. An innocent party also has the option to treat a broken condition as a broken

---

77 [1991] 3 All ER 1.
78 *Wickman Machine Tools Sales Ltd v Schuler AG* [1974] AC 235.
79 Cap 230.
80 See also Sale of Goods Act 1986 23 MIRC Cap 1 (Marshall Islands), s 13(2).
81 See Sale of Goods Act 1893 (UK), s 11(b).
82 (1876) 1 QBD 183.
83 (1876) 1 QBD 410.
84 See further chapter 18.

warranty. In other words, a party may elect to sue for damages, and not to terminate the contract.[85]

2.5.2. *Warranties*

A warranty is a term collateral to the main purpose of the contract, breach of which only entitles the innocent party to damages.[86]

In *Taubmans Paints (Fiji) Ltd v Faletau*,[87] the Supreme Court of Tonga held that failure to pay for a consignment of paint was not sufficient to entitle the plaintiff to terminate a sole agency agreement with the defendant. To justify cancellation of the agreement there must be breach of a term that is 'fundamental, going to the root of [the contract]'.

With regard to goods, there is a statutory definition. Section 2(1) of the Sale of Goods Act of Fiji, for example, defines warranty in relation to sale of goods as:

> an agreement with reference to goods which are the subject of a contract of sale but collateral to the main purpose of such contract the breach of which gives rise to a claim for damages but not to a right to reject the goods and treat the contract as repudiated.

Section 2(1) of the Sale of Goods Acts of Samoa[88] and Marshall Islands[89] and s 62 of the English Sale of Goods Act make similar provision.

The sale of goods legislation contains other provisions regarding conditions and warranties. For example, s 11 of the Sale of Goods Act of Fiji[90] provides that time is not of the essence (and therefore does not qualify as a condition) unless the contract specifies that this is the case.

The test of whether a term amounts to a warranty is whether this was the intention of the parties, judged objectively, at the time when the contract was made. In contrast to a condition, where the parties' description is not conclusive, the fact that the contract describes a term as a warranty will normally be decisive.

2.5.3. *Innominate Terms*

The category of innominate terms, sometimes referred to as 'intermediate terms', has been created by the courts to take account of the fact that complex

---

85 See also Sales of Goods Acts, which provide that if the buyer has accepted the goods or part of them, the seller can only treat the breach as a breach of warranty, unless the contract says otherwise: e.g. Sale of Goods Act Cap 230 (Fiji), s 12(3); Sale of Goods Act 1986 23 MIRC Cap 1 (Marshall Islands), s 13(3); Sale of Goods Act 1975 (Samoa), s 12(3).

86 *Bettini v Gye* (1876) 1 QBD 183.

87 [1999] TOSC 2.

88 Sale of Goods Act 1975 (Samoa).

89 Sale of Goods Act 23 MIRC Cap 1 (Marshall Islands).

90 Cap 230. See also e.g. Sale of Goods Act 1986 23 MIRC Cap 1 (Marshall Islands), s 12; Sale of Goods Act 1975 (Samoa), s 11.

contractual undertakings cannot always be categorised as either a condition or a warranty. The focus in categorising terms as innominate is on the gravity of the breach and of its consequences.

The founding case is *Hong Kong Fir Shipping Co Ltd v Kawasaki Kisen Kaisha Ltd*.[91] There, the plaintiffs chartered to the defendants the *MV Hongkong Fir* for a period of 24 months on the term that she was in every way fitted out for ordinary cargo service. The vessel was an old one and by reason of age needed to be maintained by experienced crew, which the plaintiff did not provide. The Chief Engineer was addicted to drink and inefficient, and there were not enough other engine room crew, with a result that there were many serious breakdowns. In the first seven months, she only spent eight and a half weeks at sea. The rest of the time was taken up with breakdowns and repairs. The vessel was eventually made seaworthy, but the defendant charterers refused to continue with the charterparty. It was argued on behalf of the defendants that the shipowner's obligation to provide a seaworthy vessel was a condition, any breach of which entitled the charterers to treat themselves as discharged.

The Court of Appeal rejected this contention. The undertaking as to seaworthiness was not a condition but an intermediate term. Breach of such a term would not give rise to a right to repudiate unless the conduct of the shipowners and the consequences of the breach were so serious as to frustrate the commercial purpose of the venture. The court pointed out that to hold otherwise would mean that if a nail was missing from one of the timbers, or two of several anchors not on board, the owners would be in breach. The court considered that it was contrary to common sense to allow a party to treat a contract as at an end for a trifling breach.

In summary, in *Hong Kong Fir* it was said that complex contractual undertakings cannot always be categorised as being 'conditions' or 'warranties'. Where categorisation is not possible, the innocent party may treat the contract as at an end only if the event which occurs as a result of the default substantially deprives him or her of the benefit of the contract.

This approach sacrifices certainty, as it is not possible to classify terms and predict the consequences of their breach from the outset. On the other hand, it avoids unfairness in cases where a condition is breached in a minor way.

In *Wickman Machine Tools Sales Ltd v Schuler AG*,[92] the House of Lords confirmed the existence of this category did not relieve the courts from attempting to categorise terms as conditions or warranties. In cases where it was clearly the intention of the parties that a term should operate as a condition or a warranty, then effect should be given to that intention.

---

91 [1962] 2 QB 26 (CA).
92 [1974] AC 235.

Hong Kong Fir was also considered in *Bunge Corporation New York v Tradax SA*,[93] which shed further light on how the courts should be dealing with the categorisation of terms. In that case, the sellers were required by 30 June 1975 to load the goods on board ship at a single United States Gulf port to be nominated by them. The contract further provided that the buyers should give to the sellers at least 15 consecutive days' notice of probable readiness of the vessel, and the approximate quantity required to be loaded. The buyers were two days late with the notice, and were therefore in breach of the term requiring 15 days' notice. The sellers declared them to be in default and claimed damages for repudiation of the contract. The House of Lords agreed that there was a third category of terms, consisting of 'innominate' or 'intermediate' terms, but stressed that it was not to be used unless there was ambiguity or doubt as to whether a term was a condition or warranty.

In accordance with these decisions, the first step is to decide what type of term the parties intended. If it is clearly a condition then the innocent party will be entitled to damages and rescission. If it is clearly a warranty then only damages will be available. Only if there is no clear intention may the court go on to the second step and the clause be termed innominate, the gravity of the breach and the seriousness of the consequences being considered. As stated by Lord Roskill:[94]

> I do not believe Diplock LJ ever intended his judgment to afford an easy escape route from the normal consequences of rescission to a contract breaker who had broken what was, upon its true construction, clearly a condition of the contract by claiming that he had only broken an innominate term.

It has been made clear in *Cehave NV v Bremer Handelgesellschaft mbH*[95] that the Sale of Goods Act (UK) does not prevent contracts falling under its ambit having their terms classified as conditions or warranties. This case provides persuasive authority in support of the application of the principles in *Hong Kong Fir* in contracts governed by regional sale of goods Acts.

3. EXEMPTION CLAUSES

An exemption clause may have one of two purposes:

(a) to exclude liability (an 'exclusion clause'); or
(b) to limit liability (a 'limitation clause')

---

93 [1981] 1 WLR 711.
94 *Bunge Corporation New York v Tradax SA* [1984] 1 WLR 711, 725–26.
95 [1976] QB 44 (CA).

of the person inserting the clause, who is known as the 'proferens'. The proferens may seek to escape from, or limit, the consequences of some wrongful act, for example breach of contract or commission of a tort. Such clauses are found often in standard form contracts. Because of the injustices which have arisen from this practice, the courts tend to view such clauses with suspicion. Before a court will allow a contractor to take the benefit of such a clause, clear proof is required that:

(a) the clause must be incorporated as a term of the contract; and
(b) on its true construction, the clause covers the event which occurred.

These requirements will be examined separately.

3.1. INCORPORATION OF A CLAUSE

The rules that govern the incorporation of an exemption clause apply equally to incorporation of other types of terms. However, they arise more frequently in the context of exemption clauses. Broadly speaking, terms may be incorporated by being contained in a document signed by the person to be bound or by sufficient notice having been given.

3.1.1. Signed Documents

A party who signs a document embodying the terms of a contract is generally bound by those terms. As stated in *Fiji Development Bank v Raqona*:[96]

> The general rule is that a party of full age and understanding is normally bound by his signature to a document whether he reads or understands it or not.

Signatories cannot escape liability later by claiming ignorance of those terms, even if they failed to read the document before signing or were ignorant of their precise legal effect.[97]

The distinction between signed and unsigned documents is illustrated by *Maeaniani v Saemala*.[98] In that case, the defendant signed a document stating that he had received money from the plaintiff as full settlement for his land. He later refused to execute the transfer document and the plaintiff sued for specific performance. The defendant said that he had not read the document as he was illiterate and that it had been explained to him as being a document concerning

96 (1984) 30 FLR 151, 153.
97 *L'Estrange v Graucob* [1934] 2 KB 394. See further M. Chapman, 'Common Law Contract and Consent: Signature and Objectivity' (1998) 49(4) *North Ireland Legal Quarterly* 363.
98 [1982] SILR 70.

a loan by the plaintiff to the defendant to purchase tools and equipment to build a house on the land as a joint enterprise. Daly CJ explained the rule and the reasons for it in the following way:

> The general rule in law is that where a person, who is of full legal capacity, signs a document then it is binding upon him whether or not he has read it. The reasons for this rule are obvious; there must be some degree of certainty in business dealings and a written document duly signed must be regarded as embodying certainty to the extent that the law will regard it as the formal acknowledgement by the person who signs it that he accepts the contents of the document.[99]

There are exceptions to this rule. An exemption clause will not normally be allowed to exclude or limit liability arising from a term implied by statute.[100] There are also general exceptions to the principle that a person is bound by signature of a document containing an exemption clause. These include a plea of *non est factum*,[101] misrepresentation and fraud.[102] The first two of these general exceptions require further explanation.

3.1.1.1. *Non Est Factum*

In rare circumstances, a person who signs a document may escape liability on the basis that there was a substantial difference between the document signed and the document the signatory thought they were signing. This is known as a plea of *non est factum*, which means 'it is not my deed'. Thus, in *Foster v MacKinnon*,[103] the defendant, an elderly man, was fraudulently induced to sign a bill of exchange for £3,000, on the assurance that it was a guarantee of a similar nature to one which he had previously signed. Later the bill was transferred to the plaintiff, who took it in good faith. It was held that the document was void for mistake.

However, the courts are reluctant to allow this plea and a person relying on it bears the burden of proving it on the basis of convincing evidence.[104] The older authorities were reviewed by the House of Lords in *Gallie v Lee*,[105] where Wilberforce LJ explained the principle on which *non est factum* operates as follows:

> A document should be held to be void (as opposed to voidable) only when the element of consent to it is totally lacking, that is, more concretely, when the transaction which

99 Ibid., 73, applying *Gallie v Lee* [1970] 2 WLR 1078.
100 *Hunt v Australasian United Steam Navigation Co Ltd* [1919] 2 FLR 72.
101 See e.g. *Maeaniani v Saemala* [1982] SILR 70.
102 *S Pearson & Son v Dublin Corporation* [1907] AC 357.
103 (1869) LR 4 CP 704.
104 *Gallie v Lee* [1971] AC 1004, 1084, 1092.
105 [1971] AC 1004.

> the document purports to effect is essentially different in substance or in kind from the transaction intended.

In addition to proving lack of consent, lack of negligence in signing the document must be shown.[106]

In *Maeaniani v Saemala*,[107] the facts of which are set out above, the defendant sought to set up a plea of *non est factum*. Referring to relevant passages from *Gallie v Lee*,[108] Daly CJ distinguished between cases where the signatory was adult and literate and those involving persons who were illiterate, blind or lacking in understanding. In the former case, a successful plea of *non est factum* would be very rare. The latter situation placed the law in the dilemma of protecting a disadvantaged group with the need to protect innocent third parties. His Lordship agreed with the view of Lord Wilberforce that:

> The law ought … to give relief if satisfied that consent was truly lacking but will require of signers even in this class that they act responsibly and carefully according to their circumstances inputting their signature to legal documents.

This distinction between literate and illiterate signatories has particular relevance in developing countries of the South Pacific. This was recognised by Daly CJ, who went on to explain the application of the plea of *non est factum* in Solomon Islands:

> At the early stages of development to which we have attained we still have many people who are not familiar with the written word or with the implications of signing documents. Nevertheless, the words with which Lord Wilberforce ends the passages cited above remain entirely apt to our circumstances. On the facts of an individual case a court may be more ready in Solomon Islands to conclude that the consent of a man from, for example, a rural area was truly lacking and that nevertheless he acted responsibly and carefully according to his own circumstances in signing or affixing his mark to the document. But the test remains the same; it is the evidence and circumstances which differ. I venture to suggest that a Solomon Islands Court would always approach the evidence as befits this nation rather than as befits a country at a different stage of development.

In this case the plea of *non est factum* was not established. Daly CJ took account of the fact that the defendant was a carpenter and builder, who had lived and worked in the capital for 25 years, before returning to Malaita Island. He operated a number of taxis in the capital, was articulate and intelligent, and could be described in the broader sense as a businessman.[109]

---

106 Ibid., 1091.
107 [1982] SILR 70.
108 [1971] AC 1004.
109 [1982] SILR 70, 75.

Contractual documents will normally be in English rather than the vernacular. They are also likely to refer to Western European concepts of commerce and contract. Where a signatory's orientation may be described as 'customary' rather than 'commercial' other regional courts, in addition to those of Solomon Islands, may find a plea of *non est factum* more convincing.

3.1.1.2. Misrepresentation

A person who has misrepresented the effect of an exemption clause, either personally or through an employee or agent, will not be allowed to rely on it. For example, in *Curtis v Chemical Cleaning Co*,[110] the plaintiff took a white satin wedding dress, trimmed with beads and sequins to the defendant's shop for dry-cleaning. The shop assistant gave her a document headed 'receipt' and requested her to sign it. The plaintiff asked what it was for, and the assistant said that it exempted the defendant from certain risks, and in the present case, from damage to beads and sequins. The plaintiff signed. In fact, the document exempted the defendant from all damage. When the dress was returned it was stained. In an action for damages the defendant tried to rely on the exemption clause. It was held that, as the assistant had represented the effect of the document as only limiting certain types of liability, the defendant was precluded from relying on it for other purposes.

3.1.2. Unsigned Documents

If a document is not signed, but merely delivered, it will only be incorporated into the contract if the other party has reasonable notice of it. Notice may be one of two types:

- *Actual notice*: if a party knows of the exemption clause he or she will be bound by it.
- *Constructive notice*: the other party will be deemed to have notice if the following conditions are fulfilled.

3.1.2.1. The Document Must be Contractual in Nature

The document must be of such a kind that it would be assumed by a reasonable person to be a contractual document rather than, for example, a receipt. This condition is illustrated by *Chappelton v Barry UDC*.[111] In that case, the plaintiff hired a deckchair on a beach controlled by the defendant. He paid a fee for use

---

110 [1951] 1 KB 805 (CA).
111 [1940] 1 KB 532.

of the deckchair and received a ticket. The printed terms on the back of the ticket excluded liability in the event of any accident or damage arising from the use of the chair. When the plaintiff sat on the chair it collapsed and he was injured. The plaintiff sued and the defendant tried to rely on the clause. It was held that the plaintiff had not had actual notice, and the ticket could not constitute constructive notice as a reasonable man would have assumed the ticket to be no more than a receipt.

3.1.2.2. Reasonable Steps Must be Taken to Give Notice

If the party in question has not had actual notice, it must be shown that reasonable steps were taken to give notice. Whether the notice is reasonably sufficient is a question of fact to be judged objectively in all the circumstances of the case. In *Parker v South Eastern Railway Co*,[112] the plaintiff deposited a bag in the cloakroom of a railway station belonging to the defendant. He received a ticket which said on the face, 'see back'. On the back were a number of printed conditions, including a condition limiting liability for any package to £10.00. The plaintiff admitted that he knew there was writing on the ticket, but stated that he had not read it, and did not know or believe that the writing contained conditions. The bag was lost, and the plaintiff claimed £24.10 for its value. The plaintiff was bound by the exclusion clause.

As the test is objective, the proferens is only required to take reasonable steps that are necessary to bring the clause to the attention of a normal person of the same class as plaintiff. It is not necessary to cater for individual peculiarities of a party, unless that peculiarity is known to the other party.[113] For example, in *Thompson v London, Midland and Scottish Railway Co*,[114] the plaintiff who could not read gave her niece money to buy her a railway excursion ticket. On the face of it were the words 'for conditions see back'. The back of the ticket referred the reader to the defendant's timetables. The timetables contained a clause exempting liability in respect of injury. The plaintiff was injured and claimed that this was due to the defendant's negligence. The Court of Appeal held that the notice given was sufficient, since the ticket referred on its face to conditions under which it was issued. The conditions were therefore incorporated in the contract.

Special care must be taken to draw attention to any unusual clause.[115] In *Interfoto Picture Library v Stiletto Visual Programmes Ltd*,[116] the Court of Appeal

112 (1877) 2 CPD 416.

113 See *Geier v Kujawa, Weston and Warne Bros* [1970] 1 Lloyd's Rep 364 for an example of a case where the notice was insufficient as the defendant knew that the plaintiff did not speak English.

114 [1930] 1 KB 41.

115 *Spurling v Bradshaw* [1956] 2 All ER 121; *Thornton v Shoe Lane Parking Ltd* [1971] 2 QB 163.

116 [1988] 1 All ER 348.

re-affirmed the principle that where a term in a contract was particularly onerous or unusual and would not generally be known to the other party, the proferens must show that it had been fairly and reasonably brought to the other party's attention. This applied to all terms, whether or not they contained an exemption clause.

3.1.2.3. The Steps were Taken Before or at the Time the Contract was Made

Notice of the exclusion clause must be communicated to the other party before or at the time when the contract is made. In *Olley v Marlborough Court*,[117] a notice in a hotel bedroom purporting to exclude liability for loss of luggage was not incorporated in the contract between the proprietor and guests. The contract was made at the registration desk, before the plaintiff entered her bedroom and before she had an opportunity to read the notice.

Similarly, in *Thornton v Shoe Lane Parking Ltd*,[118] the plaintiff drove into a car park, receiving a ticket from an automatic machine as he did so. The ticket said that it was issued subject to conditions displayed on the premises, but the plaintiff did not read the ticket. The displayed conditions purported to exclude all liability, including injury to customers. When the plaintiff returned to his car, there was an accident in which he was injured. The defendant tried to rely on the exemption clause. It was held that liability could not be restricted by conditions which were brought to the plaintiff's attention only after he had put his money into the machine, as at that stage the contract was complete. Lord Denning expressed his view in the following words:

> The customer pays his money and gets a ticket. He cannot refuse it. He cannot get his money back. He may protest to the machine, even swear at it. But it will remain unmoved … He is committed at the very moment when he puts his money into the machine. The contract was concluded at that time … [T]he offer is made when the proprietor of the machine holds it out as being ready to receive the money. The acceptance takes place when the customer puts his money into the slot.

3.1.3. Cases where Exemption Clauses may be Implied

If the parties to a contract have done business before, an exemption clause may in some circumstances be implied. This is discussed further below under implied terms (section 4).

---

117 [1949] 1 KB 532.
118 [1971] 2 QB 163.

3.2. INTERPRETATION OF EXEMPTION CLAUSES

Even if an exemption clause is incorporated in the contract, that is not the end of the matter. The court will examine the clause carefully to ensure that it covers the circumstances in which it is being relied on. For example, an exemption clause covering damage to property will not cover personal injury and an exemption clause covering contractual liability will not cover negligence.

Generally, an exemption clause must be interpreted like any other clause, accordingly to its natural and ordinary meaning, read in the light of the contract as a whole.[119] Thus if it clearly exempts liability, the courts will give effect to that meaning.[120]

Whilst exemption clauses must generally be interpreted like any other clause, there are a number of particular rules of construction which assist in interpreting them. These will now be discussed in turn.

3.2.1. *The Clause will be Read* Contra Proferentem

Exclusion clauses are interpreted *contra proferentem.* As stated in *Suva City Council v Koroi*:[121]

> Contra preferentem is a rule of contractual interpretation which provides that an ambiguous term will be construed against the party responsible for its inclusion in the contract.

In *Wallis, Son & Wells v Pratt and Haynes*,[122] the defendants sold the plaintiffs seeds described as 'common English sainfoin'. It was an express term of the contract that the seller gave 'no warranty express or implied as to growth, description or any other matter'. The seeds supplied turned out to be 'giant sainfoin', which was inferior. The plaintiffs sued for damages and the defendants relied on the exemption clause. It was held that the exemption clause did not apply to breach of a condition, but only to breach of a warranty. It was clear that it was a condition that had been breached, as the Sale of Goods Act implied a condition that goods sold by description must correspond with that description.

Another aspect of this rule is that a clause inserted in favour of one party cannot operate to exclude the liability of the other party.

---

119 But see the views of Denning LJ in *Photo Production Ltd v Securicor Transport Ltd* [1978] 3 All ER 146, 153.
120 *'Istros' v FW Dahlstroem & Co* [1931] 1 KB 247.
121 [2013] FJCA 97.
122 [1911] AC 394.

An example of the courts' tendency to construe clauses strictly is *Lal v Chand.*[123] There, the Court of Appeal of Fiji held that a clause inserted in favour of one party, in that case a clause entitling the purchaser of a new house to have defects remedied within a certain period after the purchase, cannot operate to exclude liability of the other party in respect of defects discovered after that period. However, this case must be read in light of *BHP Petroleum Ltd v British Steel plc*,[124] where a contract excluded all liability for defects in the piping supplied, except those defects becoming apparent within two years of purchase. The plaintiff alleged that the clause should be construed *contra proferentem* and that the clause only operated to confer additional mutual rights for a limited period. It was held that this clause was effective to exclude all liability. Had the clause in *Lal v Chand* clearly excluded liability on the part of the defendant after expiry of the defects period, it seems likely that he would have been allowed to rely on it.

In recent times, interpretation *contra proferentem* has declined. In England, the House of Lords has suggested that there is no longer any need for the courts to strain the facts in order to restrict the application of exemption clauses, as unfair clauses are now controlled by the Unfair Contract Terms Act 1977. This Act, which is discussed below in section 3.3.1, does not apply in the region, so courts may still be required to use the rules of interpretation creatively in order to achieve a just result. In *Kumar v National Insurance Company of Fiji*[125] the court stated, obiter, that much depends on the context of the commercial document being construed.

3.2.2. Rules Governing Exclusion of Liability for Negligence

In the Fiji case of *Burns Philp (South Seas) Co v Marine Pacific*,[126] Gould VP reviewed the English case law on the interpretation of clauses attempting to exclude liability for negligence. His summary of the law gives rise to the following rules.

3.2.2.1. Express Exclusion is Effective[127]

There is no rule which prevents the exclusion of liability for negligence. However, the words used must be clear.[128]

---

123 (1983) 29 FLR 71.

124 [1999] 2 All ER (Comm) 544.

125 [2012] FJSC 10, [19].

126 Unreported, Court of Appeal, Fiji, Gould VP, Spring and Henry JJA, 12 July 1979.

127 See dicta in *Betham Brothers Enterprises Ltd v Big Save Timbers Ltd* [1994] WSSC 8, 12. See also *BHP Petroleum Ltd v British Steel plc* [1999] 2 All ER (Comm) 544.

128 See also *Gillespie Bros & Co Ltd v Roy Bowles Ltd* [1973] 1 QB 400.

3.2.2.2. Negligence may be Excluded if it is the Only Cause of Action

Where the only possible cause of action against the defendant is an action for damages in negligence, then the court will interpret a 'wide' clause to cover the defendant's liability for negligence.

In *Burns Philp (South Seas) Co v Marine Pacific*, Gould VP said:[129]

> [T]he parties thought fit to add a further exclusion, by words 'without responsibility for loss or damage however caused'. The addition advantaged the respondent little if it did not extend to negligence. I think a further guide to the intention of the parties emerges from this consideration.

Gould VP referred to *Alderslade v Hendon Laundry.*[130] In that case, the plaintiff sent items to the laundry which were not returned. The contract contained a clause restricting recovery for lost items to 20 times the laundering charge. Since the laundry's only liability for lost items was in negligence, the limitation clause was meaningless unless taken as applying to such liability, and so the court found that the defendant was able to rely on it.

3.2.2.3. Where there are Other Causes of Action Negligence will not be Excluded

Where the claim may be based on some ground other than negligence, a 'wide' clause must be confined to the heads other than negligence.

In *Hollier v Rambler Motors (AMC) Ltd*,[131] the plaintiff agreed with the manager of the defendant's garage that his car should be towed to the garage for repair. While at the garage, the car was damaged by fire as a result of the defendant's negligence. The defendant argued that the transaction was subject to its usual terms, which included a term that the company was 'not responsible for damage caused by fire to customers' cars on the premises'. The defendant argued that in the circumstances the only way in which it could be liable for damage by fire was if they were negligent and that the words were therefore appropriate to exclude liability for negligence. The Court of Appeal held that, even if the exclusion clause were incorporated into the contract, it would not operate to provide a defence. The clause could be read by a reasonable customer as a warning that the defendant would not be responsible for a fire caused without negligence. It was not therefore sufficiently unambiguous to exclude liability for damage caused by negligence.

---

129 Unreported, Court of Appeal, Fiji, Gould VP, Spring and Henry JJA, 12 July 1979, 411.

130 [1945] 1 KB 189.

131 [1972] 2 WLR 401.

Similarly, in *White v John Warwick & Co Ltd*,[132] the plaintiff hired a bike from the defendants under a contract which provided that 'nothing in this agreement shall render the owners liable for any personal injury'. The saddle tilted forward while the plaintiff was riding the bike, and he suffered injuries. The court held that the words used were sufficient to exclude strict liability in contract for hiring a defective bicycle, but not their tortious liability, if any, for negligence.

3.2.2.4. Exclusion Must be Fair and Reasonable

A party will only be allowed to rely on an exemption clause if it is fair and reasonable to allow this. Factors influencing this will include whether it is in standard form, whether there was equality of bargaining power, and the nature of the breach.

As far as this last rule is concerned, *Burns Philp (South Seas) Co v Marine Pacific* is of doubtful authority. The Fiji Court followed the Court of Appeal's decision in *Photo Production Ltd v Securicor Transport Ltd.*[133] However, that case went on appeal to the House of Lords, where it was confirmed that there is no common law power entitling the courts to refuse to apply a valid and applicable exemption clause merely because it is unreasonable. Further, in a later decision, the Court of Appeal of Fiji held that if the terms of the contract are stipulated, the court cannot embark on an inquiry as to whether those terms are fair.[134] In England, the Unfair Contract Terms Act 1977, which is discussed below in section 3.3.1, provides statutory power to defeat an unfair exemption clause.

3.2.3. The Repugnancy or Total Non-Performance Rule

At one time it was thought that there was an absolute rule prohibiting an exemption clause being used to avoid liability for fundamental breach (that is, failure to perform a primary obligation, depriving the other party of the main benefit of the contract). However, in *Suisse Atlantique Societe D'Armament Maritime v Rotterdamsche Kolen Centrale*,[135] the House of Lords made it clear that the rule that a party should not be deprived of the main purpose of the contract was only a rule of construction. There is nothing to prevent exclusion of the main purpose of the contract, provided the exemption clause is sufficiently wide and clear.

Suisse Atlantique was re-affirmed in *Photo Production Ltd v Securicor Transport Ltd.*[136] In that case, the defendant contracted to provide security for

---

132 [1953] 1 WLR 1285.
133 [1978] 3 All ER 146, 153.
134 *Naidu v Singh* (unreported, Court of Appeal, Fiji, Speight P, Mishra and Barker JJA, 27 July 1984).
135 [1967] 1 AC 361.
136 [1980] 1 All ER 556.

the plaintiff. The contract excluded liability for acts of employees, unless those acts could have been prevented by due diligence on the part of the defendant. It also exempted liability for loss caused by fire. The defendant's duty patrolman deliberately started a fire, and it caused extensive damage. The House of Lords held that the rules governing construction of an exemption cause seeking to exclude liability for serious or 'fundamental' breach were no different from the rules governing other exemption clauses. In this case, the defendant had made it clear that it did not accept this kind of risk and therefore it was not liable.

In *Burns Philp (South Seas) Co v Marine Pacific*,[137] it was accepted, obiter, that establishment of a fundamental breach would negate an exclusion clause. However, this case precedes *Photo Production Ltd v Securicor Transport Ltd*[138] and it can be assumed that this view is no longer current in Fiji or the rest of the region.

The rule that courts will lean against giving effect to an exclusion clause which excludes liability for carrying out the main undertaking of the contract is illustrated by *Sze Hai Tong Bank Ltd v Rambler Cycle Co Ltd.*[139] In that case, the defendant contracted to deliver bikes to sub-purchasers in Singapore, on production of the correct documentation. The defendant released the bikes without production of the correct documentation, as a result of which the plaintiff was not paid. The plaintiff's contract with the defendant provided that the defendant's responsibility would 'cease absolutely' once the goods were discharged from the ship. The defendants were held not to be exempt from liability because, in the absence of express words, they could not exclude liability for performing the main obligation under the contract, the delivery of goods to the person specified.

3.3. STATUTORY REGULATION OF EXEMPTION CLAUSES

As mentioned above, there is no power at common law to refuse to apply an exemption clause merely because it is unreasonable.[140] However, there is statutory power to do this in some countries of the region.

3.3.1. *The Unfair Contract Terms Act 1977 (UK)*

The most far-reaching legislation is the Unfair Contract Terms Act (UK) and Regulations passed under it in 1999.[141] This Act formerly applied in Tonga, as an

137 Unreported, Court of Appeal, Fiji, Gould VP, Spring and Henry JJA, 12 July 1979, where it was accepted, obiter, that establishment of a fundamental breach would negate an exclusion clause. Cf. *Photo Production Ltd v Securicor Transport Ltd* [1980] 1 All ER 556.

138 [1980] 1 All ER 556.

139 [1959] AC 576.

140 *Photo Production Ltd v Securicor Transport Ltd* [1980] 1 All ER 556.

141 Unfair Terms in Consumer Contracts Regulations 1999 (SI 1999/2083 (UK)).

Act of general application, but is no longer in force. The Unfair Contract Terms Act limits, and in some cases removes, the right to rely on exemption clauses in certain business transactions.[142] The Act mainly protects a person dealing as a consumer. The Act and Regulations are discussed below, as they provide a useful starting point for the consideration of regional reform.

3.3.1.1. Clauses which are Void

Clauses or notices excluding or restricting liability for the following conduct are void:

- negligence causing death or personal injury;[143]
- negligence causing defects in goods which results in loss or damage, in the case of manufacturer's guarantees;[144]
- breach of seller's implied undertaking as to title in contracts for the sale of goods[145] or hire purchase;[146]
- breach of seller's implied undertakings as to conformity of goods with description or sample or as to quality or fitness in contracts for the sale of goods[147] or hire purchase;[148]
- breach of seller's implied undertakings as to title[149] and as to conformity of goods with description or sample or as to quality or fitness in consumer contracts not covered by the preceding paragraph, for example contracts of hire.[150]

3.3.1.2. Clauses which are Valid Only if they are Reasonable

Clauses or notices excluding or restricting liability for the following conduct will only be upheld if they are reasonable:

- negligence causing loss or damage to property;
- breach of contract in a consumer or standard form contract;

---

142 It also prevents exclusion of implied terms in sale of goods and hire purchase agreements, whether or not the transaction is in the course of business: Unfair Contract Terms Act 1977 (UK), s 6.

143 Unfair Contract Terms Act 1977 (UK), s 2.

144 Ibid., s 5.

145 Ibid., s 6(1)(a).

146 Ibid., s 6(1)(b).

147 Ibid., s 6(2)(a).

148 Ibid., s 6(2)(b).

149 Ibid., s 7(3A).

150 Being those contracts covered by the Supply of Goods and Services Act 1982 (UK): ibid., s 7(2).

- failure to perform at all or rendering substantially different performance from that reasonably expected;
- breach of seller's implied undertaking as to title in contracts other than contracts for the sale of goods or hire purchase, for example contracts of hire, where the claimant is not a consumer;[151]
- breach of seller's implied undertakings as to conformity of goods with description or sample or as to quality or fitness in contracts for the sale of goods or hire purchase, where the claimant is not a consumer;[152]
- breach of seller's implied undertakings as to conformity of goods with description or sample or as to quality or fitness in contracts not covered by the preceding paragraph, for example contracts of hire, where the claimant is not a consumer;[153]
- misrepresentation.[154]

3.3.1.3. Reasonableness

Reasonableness[155] is defined in s 11(1) of the Unfair Contract Terms Act:

> In relation to a contract term, the requirement of reasonableness for the purpose of this Act ... is that the term shall have been a fair and reasonable one to be included having regard to the circumstances which were, or ought reasonably to have been known to or in the contemplation of the parties when the contract was made.

Further assistance in deciding whether a clause is reasonable can be found in s 11(4), which provides that, in determining whether the term or notice satisfies the requirement of reasonableness, regard shall be had to:

(a) the resources which an individual could expect to be available to him for the purpose of meeting the liability should it arise; and
(b) how far it was open to him to cover himself by insurance and the respective bargaining power of the parties.

The onus of proof is on the person seeking to uphold the clause.[156]

---

151 Ibid., s 7(4).
152 Ibid., s 6(3).
153 Ibid., s 7(3).
154 Ibid., s 8.
155 See e.g. *British Fermentation Products Ltd v Compair Reavell Ltd* [1999] 2 All ER (Comm) 389 for a recent example of a case where the statutory test of reasonableness was satisfied. Compare *Sovereign Finance Ltd v Silver Crest Furniture Ltd* [1998] CLY 852, where a clause was held to be unenforceable as it purported to exclude all liability.
156 Unfair Contract Terms Act 1977 (UK), s 11(5).

In *Phillips Products v Hyland*,[157] the court was called on to decide whether an exclusion clause in a hire contract was unreasonable. The plaintiff hired an excavator and a driver from the defendant. The driver negligently drove into the plaintiff's building causing damage. The plaintiff sued. The hire contract provided that responsibility for any damage caused by the driver should lie with the plaintiff. The defendants argued that the clause was not an exclusion clause (but rather that it defined a duty) and therefore did not fall within the Act. They also argued that even if the clause was governed by the Act, it was a reasonable clause. The Court of Appeal held that the clause was covered by the Act and that it was unreasonable and therefore void. The court looked at the factors in s 11 and, in particular, noted that the plaintiff only hired excavators occasionally and for short periods, whereas it was the defendants' main business. Accordingly, the defendants were in the best position to assess the risk and provide themselves with appropriate insurance cover.

3.3.1.4. Contracts Outside the Act

Some important classes of contracts are specifically excluded from the Act. These include contracts of insurance,[158] contracts of employment (except in favour of an employee),[159] and contracts for the international supply of goods.[160] In general, the Act does not apply to contracts of marine salvage or towage, commercial charter parties,[161] or to contracts of the carriage of goods by sea.[162] Any part of a contract relating to the creation or transfer of an interest in land[163] or intellectual property,[164] or the creation or transfer of securities[165] is also exempt.

3.3.2. *The Unfair Terms in Consumer Contracts Regulations 1999*

In 1999, the Unfair Contract Terms Act was supplemented by the Unfair Terms in Consumer Contracts Regulations 1999,[166] which are based on a European Union Directive.[167] The main provisions of the Regulations have been summarised below, as they may provide a starting point for reform in regional counties.

---

157 [1987] 1 WLR 659. See also *Smith v Bush* [1989] 2 All ER 514 and *George Mitchell (Chesterhall) Ltd v Finney Lock Seeds Ltd* [1983] 2 AC 803 for discussion of the matters to be taken into account in considering whether a clause is reasonable.
158 Unfair Contract Terms Act 1977 (UK), Sch. 1, para. 1(a).
159 Ibid., Sch. 1, para. 4.
160 Ibid., s 26.
161 Ibid., Sch. 1, para. 2.
162 Ibid., Sch. 1, para. 3.
163 Ibid., Sch. 1, para. 1(b).
164 Ibid., Sch. 1, para. 1(c).
165 Ibid., Sch. 1, para. 1(d).
166 SI 1999/2083.
167 Council Directive 93/13/EEC on unfair terms in consumer contracts [1993] OJ L95/29.

3.3.2.1. Unfair Terms

The Regulations make provision for dealing with terms contained in standard form contracts or which form part of such a contract in the following way.

1. A contractual term in a consumer contract, which has not been individually negotiated will be regarded as unfair if it causes a significant imbalance in the parties' rights and obligations arising under the contract, to the detriment of the consumer.[168]
2. Terms in standard pre-printed forms will not be regarded as individually negotiated as the consumer will not have had an opportunity to negotiate those terms.[169]
3. Even if a specific term or certain parts of a contract have been individually negotiated, the Regulations apply to the rest of a contract if, looked at as a whole, it is a standard pre-printed contract.[170]
4. The burden of proof in establishing that a term was individually negotiated is on the seller or supplier who makes that claim.[171]
5. Schedule 2 to the Regulations contains a list of the types of terms which will be regarded as unfair, but it is not exhaustive.[172]

3.3.2.2. Assessment of Unfair Terms

Unfairness is assessed in the context of the contract as a whole, taking into account the nature of the goods or services concerned and all the surrounding circumstances. Provided that the terms are readily intelligible, the definition of the main subject matter of the contract and the adequacy of the price will not be assessed for fairness.[173]

3.3.2.3. Written Contracts

The Regulations also put the onus on sellers and suppliers to ensure that any written contract terms are in intelligible language. In case of doubt, the meaning most favourable to the consumer will prevail.[174]

---

168 European Economic Agreement [1992] OJ L1/3; Unfair Terms in Consumer Contracts Regulations 1999 (SI 1999/2083), reg. 5(1).
169 Unfair Terms in Consumer Contracts Regulations 1999 (SI 1999/2083), reg. 5(2).
170 Ibid., reg. 5(3).
171 Ibid., reg. 5(4).
172 Ibid., reg. 5(5).
173 Ibid., reg. 6.
174 Ibid., reg. 7.

3.3.2.4. Effect of Unfair Terms

Unfair terms in consumer contracts are not binding on the consumer. The rest of the contract will be enforceable if the offending term is severable.[175]

3.3.2.5. Consideration of Complaints by the Director General of Fair Trading

The Regulations provide for complaints about unfair contract terms to be considered by the Director General of Fair Trading or by a qualifying body (statutory regulators, trading standards departments and consumers' associations). If they are of the view that the term is unfair, they may apply for an injunction to prevent the continued use of the unfair term.

3.3.3. Regional Legislation and the Sale of Goods Act (UK)

As mentioned above, the Unfair Contract Terms Act (UK) does not apply in the region. Whilst none of the regional countries have made such extensive provision as the 1977 Act and Regulations, there is some relevant legislation applying in the region which limits the effect of exclusion clauses in sale of goods contracts, consumer transactions and hire purchase contracts. This is discussed below in relation to implied terms.

4. IMPLIED TERMS

4.1. INTRODUCTION

In addition to the terms of a contract upon which the parties expressly agree, there are a number of circumstances in which a term may be implied into a contract.[176] In *Digicel (Fiji) v Fiji Rugby Union*,[177] it was said that it 'is trite law that terms may be implied into contracts through statutes or by courts'. The circumstances in which the common law will imply terms are limited, because the courts take the view that it is not their task to make contracts for the parties concerned, but only to interpret contracts already made. Accordingly, in *GK Enterprises Ltd v Korean Enterprises Ltd*,[178] the Court of Appeal stated that a term could not be implied into a transaction were the parties were not at one over the subject matter of the agreement.

175 Ibid., reg. 8.
176 It is not open to a party to allege that a term is express and implied as it cannot be both: *Mudaliar v Gibson* (1987) FLR 56.
177 [2016] FJSC 40, [73].
178 [2016] SBCA 2, [15].

The position regarding implying terms into concluded contracts was explained by Marsack VP in *Lee v Mitlal*:[179]

> [T]he Court is not entitled to read into the agreement any clause which is not there, which is not expressed or which does not logically and inevitably follow from the wording of the agreement itself. As is said by Lord Esher in Hamlyn v Wood [1891] 2 QBD 488 at 491: 'I have for a long time understood that rule to be that the court has no right to imply in a written contract any such stipulation, unless, on considering the terms of the contract in a reasonable and business manner, an implication necessarily arises that the parties must have intended that the suggested stipulation should exist. It is not enough to say that it would be a reasonable thing to make such an implication. It must be a necessary implication in the sense that I have mentioned.'

A term cannot be implied if this is inconsistent with the express terms of a written contract. Thus, in *Keil v Polynesian Airlines Ltd*,[180] it was held that a term preserving the right to make a claim by way of grievance and the further right of appeal could not be implied as this would be contrary to express provisions in the contract as to termination. In Australia, it has been made clear that the rule prohibiting implied terms that are inconsistent with express terms must not be taken too literally; the mere fact that the contract provides for matters related to the point sought to be covered by the implied term need not prevent its implication.[181] As mentioned above, a term cannot be implied if it appears on the face of the document that the parties deliberately rejected it or deliberately abstained from dealing with it.[182]

Terms may be implied by the common law or by statute. These two situations will now be discussed in more detail.

4.2. TERMS IMPLIED BY COMMON LAW

Generally, the intention of the parties is the dominant consideration in deciding whether a term is implied at common law.[183] The courts will normally imply a term only if they are convinced that this is what the parties intended. In *BP Refinery (Westernport) Pty Ltd v Shire of Hastings*,[184] it was held that

> for a term to be implied, the following conditions (which may overlap) must be satisfied: (1) it must be reasonable and equitable; (2) it must be necessary to give

---

179 (1966) 12 FLR 4, 20.

180 [1980–93] WSLR 222.

181 *BP Refinery (Westernport) Pty Ltd v Shire of Hastings* (1977) 52 ALJR 20.

182 *Maritime National Fish Ltd v Ocean Trawlers Ltd* [1935] AC 524.

183 See e.g. *Ponape Transfer & Storage Inc v Wade* (1992) 5 FSM Interm 354 (Pon. 1992).

184 (1977) 180 CLR 266 (PC). Approved in *Marks and Spencer plc v BNP Paribas* [2016] AC 742, [18].

business efficacy to the contract, so that no term will be implied if the contract is effective without it; (3) it must be so obvious that 'it goes without saying'; (4) it must be capable of clear expression; (5) it must not contradict any express term of the contract.

This decision was cited with approval in *Fai Insurance (Fiji) v Prasad's Nationwide Transport Express Courier Ltd.*[185] In that case, the respondent insured a truck which it had leased from the bank with the appellant. The vehicle was damaged and the respondent claimed on the policy. Nearly 12 months after the accident, the appellant had still not repaired or re-instated the vehicle or paid the respondent money for it, at which point it was seized by the bank. The respondent sued the appellant for breach of contract in that the repairs were not carried out within a reasonable time. There was no express term in the policy that provided that the appellant had to perform its obligations of repair, replacement or payment within a reasonable time. However, the court found that such a term satisfied the five tests in *BP Refinery (Westernport)*, and could be implied because if 'an insurer could delay repairing or replacing a damaged vehicle indefinitely its obligations under the Policy would have no value'.[186]

The five principles were also applied by the Court of Appeal of Kiribati in *Metutera v Kiribati Shipping Services Ltd.*[187] The plaintiff was the master of a ship owned by the defendant. Mechanical problems prevented the ship from sailing and the board of the defendant company held the plaintiff responsible and dismissed him without notice. The plaintiff sued for wrongful dismissal, contending on appeal that there was an implied term in his employment contract that he would be given notice and a reasonable hearing before dismissal. Applying the *BP Refinery* principles, the court held that there could be no doubt that the term was reasonable, went without saying, was capable of clear expression, and did not contradict any express term. It was also necessary for business efficacy because the other terms of service in the contract could not operate reasonably and effectively without the implied term.

In certain classes of contract, terms may be implied because that is what is commonly intended in such contracts, rather than because it was the actual intention of the particular parties. In that case, the term is implied as a matter of law.

---

185 [2008] FJCA 101, [26]. Approved in *Fiji Longshoremen and Staff Association v Fiji Ports Corporation Ltd* [2013] FJET 2.

186 [2008] FJCA 101, [29].

187 [2007] KICA 16.

4.2.1. By Custom or Usage

The court may allow terms prevailing in the trade or locality in question to be implied into a contract, provided that:

1. *No contrary intention is shown.*[188]
   If the custom or trade is inconsistent with an express term of the contract it will not be implied.
2. *The custom must be notorious.*[189]
   The custom must be so well known that everyone contracting in the subject matter must be taken to have intended it to apply by not expressly excluding it.
3. *The custom must be certain and reasonable.*

An example of a term implied by custom is *Vaioleti v Cross.*[190] In that case, the defendant advertised a prize draw for which only its employees who were not late or absent during a specified period were eligible for entry. The plaintiff went to work every day but one during the specified period, and on that day she arranged for a replacement to do her shift for her. Further, in the week of her absence the plaintiff did extra shifts herself, completing 44–48 hours altogether, whereas one shift each day, as required to qualify for the draw, would only have totalled 40 hours. The draw was cancelled by the Board on the basis that none of its employees had qualified. It was held that the plaintiff qualified for the draw and judgment was given in her favour. The express terms of the unilateral contract, contained in the advertisement of the draw, were intended to be supplemented by terms implied from known custom and usage (in this case, the usage of allowing an employee to arrange a stand-in to replace them during a shift).

Similarly, in the English case of *Hutton v Warren*,[191] the plaintiff had been given notice to quit a farm, which he occupied as a tenant. He claimed that tenant farmers could take advantage of a local custom that an outgoing tenant was entitled to reasonable reimbursement for seed and labour expended on the land even though the lease did not mention this. It was held that the local custom was be implied into the lease and the plaintiff was entitled to reimbursement.

In *R v Apia Stevedoring Co Ltd*,[192] the court refused to imply a term that strict liability would not be enforced in a lighterage[193] contract on the basis of local

---

188 *R v Apia Stevedoring Co Ltd* [1950–69] WSLR 117.

189 Ibid.

190 [1990] TLR 108. See further in relation to terms implied in raffles *Kimbe International Primary School v Narpal* [1987] PNGLR 442.

191 [1836] 150 ER 517.

192 [1950–69] WSLR 117.

193 A contract to transport goods between the wharf and ships.

custom and usage. The defendant failed to discharge the burden of proving it was longstanding and notorious.

In *British Crane Hire Corporation Ltd v Ipswich Pant Hire Ltd*,[194] both parties were companies engaged in the business of hiring out earth-moving equipment. The defendant hired a crane from the plaintiff but did not receive the printed form containing the terms of hire until after the contract was made. The terms were based on a model supplied by a trade association to which both parties belonged and were well known in the trade. It was held that the terms were incorporated into the contract on the basis of the common understanding of the parties that any contract would be on the standard terms of the trade.

4.2.2. To Give Business Efficacy

If the parties, through forgetfulness or bad drafting, fail to incorporate a term which they would certainly have included if they had thought about it, the court may be prepared to write it in in order to give business efficacy to the contract. Here the courts are said to be implying a term as a matter of fact.

In *The Moorcock*,[195] the court laid down a test for a term to be implied, based on necessity. In that case, the defendants contracted to allow the plaintiff to use their wharf to load and discharge his ship, and the plaintiff was to pay the defendant for the hire of cranes and other facilities at the wharf. Whilst unloading at low tide, the ship came to rest on a hard ridge of ground beneath the mud and sustained damage. The plaintiff sued. It was held that the plaintiff could recover as the parties must have intended to contract on the basis that the berth was reasonably safe for the purpose of loading and unloading.

This case was approved in Fiji in *Chase Corporation Fiji Ltd v Minister for Works and Energy*,[196] where the Fiji High Court found that a contract between the plaintiff and the defendant for the hire of excavators included certain terms, for example to return the excavators in the same condition, and to pay for hours even if the machinery was not in use. These were implied in order to give business efficacy to the contract.

Another regional example is *Philipp v LT Endermann & Co Ltd*.[197] In that case, the plaintiff signed a construction contract with the defendants, who purported to be acting on behalf of Samo Handcraft Incorporated. After the first progress payment, the defendants failed to pay anything more. It transpired that the company had not been incorporated. It was held that there was an implied warranty in the contract that if the company did not exist the defendants would be personally liable.

---

194 [1975] QB 303 (CA).
195 (1889) 14 PD 64.
196 [2012] FJHC 1319.
197 [1950–69] WSLR 539.

4.2.3. *On the Basis of Obvious Intention*

An alternative approach to the 'business efficacy' test is what has become known as the 'officious bystander' test. In *Shirlaw v Southern Foundries*,[198] MacKinnon LJ said:

> Prima facie that which in any contract is left to be implied and need not be expressed is something so obvious that it goes without saying; so that, if while one of the parties were making their bargain, an officious bystander were to suggest some express provision for it in the agreement, they would testily suppress him with a common, 'oh, of course'.

According to the 'officious bystander' test, a term will only be implied if it is so obvious that it goes without saying. In that case a company managing director was appointed for 10 years. When facing dismissal, he sought to say that the contract implied: first that the company would not remove him during that time, and second that the Articles of Association would not be altered to enable him to be removed. The court took the view that the former could be implied, but that the latter could not.

This officious bystander test was applied in *CP Homes Ltd v Ali*.[199] In that case, the written contract between the parties came to an end. The defendant continued to use one of the bulldozers hired under the agreement and Palmer J found from the conduct of the parties an intention to continue its existence. No hire fee was specified and Palmer J noted that it was 'not for the court to impose any new term, or even consider what is reasonable'. However, he took it to be implied as a matter of 'business efficacy' that the rate previously agreed was to apply, as he regarded this as 'so obvious that it goes without saying'.

There is a large overlap between the business efficacy test and the officious bystander test. A term may be implied under either head if there would be no point in entering into the contract without it or if it can be shown to go the essence of the contract. On this basis, the Fiji Court of Appeal implied a term that goods stored would be kept continuously refrigerated into a contract of refrigeration storage.[200] The tests were dealt with together in the Samoan case of *Keil v Polynesian Airlines Ltd*,[201] where Bathgate J said that 'terms may be implied to carry out the obvious and unexpressed intention of the parties, by necessary implication, or to give business efficacy to a contract'. He went on to run the tests together by the use the term 'obvious necessity' to describe the test

---

198 [1939] 2 KB 206, 227.

199 [1995] SBHC 115.

200 *Ram Padarath Brothers Ltd v National Marketing Authority* (unreported, Court of Appeal, Fiji, Helsham P, Tikaram and Kapi JJA, 1 July 1992).

201 [1980–93] WSLR 222, 232–33.

for implying a term into a contract. His Lordship gave the example of a term that neither party will prevent the other from performing the contract as one that would normally be implied on this ground.

Obviously there is a fine line between an agreement which is uncertain and an agreement where the court will be prepared to give effect to a document by implying a term. *Sidha v Dairaj*[202] is an example of a case where one term was read in, thus saving the agreement from uncertainty, but another, which would have allowed the defendants to escape liability, was held not to be implied. The facts were that the appellants covenanted by deed to maintain the respondent, their widowed sister-in-law, until her death or remarriage, whichever should occur first. At the time when the deed was executed the respondent was living in the family home. She left because she was treated so badly. The deed made no mention of the level or place of maintenance. It was held to be the clear intention of the parties that the respondent should be maintained in 'a reasonable manner according to her station in life'. Accordingly, that term was implied. However, the court refused to imply a term that she was bound to remain in the family home, and that she would only be maintained whilst she was there, as this was not a clear intention.

4.2.4. Into Contracts of a Particular Class

In certain classes of contracts, implied terms have become standardised, and they will be implied automatically by the courts in the absence of contrary intention. Here the courts are said to be implying a term as a matter of law as opposed to fact. The court is not saying that the parties intended these terms, but that in this type of contract such a term was so common as to have become implied by law.

One exception is that an oral agreement between landlord and tenant whereby the tenant pays rent in exchange for exclusive occupation is deemed to be a periodic tenancy, the period being equal to the period for which rent is payable.[203]

Terms are also routinely implied in contracts between employer and employee. An example can be seen in *Banque Indosuez Vanuatu Ltd v Ferrieux*,[204] where the court implied a term that the employer would not conduct itself in a manner calculated to damage or destroy the relationship of confidence and trust between the contracting parties.[205] In *Leiola Group Ltd v Moengangongo*,[206] whilst ultimately deciding on the circumstances of the case and the written

---

202 [1962] 8 FLR 91.

203 See *Taba'a v Hyundai Timber Company Ltd* [1997] SBHC 3, 5. This principle is also embodied in statute, see Land and Titles Act Cap 133, s 145.

204 (1989–94) 2 VLR 490.

205 See also *Helu v Koloa* [2000] Tonga LR 299.

206 [2010] TOCA 10.

terms of employment that there was no implied term for reasonable notice, the court expressly noted that the common law in Tonga would 'ordinarily imply a term into contracts of employment that the employer can dismiss an employee by giving the employee reasonable notice'.

However, in *Brighouse v National Bank of Samoa*,[207] the Supreme Court of Samoa refused to follow New Zealand authorities implying extensive terms into employment contracts, as the Court considered the employment environment in that country to be very different from Samoa's. In this case, the plaintiff sued for wrongful dismissal and relied on implied terms, including a duty to maintain trust and confidence and to act reasonably and fairly, which he contended were part of his contract of employment. The Court followed the decision of the Court of Appeal in *Keil v Polynesian Airlines Ltd*,[208] where it was held that a term would not be implied into an employment contract if the contract was effective or made good sense without it. On this basis, it was held that none of the proposed terms could be applied.

Terms are implied into contracts for the sale of goods, management agreements,[209] and contracts for the supply of labour and materials. An example of terms implied into contracts for the sale of goods can be seen in *Hoteshwarlal v SE Tathem (Fiji) Ltd*.[210] It was held to be an implied condition of *fob* contracts for perishable goods that the goods were of merchantable quality and that they were able to endure the normal journey and be in reasonable condition on arrival.

In contracts where money is paid in instalments, in the absence of agreement to the contrary, there is an implied term that money received will be applied first to the oldest debt.[211]

Where a contract is signed on behalf of a company, the law does not imply a term that the signatory agrees to be personally liable. But such a term could be implied as a matter of fact from the conduct of a party.[212]

4.2.5. From a Previous Consistent Course of Dealing

As discussed in chapter 4, the courts have been prepared to save an agreement from failing on the grounds of uncertainty if the parties' intention can be ascertained from their previous dealings. For example, in *Hillas & Co Ltd v Arcos Ltd*,[213] the plaintiff agreed to buy from the defendant '22,000 standards of softwood goods of fair specification over the season 1930'. The written agreement

---

207 [2004] WSSC 1.
208 [1980–93] WSLR 395, 398–99.
209 *AG Smyth and Company Ltd v Namai Fa'apu'u* [1950–59] WSLR 137.
210 (1973) 19 FLR 33.
211 *Kulamma v Manadan* (1964) 10 FLR 252. See also *Bishop of Melanesia v Maile* (1973) 19 FLR 49.
212 *Philipp v LT Endermann & Company Ltd* [1980–93] WSLR 539.
213 (1932) 147 LT 503.

contained an option to buy 100,000 standards in 1931, but without particulars as to the kind or size of timber or the manner of shipment. No difficulties arose on the original purchase for 1930, but when the buyers sought to enforce the option for 1931, the defendant alleged that the terms had yet to be agreed and that the provision was only a basis for future agreement. The House of Lords held that the language used, interpreted in light of the previous course of dealing between the parties, showed a sufficient intention to be bound.

This approach extends to exemption clauses. For example, in *Henry Kendall & Sons v William Lillico & Sons Ltd*,[214] a poultry producers' association, SAPPA, bought contaminated food from the defendant under an oral contract evidenced by a later written note, referred to as a 'sold note'. The sold note expressly stated that 'the buyer takes the responsibility of any latent defects'. The defendant argued that, even though the sold note was submitted too late to form part of the express terms of the contract, the exemption clause it contained was incorporated through the parties' prior course of dealings. The prior dealings had taken place three to four times per month for the previous three years and, in each case, there had been an oral contract followed immediately by a written sold note. The notes had all contained the standard clause. It was held that even though SAPPA had never actually read any of the sold notes, it knew that the clauses existed and that the defendant always dealt on the basis that the clauses applied. Therefore, the clause was implied into the present sale agreement through the past course of dealing.

4.3. TERMS IMPLIED BY STATUTE

In addition to terms implied by common law, terms are sometimes implied by statute. In some cases, terms implied by statute may be expressly excluded by the parties, but in others they may not.

Generally statutory terms are implied to protect the consumer where there is unequal bargaining power to make freedom of contract a reality. The region has been slow to provide such protection by legislation. Fiji, Marshall Islands and Samoa are the only countries that have their own Sale of Goods Acts, which provide some protection against bad bargains in sale of goods contracts. In Tokelau, the Contract Rules 2004 govern sale of goods contracts. Fiji passed the Fair Trading Decree in 1992 to provide protection against unfair exemption clauses, which was repealed and substantially re-enacted in the Commerce Commission Decree 2010 (Fiji). In Kiribati, the Consumer Protection Act 2001, as amended by the Consumer Protection (Amendment) Act 2009, implies certain terms into consumer contracts. In some other Pacific countries, the English Sale of Goods Act applies. The main legislation on implied terms applying in the region is outlined below.

[214] [1969] 2 AC 31.

4.3.1. *Sale of Goods*

As discussed earlier in this chapter, the Sale of Goods Acts applying in the region imply certain terms into contracts to protect purchasers of goods. These conditions and warranties were originally implied by the common law, but were given statutory force by ss 12–15 of the English Sale of Goods Act 1893.

In Fiji, the Sale of Goods Act[215] only extends to 'goods' and does not regulate terms in contracts dealing with land or interests in land, such as leases. The Act implies the following terms into a contract for the sale of goods:

- that the seller has the right to sell (s 14);
- that goods sold by description will correspond with the description (s 15);
- in a sale by sample, that the goods will correspond with the sample (s 17).

Where goods are sold in the course of business, the following terms are also implied:

- that the goods are of merchantable quality (s 16(2));
- that the goods are fit for the purpose for which the buyer has indicated they are being bought (s 16(3)).

Section 16(2) does not apply to defects specifically drawn to the buyer's attention, or where the buyer examines the goods, as regards defects which that examination ought to reveal. Section 16(3) does not apply in circumstances where the buyer does not rely on, or it is unreasonable for him to rely on, the seller's skill or judgment.[216]

The Act does not allow parties in a consumer transaction to exclude these implied undertakings, unless it is fair and reasonable.[217] However, a term that goods are sold 'as is where is' may assist a seller to show that the buyer did not rely on the seller's skill or judgment.[218] In other contracts they may not exclude the undertaking as to title, and may only exclude the other undertakings if it is fair and reasonable.[219]

In Marshall Islands, the Sale of Goods Act 1986 also implies terms into sale of goods contracts,[220] but specifically provides that they may be excluded by express agreement. They may also be excluded or varied if there is a course of dealing which makes it clear that the parties did not intend the protective

215 Cap 230.
216 *Uluivutia v Western Wreckers Ltd* [2004] FJHC 330.
217 Sale of Goods Act Cap 230 (Fiji), s 55.
218 See e.g. *Uluivutia v Western Wreckers Ltd* [2004] FJHC 330.
219 Sale of Goods Act Cap 230 (Fiji), s 55.
220 Sale of Goods Act 1986 23 MIRC Cap 1 (Marshall Islands), ss 14–16.

provisions to apply, or if there is a usage to that effect, provided that usage binds both parties to the contract.[221]

The Samoan Sale of Goods Act 1975 implies equivalent protection in ss 13–16. As in Marshall Islands, these implied terms may be excluded or varied by the parties.[222]

In Tokelau, similar protection is provided by Rule 37 of the Contract Rules 2004. As in Marshall Islands and Samoa, the relevant clauses may be excluded.[223]

For countries outside Fiji, Marshall Islands, Samoa and Tokelau, the English Sale of Goods Acts may apply. However, the 1893 Act, which applies in Kiribati, Nauru, Solomon Islands and Tuvalu, does not prevent exclusion of implied terms. This reform was not introduced until 1973, when s 55 was amended by the Supply of Goods (Implied Terms) Act 1973. The 1973 Act appears to apply to contracts governed by English law in Vanuatu.[224] The 1973 reform was carried forward in the Sale of Goods Act 1979 (UK), but this does not apply in the region.[225]

In Cook Islands and Niue, the Sale of Goods Act 1908 of New Zealand applies.[226] Like the Marshall Islands and Samoan Acts, this Act allows the implied protections to be negated or varied.[227]

In Kiribati, the Consumer Protection Act 2001 implies terms into consumer contracts, including an implied warranty in a contract of service that the services will be rendered with due care and skill and that any materials supplied in connection with these services will be reasonably fit for the purpose for which they are supplied.[228] In *Bongia v Manager TTT Enterprises*,[229] the High Court of Kiribati was called on to consider whether there was an implied term that marine plywood purchased by the plaintiff from the defendant was fit for the purpose, as required by the Consumer Protection Act. Two weeks after the plywood had been used to repair the plaintiff's boat, a swollen bulge appeared on the part of the boat where the plywood had been placed and the plaintiff sued for return of the purchase price. The Court found that the marine plywood was fit for purpose and of a merchantable quality as it was the kind normally supplied by the defendant and used by him to build boats.

---

221 Ibid., s 55.

222 Sale of Goods Act 1975 (Samoa), ss 13–16, 54.

223 Contract Rules 2004 (Tokelau), R 5.

224 French law will govern contracts in French and between French parties. See further chapter 1. The 1893 Act has been held to apply: *ANZ v Marchand* [2001] VUCA 2, but there is no authority applying the 1973 Act.

225 The Unfair Contract Terms Act 1977 (UK), s 6, also applies to prevent exclusion of implied protections in Tonga.

226 Cook Islands Act 1915 (NZ), s 638; Niue Act 1966 (NZ).

227 Sale of Goods Act 1908 (NZ), s 56.

228 Consumer Protection Act 2001, s 21.

229 [2015] KIHC 37.

In Fiji, the Commerce Commission Decree 2010 is also relevant. This Decree overlaps with the Sale of Goods Act as it repeats the implied warranties in the Sale of Goods Act. However, the Decree goes further by prohibiting restrictive and unfair trade practices and prescribing penalties for such behaviour. The Decree also prohibits contracting out of the implied protections. This Decree is discussed further in chapter 12.

The sale of goods legislation also implies terms as to price. Where no price is specified, the buyer must pay a reasonable price. What is a reasonable price will depend on the circumstances of the case.[230] The Acts also contain provisions governing the time at which property in goods and the risk passes to the buyer.[231]

4.3.2. *Hire Purchase and Supply of Goods and Services*

The Hire Purchase Act 1986 of Cook Islands implies terms into contracts of hire purchase, where sale is not outright, but goods are hired, with an option to purchase. Terms implied are similar to the terms implied into sale of goods contracts, discussed above.[232] The Act does not allow contracting out.[233] The English Hire Purchase Act 1938 will apply terms into hire purchase contracts in some countries of the region, such as Solomon Islands. However, it only applies to contracts involving an amount below £100.[234] The 1938 Act was repealed by the Hire Purchase Act 1965, which may apply in Nauru.[235] The Supply of Goods (Implied Terms) Act 1973 (UK), which is applicable in Vanuatu, implies the same protective terms as apply in sale of goods contracts to hire purchase contracts.[236]

The Supply of Goods and Services Act 1982 (UK) implies statutory terms into contracts for work and materials, contracts for hire and contracts for the supply of services,[237] but is not applicable in the region.

4.3.3. *Leases*

Legislation in the United Kingdom and throughout the region implies certain obligations into leases; for example, the Land and Titles Act of Solomon Islands implies standard obligations on lessors and lessees.[238] It also deems a person in

---

[230] See e.g. Sale of Goods Act Cap 230 (Fiji), s 10.

[231] See e.g. Sale of Goods Act 1975 (Samoa), ss 18, 21, discussed in *Paulo v Va'atiuola* [2012] WSSC 110.

[232] Hire Purchase Act 1986 (CI), ss 11–14.

[233] Ibid., s 50.

[234] In the case of motor vehicles or railway rolling stock the amount is £100 and in the case of livestock £500.

[235] The Hire Purchase Act 1965 (UK) has been replaced by the Consumer Credit Act 1974.

[236] Supply of Goods (Implied Terms) Act 1973 (UK), ss 8–11.

[237] Supply of Goods and Services Act 1982 (UK), ss 7–10.

[238] Land and Titles Act Cap 93 (SI), ss 147, 148. See *Lee Kwok Kuen v Pongi* [1997] SBHC 4.

exclusive possession paying rent without a written agreement to be in a periodic tenancy.[239]

Similar terms are implied into agricultural leases in Fiji by the Agricultural Landlord and Tenant Act.[240] Section 9(g) also implies terms regarding reassessment of rent. This legislation is capable of overriding express terms to the contrary in the lease. For example, in *Native Land Trust Board v Dass*,[241] the Trust Board granted the respondent a lease for 30 years at a rent to be reassessed after 15 years, but not so as to exceed 6% of the unimproved value. Four years later, legislation was passed providing that every lease of this kind should have its rent reassessed every five years without any stipulated maximum. The Court of Appeal held that this term was implied into the contract, overriding the express terms.

4.4. CARRIAGE OF GOODS BY SEA

At common law, contracts for the carriage of goods by sea contain an implied warranty that the ship will be seaworthy in all respects.[242] The Sea Carriage of Goods Ordinance 1906 encapsulated this implied term in legislation. This implied term was examined in *Hunt v Australasian United Steam Navigation Co Ltd*.[243] The implied warranty of seaworthiness was held not to be limited to mere fitness to encounter sea perils, but to include matters such as the fitness of the machinery controlling the insulating chamber.[244] This legislation has now been repealed and the position is governed by the Sea Carriage of Goods Act.[245] This Act gives effect to the Hague-Visby Rules[246] and replaces the implied warranty of seaworthiness with an implied obligation to exercise due diligence to make the ship seaworthy.[247] In the event of an accident, the onus of proving that this obligation was complied with is on the carrier. Similar legislation containing implied terms is in force in other jurisdictions.[248] In some cases, the carrier is only bound to exercise due diligence to make the ship seaworthy.

---

239 Land and Titles Act Cap 133 (SI), s 145. See *Taba'a v Hyundai Timber Company Ltd* [1997] SBHC 3.

240 Cap 270, ss 9(1)(e), (f).

241 Unreported, Court of Appeal, Fiji, Civ App 30/1981.

242 *Kopitoff v Wilson* (1876) 1 QBD 377.

243 [1919] 2 FLR 72.

244 It was also held that the implied warranty could not be excluded.

245 Cap 231.

246 International Convention for Unification of Certain Rules of Law Relating to Bills of Lading (Hague-Visby Rules, as amended), opened for signature 25 August 1924, TS17 (1931), cmd. 380.

247 Sea Carriage of Goods Act Cap 231 (Fiji), Sch., Art. III, R 1.

248 See e.g. Carriage of Goods by Sea Act Cap 158 (SI), Sch., Art. III, R 1; Carriage of Goods by Sea Act Cap 7 (Kiribati), Sch., Art. III, R 1; Carriage of Goods by Sea Act Cap 141

4.5. DO TERMS IMPLIED BY STATUTE APPLY RETROSPECTIVELY?

Where a statute is amended after the contract is formed to imply terms into a contract or vary terms that are already implied, the question arises whether this will affect a contract that has already been formed. The answer depends to some extent on the wording of the statute and the contract. The question was considered, although not directly answered, in *Public Service Commission v Fukofuka*.[249] In this case, the respondent was appointed as head of a government ministry on 1 January 2007. The contract was varied in 2008 to provide certain additional benefits to the respondent and then extended for a further period ending on 1 January 2012. Clause 21 of the contract stated that the provisions of the Public Service Act 2002 applied to the parties. The Act provided that public servants had to take a leave of absence on registering as a candidate for election to the Legislative Assembly and that they had to resign if elected. In 2010, the Act was amended by the Public Service (Amendment) Act 2010, which replaced this provision with a requirement that public servants had to resign on registering as a candidate for election. The respondent wished to register as a candidate and wrote to the Public Service Commission maintaining that the amending Act did not apply to him because his contract was signed before the Act was amended. He invoked the provisions of the Constitution prohibiting the enactment of retrospective laws and maintained that his position if he registered as a candidate would be governed by the Act as it stood at the time his contract was signed. The Commission replied advising him that it did not agree and that if he proceeded with registration he would be deemed to have resigned from the public service. Notwithstanding, the respondent registered as a candidate. The Commission determined that he was deemed to have resigned and paid him a gratuity payment together with his other entitlements. The respondent was not elected and brought proceedings seeking damages for unlawful termination of his contract. At first instance, the Chief Justice found in favour of the respondent. It was held that because of the necessity for certainty, the terms implied by the Act must be those existing at the time of the contract, which included the rights to take leave of absence on registering as a candidate. His Lordship also referred to clause 20 of the Constitution, which prohibits the enactment of retrospective laws insofar as they curtail rights or privileges existing at the time those laws are passed. On appeal, the Court of Appeal

(Tonga), Sch. I, Art. III, R 1; Carriage of Goods by Sea Act Cap 48.04 (Tuvalu), Sch., Art. III, R 1; Maritime Act Cap 131 (Vanuatu), s 70(1); Carriers Act 1975 (Samoa); Carriage of Goods Act 1940 (NZ), s 3, in force in Cook Islands and Niue. See also Carriage of Goods by Sea Act 1971 (UK).

249 [2014] TOCA 4.

held that clause 21 of the contract was not specific enough to incorporate all the provisions of the legislation as terms of the contract. Rather, the purpose of the clause was just to draw the attention of parties to the contract to statutes and regulations that were relevant to their duties. The Court held there was no question of retrospectivity; the provisions of the new s 20 only affected those registering as a candidate from the time of its enactment and allowed the appeal.

CHAPTER 10
FORMALITIES

1. INTRODUCTION

As a general rule, a simple contract is not required to be made in writing, or to be in any particular form.[1] Contracts under seal, on the other hand, rest on their form. Unlike simple contracts, it is unnecessary to show that a contract under seal is the result of an agreement or that consideration has passed from the promisee.

Whilst simple contracts are not generally required to be in writing, there are some statutory exceptions to this rule. Some simple contracts are required not only to be supported by consideration, but also to be in writing or evidenced in writing. In such cases, the contract will be unenforceable at law, although there may be an avenue for equitable relief, for example if a plea of estoppel is available.[2]

The requirement of writing serves several functions, which can be summarised as follows:

- it encourages serious consideration before contracting;
- it helps to avoid entry into a contract on impulse, by accident or under pressure;
- it assists in rendering the contents of a contract and the fact that a contract exists more certain;[3]
- it serves an evidentiary function, including the prevention of manufactured evidence.

2. CONTRACTS UNDER SEAL

A contract under seal is sometimes referred to as a 'deed'. It is a promise made by written agreement. A deed will be enforceable whether or not consideration

---

1 *Media Enterprises Pty Ltd v Fiji Broadcasting Commission* [1999] FJHC 80; *GMR Muhammed & Sons v Wati* [2014] FJMC 161.

2 See further chapter 6.

3 For a discussion of the history and the policy behind the requirement, see M.P. Furmston, *Cheshire, Fifoot and Furmston's Law of Contract*, 17th ed., Oxford University Press, Oxford 2017, pp. 270–73.

has passed from the promisee. It is usually made by signing in front of a witness or witnesses, who must not be a party to the agreement, and delivering the document to the other party. Traditionally, a seal was required to be attached,[4] but in most jurisdictions this is no longer required. For example, s 4 of the Property Law Act (Fiji)[5] removes the requirement for a seal, except in the case of a company. It also removes the need for delivery, in order for a document to qualify as a deed. All that is required is evidence of intention to execute a deed. Similarly, in Vanuatu, the Law Reform (Contract Law) Act 2009 provides that a deed must be signed by every party to be bound by it and attested by at least one independent witness. It must also be described as a deed or as an agreement under seal.[6] However, it need not be sealed, delivered or indented.[7]

To qualify as a deed under English law, the Law Reform (Miscellaneous Provisions) Act 1989 (UK) provides that the only requirement is that it is clearly intended by the maker or parties to be a deed.[8] The Act does not prescribe how this intention must be manifested, but makes it clear that description as a deed or an appropriately worded execution clause will suffice.[9]

Some statutes require agreements to be in the form of a deed, most commonly those relating to land, as for example under the Property Law Act of Fiji. They may also be required for tax purposes, in the case of gifts to charities. Additionally, they may be employed where a greater sense of formality is regarded as desirable. They are also commonly used in the case of multilateral contracts.

3. CONTRACTS REQUIRED TO BE MADE IN WRITING

Certain contracts are void unless they are made in writing. Some may not only have to be in writing, but be in a specific form. The principal legislation imposing a requirement of writing within the region is discussed below.

3.1. BILLS OF EXCHANGE

Bills of exchange are a form of negotiable instrument. As mentioned in chapter 8, a negotiable instrument is a document containing a promise of payment which, when transferred, passes all right to payment to the transferee, for example a cheque. Bills of exchange are governed by legislation.

4 There was at one time a practice of placing a finger on the seal and saying, 'I deliver this as my act and deed'.
5 Cap 130.
6 Law Reform (Contract Law) Act 2009 (Vanuatu), s 3(1).
7 Ibid., s 3(2).
8 Law Reform (Miscellaneous Provisions) Act 1989 (UK), s 1.
9 Ibid., s 1(2)(a). They are also commonly used in the case of multilateral contracts.

Bills of Exchange Acts have been enacted in Fiji,[10] Tonga[11] and Samoa.[12] These Acts are modelled on the Bills of Exchange Act 1882 (UK), which provides that a bill of exchange or a promissory note[13] and the acceptance of a bill of exchange must be made in writing.[14] This Act applies in Solomon Islands, Kiribati, Tuvalu and Vanuatu. Papua New Guinea has its own Bills of Exchange Act, which requires a bill of exchange to be in writing.[15]

In Cook Islands, Niue and Tokelau, the Bills of Exchange Act 1908 (NZ) applies.[16]

3.2. CONTRACTS OF MARINE INSURANCE

Contracts of marine insurance are void unless made in writing in the form of a policy. Fiji, Samoa and Tonga have their own Marine Insurance Acts, being the Marine Insurance Act (Fiji),[17] the Marine Insurance Act 1975 (Samoa),[18] and the Marine Insurance Act (Tonga).[19]

In Solomon Islands, Kiribati, Tuvalu and Vanuatu, the Marine Insurance Act 1906 (UK) would appear to apply.[20] The Marine Insurance Act 1908 (NZ) applies in Cook Islands,[21] Niue[22] and Tokelau.[23]

3.3. CONSUMER CREDIT

In Fiji, the Consumer Credit Act 1999 provides that a credit contract must be in written form.[24] A credit agreement is defined to include any agreement for the

---

10 Bills of Exchange Act Cap 227 (Fiji), ss 3(1), 17(2).
11 Bills of Exchange Act Cap 108 (Tonga), ss 3(1), 17(2).
12 Bills of Exchange Act 1976 (Samoa), ss 3(1), 17(2).
13 An unconditional promise to pay money, signed by the maker of the note.
14 Bills of Exchange Act 1882 (UK), ss 3(1), 17(2).
15 Bills of Exchange Act Cap 250 (PNG), s 8(1).
16 Bills of Exchange Act 1908 (NZ), ss 3(1), 17(2), applying in Cook Islands (Cook Islands Act 1915, s 625). The Bills of Exchange Amendment Act 1971 also applies in Cook Islands (NZ Laws Act (No. 2) 1973 (CI)) and in Niue (Niue Act 1966 (NZ), s 682). The 1908 Act applies in Niue as amended by the Legislation (Correction of Errors and Minor Amendment) Act 2004 (Niue), s 10, and in Tokelau (Application of New Zealand Laws Rules 2004, R 3(1)(i) and 3(2)(ii)). All amendments would appear to apply as the Rules state that 'Acts passed in substitution will apply': R 3(2)(vii)).
17 Cap 218, s 23.
18 Section 22.
19 Cap 144, s 22.
20 Marine Insurance Act 1906 (UK), s 22.
21 By virtue of Cook Islands Act 1915 (CI), s 631.
22 By virtue of Niue Act 1966 (NZ), s 693.
23 Application of New Zealand Law Rules 2004, R 3(1)(ii), (2)(iii).
24 Consumer Credit Act 1999 (Fiji), s 12. Section 13 provides that regulations may authorise the making of specified credit contracts without a written agreement.

provision of credit, for example a loan agreement or hire purchase agreement. The document must be signed by both parties, or in the case of a written offer of credit, expressed to be capable of acceptance by performance by the debtor, for example by drawing down a loan. It must also be in a specified form and contain specified information.

In Tokelau, the Contract Rules 2004 provide that credit contracts for more than $500 are unenforceable unless they are in writing.[25]

In England and Wales, the relevant legislation is the Consumer Credit Act 1974, s 60. This is capable of applying in Vanuatu but would not appear to be an Act of general application.[26]

3.4. BILLS OF SALE

Bills of sale are documents intending to transfer ownership of chattels[27] without actually parting with possession. Bills of Sale Acts in force within the region provide that a bill of sale must be made in writing and in a certain form.[28]

There are two types of bills of sale:

- a broad category, including all absolute transfers of ownership; and
- a narrower category, applying to goods transferred by way of mortgage. The bill of sale is for the purpose of creating a security with a right of redemption when the money secured is repaid.

The following regional Acts provide that bills falling within the first category are only void as against the trustee in bankruptcy or an execution creditor if not made in the proper form and registered under the Act. Bills falling within the second category are absolutely void if they do not comply with these requirements:

- Bills of Sale Act Cap 225 (Fiji)[29]
- Bills of Sale Ordinance Cap 4 (Kiribati)[30]
- Bills of Sale Act Cap 71 (Solomon Islands)[31]
- Bills of Sale Act Cap 40.04 (Tuvalu)[32]
- Bills of Sale Act Cap 23 (Vanuatu)[33]

---

25 Contract Rules 2004 (Tokelau), R 21(3).
26 See further chapter 1.
27 All property other than freehold land.
28 Bills of Sale Act 1878 (UK), s 9.
29 Section 7.
30 Section 5.
31 Section 6.
32 Section 5.
33 Section 9.

These Acts were modelled on the Bills of Sale Act 1878 (UK), as amended by the Bills of Sale Act Amendment Act 1882 (UK).

In Niue,[34] the Chattels Transfer Act 1924 (NZ) requires documents evidencing transfer of ownership of chattels to be in writing and registered. Failure to register the transfer within the prescribed period renders the transfer void as against the trustee in bankruptcy, an execution creditor or a bona fide purchaser for value. In Cook Islands,[35] the Chattels Transfer Act 1924 has been repealed by the Personal Property Securities Act 2017. In Tokelau, the Chattels Transfer Act 1924 (NZ) may be in force where the Personal Property Securities Act 1999 (NZ) does not apply.[36]

In Papua New Guinea, the position was formerly governed by the Instruments Act.[37] This Act was repealed by the Personal Property Securities Act 2011, which commenced operation in 2016. This provides for 'security interests', including nearly all interests in property other than land, to be registered in order to retain protection against interests acquired by a third party.

3.5. HIRE PURCHASE

The Hire Purchase Act 1986 of Cook Islands requires contracts of hire purchase to be in writing.[38]

In Papua New Guinea, hire purchase agreements are governed by the Personal Property Securities Act 2011. As mentioned above, this provides for 'security interests', including those arising under hire purchase agreements, to be registered in order to retain protection against interests acquired by a third party.

The Hire Purchase Act 1938 (UK), as amended in 1964, requires a hire purchase agreement to be in writing.[39] It is unclear whether this Act qualifies as an Act of general application, thus making it part of the law within some regional countries. The Hire Purchase Act (UK) was repealed by the Consumer Credit Act 1974 (UK).

---

34 Niue Act 1966 (NZ), s 684. The Act applies as amended by the Legislation (Correction of Errors and Minor Amendment) Act 2004 (Niue), s 16.

35 Cook Islands Act 1915 (NZ), s 626.

36 Contract Rules 2004 (Tokelau), R 19; Tokelau (New Zealand Laws) Regulations 1975 (NZ), reg. 3, as amended by the Tokelau Amendment Act 1986 (NZ), s 15. The Chattels Transfer Act applies as amended by the Legislation (Correction of Errors and Minor Amendment) Act 2004 (Tokelau), s 16.

37 Cap 254. See *Morne Industries PNG Ltd v Kina Finance Ltd* [2004] PGNC 40, the first case to consider the effect of the invalidity of bills of sale under the Instruments Act.

38 Section 5. See *Cook Islands Motor Centre Ltd v Mariki Associates Ltd* [1988] CKHC 1. The Hire Purchase Act No. 2 of 2013 (CI) is not yet in force.

39 Section 3(1). Until 1964, only a note or memorandum of the agreement was required in order for the agreement to be enforceable.

4. CONTRACTS TO BE MADE OR EVIDENCED IN WRITING

Under s 4 of the English Statute of Frauds 1677 (Imp), there are several types of agreement that must, at least, be evidenced by a note or memorandum in writing and signed by the person against whom it is sought to enforce the contract. The provisions in the section governing contracts for the sale of interests in land were substantially re-enacted in s 40 of the Law of Property Act 1925 (UK). The categories of contract to which these Acts apply are:

- contracts of guarantee (but not contracts of indemnity);[40]
- contracts for the sale or other disposition of land;
- contracts made in consideration of marriage;
- contracts not to be performed within one year of their making; and
- contracts by an executor or administrator to be responsible for the deceased's debts out of his own money.

The Statute of Frauds and s 40 of the Law of Property Act 1925 (UK) apply in several countries of the region. The Act does not apply in Chuuk State, and this may also be the case in other parts of the Federated States of Micronesia.[41] The Law of Property Act 1925 (UK) was repealed in part by the Law Reform (Enforcement of Contracts) Act 1954 (UK). This abolishes the requirement of evidence in writing in the last three of the five categories of contract mentioned above. The 1954 Act would appear to apply in Solomon Islands,[42] Kiribati and Tuvalu. Accordingly, only contracts of guarantee and contracts for the sale of interests in land are required to be in writing in those countries.

Section 40 of the Law of Property Act, as amended in 1954, also applies to certain dispositions of land in Vanuatu. In *Nutley v Kam*,[43] the owner of land entered into a written agreement to sell it to the plaintiff and a transfer document was executed, following two payments and registration fees. The defendant lodged a caution based on the fact that he had loaned the owner the money to purchase the land and that they had orally agreed that the land would be transferred to the defendant if the owner failed to repay the loan. The court upheld the plaintiff's claim, as the unwritten agreement was unenforceable as it did not comply with s 40 of the Law of Property Act 1925 (UK).

---

40 *Yeoman Credit Ltd v Latter* [1961] 1 WLR 828.

41 See *Nakamura v Moen Municipality* [2007] FMCSC 14; *Marcus v Truk Trading Corporation* [2001] FMSC 33.

42 Where the subject matter of the contract is registered land, the position is governed by the Land and Titles Act Cap 133, s 117.

43 [2003] VUCA 29.

However, the Act has been held not to apply to registered leases. In *Laau v Wong*[44] it was held that such instruments are not subject to s 40 of the Law of Property Act, but are governed by the Land Leases Act. Section 77(1) of that Act requires every instrument evidencing a disposition of land to be signed by the proprietors of the interest and all other parties to the instrument. This imposes a more rigorous requirement than the English Act, as an 'instrument' is required and all parties must sign it.

In 1989, the English law relating to contracts for the sale of interests in land was fundamentally changed by the Law of Property (Miscellaneous Provisions) Act. This requires such contracts to be made in writing rather than merely evidenced in writing. The contract must either be in a single document signed by both parties or, where the parties have arranged for exchange of contracts, each party must sign the copy they intend to exchange. This Act does not apply in the region.

Some countries of the region have made their own provision requiring contracts to be evidenced in writing. In Cook Islands, s 40 of the Law of Property Act has been repealed by the Personal Property Securities Act 2017,[45] which requires security agreements to be in writing and signed.[46]

In Niue, it only applies to contracts made before the commencement of the Niue Act 1966.[47] After that date, the position is governed by the Property Law Act 1952 (NZ).[48] Subsequent contracts, whether made orally or in writing by Niueans, are enforceable at the discretion of the court, having regard to the interests of the Niuean.[49] In relation to guarantees, the Niue Act 1966 provides:[50]

> No special promise by any person to answer for the debt, default, or miscarriage of another person, being in writing and signed by the party to be charged with it or some other person lawfully authorised by him, shall be deemed invalid to support an action or other proceedings to charge the person by whom the promise was made by reason only that the consideration for the promise does not appear in writing or by necessary inference from a written document.

The Statute of Frauds does not apply in Samoa.[51] However, the Property Law Act 1952 (NZ), s 10, does apply and requires leases, assignments and partitions

44 [1993] VUSC 5.
45 This Act governs the creation, registration, priority and enforceability of security interests.
46 Section 8. Such security interests must be perfected by creation of a registrable note and registration of a Finance Notice: Part V.
47 Section 711(2).
48 As amended by the Legislation (Correction of Errors and Minor Amendment) Act 2004 (NZ), s 55.
49 Section 711(1).
50 Ibid., s 710.
51 *Richard Lang & Co v R* [1930–49] WSLR 52.

of land to be by deed. The Contracts Enforcement Act 1958 (NZ), s 2, which requires contracts for the sale of land to be in writing, also applies in Samoa.[52]

In Papua New Guinea, the position is governed by the Frauds and Limitations Act 1988, which requires contracts for the disposition of land to be evidenced in writing.[53]

In Fiji, the position is covered by s 59 of the Indemnity, Guarantee, and Bailment Act,[54] which is substantially the same as s 4 of the Statute of Frauds.[55] In *Nandan v Datt*,[56] Speight J stated that s 59 was invoked by a submission on lack of evidence in writing in respect of a sale of land, which was the Fiji equivalent of s 4 of the Statute of Frauds 1677 (UK).[57]

More recently, s 59 was discussed in *Vision Properties Ltd v Northern Projects Fiji Ltd*.[58] In that case, the plaintiff applied for specific performance of a contract for the sale and purchase of land. The defendant argued that the sale agreement had been sent to the plaintiff in error and that it was only a draft. In considering whether the agreement complied with s 59, the court commented as follows:

> This has been taken from the English Statute of Frauds, and though Fiji does not have a statute of frauds the English and common-law authorities on this is equally applicable in Fiji. If there is a contract for the sale of land, that contract, or some memorandum or note of it, must be in writing and signed by the party to be bound, or by someone lawfully authorized to sign on that party's behalf before the contract will be enforced at common law.

The court held that the evidence did not support the contention that it was not meant to be sent to the plaintiff and that it contained all the essential terms of the agreement. However, the court was also faced with the fact that the document had not been signed by the defendant. In this case, the court was prepared to apply the 'authenticated signature fiction', by virtue of which, in certain limited circumstances, a document is deemed to have been signed. This principle is discussed further in section 4.1.2.

The position in Tonga was formerly governed by the Contract Act, which laid down that certain contracts must be in writing. That Act was repealed by the Contract (Repeal) Act 1990. However, the Contract Act still applies to contracts

---

52 Reprint of Statutes Act 1972 (Samoa).
53 Section 4. See e.g. *Seafright v Bishop Shipping Services* (1976) PNGLR 22.
54 Cap 232. See further *Kumar v Arjun* [2019] FJHC 667.
55 See the comments on point in *Nair v Public Trustee of Fiji* (unreported, High Court, Fiji, Lyons J, 8 March 1996), 29. See also *Kulamma v Manadan* (1964) 10 FLR 252, where the Law of Property Act 1925 (UK) was held not to apply to Fiji, as it was passed after the cut-off date.
56 [1984] FJCA 5.
57 Ibid., 5.
58 [2011] FJHC 204.

made before the repealing Act, which came into force on 15 February 1991. It may only be pleaded as a defence by an individual, not a corporation.[59] Between 1991 and 2003, the Law of Property (Miscellaneous Provisions) Act 1989 may have applied in Tonga as an Act of general application.[60]

The legislation discussed here governs the making of contracts. It should be noted that, in relation to land, legislation in force within most countries of the region requires a sale of land to be 'completed' by the execution of a document in a prescribed form, which must then be registered at the relevant registry.[61] Other interests in land, including long leases, are also often required to be in a prescribed form and registered at the lands registry.[62]

4.1. THE FORM REQUIRED

The legislation discussed above provides that if the agreement itself is not in writing, it must be evidenced by a sufficient memorandum or note. This raises the question of what will be 'sufficient'.

4.1.1. What Constitutes a Sufficient 'Memorandum or Note'?

It is clear that there need be no intention for the note or memorandum to serve as written evidence of the contract, provided it acknowledges the existence of a contract. For example, in *Tiverton Estates v Wearwell Ltd*,[63] a letter which would otherwise have satisfied the statute went on to refer to the agreement as 'subject to contract'. It was clear that the signatory did not consider that a contract had been formed.

Whilst the material terms must be evidenced in writing, they need not all be in the same document; a memorandum or note may be proved from several papers or a series of correspondence, provided they are connected, and the connection appears from the documents themselves.[64]

The sufficiency of the written evidence has received some attention within the region. In the Solomon Islands case of *Maeaniani v Saemala*[65] a document

59 *Teta v Ullrich Exports Ltd* [1981–1988] Tonga LR 127; *The Free Wesleyan Church of Tonga v Fua & Lawton Construction Ltd* [1992] Tonga LR 21.

60 Acts of general application were repealed in Tonga by the Civil Law (Amendment) Act 2003. The Law of Property (Miscellaneous Provisions) Act 1989 (UK) has been held to apply in other Commonwealth countries, see e.g. *Uganda Printing and Publishing Co v Kabangala* (1921) 3 ULR 77, but see *Bennett v Garvie* (1917) 7 EAPLR. Note that the Act was later excluded by the Contract Act Cap 75 (Uganda).

61 See e.g. Land and Titles Act Cap 133 (SI), ss 116, 172.

62 See e.g. Land and Titles Act Cap 133 (SI), s 146. See *Lee Kwok Kuen v Pongi* [1997] SBHC 4.

63 [1975] Ch 146 (CA).

64 *Stokes v Whicher* [1920] 1 Ch 411.

65 [1982] SILR 70.

worded as follows was held to constitute sufficient evidence of a contract for the sale of land:

> Receipt Date 23-9-80
>
> Received from Mr J Maeaniani the sum of one thousand, three hundred and sixteen dollars; as full settlement for my land (and plan, fees and other account) shown as parcel 192-002-9 on Lot 1375 (VI) on[66] Panatina Ridge.
>
> I agreed that the title of land will be in my name until such time Mr J MAEANIANI wishes to transfer it into his own name.
>
> Signature: Jack Sae Witness: J Maeaniani
> Date: 23/9/80

The question of what constitutes a 'memorandum or note' was considered more recently in Solomon Islands in *Hue v Bochman*,[67] which involved a claim for possession of land. A letter written and signed by the plaintiff when he wrote to the local council giving his consent for the defendant developing the land while awaiting the official transfer, together with his solicitors' subsequent repudiation of the agreement in another letter, were accepted as a 'memorandum or note'.

It is essential that the memorandum or note contains all the essential terms of the contract. What is essential will depend on the type of contract, but will invariably include:

- the names of the parties, or a description sufficient to identify them with certainty;
- the subject matter of the contract, for example the address and size of the land;
- the consideration;[68] and
- any special terms.

In *Prasad v Hussein*,[69] the plaintiff relied on a note or memorandum consisting of written instructions signed by both parties and addressed to a solicitor, asking him to prepare a sale and purchase agreement. The instructions contained the following wording:

PROPERTY:	S PRAAD'S house at Lakemba Street.
PRICE:	£3,300.0.0
DEPOSIT:	£1,000.
BALANCE:	Under New Zealand Bank

66 In the Report this word is shown as 'Hon'.
67 [2018] SBHC 7.
68 *Lee v Mitlal* (1966) 12 FLR 4, 27.
69 (1967) 13 FLR 98.

We undertake to pay £82.0.0 re costs and disbursements

X
Left thumb of Ali Hussein
Sgd. Shambhu Prasad
Witness: Sgd Muni Deo

Hammett J held that there were a number of material matters missing from this note, for example the intended date of transfer and the date of possession. It was held that the dealings between the parties did not amount to a completed contract but only to an agreement to make an agreement, the complete terms of which had not been settled.

In *Motibhai & Co Ltd v Civil Aviation Authority of Fiji*,[70] it was held that the essential terms of a lease were:

- the identity of the lessor and the lessee;
- the description of the premises;
- the commencement date and the term of the lease; and
- the amount of the rent or details of the other consideration to be paid.

The requirement of sufficiency has been interpreted strictly. In *Narayan v Shah*[71] the Privy Council held that all the material terms must be precisely recorded. The case involved an agreement for the sale of two parcels of land and some chattels by Narayan to Shah for £5,000. Narayan signed a written memorandum of the agreement, which specified the price and the land, but not the chattels. Narayan refused to complete. The Privy Council held that the memorandum was insufficient for the purposes of s 59 of the Indemnity, Guarantee, and Bailment Act, as the contract was an indivisible one for an indivisible price, and all the subject matter was not described. However, the Court made it clear that a term which is not of major importance and is only of benefit to one party may be waived by that party.[72]

4.1.2. Signature

The memorandum or note must normally be signed by the person sought to be made liable or a person expressly authorised to sign. The signature need not be the actual subscription of a party's name, but can be a mark, printed or stamped name, and need not necessarily be at the end of the document.

---

[70] Unreported, High Court, Fiji, Sadal J, 3 December 1993.
[71] [1979] 1 WLR 1349.
[72] See also *Kumar v Arjun* [2019] FJHC 667.

The document need not be signed by both parties. Thus, a person who has not signed can enforce it against the party who has.

The signature requirement could operate unjustly, and to prevent this, courts in England, Australia and particularly New Zealand have developed the 'authenticated signature fiction'.[73] This applies where one party, either personally or by an agent, induces the other party to sign a note or memorandum of sale, by representing that they regard themselves as bound by it even though they have not signed it. In *Bala v Dewan*,[74] the Court of Appeal of Fiji accepted that this gloss could be applied in respect of s 59 of the Indemnity, Guarantee and Bailment Act,[75] but pointed out the danger in putting a gloss upon a statutory provision and refused to apply the fiction in a situation which would expand its scope.

More recently, the 'authenticated signature fiction' was applied in Fiji in *Vision Properties Ltd v Northern Projects Fiji Ltd.*[76] The court cited the New Zealand decision of *Sturt v McInnes*,[77] where it was held that the authenticated signature fiction applies if the following three conditions are fulfilled:

1. The contract or some memorandum or note thereof containing the terms of the contract must have been prepared by the party sought to be charged, or by his agent duly authorised in that behalf, and must have that party's name written or printed on it.
2. It must be handed or sent by that party, or his authorised agent, to the other party for that other party to sign.
3. It must be shown, either from the form of the document or from the surrounding circumstances, that it is not intended to be signed by anyone other than the party to whom it is sent and that, when signed by him, it shall constitute a complete and binding contract between the parties.

4.2. PART PERFORMANCE

The lack of evidence in writing does not invalidate a contract, it merely renders it unenforceable in law. Under the equitable doctrine of part performance, even if there is no written memorandum or note, the plaintiff may obtain specific performance of an oral contract, if the plaintiff can show sufficient acts of part performance. This equitable principle was endorsed by s 40(2) of the Law of Property Act 1925 (UK), which states that: 'this section … does not affect the

---

73 *Sturt v McInnes* [1974] 1 NZLR 729.
74 [1998] FJCA 54.
75 Cap 232.
76 [2011] FJHC 204.
77 [1974] 1 NZLR 729.

law relating to part performance'. However, the doctrine of part performance no longer applies to contracts for the disposition of interests in land in England, where the Law of Property (Miscellaneous Provisions) Act 1989 requires such contracts to be made in writing, rather than merely evidenced in writing. However, other equitable remedies may be available and this is discussed further in chapter 20.[78]

This doctrine of part performance continues to apply within the region. The following explanation of the doctrine by Lord Reid *Steadman v Steadman*[79] is useful:

> If one party to an agreement stands by and lets the other party incur expense or prejudice his position on the faith of the agreement being valid he will not then be allowed to turn around and assert that the agreement is unenforceable. Using fraud in its older and less precise sense, that would be fraudulent on his part and it has become proverbial that courts of equity will not permit the statute to be made an instrument of fraud.
>
> It must be remembered that this legislation did not and does not make oral contracts relating to land void: it only makes them unenforceable. And the statutory provision must be pleaded; otherwise the court does not apply it. So it is in keeping with equitable principles that in proper circumstances a person will not be allowed 'fraudulently' to take advantage of a defence of this kind. There is nothing about performance in the Statute of Frauds. It is an invention of the Court of Chancery and in deciding any case not clearly covered by authority I think that the equitable nature of the remedy must be kept in mind.
>
> In my view, unless the law is to be divorced from reason and principle, the rule must be that you take the whole circumstances, leaving aside evidence about the oral contract, to see whether it is proved that the acts relied on were done in reliance on a contract: that will be proved if it is shown to be more probable than not.

In *Nandan v Datt*,[80] the Court of Appeal held that the doctrine of part performance of an agreement applies in Fiji, in spite of the fact that s 59 of the Indemnity, Guarantee and Bailment Act does not include the equivalent of s 40(2) of the Law of Property Act 1925 (UK).[81] His Lordship referred to the history of part performance as evidence of the existence of a contract for sale of land and to the discussion of this in *Steadman v Steadman*,[82] particularly in the judgment of Lord Reid. As the doctrine was developed as an answer to the defence based on the Statute of Frauds and that Statute, 'given modernisation of

---

78 See e.g. *Yaxley v Gotts* [1999] 2 FLR 941, where the plaintiff succeeded in establishing an interest in property on the basis of proprietary estoppel.

79 [1976] AC 536, 540.

80 [1984] FJCA 1.

81 See also *Kumar v Nasinu Land Company Ltd* [2016] FJHC 318.

82 [1976] AC 536.

language', was repeated in s 59 of the Fiji Act, the Court considered the doctrine still applicable in Fiji.

The doctrine is strictly limited, and the following requirements must be satisfied before it can apply.

4.2.1. The Acts Must Lead to the Conclusion that a Contract Exists

An equivocal act will not suffice as an act of part performance. For example, payment of a sum of money such as a deposit or first instalment will not usually be sufficient. In *Jeet v Chotelal*,[83] the plaintiff paid the defendant £534 in cash at the rate of £6 per month in consideration of an alleged agreement by the defendant to transfer to the plaintiff a one third interest in a Crown Lease. In an action for specific performance, the defendant relied on the absence of a note or memorandum in writing. At the hearing, counsel for the plaintiff abandoned the claim for specific performance, apparently accepting that the payment of money could not amount to part performance.[84]

Similarly, in *Bowring v New Guinea Goldfields Ltd*,[85] the defendant agreed verbally to lease certain land to the plaintiff, provided that she paid outstanding rents and fines relating to the lease. After she had paid, the defendant decided to forfeit the head lease. The plaintiff sued for specific performance. It was held that the payment of the outstanding rents and fines was not sufficient to constitute an act of part performance. It was a mere money payment and did not change the relative position of the parties (although it might give rise to a claim for recovery of the money paid). Something more, such as entering into possession, was required. Accordingly, the contract was unenforceable as it did not comply with the requirement for the agreement to be evidenced in writing imposed by the legislation in force at the time.[86]

However, payment of money may suffice if the surrounding circumstances make it clear that the payment can only relate to the contract. For example, in *Nandan v Datt*,[87] the plaintiff succeeded in his claim to a right of way over the defendant's land, which was not evidenced in writing. Immediately after the agreement was made, the plaintiff commenced paying instalments of the purchase price for the land, which he was occupying, and to which the right

---

[83] (1962) 8 FLR 209. But see *Nandan v Datt* [1984] FJCA 1, 6–7, where Speight JA interpreted *Steadman v Steadman* [1976] AC 536 as authority for the proposition that payment of part of the purchase price would be a sufficient act of part performance.

[84] It was also held in this case that such monies cannot be recovered unless there is an implied promise to repay.

[85] Unreported, Supreme Court, New Guinea, 9 October 1952. Cited in R.W. James, *Land Law and Policy in Papua New Guinea*, Monograph No. 5, Law Reform Commission of Papua New Guinea, Port Moresby July 1985, 96.

[86] Statute of Frauds and Limitations 1867 (Qld).

[87] [1984] FJCA 1.

of way was the only access. He continued to pay until he had made sufficient payments to entitle him to call for a conveyance. It was held that these payments could only be referable to the purchase price of the land as, at the time, the plaintiff was occupying the land as sub-lessee of a third party and had no other reason to pay money to the defendant's predecessor in title.

Similarly, in *Steadman v Steadman*,[88] it was held that the payment of £100 arrears of maintenance made in the context of the signing of a related indivisible maintenance agreement and preparation of a transfer deed were unequivocally referable to the existence of a contract, one of the terms of which was that the wife would sell the husband her interest in the matrimonial home for an agreed sum.

An example of an unequivocal act can be found in *Rawlinson v Ames*.[89] In that case, the defendant entered into an oral contract with the plaintiff to take the lease of a flat. It was agreed that certain alterations would be carried out by the plaintiff, and, while these were being carried out, the defendant constantly inspected the progress and made suggestions about the work. On completion of the alterations, the defendant repudiated the contract and set up the defence that there was no sufficient note or memorandum in writing. It was held that the acts of the plaintiff in complying with the requests of the defendant inevitably suggested the conclusion that the defendant had entered into a contract giving her some interest in the property.

4.2.2. *The Acts Must be Done by the Person Seeking to Enforce the Contract*

The plaintiff cannot rely on acts carried out by the defendant. The doctrine requires that the plaintiff should have been induced or allowed by the defendant to alter his or her position on the basis of the contract, so that it would be a fraud on the part of the defendant to set up the legal unenforceability of the contract. If only the defendant has acted in reliance on the contract this cannot be a fraud on the plaintiff.

4.2.3. *The Contract Must be Specifically Enforceable*

The contract must be one which if it were evidenced in writing would have been specifically enforceable. To put it another way, the only impediment to specific performance must be the lack of writing. For example, in *Britain v Rossiter*,[90] the plaintiff sued for wrongful dismissal in breach of an oral employment contract of service. The contract was for more than one year, and under the law at that time

---

[88] [1976] AC 536.
[89] [1925] Ch 96.
[90] (1879) 11 QBD 123.

was required to be in writing. The contract had been partly performed, and the plaintiff sought to have it specifically enforced. The Court of Appeal held that the doctrine could not be applied, as equity would not order specific performance of a contract of service.

4.2.4. *There Must be Proper Evidence of the Contract*

There must be clear and proper evidence of the contract, whether written or oral. As pointed out in *Prasad v Hussein*,[91] the doctrine cannot be used to finalise a contract which is still being negotiated or which would otherwise fail for uncertainty.

---

91 (1967) 13 FLR 98. See above section 4.1.1 for further discussion.

CHAPTER 11
INCAPACITY

1. INTRODUCTION

The development of the common law of contract has been dominated by a policy of individualism. However, it has long been recognised that this policy must be balanced against the policy requiring the law to protect those suffering from a disability, who cannot govern their own affairs.[1] The categories of individuals who require protection from the consequences of entering into a disadvantageous contract are minors, persons of unsound mind and drunken persons. There are also special rules relating to the contractual capacity of companies. This chapter deals mainly with minors, but also looks briefly at the other categories of incapacity. The rules for contracting with the Crown and government agencies are not discussed.

2. A MINOR'S CAPACITY TO CONTRACT

2.1. WHO IS A MINOR?

A minor is any person under the age of majority. At common law the age of majority was 21 years. A person under that age was referred to as an 'infant'. 'Minor' is now the preferred term. The common law is supplemented in the case of interpretation of the written law in some countries of the region by interpretation Acts. For example, Fiji's Interpretation Act provides that: '"Infant" or "Minor" means a person under twenty-one years of age'.[2] The age of majority has been lowered to 18 by statute in some countries of the region, namely Cook Islands,[3]

---

1 Infants Relief Act 1874 (UK).

2 Interpretation Act Cap 7 (Fiji), s 2.

3 Infants Act 1908 (NZ), s 2(3) inserted by Infants Amendment Act 2009 (CI), s 2. The Infants Act applies by virtue of the Cook Islands Act 1915 (NZ), s 630. The Infants Act Amendment Act 1967 (NZ) is also in force by virtue of the New Zealand Laws Act 1967 (CI).

Marshall Islands[4] and Nauru.[5] In Samoa, the Infants Ordinance 1961 provides that the age of majority is 21.[6] The Minors Contracts Act 1969 (NZ) also retains the age of majority at 21 in Niue, but restricts the protection given to minors over the age of 18.[7] The Contract Act reduced the age of majority to 16 in Tonga,[8] but that Act has since been repealed.[9]

In England, the age of majority was reduced from 21 to 18 by the Family Law Reform Act 1969.[10] Assuming this to be an Act of general application, it will apply in Vanuatu.

In the other countries of the region, although there are instances of statutes reducing the age of majority for other purposes, such as marriage[11] or voting,[12] generally a person is not regarded as having full contractual capacity until reaching 21. Employment contracts may be subject to special age limits, prescribed by regional employment legislation.[13] Many people in their late teens and early twenties will have been in the work force for some time and may even own their own businesses. Accordingly, they are more likely to enter into contracts and consequently, there is greater scope for a plea of incapacity within the region than in countries where the restriction on contractual capacity applies only to individuals under the age of 18. Surprisingly, regional law reports reveal little evidence of the plea being raised. One reason for this may be the evidential difficulty of proving incapacity within the region, where many people do not hold a birth certificate. Even oral evidence may be problematic, as some people do not know their date of birth. It is not unusual for people to assess their approximate age, and that of family members, by reference to an important event, for example the date of independence.

---

4 Domestic Relations Act 26 MIRC Cap 1 (Marshall Islands), s 7. Whilst this Act deals with domestic relations rather than contracts, it appears to lower the age of majority for all purposes.

5 Interpretation Act 2011 (Nauru).

6 Infants Ordinance 1961 (Samoa), s 2.

7 Minors Contracts Act 1969 (NZ), s 5. The Act applies by virtue of the Niue Act 1966 (NZ), ss 676, 692. A married or widowed minor is taken to be of full contractual capacity, even if he or she is under 21: s 4.

8 Contract Act Cap 26 (Tonga), s 2.

9 Contract (Repeal) Act 1990 (Tonga). The Act still applies to contracts made before it came into force on 15 February 1991.

10 Section 1.

11 See e.g. Islanders Marriage Act Cap 171 (SI), s 10, which prescribes the marriageable age at 18, or 15 with the consent of the father.

12 See e.g. Constitution of Solomon Islands 1978, s 55(1)(b), which prescribes the qualification age for electors as 18.

13 See e.g. Labour Act Cap 73 (SI), Pt. VII.

2.2. THE EFFECT OF MINORITY

The common law position required consideration of three separate categories, being:

- contracts binding on minors;
- contracts binding on minors unless repudiated; and
- contracts not binding unless ratified.

The common law was first altered in England by the Infants Relief Act 1874. This Act removed the third category by providing that ratification was ineffective.[14] The 1874 Act appears to apply to all countries of the region, other than Samoa, Cook Islands, Marshall Islands, Niue, Tokelau and Tonga.[15] The Act was finally repealed in England by the Minors Contracts Act 1987. This Act does not apply in the region.

Cook Islands is subject to Parts I and II of the Infants Act 1908 (NZ).[16] In Niue, the Minors Contracts Act 1969, which repealed the Infants Act 1908 in New Zealand, applies.[17] Nauru is specifically stated to be subject to the common law of England relating to contractual liability of minors.[18] Since 2003, minors' contracts have also been governed by the common law in Tonga.[19] As mentioned above, Samoa has its own Act, the Infants Ordinance 1961, which is based on the Infants Act 1908 (NZ), but has its own peculiarities. Tokelau also has its own legislation, the Contract Rules 2004, pursuant to which the age of majority is 16.

In Marshall Islands, the Sale of Goods Act regulates contracts for the sale of goods to minors.[20] Other contracts would appear to be governed by the common law of the United States.[21]

To deal with the law throughout the region it is therefore necessary to examine the common law position, the Infants Relief Act 1874 (UK), the New Zealand Acts of 1908 and 1969, the Samoan Act, and the Tokelau Rules. The common law categories will be used as the starting points for this exercise,

---

14 Infants Relief Act 1874 (UK), s 2.

15 See further chapter 1 and sections 2.2.3 and 2.2.4.

16 Cook Islands Act 1915 (NZ), s 630, continued in force by Cook Islands Constitution Act 1964 (NZ), Art. 77. The Infants Act 1908 (NZ) applies as amended by the Infants Amendment Act 2009 (CI), s 2. The Infants Act Amendment Act 1967 (NZ) is also in force by virtue of the New Zealand Laws Act 1967 (CI).

17 Niue Act 1966 (NZ), ss 676, 692.

18 Custom and Adopted Laws Act 1971 (Nauru), proviso to the First Schedule, as amended by the Custom and Adopted Laws (Amendment) Act 1976, s 4(e).

19 Civil Law (Amendment) Act 2003 (Tonga).

20 Sale of Goods Act 23 MIRC Cap 1 (Marshall Islands), s 4.

21 Constitution of Marshall Islands 1979, Art. XIII.

with an explanation of the statutory changes which have been made by the British Acts and regional Sale of Goods Acts to each category. The New Zealand and Samoan Acts and the Tokelauan Rules will then be outlined to explain the position in Cook Islands, Niue, Samoa and Tokelau.

2.2.1. Contracts Binding on Minors

The common law has attempted to balance two conflicting policies in the case of minors: on the one hand, the need to protect them from their own inexperience; and on the other, the need to ensure that traders and employers are not completely deterred from dealing with minors. For this reason, there are two types of contracts that remain binding on minors in all jurisdictions:

- contracts for necessaries; and
- beneficial contracts of service.

2.2.1.1. Contracts for Necessaries

Contracts for the supply of necessaries to a minor are prima facie valid. The policy that minors should not be bound by contracts is relaxed in this instance for the benefit of the minor, as it would be counterproductive not to allow contracts to be made for things which a minor needs. Traders might be unwilling to deal with minors if their right to payment was binding only in honour.

However, the transaction will only be free of risk for the trader if the goods are clearly 'necessaries'. Unfortunately, there is no precise definition of this term provided by the law. There is some guidance in the case of contracts for the sale of goods. For example, s 4 of the Fiji Sale of Goods Act provides:[22]

> 'Necessaries' ... means goods suitable to the condition in life of such infant or minor or other person and to his actual requirements at the time of the sale and delivery.

However, this only poses the question of what goods are suitable to a minor's condition in life and to his or her actual requirements.

There are really two questions involved in determining whether goods or services constitute necessaries:

- is the article or service capable of being a necessary in the eyes of the law; and, if so,
- is the article or service necessary for this minor?

---

[22] Sale of Goods Act Cap 230 (Fiji). Other Sale of Goods Acts applying in the region make similar provision. See e.g. Sale of Goods Act 1979 (UK), s 3; Sale of Goods Act 23 MIRC Cap 1 (Marshall Islands), s 4.

The first of these questions is a question of law. *Chapple v Cooper*[23] gives some guidance as to what will be regarded by the law as necessary. In that case a widow, who was a minor, was held liable for the cost of her husband's funeral. Alderson B made it clear that 'food, raiment, lodging and the like' may be necessaries, as may education, such as lessons in art, trade, intellectual, moral or religious pursuits. Services, such as doctors' visits, may also be included. The decision makes it clear that 'necessaries' are not restricted by law to things required to survive, but may include goods or services required for a reasonable existence. On the other hand, mere luxuries, whether in the form of goods or services, cannot be necessaries. However, luxurious goods or services, which have some utility, may be. For example, a china teapot may be a necessary, whereas a china ornament may not. Similarly, taking a taxi to a required destination may be necessary, whereas a joy ride in a stretch limousine will not be.

The antiquated wording used by Baron Alderson in *Chapple v Cooper*[24] carries its own warning. That case was decided in the nineteenth century. Things that were a luxury then may now be regarded as essentials. For example, a bicycle or even a mobile telephone may now qualify as necessaries in law.

Having excluded items of mere luxury, goods and services are still subject to the second question, as they must also be necessary for the particular minor. This is a question of fact. Luxurious items and services that serve some purpose will only be regarded as necessaries if they are in keeping with the minor's normal standard of living. Further, they will not be necessaries if the minor is already sufficiently supplied with goods of that kind. For example, in *Nash v Inman*,[25] a tailor supplied a Cambridge undergraduate with clothing that included 11 fancy waistcoats. When the student was sued for payment, he pleaded incapacity. Although the first question could be answered in the affirmative, as clothing was capable of being a necessary in the eyes of the law, the defence succeeded as the defendant already had a sufficient supply of waistcoats.

Further examples of unnecessary goods for a minor were given in *Ryder v Wombwell*.[26] In that case it was held that a pair of crystal, ruby and diamond solitaires and an antique goblet in silver gilt were not necessaries for a minor with an income of £500 per year, even though he was the son of a deceased baronet and moved in 'the highest society'. Further examples of unnecessary items put forward in that case were:

> earrings for a male, spectacles for a blind person, a wild animal, … a daily dinner of turtle and venison for a month for a clerk with a salary of £1 a week.

---

23 (1844) 153 ER 105.
24 Ibid.
25 [1908] 2 KB 1.
26 (1869) LR 4 Ex 32.

This case highlights the question of whether items which are regarded by the law as necessaries in England would be regarded as necessaries in the South Pacific region, and vice versa. The dinner of turtle referred to might be a common part of the menu in some countries of the Pacific. Other examples come readily to mind: a canoe may be a necessity in coastal villages of Solomon Islands, but not in metropolitan England. The answer is no doubt that the geographical and cultural situation of the minor are part of the relevant circumstances, which will determine what is necessary for that individual.

2.2.1.1.1. Loans for Necessaries

A loan of money to a minor for the purchase of necessaries was not recoverable at common law, as there was no guarantee that the money would be used for that purpose.[27] In equity, however, a loan to a minor for the purchase of necessaries is recoverable if it was lent and actually used to buy necessaries.[28] The Infants Relief Act 1874 (UK) rendered contracts of loan to a minor void.[29]

2.2.1.1.2. The Extent of a Minor's Liability for Necessaries

Even if goods qualify as necessaries, the minor is not obliged to pay the contract price. The common law position,[30] endorsed by the Sale of Goods Acts,[31] is that a reasonable price must be paid for necessary goods that the minor has accepted. The position is not so clear in the case of an unexecuted contract for necessaries. Cheshire, Fifoot and Furmston are of the opinion that such contracts are unenforceable,[32] whereas Treitel considers that a reasonable price must be paid.[33]

Payment of the contract price appears to be required for necessary services, whether the contract is executed or unexecuted.[34]

2.2.1.2. Beneficial Contracts of Service

Contracts of service, such as apprenticeships, have been held to be binding on a minor, because they allow the opportunity to earn a living. Again, to deny

27 *Earle v Peale* (1711) 1 Salk 386.
28 *Martin v Gale* (1876) 4 Ch D 428.
29 The Minors Contracts Act 1987 (UK) repeals the Infants Relief Act 1874 (UK).
30 *Nash v Inman* [1908] 2 KB 1.
31 See e.g. Sale of Goods Act Cap 230 (Fiji), s 4.
32 M.P. Furmston, *Cheshire, Fifoot and Furmston's Law of Contract*, 17th ed., Oxford University Press, Oxford 2017, pp. 533–34.
33 E. Peel, *Treitel on the Law of Contract*, 14th ed., Sweet & Maxwell, London 2015, 641.
34 See e.g. *Roberts v Gray* [1913] 1 KB 520.

capacity would be counter-productive, as it would discourage employers from dealing with minors. The contract must be substantially for the benefit of the minor. One or two prejudicial terms will not be decisive, as the court will look at the contract as a whole, weighing the onerous with the advantageous. The position is well summarised by the words of Fry LJ in *De Francesco v Barnum*:[35]

> I approach this subject with the observation that it appears to me that the question is this, Is the contract for the benefit of the infant? Not is any one particular stipulation for the benefit of the infant. Because it is obvious that the contract of apprenticeship or the contract of labour must, alike any other contract, contain some stipulation for the benefit of the one contracting party, and some for the benefit of the other. It is not because you can lay your hand upon a particular stipulation which you may say is against the infant's benefit, that therefore the whole contract is not for the benefit of the infant. The court must look at the whole contract having regard to the circumstances of the case, and determine, subject to any principles of law which may be ascertained by the cases, whether the contract is or is not beneficial. That appears to me to be in substance a question of fact.

In that case a 14-year-old had entered into a deed of apprenticeship in choreography with the plaintiff. The plaintiff was to teach the minor stage dancing. During the period of apprenticeship, the minor was not to take any professional engagement without the plaintiff's consent, nor was she to marry. She was to receive certain payments for any performances she might give, but there was no provision for any other pay, and the plaintiff did not undertake to find her work. It was held that the effect of the deed was to place the minor entirely at the plaintiff's disposal. As it was not beneficial to the minor, it was unenforceable.

This case can be contrasted with *Roberts v Gray*,[36] in which the plaintiff agreed to take the defendant, a minor, on a billiard tour to instruct him in the profession of billiard player. The defendant repudiated the contract. The court awarded damages in favour of the plaintiff.

The law applies equally to contracts which are not strictly contracts of service, but allow a minor to earn a living. Thus, in *Doyle v White City Stadium*,[37] the Court of Appeal upheld a contract between a minor boxer and the British Boxing Board of Control, by virtue of which he was granted a boxing licence in return for agreeing to abide by their rules.

Contracts for necessaries and beneficial contracts of service are unaffected by the English legislation regulating minors' contracts.

---

35 (1890) 45 Ch D 430.
36 [1913] 1 KB 520.
37 [1935] 1 KB 110.

2.2.2. *Contracts Binding on Minors Unless Repudiated*

At common law, contracts which confer an interest in property on the minor, which involves continuous or recurring obligations, are valid unless repudiated. Examples are contracts for the purchase of shares,[38] where calls may be made from time to time, and leases,[39] where rent may be payable on a recurring basis.

The repudiation must take place during the minority, or within a reasonable time afterwards. What is reasonable is a question of fact, to be considered in the circumstances of each case. In *Edwards v Carter*,[40] the House of Lords held that four years and eight months was too long to be reasonable.

The common law position on contracts of this nature has not been affected by English legislation.

2.2.3. *Contracts not Binding Unless Ratified*

Contracts which neither involve necessaries nor confer an interest in property involving continuous or recurring obligations are void. However, under the common law they may be ratified after the minor reaches majority. It is not a question of the minor saying, 'I will not be bound' and thereby rejecting a voidable agreement; rather, it is a question of the minor saying, 'I will be bound', and thereby validating an otherwise void agreement. An example of such a contract is any trading contract where the minor is the supplier.[41]

The Infants Relief Act 1874 (UK) renders such contracts incapable of being ratified, even if fresh consideration is given.[42] Accordingly, in countries of the region other than Cook Islands, Marshall Islands, Niue, Samoa, Tokelau and Tonga, ratification is no longer an option and all such contracts are void.

Whilst there are no regional cases involving the application of the Infants Relief Act, the case of *Bank of India v Rai Bahadur Singh*[43] is an interesting example from Singapore. In that case, two minors executed a letter of set-off in favour of the appellant bank, giving it the right to set off all moneys deposited by them, in favour of a named company. The total deposits were appropriated by the bank. After they reached majority, the minors sought to recover this money.

---

38 *Dunlop and Wicklow Railway v Black* (1852) 8 Exch 181.

39 *North Western Railway Co v M'Michael* (1850) 5 Exch 114; *Davies v Beynon-Harris* (1931) 47 TRR 424.

40 [1893] AC 360.

41 *Mercantile Union Guarantee v Ball* [1937] 2 KB 498.

42 Infants Relief Act 1874 (UK), s 2.

43 [1994] 4 LRC 264.

The contract of set-off was held to be void pursuant to the Infants Relief Act, which applied by virtue of s 5(1) of the Civil Law Act (Singapore).[44]

The Minors Contracts Act 1987 (UK) repeals s 2 of the Infants Relief Act, reinstating the common law position allowing ratification, either expressly or by implication, after a minor reaches majority. As mentioned, this Act does not apply in the region. However, in countries where the common law remains intact, ratification is still possible and will result in the contract being enforceable on both sides.

2.2.4. *Void Contracts*

The Infants Relief Act 1874 (UK) introduced a new class of minors' contracts, which are absolutely void. These are loan contracts, contracts for the supply of non-necessaries other than those regarded as voidable, and accounts stated (that is, acknowledgements that money is owed).

This provision has been repealed by the Minors Contract Act 1987 (UK). The Minors Contract Act also empowers the court to order a minor to return property transferred, or any property representing it, to the adult in any case where it is 'just and equitable to do so'.[45] As this Act does not apply in the region, the Infants Relief Act will render these contracts void in the countries where it applies.

2.2.5. *The Position in Cook Islands, Niue, Samoa and Tokelau*

In Cook Islands, the Infants Act 1908 (NZ) applies.[46] This Act retains the common law position on contracts for necessaries and beneficial contracts of service. The Act deals with other contracts in the same way as the Infants Relief Act 1874 (UK), which is discussed above. However, the Statutes Amendment Act 1951 (NZ) introduced a new s 12A into the 1908 Act which gives the minor or the minor's parent or guardian the option to apply to the magistrates' court for approval of a contract prior to entering into it. If such approval is granted, the contract will be valid whatever its nature.

In Samoa, the Infants Ordinance 1961 is based on the Infants Act 1908 (NZ), as amended. The Samoan Act, like the New Zealand Act of 1908, only deals with contracts that would be void or voidable at common law, thus leaving intact the law relating to contracts for necessaries and beneficial contracts of service. Outside these categories, the common law no longer applies in Samoa. Instead,

---

44 Cap 43.

45 Minors Contract Act 1987 (UK), s 3.

46 Cook Islands Act 1915 (NZ), s 630. The Infants Act Amendment Act 1967 (NZ) is also in force by virtue of New Zealand Laws Act No. 13 of 1967 (CI).

minors' contracts will be enforceable at the discretion of the court, taking into account the following factors:[47]

(a) the age, appearance, financial resources, and business competence of the infant at the time of entering into the contract;
(b) the extent of any steps taken by any other party prior to the contract to satisfy himself or herself as to the age, financial resources, and business competence of the infant;
(c) the fairness of the terms of the contract;
(d) the extent and nature of the benefit accruing to the infant under the contract; and
(e) any other circumstances which the Court considers material.

This section applies equally to actions to enforce a contract to meet any obligation incurred during minority and to actions to enforce ratification of such obligations made after the minor reaches 21, whether or not there is fresh consideration.[48]

Alternatively, under s 22, which is very similar to s 12A of the Infants Act 1908 (NZ), the court's approval may be obtained by a minor, or the parent or guardian of a minor, prior to entry into the contract, in which case the minor will always be bound. In *Peseta v Siliato*,[49] the plaintiff sued the defendants for failure to pay for the cost or the repairing the windscreen of his vehicle, which had been broken by the defendant. It was held that no contract existed; accordingly, it was not necessary for the court to consider the defence of incapacity.

In Niue, the Minors' Contracts Act 1969 (NZ) applies.[50] This Act introduces a comprehensive approach to minors' contracts and departs 'entirely from the common law distinction between contracts for necessaries and other types of contract'.[51] Since 2004, the Act only applies where the issue of incapacity arises in civil proceedings and where the consideration for the promise or act of any minor under the contract is no more than $2,000.[52] The Minors' Contracts Act draws a distinction between contracts with minors under 18 and contracts with minors over 18. The latter will be valid unless the court is satisfied:

- that the consideration given to the minor was so inadequate as to be unconscionable; or
- that any obligation imposed on the minor was harsh or oppressive.

---

47 Section 21(2).
48 Section 21(4).
49 [2016] WSDC 53.
50 Niue Act 1966 (NZ), ss 676, 692.
51 *Morrow & Benjamin v Whittington* [1989] LRC (Comm) 511, 513–14. See further J.F. Burrows, 'Minors Contracts Act 1969 (NZ)' (1973) 47 *Australian Law Journal* 657.
52 Legislation (Correction of Errors and Minor Amendment) Act 2004, s 39, amending Minors' Contracts Act 1969 (NZ), s 14.

This distinction does not apply to contracts for services, which will be dealt with in accordance with the same principles, whether the minor is under or over 18.

In general, contracts, other than contracts of service, entered into by a minor below the age of 18 are unenforceable against the minor unless they are fair and reasonable.[53] Even if the contract is fair and reasonable, the court still has to exercise its discretion as to whether to enforce the contract in whole or in part. The factors to be taken into account by the court in the exercise of its discretion are:[54]

(a) The circumstances surrounding the making of the contract;
(b) The subject-matter and nature of the contract;
(c) In the case of a contract relating to property, the nature and the value of the property;
(d) The age and the means (if any) of the minor;
(e) All other relevant circumstances.

The court is also empowered to make such orders as it thinks fit for compensation or restitution in favour of any party to the contract.[55] Accordingly, if it declares a contract unenforceable it may nevertheless order the minor to return property to another party.

In *Morrow & Benjamin v Whittington*,[56] the plaintiff was a firm of stockbrokers. The plaintiff purchased shares for the defendant over a number of years when he was aged between 15 and 17. In 1987 the stock market collapsed and the plaintiff claimed $30,250 from the defendant, being the balance owed for shares purchased on his behalf. In considering whether the contract was fair and reasonable, the High Court of New Zealand interpreted the term 'reasonable' as having its normal meaning. It was not enough to show that there was consideration and that the contract was not harsh or oppressive. In this case, taking into account all the factors specified in s 6(3), the court considered that the contract was unreasonable at the time it was made. Even if that conclusion was wrong, the court considered the fact that a substantial firm allowed a 17-year-old, who it regarded as having a casual and arrogant attitude, over $35,000 credit to purchase highly speculative stocks, at a time when the firm itself recognised that the market was in a chaotic state, dictated against the exercise of discretion in the plaintiff's favour.

---

53 Minors' Contracts Act 1969 (NZ), s 6(2).
54 Ibid., s 6(3).
55 Ibid., s 7.
56 [1989] 3 NZLR 122.

Like the Infants Act 1908 (NZ) and the Infants Ordinance 1961 (Samoa), the Minors Contract Act 1969 (NZ) also gives the option of applying to the court for approval of a contract prior to entering into it.[57] However, this Act allows such application to be made to the magistrates' court by any party to the proposed contract, not just the minor or the minor's parent or guardian.[58] If such approval is granted, the contract will be valid whatever its nature.

The Tokelau Contract Rules 2004 provide that a contract made by a person under 16 is unenforceable, 'unless it can be shown that enforcement would be fair and reasonable'.[59] The Rules provide that 'all circumstances must be taken into account', and in particular:[60]

(i) the nature and value of the benefits to which that person is entitled under the contract;
(ii) the burden imposed by the contract obligations;
(iii) the actual and apparent ability of that person to carry out the contract obligations;
(iv) the actual and apparent age of that person if aged less than 16 years;
(v) the actual and apparent intelligence or mental capacity of that person;
(vi) whether that person's parent or guardian has consented to or approved the making of the contract;
(vii) any misrepresentations made by that person relating to any of the matters referred to in subparagraphs (iii) to (vi).

2.3. LIABILITY OF A MINOR IN TORT

Generally, there is no age limit on tortious liability and a minor is liable for torts such as defamation, conversion or negligence. However, a minor will not be liable for a tort connected with a contract that is not binding on the minor. To hold the minor liable in such a case would be to indirectly enforce an otherwise unenforceable contract. If on the other hand the tort can be separated from the contract, the minor may be liable under general tortious principles.

In order to determine whether the tort can be independently enforced, it is necessary to determine whether the wrongful conduct was contemplated by the contract. If it was, then no action can be brought. If it was not, then an action will lie in tort. Another way of putting this would be to ask whether the tort was committed in the process of performing the contract. Alternatively, was it committed outside what was contemplated by the contract?

---

57 Minors Contract Act 1969 (NZ), s 9.
58 Ibid., s 9(2).
59 Contract Rules 2004 (Tokelau), R 9(1).
60 Ibid., R 9(2).

A useful comparison can be made between *Jennings v Randall*[61] and *Burnard v Haggis*.[62] In the former, a minor hired a horse and injured it through excessive and improper riding and was found not liable. In the latter, the minor was held liable for the death of a horse through jumping, which had been expressly forbidden by the contract of hire.

A more modern example is *Ballett v Mingay*,[63] where a minor was successfully sued in detinue for failure to return a microphone and amplifier which he had hired and lent to a friend in breach of the contract.

It follows that, where a minor fraudulently represents that he or she is of age, the defence of lack of capacity is still available in answer to an action for breach of contract. However, this does not mean that the minor will be unimpeachable. Equity may provide a remedy in the case of fraud, through the doctrine of restitution. Where the property is still in the possession of the minor, the court may order its return.[64] As discussed above, a similar remedy is provided by s 3 of the Minors Contract Act 1987 (UK), but as this Act does not apply in the region, the equitable remedy is still of great importance.

If money obtained under a contract has been spent or goods parted with, equity cannot assist. In *R Leslie Ltd v Sheill*,[65] the plaintiff was a firm of registered money lenders. It sued the defendant, to whom it had made two loans of £200 each, to recover £475, being the balance of the loan with interest. At the time of obtaining the loans, the defendant was a minor but he had falsely represented to the plaintiffs that he was of full age. The money had been spent. The Court of Appeal held that no action could be maintained to recover the money because the Infants Relief Act rendered the contract void.

2.4. UNSOUND MIND AND INTOXICATION

The contracts of persons of unsound mind are outside the control of the court, and contracts of drunken persons are generally dealt with in the same way as minors' contracts were at common law. It is unclear whether the defence of incapacity extends to a person whose incapacity is the result of drug use. This is arguably the case in Tokelau, where the Rules render unenforceable a contract made by any 'person who lacks capacity to understand the nature of the obligations under the contract'.[66] Persons under such disability will be liable

61 (1799) 8 TR 335.
62 (1863) 14 CB (NS) 45.
63 [1943] KB 281.
64 *Stocks v Wilson* [1913] 2 KB 235.
65 [1914] 3 KB 607.
66 Contract Rules 2004 (Tokelau), R 9(1).

to pay a reasonable price for necessary goods and, it would seem, for necessary services. The common law position regarding necessary goods is retained by the Sale of Goods Acts in force in the region, for example the Fiji Sale of Goods Act, s 4.

Contracts which do not involve necessaries will be enforceable unless it can be proved that at the time of making the contract:

- the person relying on the disability was unable to appreciate the nature of the transaction they were entering into; and
- the other party knew of this condition.[67]

Contracts within this category are voidable rather than void. Accordingly, the defence cannot succeed if the contract had been ratified after the disability ceases. In *Matthews v Baxter*,[68] for example, the defendant, whilst intoxicated, agreed to purchase certain houses and land from the plaintiff at auction. When he sobered up he affirmed the contract, but later changed his mind. The defence of intoxication was not available.

Within the region, legislation provides for persons of unsound mind to be made the subject of a 'reception' or similar order and to be detained in a mental hospital.[69] The court will normally appoint a relative or friend or the public trustee to manage the affairs of a person of unsound mind, and this will include the right to enter into contracts on that person's behalf.[70] It is unclear whether a person of unsound mind who is subject to a management order retains any capacity to contract or whether such contracts will be unenforceable.[71]

A person who has been declared a 'patient' under the Mental Health Act 1983 (UK) is regarded as incapable of entering into a valid contract. This power is taken over by the court and any contract made with the 'patient' appears to be unenforceable.[72] This Act does not apply in the region.

Mental disability that falls short of preventing understanding of the nature of a contract or mere lack of business acumen is not sufficient to sustain a plea of

67 *Imperial Loan Co v Stone* [1892] 1 QB 599; *Gore v Gibson* (1843) 153 ER 260. See also *Hart v O'Connor* [1985] 2 All ER 880.

68 (1873) LR 8 Ex 132.

69 See e.g. Mental Treatment Act Cap 103 (SI).

70 Ibid., Pt. VIII.

71 There is conflicting authority on the equivalent British legislation: Lunacy and Mental Treatment Acts 1890 to 1930 (repealed). See further G.H.L. Fridman, 'Mental Incompetency, Part II' (1964) 80 *Law Quarterly Review* 84.

72 There is no authority on the relevant provisions of the Mental Health Act 1983 (UK), but with regard to the Lunacy and Mental Treatment Acts 1890 to 1930 (repealed), see Fridman, above n. 71.

incapacity, but it may be relevant to a plea of undue influence or unconscionability, which are discussed in chapter 13.

2.5. CORPORATIONS

Under the regional legislation regulating companies, an incorporated body is regarded as a separate legal entity, which can sue, be sued, and acquire and own property. If the incorporation has not been completed, the organisation will not have the capacity to contract.[73] A contract with a firm operating as a partnership, on the other hand, must be made with the individual partners, as the partnership has no separate legal identity and cannot contract in its own right.[74] It is therefore very important to know whether a particular business is incorporated or not, in order to know whether it has the capacity to contract in its own right.

Further, although companies are regarded in law as separate legal entities, they cannot physically act, and therefore they must do so through officers of the company. It is therefore also essential to ensure that an officer has the requisite power to represent and bind the company. This will usually be apparent from the role that the person takes in the company.[75]

Further, in some countries of the region, a company's power to contract is limited by its Memorandum of Association. The 'objects' for which the company is established will set the boundaries for the matters in respect of which it may contract.[76] Contracts outside those boundaries are said to be 'ultra vires', that is, outside the company's powers, and will be void. For example, if a company executes a guarantee and this is not authorised by its objects clause, the guarantee will be void.[77] In *Ashbury Railway Carriage and Iron Co Ltd v Riche*,[78] a contract for construction of a railway line made by a company that was restricted by its objects clause to making and selling rolling stock was held to be ultra vires and therefore void.

---

73 *Prasad v Sunrise Corporation Ltd* [2005] FJCA 23.

74 *Bradley Egg Farm Ltd v Clifford* [1943] 2 All ER 378.

75 In the absence of actual authority, ostensible authority may suffice. See further *Media Enterprises Pty Ltd v Fiji Broadcasting Commission* [1999] FJHC 80.

76 *Ashbury Railway Carriage and Iron Co Ltd v Riche* (1875) LR 7 HL 653, 668.

77 The power to execute a guarantee cannot be implied.

78 (1875) LR 7 HL 653.

Amendments have been made to the Companies Acts of some regional countries, such as Fiji,[79] Kiribati,[80] Tonga,[81] Tuvalu[82] and Vanuatu.[83] These amendments have abolished the doctrine of ultra vires. In those countries, a contract which goes outside the objects of a company will be binding unless the other party to the contract was acting in bad faith. It would appear that knowledge that the contract is ultra vires is not in itself enough to show bad faith.[84] Notwithstanding, a person with such knowledge would be unwise to proceed with the contract.

79 Companies Act Cap 247 (Fiji), s 8.
80 Companies Ordinance Cap 10A (Kiribati), s 17.
81 Companies Act 1995 (Tonga), s 20.
82 Companies Act Cap 40.08 (Tuvalu), ss 34, 35. See also Companies Act 1985 (UK), s 35, substituted by Companies Act 1989, s 108, which prevents a contract failing on the grounds of incapacity.
83 Companies Act Cap 191 (Vanuatu), proviso to s 45(1).
84 *International Sales and Agencies Ltd v Marcus* [1982] 3 All ER 551.

CHAPTER 12
MISREPRESENTATION

1. INTRODUCTION

Some statements made in the course of negotiations fall short of terms of the contract and are categorised as 'mere representations'. If they turn out to be false, no action lies for breach of contract. However, if the representations were made to induce a party to enter into a contract, there may be a remedy for misrepresentation.

This chapter examines the elements of actionable misrepresentation and the different types of misrepresentation. It also discusses the remedies available, both common law and statutory.

2. THE ELEMENTS OF ACTIONABLE MISREPRESENTATION

The false statement may be in writing, oral or consist of conduct.[1] It need not be express. For example, in *Bank of Western Samoa v Suisala*,[2] the plaintiff bank provided a company with an overdraft, guaranteed from the defendants, three of whom were directors of the company. The bank prepared the guarantee documentation. The form contained the name of an additional director, who was also a director of the bank, in the space provided for the names of guarantors. This director did not sign, as it was contrary to the bank's policy for its directors to guarantee customer's overdrafts. The defendants gave evidence that they would not have signed the guarantee had they known this. It was held that placing the bank's director's name on the form was a misrepresentation that he was acceptable to the bank as a guarantor. Accordingly, the defendants were entitled to rescind the guarantee.

1 *Horsfall v Thomas* (1862) 1 H&C 90.
2 (1991) Samoa LR 1.

In order to succeed in an action for misrepresentation, it must be shown that:

- a false statement of existing or past fact was made by one party ('the representor');
- the statement was addressed to the other party ('the representee');
- it was made before or at the time the contract was made;
- it was intended to and did induce the representee to enter into the contract.

The first and last of these elements require further explanation.

2.1. A FALSE STATEMENT OF EXISTING OR PAST FACT MADE BY A PARTY

The misrepresentation must normally have been made by the defendant or the defendant's agent.[3] However, whilst misrepresentation by someone who is not an agent of the defendant may not be sufficient in itself, it may assist the court in drawing an inference that the defendant is guilty of misrepresentation.[4]

However, the statement must be of fact.[5] Statements of fact must be distinguished from the following types of statement.

2.1.1. Representations of Law

Representations of law do not qualify as actionable statements. This rule is simple to state, but is often difficult to apply. If the statement is a general one about the state of the law, it will be a representation of law, and will not amount to misrepresentation. On the other hand, if it is a statement about the law applying to facts that are essential to the contract, it may be a representation of fact. For example, a statement that 'planning permission is not required for buildings in Suva' may be a representation of law. On the other hand, a statement that 'planning permission was not required for the erection of this shed' is more likely to be a statement of fact.

---

3 *Saville Heaton & Co Ltd v United Apparel (MGF) Ltd* (unreported, High Court, Fiji, Scott J, 9 April 1996). The decision in this case was upheld by the Court of Appeal and the Supreme Court, but this point as not discussed: *United Apparel (MFG) Ltd v Saville Heaton & Co Ltd* [1997] FJCA 40; *United Apparel (MFG) Ltd v Saville Heaton & Co Ltd* [1998] FJSC 9.

4 *Lal v Chand* (1983) 29 FLR 71, 74.

5 See e.g. *Motil v North (Fiji) Group Ltd* [2013] FJHC 446.

2.1.2. *Representations as to Future Intention*

Generally, a statement of future intention will only be binding if it is incorporated into the contract. However, the exception to this is where the representor did not, at the time the statement was made, have any such intention. For example, in *Edgington v Fitzmaurice*,[6] directors of a company issued a prospectus inviting subscriptions for debentures, stating that the issue was for investment purposes. The plaintiff advanced the money in reliance on the statement and in the erroneous belief that the debenture holders would have a charge upon the property of the company. It transpired that the real object of the loan was to enable the directors to pay off pressing debts. The Court of Appeal held that the plaintiff was entitled to rescind on the basis of misrepresentation. Although the statement was of intention, the court held that the directors had no intention of keeping to this at the time the statement was made in the prospectus.

2.1.3. *Expressions of Opinion*

The statement of an opinion or a belief will not form the basis of a claim for misrepresentation. For example, in *Bisset v Wilkinson*,[7] the defendant, whilst in the process of selling his farm, was asked by the purchaser how many sheep the land could support. The farm had not previously been used for sheep, but the vendor gave an opinion, which turned out to be incorrect. It was held that this was merely an honest expression of an opinion, and not a statement of fact as to the actual capacity of the farm.

However, where a person giving an opinion was in a position to know the true facts, and could not reasonably have held the opinion expressed, then his or her opinion may be treated as a statement of fact. For example, in *Smith v Land and House Property Corporation*,[8] the plaintiff put his hotel up for sale, stating that it was let to a 'most desirable tenant'. The defendant agreed to buy the hotel. The tenant was bankrupt. As a result, the defendant refused to complete and was sued for specific performance. The Court of Appeal held that the plaintiff's statement was not mere opinion but was one of fact.

In recent years, the courts appear less inclined to allow a person with special skill and knowledge to escape a finding of misrepresentation on the basis that it was mere opinion or a future prediction. The courts have been prepared to uphold a plea of misrepresentation where a forecast can be said to represent as a fact that the maker exercised reasonable care in making it. For example,

6 (1885) 29 Ch D 459.
7 [1927] AC 177.
8 (1884) 28 Ch D 7.

in *Esso Petroleum v Marden*,[9] a petroleum company that offered an inaccurate forecast of the sales potential of a service station was liable in damages to a tenant who contracted with the company on the basis of the forecast.

2.1.4. Silence

Generally, non-disclosure of a fact does not amount to misrepresentation. There must be a positive statement or at least some conduct from which a statement may be implied, although it has been said that '[a] nod or a wink, or a shake of the head or a smile' may suffice.[10] If one party is labouring under a misapprehension, there is no duty on the other party to correct it. For example, in *Keates v Lord Cadogan*,[11] the defendant let a house to the plaintiff. The defendant was aware that the house was required for immediate occupation, but failed to reveal that it was in ruins. It was held that it was for the plaintiff to make proper investigation and that the defendant was not liable in respect of the non-disclosure.[12]

There are four exceptions to the rule that silence does not amount to misrepresentation.

2.1.4.1. Partial Disclosure

A partial disclosure may amount to misrepresentation. This will be the case if suppression of material facts renders facts which are stated untrue. For example, in *Dimmock v Hallett*,[13] the vendor of land told the purchaser that the farms on the land were all let, but omitted to say that the tenants had given notice to quit. This was held to amount to misrepresentation.

A regional case example of half-truths amounting to misrepresentation is *Lallu v Ranchod*.[14] In that case, the plaintiff was equal partner with the defendant, her late husband's brother, in the business of merchants and theatre proprietors. The business also owned certain properties. In 1990, the defendant was convicted of assaulting the plaintiff, who was forced to move out of the house she shared with the defendant and his family into accommodation behind the theatre. After various meetings with the defendant and members of the Gujarati Indian community, the plaintiff and defendant executed a deed providing for the dissolution of the partnership with all assets to be transferred to the defendant and $50,000 to be paid to the plaintiff. After execution of the deed, the plaintiff

---

9 [1976] QB 801.
10 *Walters v Morgan* (1861) 3 De GF & J 718, 725; 45 ER 1056, 1059.
11 (1851) 10 CB 591.
12 See also *Smith v Hughes* (1871) LR 6 QB 597. Cf. *Muri v Shin* [2018] VUMC 16.
13 (1866) LR 2 Ch App 21.
14 Unreported, Court of Appeal, Fiji, Savage, Dillon, and Hillyer JJA, 30 August 1996.

became aware that she would only receive $50,000, and not the money and the theatre as she had thought. Some information regarding the value of the business had been given to the plaintiff. However, the Court of Appeal stated that non-disclosure of matters of importance – namely profits of the partnership, sales forming a substantial part of trading operations, acquisition of land in an individual partner's name with partnership funds, and questions regarding gross profits in a period following serious damage to the trading premises – constituted misrepresentation.

A broader approach to partial disclosure was endorsed by the Kiribati High Court in *Kiribati Supplies Company Ltd v Raiha*.[15] In that case, the plaintiff had previously done business with the defendant on the basis that the defendant would order and import goods from overseas and the plaintiff would be responsible for paying customs duties and port charges. Normally, the port charges were modest, as the plaintiff cleared the cargo immediately. On this occasion the goods were imported by the defendant for another customer, but that deal fell through and the goods were not collected. The defendant offered them to the plaintiff, who agreed to buy them, not knowing that the port charges were already running. The court held that failure to warn the plaintiff of this amounted to a misrepresentation. Accordingly, in Kiribati, it would seem that failure to disclose a change in terms, or at least that charges relating to the goods will differ significantly from a past course of dealing, may be sufficient to constitute misrepresentation.

2.1.4.2. Where a Representation becomes False

If a person makes a representation which is true, but circumstances later change rendering the representation false, the representor must set the record straight. In *With v O'Flanagan*,[16] a medical practice became valueless between the time of making the statement as to its worth and the date of sale. It was held that the vendor should have communicated this to the purchaser.

2.1.4.3. Active Concealment

A positive act taken to conceal defects in goods will constitute misrepresentation. For example, in *Horsfall v Thomas*,[17] the vendor of a gun inserted a plug to conceal a defect in workmanship. This conduct constituted misrepresentation.

---

15 [2010] KIHC 46.
16 [1936] Ch 575.
17 (1862) 1 H&C 90.

2.1.4.4. Contracts *Uberrimae Fidei*

In contracts *uberrimae fidei* (of utmost good faith), there is a duty of full disclosure.[18] Merely refraining from misrepresentation is not enough to fulfil this duty. There must be complete disclosure of all material facts. The main contracts that come within this category are contracts of insurance,[19] family settlements and contracts where there is a fiduciary relationship. A fiduciary relationship is one in which the parties are in a special relationship of confidence and trust. The categories of fiduciary relationships remain open, but examples are solicitor and client,[20] trustee and beneficiary, bank manager and client, and inter-family agreements. Employers and employees are not normally in a fiduciary relationship.[21]

2.2. THE REPRESENTATION MUST INDUCE THE CONTRACT

There can be no liability in respect of a falsehood that does not induce the other party to enter into the contract. In other words, there can be no inducement without reliance. Accordingly, statements made after the contract has been entered into cannot constitute misrepresentation, although they may provide evidence in support of a claim that statements made beforehand constituted misrepresentation.[22] Common cases where it has been held that there is no reliance, and consequently no inducement, are discussed in the following sections.

2.2.1. Where the Misrepresentation did not Come to the Plaintiff's Notice

If the misrepresentation did not come to the plaintiff's notice prior to entry into the contract, it cannot amount to an inducement. For example, in *Horsfall v Thomas*,[23] the defendant was not allowed to rely on misrepresentation consisting of concealment of a defect in a cannon as he had not inspected the gun prior to purchase.

---

18 *Dominion Insurance Ltd v Union Electrique Du Vanuatu* [2013] VUSC 113.

19 See e.g. *Rentway Rentals Ltd v National Pacific Insurance Ltd* [1980–1993] WSLR 327.

20 *Midland Beach Estate Ltd v Balgovind* [2012] 1 FLR 450, [31].

21 *Bell v Lever Brothers* [1932] AC 161. Compare *Sybron Corporation v Rochem Ltd* [1983] 2 All ER 707.

22 *Midland Beach Estate Ltd v Balgovind* [2012] 1 FLR 450, [25].

23 (1862) 1 H&C 90.

2.2.2. *Where the Representee is not Influenced by the Statement*

Where the representee relies on his or her own judgement, there can be no action for innocent or negligent misrepresentation. For example, in *Attwood v Small*,[24] the plaintiffs negotiated with the defendant for the sale of certain mines. The plaintiffs asked about the capabilities of the property. The engineer appointed by the plaintiffs verified the defendant's answer. Six months after the sale, the plaintiffs found that the defendant's representation was untrue and the plaintiffs sought to rescind. It was held that rescission was not available, as the plaintiffs had not been induced to enter the contract by the defendant's statement; rather, they had relied on their own engineer's report.

Where the misrepresentation is fraudulent, it is not open to the representor to say that the representee relied on his or her own judgement.[25] Neither is it an answer to a claim for misrepresentation to say that the representee was afforded the opportunity to verify the statement, but chose not to do so. For example, in *Redgrave v Hurd*,[26] the representee was induced to purchase a solicitor's house and practice by innocent misrepresentations as to the value of the practice. He was allowed to rescind even though the books and papers, which he had been invited to examine and did not, would have revealed the true position.

2.2.3. *Where the Statement is Immaterial*

The statement must relate to a material fact in order to have induced the contract. A fact will be material if it is likely to influence a person's decision to enter into the contract.[27]

3. THE DIFFERENT TYPES OF MISREPRESENTATION

Once misrepresentation has been established, it is necessary to establish the nature of the misrepresentation, as this determines the available remedies. In all cases, the innocent party has the option to rescind the contract. The right to damages is more restricted.

Originally there were only two types of misrepresentation recognised by law: fraudulent and innocent. The law has developed, both through the common

---

24 (1838) 6 Cl & Fin 232; 7 ER 684.

25 *Pearson v Dublin Corporation* [1907] AC 351.

26 (1881) 20 Ch D 1.

27 *Bank of Western Samoa v Suisala* (1991) Samoa LR 1.

law and by the intervention of statute. There are now three categories of misrepresentation:

- fraudulent;
- negligent; and
- innocent.

3.1. FRAUDULENT MISREPRESENTATION

In *Parbhubhai v Prasad*,[28] the Fiji Court of Appeal held that a party alleging fraudulent misrepresentation assumes the onus of proving:

> (a) That the alleged representation consisted of something said which amounted in law to a representation.
> (b) That the representation was made by the respondent to the appellant.
> (c) That the representation was material and induced the appellant to enter into the contract.
> (d) That the representation was false.
> (e) That the representation was made by the appellant fraudulently.
> (f) That by reason of acting upon the representations the appellant suffered damage.

In order to satisfy (e), and establish that the misrepresentation was fraudulent, it is necessary to show that it was made:

- knowingly; or
- without belief in its truth; or
- recklessly, not caring whether it is true or false.[29]

In *Midland Beach Estate Ltd v Balgovind*,[30] the plaintiff company entered into a contract to sell land to the defendant. The sole directors and shareholders of the plaintiff were principals of a firm of solicitors. That firm acted for both parties in the sale. After the defendant had paid a deposit of F$100,000 into the solicitors' account, the plaintiff terminated the contract before the settlement date, claiming breach of covenants, and subsequently sold the land to a

---

28 (1959) FLR 118.

29 *Derry v Peek* (1889) 14 App Cas 337, 374 (Lord Herschell); *Motil v North (Fiji) Group Ltd* [2013] FJHC 446. See e.g. *Fletcher v James* [1958] PGSC 12.

30 (2012) 1 FLR 450, [46].

third party. The defendant lodged a caveat which prevented the registration of the land by the new owner. The plaintiff applied for the removal of the caveat and a declaration that the defendant had no rights to the property. The defendant counter-claimed, inter alia, for misrepresentation, on the basis that his solicitor had told him the property belonged to a third party and had not revealed his conflict of interest. His solicitor had also stated that his cousin would co-purchase the property with the defendant and that the cousin had paid his share of the purchase price. The defendant sought orders that the contract was void ab initio and damages. The court, citing *Krakowski v Eurolynx Properties*,[31] held that to 'succeed in fraud, a representee must prove, inter alia that the representor had no honest belief in the truth of the representation in the sense in which the representor intended it to be understood'. The court found in favour of the defendant, holding that the solicitor was fully aware that the representations were false and that he made them with the deliberate intention of fraudulently inducing the defendant to enter into the contract.

An example from Samoa can be found in *Selevae v Tanielu*,[32] where the plaintiff purchased a car from the defendant, which he intended to use as a taxi. The defendant stated that the car was roadworthy. The day after purchase, the car broke down and the defendant repaired it. A week later, the brakes failed and it was again repaired by the defendant. Two days later, further problems arose and the car was returned to the defendant on the basis that it was faulty. The plaintiff sued on the basis of fraudulent misrepresentation and breach of the implied condition of merchantable quality. The court found that the defendant knew or ought to have known what was wrong with the vehicle and by knowingly uttering a false statement to the plaintiff, he intended to induce the plaintiff to act on it, which the plaintiff did. It was held that the plaintiff was entitled to rescind the contract and to recover the purchase price.

A negligent statement will not amount to fraudulent misrepresentation, however gross the negligence.[33] However, a party may be guilty of both. In *Quarter Enterprises Pty Ltd v Allardyce Lumber Company Ltd*,[34] the High Court of Solomon Islands found that the defendant's conduct was both negligent and fraudulent. In that case, the defendant had entered into an agreement to provide logs to the plaintiff on the basis that the plaintiff would underwrite a loan to the defendant to buy associated machinery and equipment. The plaintiff alleged that the defendant was not in sound financial condition when it entered into that agreement and claimed damages. It was held that the defendant's managing

31 (1995) 183 CLR 563.
32 [2006] WSSC 45. See also *Afolau Construction v SSFA* [2013] WSSC 73.
33 *Derry v Peek* (1889) 14 App Cas 337.
34 [2007] SBHC 118.

director was negligent in that he had material available to him to give grounds to suspect the veracity of the official survey of the area of land he had available to source logs from and knew that the plaintiff was relying on him for the accuracy of that survey. Further, the representations that were made about the defendant's strong financial position were 'manifestly wrong and [known] to be wrong', which amounted to fraudulent misrepresentation.

3.2. NEGLIGENT MISREPRESENTATION

As mentioned above, negligent misrepresentation was not recognised originally as a separate category. Subject to an exception in the case of a fiduciary relationship between the parties,[35] misrepresentation was either innocent or fraudulent. Only fraudulent misrepresentation gave rise to a right to rescind the contract.

This position has been changed by both common law and legislative developments.

3.2.1. Common Law Developments

In *Hedley Byrne & Co Ltd v Heller & Partners Ltd*,[36] the House of Lords had to consider whether the plaintiffs could recover for loss suffered by extending credit to a certain firm. They had been induced to do so by a reference carelessly given by the firm's bank, which in effect vouched for the firm's creditworthiness. The bank escaped liability because of an exemption clause (they had given the reference on the basis that they were doing so 'without responsibility'). However, the House of Lords made it clear that the bank would otherwise have been liable. In so doing, the court extended the duty of care in tort to negligent misstatement, where a 'special relationship' existed between representor and representee.

The case did not deal directly with misrepresentation in contract. However, in *Esso Petroleum v Marden*,[37] it was held that liability exists for negligent misrepresentation made prior to entry into a contract if the person making the statement owes a duty of care to the representee. This duty will arise where the representor has or purports to have some special skill or knowledge and knows or should know that the representee will rely on the representation. In *Howard Marine and Dredging Co Ltd v A Ogden & Sons (Excavations) Ltd*,[38] it was held

35 *Nocton v Lord Ashburton* [1914] AC 932.
36 [1964] AC 465.
37 [1976] QB 801.
38 [1978] QB 574.

that a duty of care will also arise if the representation is to be regarded as neither casual nor unconsidered but to be relied upon.

It is unclear whether a duty of care exists to found an action for negligent misrepresentation outside these situations. In *Saville Heaton & Co Ltd v United Apparel (MGF) Ltd*,[39] the High Court of Fiji seems to suggest, obiter, that the duty of care which suffices to found an action for the tort of negligence may suffice to establish liability for negligent misrepresentation. The decision in this case was upheld by the Court of Appeal and the Supreme Court, but this point was not discussed.[40]

The common law developments are of fundamental importance in the countries of the region where there is no applicable legislation. Assuming that they are applicable to the circumstances of the country, the English cases discussed are part of the introduced law in regional countries other than Niue, and if there is no legislative provision, they are likely to be followed.

3.2.2. *Legislative Developments*

The uncertainties regarding the common law principles have been overtaken by legislation in some countries of the region. In Fiji, the Sale of Goods Act governs misrepresentation relating to contracts for the sale of goods.[41] Identical provisions exist in the Misrepresentation Act 1967 (UK), which appears to apply in Nauru and Vanuatu.

There are two main differences between the common law position and the statutory position on negligent misrepresentation:

1. Where the legislation applies, there is no need to prove a special duty of care, but only that the representation induced the other party to enter the contract.[42]
2. The statute reverses the burden of proof. Once the representee proves that there was a misrepresentation, and that it induced the representee to enter into the contract, the onus is on the representor to prove both his belief in the truth of the representation and reasonable ground for his belief.

---

[39] Unreported, High Court, Fiji, Scott J, 9 April 1996, 17. It may be that this case was decided under the statutory provisions in the Sale of Goods Act, but if so it was not necessary to embark on an investigation of whether a duty of care existed.

[40] *United Apparel (MFG) Ltd v Saville Heaton & Co Ltd* [1997] FJCA 40; *United Apparel (MFG) Ltd v Saville Heaton & Co Ltd* [1998] FJSC 9.

[41] Cap 230. See e.g. *Uluivutia v Western Wreckers Ltd* [2004] FJHC 330.

[42] *Howard Marine and Dredging Co Ltd v A Ogden & Sons (Excavations Ltd)* [1978] QB 574. But see *Saville Heaton & Co Ltd v United Apparel (MGF) Ltd* (unreported, High Court, Fiji, Scott J, 9 April 1996), where Scott J appears to have regarded the existence of a duty of care as relevant. The Sale of Goods Act was not discussed. The decision was upheld by the Court of Appeal and the Supreme Court, but on different grounds: see above n 40.

These Acts are also of relevance to remedies and are discussed further in section 4 below.

3.3. INNOCENT MISREPRESENTATION

An innocent misrepresentation is one containing no element of fraud or negligence.

4. REMEDIES FOR MISREPRESENTATION

4.1. RESCISSION

Rescission is available for all categories of misrepresentation. A contract can be rescinded by giving notice to the representor. Where it is impossible to trace the other party, the requirement may be waived, provided that all reasonable steps are taken to recover the goods. In *Car and Universal Finance v Caldwell*,[43] the owner of a car was induced by fraud to sell his car to a rogue, who disappeared and could not be traced. On discovering the fraud, the owner notified the police and the Automobile Association. These actions were held sufficient to rescind the contract so that an innocent third party who had bought the car from the rogue acquired no title to it.

4.1.1. Imposition of Terms

In ordering rescission, the court may impose terms. For example, a party may be required to account for profits, or to allow for deterioration, in order to do what is practically just.

4.1.2. Bars to Rescission

There are several bars to the right to rescind.

4.1.2.1. Affirmation of the Contract

If the representee has affirmed the contract, the right to rescission will be lost.[44] This is because affirmation is an indication to the representor of an intention to continue with the contract, despite the misrepresentation.

---

43 [1965] 1 QB 525.

44 *Long v Lloyd* [1958] 1 WLR 753.

4.1.2.2. Lapse of Time

The right to rescind will be lost if the representee does not act within a reasonable time.[45] However, this bar may not apply in the case of fraudulent misrepresentation.[46] Delay will not normally act as a bar where the representee is ignorant of the truth and therefore of his or her right to rescind. However, it will still be a factor to be taken into account, and in *Leaf v International Galleries*[47] the right to rescind was barred by five years' delay, even though the representee did not discover the truth until shortly before the proceedings commenced.

4.1.2.3. Impossibility of *restitutio in integrum*

The right to rescind will be lost if *restitutio in integrum* is impossible, that is, it is no longer possible to restore the parties to the position that they were in before the contract was made.[48]

4.1.2.4. Third Party Rights

If the property is purchased in good faith by an innocent third party, prior to rescission of the contract the third party obtains good title.[49] Accordingly, rescission is no longer possible.[50] No title will pass in any property transferred after the rescission of the contract.

4.1.2.5. Statutory Bars

In Fiji,[51] and in those countries where the Misrepresentation Act 1967 (UK) applies, the court has the discretion to award damages instead of rescission.[52]

4.2. DAMAGES

4.2.1. Damages for Fraudulent Misrepresentation

Damages are available for fraudulent misrepresentation. The measure of damages is tortious.[53] This means that generally damages will be awarded to put

---

45 *Leaf v International Galleries* [1950] 2 KB 86.

46 *Armstrong v Jackson* [1917] 2 KB 822.

47 [1950] 2 KB 86.

48 *Clarke v Dickson* (1858) EB & E 145.

49 *Babcock v Lawton* (1880) 5 QBD 284.

50 *Phillips v Brooks* [1919] 2 KB 243.

51 Sale of Goods Act Cap 230 (Fiji).

52 Ibid., s 76(2); Misrepresentation Act 1967 (UK), s 2(2).

53 This is because it is treated in the same way as the tort of deceit: *Clef Aquitaine SARL and Another v Laporte Materials (Barrow) Ltd* [2000] 3 All ER 493.

representees back in the position that they would have been if the contract had never been entered into, rather than the position that they would have been in if the representation had been true. Normally, an award of damages in tort is limited by the test of remoteness, that is, the defendant will be liable only for damages that were reasonably foreseeable. However, this is not so in the case of fraud, where the 'defendant is bound to make reparation for all the actual damages directly flowing from the fraudulent inducement'.[54] In *Enterprises Pty Ltd v Allardyce Lumber Company Ltd*,[55] the court held that *Doyle v Olby*[56] was 'adopted law in the Solomon Islands'. On that basis, it was ordered that the defendant make reparation for all the actual damages directly flowing from the fraudulent inducement.

It is not essential to show actual loss in order to recover. It is enough to show that a party would have entered into a contract (either with the defendant or a third party) on more favourable terms if that party had known the truth.[57]

Contributory negligence would not appear to be a defence to an action for fraudulent misrepresentation, as it does not apply to an action for deceit.[58]

4.2.2. Damages for Negligent Misrepresentation

Damages are also available for negligent misrepresentation at common law. The measure of damages is in tort, so as to put representees back in the position that they would have been in had the contract not been entered into.[59] Unlike damages for fraudulent misrepresentation, damages for negligent misrepresentation are limited by the rules of remoteness.[60] Accordingly, only losses that are reasonably foreseeable may be recovered.[61]

---

54 *Motil v North (Fiji) Group Ltd* [2013] FJHC 446. See also *Smith and New Court Securities Ltd v Scrimgeour Vickers (Asset Management) Ltd* [1999] 4 All ER 769.

55 [2007] SBHC 118.

56 (1969) 2 QB 158.

57 *Clef Aquitaine SARL and Another v Laporte Materials (Barrow) Ltd* [2000] 3 All ER 493.

58 *Alliance and Leicester Building Society v Edgestop Ltd* [1993] 1 WLR 1462.

59 But see *South Australia Asset Management Corp v York Montague Ltd* [1997] AC 191, where damages for misinformation were limited by reference to the contractual bargain. This method of calculation has been criticised: J. Stapleton, 'The Normal Expectancies Measure in Tort Damages' (1997) 113 *Law Quarterly Review* 257.

60 *Saville Heaton & Co Ltd v United Apparel (MGF) Ltd* (unreported, High Court, Fiji, Scott J, 9 April 1996), 18, 20. The decision in this case was upheld by the Court of Appeal and the Supreme Court, but this point was not determined. See above nn. 39, 40.

61 *Esso Petroleum v Marden* [1976] QB 801.

In Fiji, damages may be awarded for negligent misrepresentation under s 76(1) of the Sale of Goods Act.[62] Section 76 of the Sale of Goods Act (Fiji) and s 2(1) of the Misrepresentation Act 1967 (UK) provide:

> Where a person has entered into a contract after a misrepresentation has been made to him by another party thereto and as a result thereof he has suffered loss, then, if the person making the misrepresentation would be liable to damages in respect thereof had the misrepresentation been made fraudulently, that person shall be so liable notwithstanding that the misrepresentation was not made fraudulently unless he proves that he had reasonable ground to believe and did believe up to the time the contract was made that the facts represented were true.

The effect of this sub-section is to confer the same right to damages for negligent misrepresentation as exist in the case of fraudulent misrepresentation.

The position is identical under s 2(1) of the Misrepresentation Act 1967 (UK). However, the measure of damages under both these statutes is unclear. The language employed suggests that a tortious measure was envisaged. The case law is conflicting, but it now appears settled in England that the measure of damages is the tortious rather than contractual measure.[63] As damages are being awarded as if 'misrepresentation had been made fraudulently', it would appear that there is no requirement of foreseeability.[64] These cases are likely to be followed in Fiji, given the similarity in the wording of the relevant provisions.

It would appear that a plea of contributory negligence may be available where there is concurrent liability in tort for negligent misrepresentation.[65] If liability arises under s 2(1) alone, the misrepesentor is liable as if 'the misrepresentation had been made fraudulently', and as contributory negligence is not a defence to fraud, it would not appear to apply.

In the countries to which the Sale of Goods Act (Fiji) and the Misrepresentation Act 1967 (UK) apply, the courts may refuse rescission and award damages instead under s 76(2) and s 2(2) respectively. It is not possible to recover twice under both s 76(1) and s 76(2) or under both s 2(1) and s 2(2).[66] Damages under s 76(1) and s 2(1) will generally be greater.

---

62 Cap 230.

63 *Royscott Trust Ltd v Rogerson* [1991] 3 All ER 294 (CA).

64 Ibid. But see *Smith New Court Securities Ltd v Citibank NA* [1997] AC 254, 283.

65 *Gran Gelato Ltd v Richcliff (Group) Ltd* [1991] Ch 560. See also the dicta in *Saville Heaton & Co Ltd v United Apparel (MGF) Ltd and the Attorney-General* (unreported, High Court, Fiji, Civ Cas 410/1992, 9 April 1996), 17. The decision in this case was upheld by the Court of Appeal and the Supreme Court, but this point was not discussed. See the discussion above accompanying nn. 39, 40.

66 Misrepresentation Act 1967 (UK), s 2(3); Sale of Goods Act Cap 230 (Fiji), s 76(3).

4.2.3. *Damages for Innocent Misrepresentation*

Prior to the developments in common law and legislation discussed above, in the absence of fraud there was no right to damages for misrepresentation. To remedy the position, equity developed the remedy of an indemnity for innocent misrepresentation. The precise principles on which an indemnity is to be assessed are not clear, but it would appear to entitle the representee to reimbursement for out-of-pocket expenses paid out pursuant to the contract.[67] In the absence of fraud, an equitable indemnity is the only remedy for innocent misrepresentation other than rescission in countries of the region which do not have the benefit of statutory reform.

Section 76(2) of the Sale of Goods Act (Fiji) and s 2(2) of the Misrepresentation Act 1967 (UK) provide that in the case of innocent misrepresentation the court may refuse the remedy of rescission and award damages instead. Thus, there is now a limited right to damages for misrepresentation in the countries to which these Acts apply. However, the remedy of damages is subject to limitations:

- it is at the discretion of the court; and
- it may only be awarded in lieu of rescission (whereas the innocent party may be awarded both damages and rescission where misrepresentation is fraudulent or negligent).

The measure to be applied where damages are awarded in lieu of rescission under the legislation is neither contractual nor tortious. Rather it is a special measure, designed to compensate for the loss caused by the refusal to allow rescission.[68] In contracts for the sale of land or goods, this will be the difference between the value of the land or goods as they were received and the value of the goods as represented.[69]

Where a court awards damages in lieu of rescission, there will be no right to an indemnity, as the indemnity is part of the remedy of rescission, awarded to restore the status quo.

4.3. SUMMARY OF AVAILABLE REMEDIES

The position regarding remedies for different types of misrepresentation is summarised in Table 6.

---

67 *Whittington v Seale-Hayne* (1900) 82 LT 49.

68 *William Sindell plc v Cambridgeshire County Council* [1994] 1 WLR 1016; *UCB Corporate Services Ltd v Thomason* [2005] 1 All ER (Comm) 601, [37].

69 *William Sindell plc v Cambridgeshire County Council* [1994] 1 WLR 1016.

Table 6. Remedies for misrepresentation

Type of Misrepresentation	Available Remedies
Fraudulent	Rescission (subject to equitable bars) *and/or* common law damages in tort (but not restricted by remoteness test)
Negligent	Rescission (subject to equitable bars) *and/or* common law damages in tort (restricted by remoteness test) or damages under s 76(1) SGA; s 2(1) MA (in countries to which they apply) in tort (but not restricted by remoteness test)
Innocent	Rescission and an indemnity (subject to equitable bars) *or* damages in lieu under s 76(2) SGA; s 2(2) MA (in countries to which they apply) (a special measure applies)

Source: Compiled by the author.

In Tokelau, the Contract and Commercial Law Act 2017 (NZ) applies.[70] Subject to any express contractual provision, the Act makes the following provides for damages for misrepresentation in sale of goods contracts:

> (1) If a party to a contract (A) has been induced to enter into the contract by a misrepresentation, whether innocent or fraudulent, made to A by or on behalf of another party to that contract (B), –
> (a) A is entitled to damages from B in the same manner and to the same extent as if the representation were a term of the contract that has been breached; and
> (b) A is not, in the case of a fraudulent misrepresentation, or of an innocent misrepresentation made negligently, entitled to damages from B for deceit or negligence in respect of the misrepresentation.[71]

5. EXEMPTION FROM LIABILITY FOR MISREPRESENTATION

As mentioned in chapter 9, it is possible to exclude or limit liability arising for breach of contract, by means of an express provision to that effect. It is also possible to exclude or limit liability for misrepresentation. However, the following special rules apply in the case of misrepresentation:

(a) it is not possible to exclude liability for fraud;[72] and
(b) s 77 of the Sale of Goods Act (Fiji) and s 3 of the Misrepresentation Act 1967 (UK) raise a presumption that such an exclusion clause is invalid. It may be upheld if it is reasonable, but the onus is on the party seeking to rely on it to establish this.

70 Contract Rules 2004 (Tokelau), R 19.
71 Section 35.
72 *Motil v North (Fiji) Group Ltd* [2013] FJHC 446.

6. FAIR TRADING LEGISLATION

Fiji and, to a more limited extent, Marshall Islands and Solomon Islands have legislation which governs misleading or deceptive conduct and modifies the common law of misrepresentation.

The Misrepresentation Act 1967 (UK) contains similar provisions to Fiji's Sale of Goods Act and modifies the common law of misrepresentation. As mentioned above, the UK Act would appear to apply in Nauru and Vanuatu.

6.1. COMMERCE COMMISSION DECREE

In 2011, the Commerce Commission Decree repealed Fiji's Fair Trading Decree 1992, which had formerly dealt with misleading or deceptive conduct. The Commerce Commission Decree overlaps with the common law of misrepresentation, as modified by s 76 of the Sale of Goods Act.[73] However, the thrust of the Act is to protect the public rather than to interfere with private contractual arrangements. It does not cover transactions outside the field of trade and commerce, for example private sale and purchase agreements. The Commerce Commission Decree is not fraught with the difficulty of proving of intention to be entitled to damages and the remedies provided are broader than those available under the common law or the Sale of Goods Act.

6.1.1. False or Misleading Representation

Section 75(1) of the Commerce Commission Decree provides:

> A person shall not, in trade or commerce engage in conduct that is misleading or deceptive or is likely to mislead or deceive.

Accordingly, in order to come within the section:

- *The person must be in trade or commerce*
  'Trade or commerce' is defined in s 4(1) as including 'any business or professional activity' and business is in turn defined as including '(a) a business not carried on for profit; (b) a trade or profession or vocation'.

- *The person must engage in conduct*
  Conduct does not necessitate continuing activity. It includes doing, or refusing or omitting to do any act.

---

73 Cap 230.

- *The conduct must be misleading or deceptive*
  This is a question of fact to be determined in the context of the facts and surrounding circumstances on the balance of probabilities.[74] It is judged objectively. It is not necessary to show an intention to mislead or deceive.

The Decree also makes provision regarding false or misleading advertisements[75] and false or misleading representations in relation to land.[76]

6.1.2. *Remedies*

Contravention of the terms of the Decree is a statutory offence, but may also give rise to civil action. Sections 145–147 provide the following remedies:

- injunction;
- damages; and
- compensation and other remedial remedies.

Other remedies include an order rendering the contract unenforceable in whole or part, variation of the contract, and repair or replacement of goods.[77] However, the provisions on remedies reveal a further limitation of the Decree, as the remedies are only available to consumers.[78]

6.2. MARSHALL ISLANDS' CONSUMER PROTECTION ACT

In Marshall Islands, the Consumer Protection Act of the Revised Code[79] declares unfair or deceptive acts in trade or commerce to be unlawful, including:

- passing off goods of those of another;
- causing likelihood of confusion or misunderstanding as to the source of goods;
- causing likelihood of confusion or misunderstanding as to connection with another body;
- deceptive representations as to geographic origins of goods or service;

74 *Jattan v Drivesmart Suva Ltd* [2015] FJHC 900. This case was decided under the equivalent provision (s 54) of the Fair Trading Decree 1992.
75 Commerce Commission Decree 2010, s 78.
76 Ibid., s 79.
77 Ibid., s 147(5).
78 Ibid., s 147(6).
79 20 MIRC Cap 4.

- representations of approval, attributes, quantities or connection regarding goods or services;
- representations of goods as original or new if they are not;
- representation as to particular standard, quality, grade, style or model of goods or service;
- false advertising;
- any other conduct which creates a likelihood of confusion or misunderstanding;
- any act or practice that is unfair or deceptive.

The Act sets up a system of investigation and restraint, to be administered by the Attorney-General.[80] It provides for a penalty of up to $1,000 per violation and a penalty of up to $10,000 for breach of an injunction granted under the Act, to be paid to the government.[81] It also allows civil action by anyone who suffers loss as a result of a prohibited act for the recovery of $100 or actual damages, whichever is the greater.[82]

6.3. SOLOMON ISLANDS' CONSUMER PROTECTION ACT

In Solomon Islands, the Consumer Protection Act[83] prohibits the making of false representations in the course of trade or business in connection with the supply or use of goods or services. There is no definition of the term 'trade or business' within the Act. The Act does not provide a civil remedy, but makes misleading or deceptive conduct an offence. In particular, it is an offence under s 25 to:

- misrepresent the standard, quality or grade of goods or services, or the style or mode of goods;
- falsely represent that they are new;
- falsely represent that goods have sponsorship, approval performance, characteristics, accessories, uses or benefits;
- falsely represent that a trader has sponsorship, approval or affiliation;
- falsely represent the need for goods, services, replacements or repairs; or
- falsely represent the existence or effect of a warranty or guarantee.

---

80 Ibid., ss 405, 409, 410–412.

81 Ibid., s 413.

82 Ibid., s 406.

83 Cap 63.

Further, s 30 prohibits misleading conduct in trade or commerce, liable to mislead the public as to the nature, characteristics or suitability or quantity of goods or services.

The penalty on first conviction under the Act is a fine of up to $3,000 or imprisonment of up to a year.[84] In the case of subsequent convictions, a fine of up to $7,000 or imprisonment for up to two years is provided.[85] The court may also order forfeiture of the goods in respect of which an offence was committed[86] and may ban the convicted person from trading for such period as it thinks fit.

---

84 Ibid., s 34(1)(a).
85 Ibid., s 34(1)(b).
86 Ibid., s 34(2).

CHAPTER 13

DURESS, UNDUE INFLUENCE AND UNCONSCIONABILITY

1. INTRODUCTION

This chapter examines the situations in which relief is available to a person who has entered into a contract because of some improper pressure. It is important to note at the outset that the pressure must be 'improper'. People may be compelled to enter into unfavourable transactions by a number of factors: the demands of their own circumstances; the lack of an alternative source for the benefits they seek; or more generally the bargaining strength of the other party. It would be contrary to the principles underlying contract law to allow a party to escape from the consequences of a transaction freely entered into merely because of restraints imposed on the exercise of freedom of choice. However, there are circumstances in which the pressure is such that the victim cannot be said to have acted freely. In certain cases of improper pressure, law or equity will afford relief.

Protection from improper pressure may arise within the following categories:

- the common law doctrine of duress;
- the equitable rules of undue influence;
- the common law doctrine of unconscionability; and
- statutory protection.

2. THE COMMON LAW DOCTRINE OF DURESS

At common law, improper pressure put on one party by another to enter into a contract may amount to duress. To amount to duress:

- the pressure must amount to compulsion of the will of the victim; and
- the pressure exerted must be illegitimate.[1]

A contract entered into under duress is voidable.

1 *Universe Tankships Inc of Monrovia v International Transport Workers' Federation* [1982] 2 All ER 67.

2.1. WHAT WILL CONSTITUTE SUFFICIENT PRESSURE?

The original common law doctrine recognised only physical pressure as sufficient to amount to duress. This required actual or threatened violence to the victim.[2] In current times, such physical duress is uncommon in the commercial field. However, one example of physical duress can be found in *Barton v Armstrong*.[3] The defendant threatened the plaintiff with death if his company did not pay a substantial sum of money to the defendant. This was held to amount to duress. The Privy Council made it clear that it is not necessary to show that the duress was the sole cause of the victim's entry into the contract. If threats were a contributory reason for entry into a contract, that will be enough. Once duress is established, the onus is on the defendant to show it had no bearing on the making of the contract.

Physical duress is more likely to occur between relatives. One regional example is *Cheon v Cheon*,[4] where a matrimonial property agreement was set aside on the ground that the applicant's consent had been obtained by force and threats. Palmer J said:

> Whilst the Court recognises on the one hand, the freedom of the parties to enter into agreements voluntarily, it should nevertheless treat very cautiously any such agreements that seek to exclude any [party's] right to litigation unless it is satisfied that independent legal advice had been given. In the circumstances of a husband and wife relationship this is all the more important as the possibility of duress occurring is very real in circumstances where you have a domineering and controlling spouse.[5]

Duress today is more likely to take the form of economic pressure, and it is now well established that this will suffice. The point was confirmed in *The Atlantic Baron*.[6] Under a ship construction contract, the building company demanded a 10% increase in instalments from the owners largely because of a devaluation of the US dollar. The owners did pay the increased rate demanded from them, although they protested that there was no legal basis for the demand. The owners were commercially compelled to pay since at the time of the threat they were negotiating a very lucrative contract for the charter of the ship to be built. Mocatta J decided that this constituted economic duress. The illegitimate pressure exerted by the building company was their threat to break the construction contract. Where accordingly a threat to break a contract had led to a further contract,

---

2 *Seear v Cohen* (1881) 45 LT 589.
3 [1976] AC 104.
4 [1997] SBHC 16.
5 Ibid., 2.
6 *North Ocean Shipping Co Ltd v Hyundai ('The Atlantic Baron')* [1979] QB 705.

that contract, even though it was made for good consideration (an increase in the return letter of credit), was voidable by reason of economic duress. However, that right had been lost as the contract had been affirmed by delay.

However, in *Pao On v Lau Yiu Long*,[7] the Privy Council refused to uphold a claim of economic duress. The Council made it clear that in a contractual situation commercial pressure is not enough. There must be some factor present 'which could be regarded as coercion of his will so as to vitiate his consent'. Lord Scarman stated that the material factors to consider were:

1. whether the party alleged to have been coerced did or did not protest;
2. whether at the time of the alleged coercion the party did or did not have an adequate legal remedy;
3. whether the party was independently legally advised; and
4. whether after entering into the contract the party took steps to avoid it.

A further important development took place in *Universe Tankships Inc of Monrovia v International Transport Workers' Federation*.[8] In that case, the defendant had blacklisted one of the plaintiff's ships and agreed to release it only on payment of a large sum of money, paid partly to the Union's Welfare Fund. After payment, the plaintiff sought recovery on the basis that the payment took place under economic duress. This plea was upheld.

This case is important in two respects:

1. It suggests that it is not necessary that the will of the victim must be 'overborne', as suggested in *The Atlantic Baron*[9] and *Pao On v Lau Yiu Long*.[10] Rather, there must be compulsion of the will.
2. It rejects the notion that in order to amount to duress, the defendants must be aware that the victim is acting under duress.

Lord Diplock stated that the rationale of economic duress is:

> that his apparent consent was induced by pressure exercised on him by that other party which the law does not regard as legitimate, with the consequence that the consent is treated in law as revocable unless approbated either expressly or by implication after the illegitimate pressure has ceased to operate on his mind.[11]

---

7 [1980] AC 614.

8 [1982] 2 All ER 67.

9 *North Ocean Shipping Co Ltd v Hyundai ('The Atlantic Baron')* [1979] QB 705.

10 *Pao On v Lau Yiu Long* [1980] AC 614.

11 *Universe Tankships Inc of Monrovia v International Transport Workers' Federation* [1982] 2 All ER 67, 75–76.

The case also made it clear that is not fatal if a party can show that there was no 'practicable choice'.[12] Failure to protest is only one factor to consider.

The need to establish coercion vitiating consent was also rejected in *Dimskal Shipping Co SA v International Transport Workers Federation*[13] and in the Australian case of *Crescendo Management Pty Ltd v Westpac Banking Corporation*.[14] Both of these authorities were cited with approval by the Court of Appeal of Tonga in *Bank of Tonga v Tulikihakau*.[15] In that case, the plaintiff was employed by the defendant bank. In June 1994, he gave one month's notice in order to take up a job with another bank. However, his new employer wanted his services urgently and agreed with the plaintiff to pay 15 days' pay to the defendant for the plaintiff's early release and to pay off his outstanding loans to the defendant. The plaintiff wrote to the bank with these terms and asked for the balance of his retirement fund to be credited to him. The defendant replied confirming early release. However, the retirement fund payment was withheld. In addition, the new employer delayed in taking over the loan. It was suggested by the defendant that the retirement fund be put towards the loans, to be reimbursed when the new employer took them over. The plaintiff refused and informed the defendant that he would go on paying off the loan by instalments until it was taken over. The plaintiff also repeated his request for his retirement fund to be paid out. It was accepted that the plaintiff was under pressure during this time, as he needed the money and that he had made this clear to the bank. The retirement fund was still not paid out, and in December the defendant wrote a letter to the plaintiff suggesting that $2,106.83 should be paid from the retirement fund towards repayment of the plaintiff's father's debt. The plaintiff replied, agreeing to a deduction of $600 from the retirement fund to be credited to his father's loan account, in the hope that this would satisfy the bank. However, the retirement funds were still not paid, and the bank wrote again insisting that he agree to a deduction of $1,100. In February, the plaintiff gave in and agreed to a deduction of $1,000 from his retirement fund. After consulting a solicitor, he applied to recover that amount. The Court of Appeal of Tonga upheld the trial judge's finding of fact that the payment of $1,000 was made under duress arising from illegitimate pressure consisting of the threat to continue withholding the plaintiff's money. The Court stated that: 'However, precisely, the effect of the pressure should be stated, it is clear that it must have been, as Lord Goff put it, "a significant cause inducing the plaintiff"'. The Court cited with approval the Privy Council's decision in *Barton v Armstrong*,[16] to the

12 *Universe Tankships Inc of Monrovia v International Trade Workers' Union Fund* [1982] 2 All ER 67, 88 (Scarman LJ).

13 [1992] AC 152.

14 (1988) 19 NSWLR 40.

15 (1999) Tonga LR 182.

16 [1976] AC 104.

effect that, once a serious threat was shown, the onus was on the defendant to prove it had no effect, and that the court need only conclude that the threat was 'a reason, not necessarily the only reason, for the plaintiff's action'.[17]

2.2. WHAT WILL CONSTITUTE ILLEGITIMATE PRESSURE?

Driving a hard bargain or exerting commercial pressure is not enough to amount to duress.[18] Facts which may indicate the existence of illegitimate pressure are threats of non-performance unless additional payment is made, coupled with the absence of any consideration. The decision to that effect in *Pao On v Lau Yiu Long*[19] was approved in *Atlas Express Ltd v Kafco (Importers and Distributors) Ltd*.[20] In that case, the defendant contracted to supply basketware to a large supermarket chain. The plaintiff contracted with the defendant to deliver the basketware to the supermarket. After the contract commenced, the plaintiff discovered that it had under-priced the contract and threatened to discontinue delivery unless the defendant paid an additional sum on each consignment. The defendant was heavily dependent on the contract with the supermarket and there would have been a severe penalty for failure to perform that contract. The defendant could not find an alternative carrier and agreed under protest to make the extra payments. The plaintiff sued for non-payment of the additional sum. It was held that the agreement was invalid for economic duress and for lack of consideration.

This case can be compared with *Williams v Roffey Bros & Nicholls (Contractors) Ltd*.[21] In that case, the defendants were the main contractors on a building contract. The plaintiffs were sub-contracting carpenters on the job and were in financial difficulty. The defendants realised that there was a risk that the plaintiffs would not complete the work. To avoid having to pay damages under the main contract if the job was not finished on time, the defendants offered the plaintiffs an extra payment. The defendants later refused to pay this extra money and said there was no consideration for the promise to pay it. It was held by the Court of Appeal that the defendants' avoidance of the risk of having to pay liquidated damages in the main contract was consideration for the promise. There was no duress in this case as the plaintiffs made no threats. Rather, the defendants made the offer of the extra payment.

---

17 *Bank of Tonga v Tulikihakau* [1999] TOCA 16.
18 *Azam v Azam* (1967) 13 FLR 115.
19 [1980] AC 614.
20 [1989] QB 833.
21 [1990] 1 All ER 512.

2.3. REMEDIES

A contract entered into under duress is voidable rather than void. The injured party is entitled to rescind the contract unless it has been affirmed.[22] It is unclear whether damages may be recovered for duress. In *Universe Tankships Inc of Monrovia v International Transport Workers' Federation*,[23] Lords Diplock and Scarman expressed differing views on this point. By analogy with the tort of intimidation, damages may be recoverable.[24] It is also unclear whether an injured party who has affirmed may recover damages in tort. According to *Chitty on Contract*, damages are available in this situation.[25]

3. THE EQUITABLE RULES OF UNDUE INFLUENCE

If one party induces the consent of the other by undue influence, the contract is voidable in equity. The court interferes, not on the grounds of fraud, but because of public policy or the prevention of victimisation by a party with influence over another.[26] There are no precise boundaries to the jurisdiction, which is applied on a case-by-case basis. In *Fonua v MBf Bank Ltd*,[27] Ward CJ cited with approval the words of Scarman LJ in *National Westminster Bank v Morgan*:[28]

> There is no precisely defined law setting limits to the equitable jurisdiction of a court to relieve against undue influence. This is the world of doctrine, not of neat and tidy rules. The courts of equity have developed a body of learning enabling relief to be granted where the law has to treat the transaction as unimpeachable unless it can be held to have been procured by undue influence. It is the unimpeachability at law of a disadvantageous transaction which is the starting point from which the court advances to consider whether the transaction is the product merely of one's own folly or of the undue influence exercised by another.

In *Latchan v Martin*[29] the Fiji Court of Appeal held that 'where a transaction is shown to have been so opposed to fair dealing that it ought not to be binding the Court will be prepared to interfere'.

---

22 *North Ocean Shipping Co Ltd v Hyundai Construction Co Ltd ('The Atlantic Baron')* [1979] QB 705.

23 [1983] 1 AC 366.

24 J. Chitty and H.G. Beale (eds.), *Chitty on Contract*, 28th ed., Vol. 1, Sweet & Maxwell, London 1999, 431. In *Universe Tankships of Monrovia v ITWF* [1983] 1 AC 366 Lords Diplock and Scarman expressed differing views on this point.

25 J. Chitty and H.G. Beale (eds.), *Chitty on Contract*, 28th ed., Vol. 1, Sweet & Maxwell, London 1999, 432.

26 But note that actual undue influence has been regarded as a species of fraud: *CIBC Mortgages plc v Pitt* [1993] 4 All ER 433.

27 (1999) Tonga LR 4; upheld on appeal to the Court of Appeal of Tonga [2000] TOCA 13.

28 [1985] AC 686, 709.

29 (1984) 30 FLR 70, citing *Chesterfield v Jansen* (1751) 2 Ves Sen 125, 155.

There are two classes of undue influence: presumed undue influence and actual undue influence. These were explained in *Kumari v Ammai*,[30] where the Court of Appeal of Fiji cited the words of Cotton LJ in *Allcard v Skinner*:[31]

> These decisions may be divided into classes: first where the Court has been satisfied that the gift was the result of influence expressly used by the donee for the purpose; secondly, where the relations between the donor and donee have at or shortly before the execution of the gift been such as to raise a presumption that the donee had influence over the donor. In such a case the court sets aside the voluntary gift, unless it is proved that in fact the gift was the spontaneous act of the donor acting under circumstances which enabled him to exercise an independent will and which justify the court in holding that the gift was the result of a free exercise of the donor's will.

The ratio of this case applies not only to gifts, but also to sales at an undervalue.

3.1. PRESUMED UNDUE INFLUENCE

Where there is a special or confidential relationship between the parties, it is presumed that undue influence was applied and the onus is on the party in whom confidence was reposed to show that undue influence was not used. Examples of such relationships are solicitor and client, doctor and patient, religious advisor and disciple,[32] partners,[33] and parent and child.

The category of spiritual advisor and disciple is of considerable importance within the South Pacific region, where the church is a powerful force.[34] As stated by Lindley J in *Allcard v Skinner*:[35]

> The influence of one mind over another is very subtle, and of all influences religious influence is the most dangerous and the most powerful, and to counteract it courts of equity have gone very far.

Apart from parent and child, family relationships, including husband and wife, have been held not to constitute a special category.[36] However, the categories are

30 [1978] FJCA 1.

31 (1887) 36 Ch D 145.

32 Ibid.

33 *Lallu v Ranchod* (unreported, Court of Appeal, Fiji, Savage, Dillon and Hillyer JJA, 30 August 1996), 9. See further J. Corrin Care, 'Case Note on *Lallu v Ranchod*' (1998) 2 *Journal of South Pacific Law* 20.

34 See e.g. the Constitution of Tonga, where religious observance has been included in the Bill of Rights.

35 (1887) 36 Ch D 145, 183.

36 *Barclays Bank plc v O'Brien* [1994] 1 AC 180.

not closed, and where it can be shown that there is a relationship of ascendency and dependency between the parties, and where a party relies on the advice and assistance of the other, the court may presume undue influence in the absence of evidence to the contrary. In *Barclays Bank plc v O'Brien*,[37] the House of Lords confirmed that no special relationship arises in law between husband and wife, but such relationship may arise in the circumstances of a particular case. This is of particular importance in those parts of the South Pacific region where women do not have a right to speak for themselves.[38]

The possibility of undue influence from relatives is also increased by the fact that social security is not provided by the state and it is very common for the elderly and infirm to be cared for by family members. In *Kumari v Ammai*,[39] the plaintiff was an elderly and illiterate woman. She went to live with her daughter and grandson. During the 19 months that she was with them, $6,709 was withdrawn from her bank account, and her house, worth $19,893, was transferred to her grandson for $8,000. The Court of Appeal held that in order for a presumption of undue influence to arise, a 'relation of confidence' must be shown. An example of such relationship was that between doctor and patient or a family relationship. In this case, the evidence showed not only a family relationship, but also a situation of dependency in practically all matters. In these circumstances, the presumption of undue influence arose and the onus of proving the absence of such influence was on the party seeking to uphold the contract. In this case, that onus had not been discharged.

Another regional example of presumed undue influence based not so much on 'family relationships' as on a customary or community relationship is *Lallu v Ranchod*.[40] In that case, the plaintiff became equal partner with the defendant, her late husband's brother, in the business of merchants and theatre proprietors. The business also owned certain properties. In 1990, the defendant was convicted of assaulting the plaintiff, who was forced to move out of the house she shared with the defendant and his family into accommodation behind the theatre. The parties were members of the Fijian Indian Gujarati community, with its own language and customs. The defendant arranged a meeting between the parties and prominent members of the community, which was a common way of dealing with disputes. After the meeting, the parties executed a deed providing for the dissolution of the partnership, with all assets to be transferred to the defendant and $50,000 to be paid to the plaintiff. After execution of the deed, the plaintiff became aware that she would only receive $50,000, and not the money and the theatre as she had thought.

---

37 Ibid.

38 See further e.g. A. Sherrill Whittington, S. Ospina and A. Pollard, *Women in Government In Solomon Islands A Diagnostic Study*, RAMSI, Honiara 2006.

39 [1978] FJCA 1.

40 Unreported, Court of Appeal, Fiji, Savage, Dillon and Hillyer JJA, 30 August 1996.

It was held that a presumption of undue influence arose from the relationship between the parties, as the defendant dominated the plaintiff and there was an inequality of bargaining power. Accordingly, the deed was set aside. It was also held that the third parties 'recruited' by the defendant exercised such a degree of domination and control over the plaintiff as to undermine her ability to make an independent decision.

This case is of considerable importance in the South Pacific. If an agreement is entered into between members of a customary group with unequal status, the presumption of undue influence would appear to arise. For example, an agreement between a village chief or noble and a member of their community group might raise the possibility of undue influence. Further, if a chief or tribal elder takes part in the negotiations leading up to entry into the agreement at the request of one party, this may also give rise to a presumption of undue influence.

Another situation that does not form a recognised special relationship is bank manager and customer.[41] However, as in the case of family relationships, if a special relationship can be shown to exist on the facts, the courts will apply the presumption. For example, in *Lloyds Bank Ltd v Bundy*,[42] a guarantee was given to the plaintiff bank by the defendant, an elderly farmer, who was a customer of the bank. The guarantee was in respect of his son's indebtedness and was secured by a mortgage of the defendant's house in favour of the bank. The bank had built up a special relationship with the Bundy family over the years, and consequently the plaintiff had trust and confidence in the bank. It was held that, as the plaintiff was liable to be influenced by the bank, which was obtaining a benefit, there was a duty on it to ensure that the plaintiff formed an independent judgment on the transaction. The duty in this case was particularly onerous as the plaintiff was mortgaging all his assets and the son's financial circumstances were unlikely to improve. It was held that the defendant had failed to discharge this duty.

In addition to the requisite relationship, it was held in *National Westminster Bank v Morgan*[43] that in order for a transaction to be set aside because of presumed undue influence, the transaction must be to the manifest disadvantage of the plaintiff. In fact, in that case, the plaintiff failed for two reasons: first, the presumption did not arise, and second there was no manifest disadvantage, as the risks involved were worth running. However, doubt has been cast on this requirement by *CIBC Mortgages plc v Pitt*,[44] where the House of Lords indicated that it might be willing to reconsider the matter. Similarly, in *Barclays Bank plc v Coleman*,[45] it was observed by Nourse LJ in the Court of Appeal that the

41 *National Westminster Bank v Morgan* [1985] AC 686; *Fonua v MBf Bank Ltd* [2000] TOCA 13.
42 [1975] QB 326.
43 [1985] AC 686.
44 [1993] 4 All ER 433.
45 [2000] QB 20, 31.

requirement of manifest disadvantage might not continue to be a necessary factor in cases of presumed undue influence.

The presumption of undue influence may be rebutted by evidence that the party seeking to set aside the contract received independent legal advice. The existence of independent legal advice was pleaded as a defence in *Kumari v Ammai*,[46] but not proved. It was also negated by the statement in the defence that the parties had both been represented by the same solicitor.

3.2. ACTUAL UNDUE INFLUENCE

Where there is no special relationship between the parties, a party alleging undue influence must prove that undue influence was exerted and that this excluded free consent to the agreement.

In *CIBC Mortgages plc v Pitt*,[47] the defendant had been induced to agree to a second mortgage on the family home as security for a loan to finance share purchases. The defendant had not wanted to go ahead with the scheme, but had given in to a campaign of sustained pressure. The court held that a transaction not entered into freely and knowingly would be set aside as such pressure was a species of fraud. This case also makes it clear that it is not necessary to prove manifest disadvantage in the case of actual undue influence.

It is important to note that where a person has been induced to enter into a contract by undue influence, actual or presumed, the courts have held that third parties will also be affected by that undue influence, if they have actual or constructive notice of it. Thus, a contract made with a bank by a husband and wife jointly may be set aside by the wife on the grounds of undue influence by the husband if the wife can show that the bank had actual or constructive notice of the undue influence exerted on her by the husband.[48] Further, the courts have held that one situation when a bank will be held to have constructive notice of undue influence over a wife is when she signs a contract to provide that property owned wholly or partly by her is to be held by the bank as security for a loan which is solely for the benefit of the husband.[49] The courts have also made it clear that a bank will be fixed with constructive notice not only in the case of a wife and husband, but whenever one party to a contract is providing property to a bank as security for a loan to another person. On the other hand, if both parties to a contract to provide property as security to the bank are to benefit

---

46 [1978] FJCA 1.

47 [1993] 4 All ER 433.

48 *Barclays Bank plc v O'Brien* [1994] 1 AC 180; *Royal Bank of Scotland plc v Etridge (No. 2)* [2002] 2 AC 773.

49 Ibid.

from the loan, the bank will not be held to have constructive notice of any undue influence that may have been exerted on one party by the other.[50]

An example of circumstances falling short of undue influence can be seen in *National Westminster Bank v Morgan*.[51] In that case, a husband and wife owned their home jointly. The husband was unable to meet his mortgage payments and made refinancing arrangements with the bank, secured by a mortgage in favour of the bank over the matrimonial home. The bank manager called at the home to get the wife to execute the charge. She made it clear that she did not wish the charge to cover her husband's business liabilities. The bank manager assured her in good faith, but incorrectly, that it did not. It was in fact unlimited. The wife signed without obtaining independent advice. The husband and wife fell into arrears with the mortgage and the bank obtained an order for possession. Shortly afterwards, the husband died without paying off the business advances. The wife sought to set aside the mortgage on the grounds of undue influence. It was held that, as there was no special relationship, actual undue influence had to be proved and this onus had not been discharged in this case.

3.3. REMEDIES

As in the case of duress, undue influence renders the contract voidable rather than void. As illustrated by some of the cases discussed above, the victim often does not seek a remedy, but relies on undue influence as a defence when sued.

Damages are not available as a remedy for undue influence.[52] The available remedy is rescission.[53] Rescission is subject to the limits imposed by equity, which were discussed in chapter 12. These can be summarised as:

- affirmation;
- lapse of time;
- impossibility of restitution; and
- third party rights.

Impossibility of restitution will only be a bar to rescission for undue influence if it is possible to do substantial justice between the parties. The court may order either party to make restitution if they have received a benefit under the contract prior to rescission.[54]

50 *CIBC Mortgages plc v Pitt* [1993] 4 All ER 433.
51 [1985] 1 AC 686.
52 *Mahoney v Purnell* [1996] 3 All ER 61.
53 See e.g. *Allcard v Skinner* (1887) 36 Ch D 145.
54 *O'Sullivan v Management Assets Agency Ltd* [1985] QB 428.

With regard to third parties, if they have acquired an interest in the subject matter of the contract in good faith and for value, they cannot be displaced by an action for rescission. However, rescission will be effective, not only against the person exercising undue influence, but also against a third party, if that party had notice that such influence had been exercised[55] or if they have not given good consideration.[56]

4. UNCONSCIONABILITY

Whilst the policy of the law is not to interfere with bad bargains,[57] there is another limited class of case where equity may intervene to set aside a contract that may be described as harsh or unconscionable.

The notion of unconscionability is difficult to define and there is no closed list of categories of behaviour to which it applies.[58] One view, espoused by Lord Denning, is that there is a wide doctrine of unconscionability, based on inequality of bargaining power, and that duress and undue influence are just part of this wider concept of unconscionability.[59] However, Lord Denning's wider approach has not been followed and was specifically disapproved by Lord Scarman in *National Westminster Bank v Morgan*.[60] In *McGoon v Ali*,[61] the Court of Appeal of Fiji regarded unconscionability as a separate principle from undue influence, although the facts in some cases might amount to both.

The Court further stated in *McGoon v Ali*[62] that a useful starting point when considering unconscionable conduct could be found in *Evans v Lloyd*,[63] where the court relied on the following passage from *Snell's Equity*:[64]

> There is a well established equitable jurisdiction to set aside a purchase from 'a poor and ignorant man' at a considerable undervalue unless the purchaser satisfies the court that the transaction was fair, just and reasonable.
>
> The doctrine applies where (1) (one party) is suffering from certain kinds of disability or disadvantage; (2) the bargain is oppressive to (that party); and (3) the other party acted unconscionably in that he or she knowingly took advantage of

55 *Barclays Bank plc v O'Brien* [1994] 1 AC 180.
56 *Bridgman v Green* (1757) Wilm 58, 65.
57 *Clarion Ltd v National Provident Institution* [2000] 2 All ER 265.
58 *Cresswell v Potter* [1978] 1 WLR 225. See also *Backhouse v Backhouse* [1978] 1 WLR 243.
59 See e.g. *Lloyds Bank v Bundy* [1975] QB 326.
60 [1985] 1 AC 686.
61 [2015] FJCA 31, [21].
62 Ibid., [27].
63 [2013] EWHC 1725, [47].
64 J. McGhee (ed.), *Snell's Equity*, 32nd ed., Sweet & Maxwell, London 2010, para. 8-036.

> that party ... Where these requirements are met the burden then passes to (the other party) to satisfy the court that the transaction was fair, just and reasonable.

With regard to the first requirement, the Court went on to say that, apart from poverty and lack of education, which were well-established disabilities or disadvantages for the purpose of the doctrine, 'illness, inexperience, impaired faculties and financial need are all matters that may affect a party's ability to make a judgment in his own best interests'.[65] In order to meet the second requirement, it is not sufficient to establish that the transaction was imprudent. It must be established that the terms were 'overreaching and oppressive and that they shock the conscience of the court'.[66]

As for the third requirement, unconscionable conduct refers 'not only to the oppressive terms but to the behaviour of the stronger party, which must be morally culpable or reprehensible'. Unequal bargaining power or unfavourable terms alone are insufficient to satisfy this requirement.[67] Further, a court will not find unconscionable conduct if a party was unaware that the other party was acting under a special disadvantage or if there was no improper behaviour during negotiations, such use of unfair or illegitimate tactics or seeking to take advantage of a mistake.[68]

In *Li v Finefuiaki*,[69] the plaintiff claimed possession of two lots of land, of which he was the registered holder. He claimed that although he had intended to subdivide the land and sell part to the defendant, the defendant had built on the wrong part of the land and had built on an area double the size that was originally agreed to be sold. The agreement was concluded orally and never put into writing. The plaintiff also claimed that, in any event, the defendant had not been paid the full contract price. It was held that although there was no clear contract of sale, the plaintiff had taken no action to prevent the defendant from building on the larger portion of land or to indicate that full payment was required before work began. It was held that the plaintiff had acted unconscionably and was estopped from evicting the defendant. In spite of the uncertainty surrounding the terms, specific performance of the contract was ordered.

The fact that a party did not receive legal advice will be a factor to be considered in assessing whether the other party has acted unconscionably.[70] In *Benaia v Khan*,[71] the plaintiff entered into an agreement to charter the defendant's vessel and paid the charter fee. The vessel was not available immediately, as the

65 *McGoon v Ali* [2015] FCJA 31, [27], citing *Blomley v Ryan* (1956) 99 CLR 362, 145.
66 Ibid., [30], citing *Evans v Lloyd* [2013] EWHC 1725, [47].
67 Ibid., [31], citing *Evans v Lloyd* [2013] EWHC 1725, [47].
68 Ibid.
69 [2013] TOLC 1.
70 See above n. 46.
71 [2005] KIHC 49.

plaintiff had thought it would be. The plaintiff claimed for recovery of the fee. The court held that the agreement was unconscionable as the plaintiff was 'naïve in business matters' and did not get independent legal advice; he spent only a few minutes perusing the document and it was not explained to him.

However, the fact that legal advice was obtained will not be fatal to a claim of unconscionability. In *McGoon v Ali*,[72] the plaintiff sued his employer for damages for personal injuries incurred as a result of an accident at work. At the pre-trial conference stage, the parties agreed to settle, and the parties eventually signed a settlement document. The plaintiff later commenced proceedings, seeking to set aside the document. Whilst the relevant part of the claim was couched in terms of undue influence, the court considered the facts alleged as possibly amounting to either undue influence or unconscionable conduct. The court found that the factors weighing in favour of a finding of unconscionability were that the plaintiff was in a 'dire financial position' and, being an employee, was the weaker party; he had been badly injured and needed money to support his family; and the employer acted knowing of this vulnerability. Against this weighed the fact that the plaintiff was not in poor health at the time of signing, he had the necessary capacity and he received independent legal advice on the day. On balance, the court concluded that the defendant's conduct was unconscionable.

The Court in *McGoon v Ali*,[73] also held that that the doctrine of unconscionability was not restricted to sale and purchase agreements, but applied to any type of agreement.

In regional countries other than Cook Islands,[74] Fiji[75] and Papua New Guinea,[76] there is no statutory provision which guards against inequality of bargaining power. In countries without such legislation, this arguably justifies a more proactive approach by the courts to abuse of a dominant position.[77] In *Taval v Maleb*,[78] the Vanuatu Supreme Court stated, obiter, that it would not enforce an unconscionable contract, especially one reflecting inequality of bargaining power. In Fiji, the more liberal approach to estoppel[79] might also suggest that the courts in that country may be inclined to follow Lord Denning's broader doctrine of unconscionability. However, it is clear that merely driving a hard bargain will not in itself amount to unconscionability.[80]

---

72 [2015] FJCA 31.
73 Ibid., [32].
74 Cook Islands Act 1915 (NZ), s 645, discussed in section 5.1.
75 Fair Trading Decree 1992 (Fiji), s 55, discussed in section 5.2.
76 Fairness of Transactions Act 1993 (PNG).
77 See also Law Reform Commission of Papua New Guinea, *Fairness of Transactions*, Report No. 6, December 1977, 5, discussed in section 5.3.
78 [2015] VUSC 21, [49].
79 *Nair v Public Trustee of Fiji* (unreported, High Court, Fiji, Lyons J, 8 March 1996).
80 See e.g. *Azam v Azam* (1967) 13 FLR 115.

The remedy in cases of unconscionable conduct is rescission. This relief is subject to the same limitations that apply in the case of undue influence.

5. STATUTORY PROTECTION

In some countries of the region, unconscionable contracts have been dealt with by statute. In Cook Islands, the legislation covers all contracts. Similar legislation is in force in the neighbouring country of Papua New Guinea. In Fiji, statutory intervention is limited to agreements to supply goods or services.

5.1. COOK ISLANDS

In Cook Islands, s 645 of the Cook Islands Act (NZ) gives the High Court discretion to alter a contract made by Cook Islands Maoris, if the court is of the opinion that it is oppressive, unreasonable or improvident. The court may either refuse to enforce it or may enforce it only to such an extent and on such terms as it thinks fit. Until 2004, a similar provision was in force in Niue.[81]

5.2. FIJI

The Fair Trading Decree 1992, discussed in chapter 12, provides that a person involved in trade or commerce, and more particularly the supply of goods or services, shall not engage in unconscionable conduct.[82] Unconscionable conduct is not defined, but a number of factors are specified as being relevant to determining whether it exists:

1. relative bargaining strengths;
2. whether the customer was required to comply with conditions which were not reasonably necessary for the protection of the supplier's reasonable interests;
3. whether the customer understood any relevant documents;
4. whether any undue influence or pressure was exerted or unfair tactics used;
5. the price and conditions upon which similar goods or services could have been obtained elsewhere.

---

81 Niue Act 1966 (NZ), s 711 provided all courts with discretion to refuse to enforce a contract made by a Niuean if the court regards the contract as oppressive, unreasonable or improvident. This section was repealed by the Legislation (Correction of Errors and Minor Amendment) Act 2004 (Niue), s 42(88).

82 Fair Trading Decree 1992 (Fiji), s 55.

The only remedies available are compensation or 'other relief', as opposed to injunctions or damages, which are not available.[83]

5.3. PAPUA NEW GUINEA

In Papua New Guinea, the Transactions with Native Acts of 1958 and 1963 required contracts with Papua New Guineans to comply with certain formalities, and empowered a court to ignore the terms of the contract and give effect to any decision that it considered equitable.[84] Those Acts were repealed by the Fairness of Transactions Act 1993, which was not brought into force until 1998.[85]

This Act was the result of a Report by the Law Reform Commission of Papua New Guinea.[86] The Commission stated that it was not convinced that the 'harsh' law of contract was suitable for the country as the assumption that most people enter contracts on equal terms was untrue in most cases. The Commission considered that most Papua New Guineans understood little contract law and entered into contracts without knowing the terms and conditions. The Act is designed to:

> (a) ensure the overall fairness of any transaction which—
> (i) is entered into between parties in circumstances where one party is for reasons of economic or other advantage predominant and the other is not able to exercise a free choice; or
> (ii) for one reason or another, without attaching any evil design or bad faith, appears to be manifestly unfair or not to be genuinely mutual; and
> (b) allow for the re-opening and review of any transaction irrespective of fault and validity, enforceability or effect of any agreement; and
> (c) ensure the fair distribution and adjustment of rights, benefits, duties, advantages and disadvantages arising out of a transaction.[87]

The concept of fairness is defined in the Act as relating to the principle of the just and equitable distribution of the rights, privileges, advantages, benefits

---

83 Ibid., s 127.

84 For an example of the court's approach before the introduction of the Fairness of Transactions Act 1993, see *Luke v Ralda* [1992] PNGLR 549.

85 Government Gazette G.111/1998.

86 Law Reform Commission of Papua New Guinea, *Fairness of Transactions*, Report No. 6, December 1977. See D.K. Srivastava, 'Note: The Law Reform Commission's Fairness of Transactions Bill' (1977) 5 *Melanesian Law Journal* 139.

87 Fairness of Transactions Act 1993 (PNG), s 1.

and duties, obligations and disadvantages of a transaction, relative to a party's standing in or contribution to the transaction, and applicable business principles and practices.

Where the parties are not on an equal footing, a transaction is deemed to be unfair if a party shows:

> (a) that he did not understand the transaction and no genuine effort was made to explain its terms to him prior to entering into the transaction; or
> (b) that the other party was in such a predominant position ... that an ordinary person with the background of the complainant was not likely to exercise a true freedom of choice ...; or
> (c) that the other party had or should have had ... information affecting the fairness of the transaction which was not disclosed to the complainant; or
> (d) that he was mistaken in or had miscalculated the likely consequences of the transaction ... to such an extent adverse to his interests that he could not reasonably be held responsible for such consequences.[88]

If the court is satisfied that the transaction is unfair, either party may apply for it to be reviewed. The powers of the court following a review are not spelt out, but presumably, as under the Transactions with Native Acts, it may make such decision as it considers equitable.[89] It is not possible to exclude the application of the Act.[90]

The first case to discuss the Fairness of Transactions Act 1993 was *Negiso Investments Ltd v PNGBC Ltd.*[91] In that case, the plaintiff obtained a loan of K600,000 from the defendant on the security of registered mortgages over its properties. On default, the defendant exercised its power of sale over one property. The first sale fell through, so it was re-advertised for sale and the defendant sold another of the plaintiff's properties. The plaintiff claimed that these dealings were 'not genuinely mutual and manifestly unfair ... within the meaning of those terms as provided in [the Act]'. The Court held, relying on an article by Owen Cox, that 'fairness' meant 'weighing the respective bargaining positions of the parties'.[92] The Court concluded that the defendant's conduct was unfair within the meaning of the Act and therefore subject to review. The sales of the properties were not diligently pursued, and the defendant was in a stronger

88 Ibid., s 5(2).
89 See above text at n. 84.
90 Fairness of Transactions Act 1993 (PNG), s 12.
91 [2003] PGNC 72.
92 O. Cox, 'Fair Trading in Papua New Guinea' (2001) 75 *Australian Law Journal* 53. Fairness is defined in s 4 of the Act.

position than the plaintiff, who was financially weak, not well educated, lacking in any business acumen, and commercially naïve. It was held that the transaction was not unlawful, but unfair. Accordingly, the Court was empowered to review the transactions under the Act.

In *Gubon v Pacific Mobile Communications Ltd*,[93] the second case to consider the Act, the Court said that the Fairness of Transactions Act was not something new, but 'what has always been the law at common under the principles of inequality of bargaining powers and unconscionable conduct, which could undo a contract or transaction'.[94] This statement was approved by the Supreme Court in *Augerea v The Bank South Pacific Ltd*.[95] In that case, the appeal against summary judgment for the respondents was set aside on the grounds that there were serious issues to be tried, including the fact that the parties were not in an equal bargaining position at the time when they had signed the various agreements that were in issue. The respondent had 'its legal and experience loan or lending team working for it and advancing its cause whilst the [appellants] were mere employees with no independent legal advice'. The appellants did not have the advantage of legal advice, and even if they had they 'were in a no win position' because there was no choice but to accept the bank's terms. In those circumstances, the burden was on the respondent to provide evidence of a fairly negotiated agreement.

The Act was also discussed in *Piokole v Logona*,[96] which involved a dispute between Air Niugini Limited and some of its pilots over whether their earlier employment contracts were still in effect or had been superseded by a later agreement unilaterally imposed by the airline. In holding that the later agreements were ineffective, the Court commented that the 'principle of fairness pre-existed the Fairness of Transactions Act, our country's independence and goes back to the time of the concept of the rule of law becoming central for the democratic world'. In this case, fairness required the airline giving the pilots ample opportunity to consider the terms of the new contracts, seek legal advice and consult their unions, and allowing for some room for negotiation to reach mutually acceptable agreements.

The power to review the contract gives a broader scope for relief than equity and other regional legislation. Accordingly, it could provide a model for the protection of Pacific Islanders in other countries of the region.

---

93 [2006] PGNC 128.

94 Referring to *Lloyds Bank Ltd v Bundy* [1975] QB 326.

95 [2007] PGSC 12.

96 [2017] PGNC 79. An appeal was allowed in this case, but on other grounds not related to the Fairness of Transactions Act: *Air Niugini Ltd v Piokole* [2019] PGSC 43.

5.4. TOKELAU

Whilst there is no direct statutory regulation of duress, undue influence or unconscionable contracts in Tokelau, it should be noted that the Contract Rules 2004 provide that, subject to those Rules, 'the law of New Zealand for the time being in force' applies to duress, undue influence and unconscionability.[97]

---

[97] Contract Rules 2004 (Tokelau), R 19.

CHAPTER 14
MISTAKE

1. INTRODUCTION

1.1. THE MEANING OF MISTAKE

'Mistake' in the context of vitiation of a contract has a narrower meaning than it bears in everyday use. The law will only intervene in a contractual agreement on the grounds of a mistake in a narrow range of circumstances. Exactly where the boundaries of an operative mistake lie is 'unsettled'.[1] However, it is clear that a court will only interfere in a limited number of cases. The courts will not assist where a party makes a mistake as to the commercial or legal consequences or effect of a contract rather than as to its subject matter or terms.[2] One reason for confining operative mistake is that it renders the contract void ab initio. This can have broad implications, not only for the parties, but also for third parties.

1.2. THE CATEGORIES OF MISTAKE

The uncertainty surrounding the doctrine of mistake that arises from conflicting case law is exacerbated by a difference of opinion amongst academics as to the correct way to categorise different types of mistake. Beatson, Burrows and Cartwright recognise two categories of mistake: 'common mistake' and 'unilateral mistake'.[3] Cheshire, Fifoot and Furmston's *Law of Contract*, on the other hand, recognises three categories: 'common mistake', 'mutual mistake' and 'unilateral mistake'.[4] This chapter follows the latter approach.

---

1 See *Khan v Mohammed* (1982) 28 FLR 94, where Rooney J referred to the law as 'unsettled'.

2 *Clarion Ltd v National Provident Institution* [2000] 2 All ER 265.

3 J. Beatson, A. Burrows and J. Cartwright, *Anson's Law of Contract*, 30th ed., Oxford University Press, Oxford 2016, p. 271.

4 M.P. Furmston, *Cheshire, Fifoot and Furmston's Law of Contract*, 17th ed., Oxford University Press, Oxford 2017, p. 296.

2. COMMON MISTAKE

The term 'common mistake' refers to the situation where both parties make the same mistake. In this type of case, the parties are in agreement, but the contract is nullified by facts unknown to them. If the mistake is sufficiently fundamental that it negates consent, then the contract will be void.

The concept of common mistake was explored in *Bell v Lever Bros Ltd*,[5] although referred to in that case as 'mutual mistake'. The plaintiffs had reached an agreement for compensation with the defendant over the early termination of his contract of employment. A large compensation payment was made pursuant to this agreement. After payment, the plaintiff found that the defendant was guilty of misconduct which would have justified termination without compensation. The plaintiff therefore argued that the compensation contract was void for mistake.

By a majority of three to two, the House of Lords held the agreement to be binding. Their Lordships considered that some types of common mistake would render the contract void, but sought to confine operative mistake within the following narrow limits:

1. the mistake must be a false and fundamental assumption going to the root of the contract;
2. both parties must have it in mind at the time the contract was made as being the basis of their agreement; and
3. it is not enough that one party can show that had if they had known the true facts they would never have made the contract.

In this case, these requirements were not fulfilled, as the parties got what they bargained for. The discovered facts did not destroy the identity of the contract. It was immaterial that they would not have entered into the contract had they known the true facts.

Bell v Lever Bros Ltd left it unclear whether the assumption must to relate to the existence of the subject matter of the contract in order to qualify as fundamental,[6] or whether it may relate to a broader range of facts.[7]

Later cases appeared to prefer the narrow interpretation of the ratio of *Bell v Lever Bros Ltd*, and to interpret the decision as not allowing a contract to be held void for a mistake about the nature (rather than existence) of a fact.[8] However, in

---

5 [1932] AC 161.
6 Ibid., 227 (Atkin LJ).
7 Ibid., 206 (Warrington LJ).
8 See e.g. *Solle v Butcher* [1950] 1 KB 671; *Leaf v International Galleries* [1950] 2 KB 86.

2002 the law relating to mistake was reviewed in *Great Peace Shipping v Tsavliris Salvage Ltd.*[9] In this case, a ship called the *Cape Providence* was on her way from Brazil to China and suffered serious structural damage while at sea. The defendant offered to assist the owners to recover the ship and this was agreed. As the ship was in danger of sinking, the defendant looked for a ship nearby to evacuate crew if necessary. A firm of brokers found the plaintiff's ship, *Great Peace*, to be nearby and, based upon its position, able to arrive within 12 hours. A contract was entered into, but unfortunately the position of the *Great Peace* was incorrect and the defendant cancelled the contract and employed a closer vessel. The plaintiff sued for the money that would have been payable under the contract.

The Court laid down five elements required in order for common mistake to avoid a contract:[10]

> (a) there must be a common assumption as to the existence of a state of affairs;
> (b) there must be no warranty by either party that the state of affairs exists;
> (c) the non-existence of the state of affairs must not be attributable to the fault of either party;
> (d) the non-existence of the state of affairs must render performance impossible; and
> (e) the state of affairs may be the existence, or a vital attribute, of the consideration to be provided or circumstances which must subsist if performance of the contractual adventure is to be possible.

In *Great Peace Shipping*, the subject matter existed in the form of the vessel, the *Great Peace*, but it was argued that both parties were mistaken as to its location, and this was fundamental to the contract. That is, if Tsavliris knew of the location, they would not have made the contract. The Court considered that the underlying basis for common mistake was the impossibility of performing the contract. The Court explained that:[11]

> The avoidance of a contract on the ground of common mistake results from a rule of law under which, if it transpires that one or both of the parties have agreed to do something which it is impossible to perform, no obligation arises out of that agreement.

In determining whether the performance of the contract was impossible, the Court regarded it as 'necessary to identify what it is that the parties agreed would

---

9 [2003] QB 679, [71]–[75]. See further P. MacFarlane, 'Case Note on Great Peace Shipping Ltd v Tsavliris Salvage (International) Ltd', (2003) 7(2) *Journal of South Pacific Law*.

10 Ibid., [76].

11 Ibid., [17].

be performed'.[12] This requires a careful examination of the express terms and any implications arising out of the surrounding circumstances to determine whether the 'contractual adventure' that is alleged is impossible. In this case, it was held that the contract was not void because performance was not impossible.

The principles set out in *Great Peace Shipping* were applied in *Cook Islands National Line Agency Ltd v Cook Islands Shipping Corporation Ltd.*[13] In this case, the plaintiff, as liquidator, sought a declaration as to the validity of an agreement for sale and purchase between the appellants (the companies in liquidation), and the respondent, a new company. The appellants, relying on *Great Peace Shipping*, argued that the agreement was void for common mistake, since the parties proceeded on a false and fundamental assumption in that they mistakenly believed that the Cook Islands government would pass legislation to authorise a new shipping monopoly in favour of the respondent, the establishment of which comprised in part the agreement. The Court of Appeal rejected this, holding that the parties contracted on the basis of an expectation that the new shipping policy, including exclusivity, would be implemented. Any mistake was a mistake as to future intention, but even if it were a mistake as to present fact it was not fundamental to the agreement, since both parties received what they bargained for. The performance of the agreement was also not impossible, as the Cook Islands government could have passed legislation to introduce the new policy, but chose not to. Applying the *Great Peace* principles, the court held that it could not be said that the contractual adventure was impossible to perform or that the nature of the arrangement had changed unalterably. At the time of contracting, the necessary legislation was still a possibility. Accordingly, the agreement was valid.

A regional case where common mistake was found to render the contract void is *Khan v Mohammed.*[14] In that case, the parties were partners. By agreement, the plaintiff withdrew from the partnership and was to be paid back his original capital contribution of $2,000 plus an equal share of the operating profit to the date of his withdrawal, which was calculated as $8,300. Unfortunately, it later transpired that the total profit had been calculated wrongly by one of the partners and the remaining partners refused to pay the plaintiff the balance owing to him. It was held that the agreement was based on a fundamental error as to the financial position of the partnership, which went to the root of the contract. The contract was therefore held to be void.

In *Tonga Development Bank v Howard*[15] the court held that the parties were acting under a common mistake as to whether land leased to the defendant

---

12 Ibid., [18].
13 [2003] CKCA 9.
14 (1982) 28 FLR 94.
15 [2001] Tonga LR 6.

included a dwelling house. However, the court refused to find the agreement void, and held that 'the mistake can be remedied because in Tonga it has been well established that, unlike most jurisdictions, houses are regarded as items of personal property rather than accretions to the land'.[16] Instead, the court issued a declaration that the lease did not include the dwelling house.

In *Zuchetto v Republic of Vanuatu*,[17] the plaintiff signed an agreement in the standard form to lease land, which was in the process of being forfeited by the lessees, from the defendant for 75 years. After the forfeiture process was completed the Minister, on behalf of the defendant, did not register the plaintiff's lease, but instead entered into a new lease with the second and third respondents. The plaintiff brought proceedings, seeking cancellation of the new lease and a declaration that his lease was valid. The Supreme Court dismissed the claim on the basis that the original lease agreement between the plaintiff and defendants was void for common mistake (being that the prior lease had been forfeited). The Court of Appeal allowed the appeal, applying the five elements of common mistake from *The Great Peace*. The Court held that only four out of the five factors from *The Great Peace* were present, and therefore the original lease agreement was invalid.

There are some recognised types of mistake that have generated a large amount of case law. These will now be examined.

2.1.1. *Subject Matter which has Ceased to Exist*

At common law, the contract is void if the subject matter is non-existent at the time of the contract (*res extincta*). Lord Atkin, in *Bell v Lever Bros Ltd*,[18] gave as an example of a contract which would be void for mistake an agreement for purchase a specific article which had in fact perished prior to the making of the contract.

In *Couturier v Hastie*,[19] the contract was for the purchase of a cargo of corn. At the time of the contract the cargo had been sold to someone else. The purchaser was held to have no liability.[20] This case is of doubtful authority, as it appears to have been decided on the basis that there was a total failure of consideration.[21]

16 Citing *Kolo v Tonga* [1997] Tonga LR 181.
17 [2014] VUCA 17.
18 [1932] AC 161, 218.
19 [1856] UKHL J3.
20 See also *Strickland v Turner* (1852) 7 Exch 208.
21 The case was distinguished on this basis in *McRae v Commonwealth Disposals Commission* (1951) 84 CLR 377.

The above cases deal with the position where the subject matter of the contract has ceased to exist at the time when the contract was made. The question arises whether the result is the same if the subject matter of the contract has never existed. In the Australian case of *McRae v Commonwealth Disposals Commission*,[22] the High Court of Australia found that it was not. In that case, the defendant invited tenders for a salvage operation in relation to an oil tanker, said to be 'lying on the Jourmand Reef', off the coast of Papua New Guinea. The plaintiffs were awarded the contract, but found that neither the reef nor the tanker existed in the area indicated by the defendants. The defendant declared that the contract was void for mistake and that it therefore had no liability. It was held that there was a contract, in that the defendant had to be taken to have warranted the existence of the tanker, and was therefore liable for damages.

Whilst this is an Australian case, it is highly persuasive and has led to a reappraisal of the law of mistake relating to non-existent goods. The case highlights that mistake as to existence of the subject matter will not always result in invalidity of the agreement. It will depend on the construction of the contract. Even if the subject matter has ceased to exist, the contract will still be valid if performance was guaranteed by one of the parties, as it was in *McRae*. The contract will also be valid if it is clear that the buyer purchased a chance – in other words, took a risk that the subject matter might not exist and undertook to pay in any event.[23]

In relation to the sale of specific goods, the common law rules governing goods that have perished prior to entry into the contract have been given statutory form. The relevant provisions are as follows:

- Sale of Goods Act 1979 (Fiji), s 8
- Sale of Goods Act 1986 (Marshall Islands), s 9
- Goods Act 1951 (PNG), s 8(1)
- Sale of Goods Act 1975 (Samoa), s 7
- Sale of Goods Act 1893 (UK), s 6
- Sale of Goods Act 1908 (NZ), s 9[24]
- Contract and Commercial Law Act 2017 (NZ)[25]

22 (1951) 84 CLR 377.

23 For a discussion of cases where the contract allocates this risk to the buyer see M. Chen-Wishart, *Contract Law*, 5th ed., Oxford University Press, Oxford 2015, p. 262. One interpretation of the decision in *Couturier v Hastie* [1843–60] All ER 280 is that the seller assumed the risk of non-existence: P.S. Atiyah, '*Couturier v Hastie* and the Sale of Non-Existent Goods' (1957) 73 *Law Quarterly Review* 340.

24 Applying in Cook Islands and Niue. See further chapter 1.

25 Contract Rules 2004 (Tokelau), Pt. 2, R 19.

The provisions are all very similar. Section 8 of the Fiji Act, for example, states:

> Where there is a contract for the sale of specific goods and the goods, without the knowledge of the seller, have perished at the time when the contract is made, the contract is void.

2.1.2. *Impossibility of Performance*

Although the subject matter of the contract still exists, performance may be impossible for some other reason. For example, in *Sheikh Bros v Ochsner*[26] the appellants, who were lessees of an estate in Kenya, granted the respondent a licence to cut and manufacture sisal (fibre made from leaves) on the estate. The terms of the licence provided that the respondents should deliver to the appellants 50 tons of manufactured sisal fibre per month. It transpired that the yield of the estate was insufficient to comply with this condition. The Privy Council held that the contract was void.

Another example of commercial impossibility is *Griffith v Brymer*,[27] where a contract for the hire of a room to view the coronation of Edward VII was held void as the procession had been cancelled prior to entry into the contract.

2.1.3. *Mistake as to Quality*

Normally a mistake as to quality will not render the contract void. The following example was given in *Bell v Lever Bros Ltd*:[28] A buys a picture from B for a high price, both A and B believing it to be the work of an old master. If it turns out to be a modern copy, A has no remedy in the absence of representation or warranty.

Similar facts arose in *Leaf v International Galleries*,[29] where the plaintiff bought a picture from the defendant, both believing it was by Constable. Several years later, when the plaintiff tried to sell it, he found out that it was not by Constable. The mistake, though fundamental, did not render the contract void. Lord Atkin made it clear that this was not to say that mistake as to quality could never be a vitiating factor:

> In such a case a mistake will not affect assent unless it is the mistake of both parties and is as to the existence of some quality which makes the thing without the quality essentially different from the thing as it was believed to be.

---

26 [1957] AC 136.

27 (1903) 19 TLR 434.

28 [1932] AC 161, 218.

29 [1950] 2 KB 86.

It has been suggested that Lord Atkin was distinguishing a separate category of mistake, consisting of mistake as to substance (or essence), which will render the contract void, as opposed to quality (or attributes), which will not.[30] However, a mistake as to substance was found not to render a contract void in *Solle v Butcher*.[31] In that case the defendant let a flat to the plaintiff at a rent of £250 per annum. Both parties assumed that, in view of the considerable alterations that had been carried out on the flat, it was not subject to rent control. The assumption was incorrect, and the maximum permitted rent was £140. The plaintiff sought the return of the overpaid rent. The defendant alleged that the lease was void for mistake. The Court of Appeal held that although there was a mutual mistake as to fact, it did not render the contract void.

Glanville Williams has argued that mistakes as to quality cannot be separated from mistakes as to substance and that qualities considered together produce the essence or substance of an article.[32] He suggests that the better approach is to focus on the intention of the parties when they entered into the contract.

Quality of subject matter in a sale of goods contract is dealt with under the Sale of Goods Acts applying in the region. For example, s 16(2) of the Sale of Goods Act Cap 230 (Fiji) provides that, in general, where a seller sells goods in the course of business, there is an implied condition that the goods are of merchantable quality.

3. MUTUAL MISTAKE

Mutual mistake refers to the situation where the parties are at cross-purposes. Each party is mistaken as to the other's intention. As opposed to common mistake, where the parties are in agreement but the contract is nullified due to facts unknown to them, in the case of mutual mistake the parties are unknowingly not in agreement at all. If the mistake is so fundamental that it negates consent, then the contract will be void.

A good example can be found in *Raffles v Wichelhaus*.[33] In that case, the defendant agreed to buy a cargo of cotton from the plaintiff to arrive 'ex Peerless' from Bombay. In fact, there were two ships called *Peerless* and both sailed from Bombay, but the defendant had in mind the one that sailed in October, whereas the plaintiff was referring to the one that sailed in December. It was held that no contract existed.

---

30 See e.g. *Kennedy v Panama, New Zealand, and Australia Royal Mail Co Ltd* (1867) LR 2 QB 580.

31 [1950] 1 KB 671.

32 G. Williams, 'Mistake as to Party in the Law of Contract: Parts I and II' (1945) 23 *Canadian Bar Review* 271.

33 [1864] Hurl & C 906.

An objective test is applied in deciding whether there has been a mutual mistake. If the contract would be understood by a reasonable person to have one meaning only, the fact that one party subjectively took it to mean otherwise will not be enough to render the contract void for mistake. In this respect, it is useful to compare *Scriven Bros v Hindley*[34] with *Smith v Hughes*.[35] In *Scriven*, there was confusion as to two lots at an auction, one being 'hemp' and the other being 'tow'. The defendant bid an unusually high price for the hemp, thinking it was tow. The contract was void. In *Smith*, the plaintiff had offered to sell oats to the defendant by sample. When delivered they were 'new' oats and of no use to the defendant. It was held that it was not enough for the defendant to be mistaken. Objectively, it was a contract for a particular consignment of oats, which is what the defendant got.

4. UNILATERAL MISTAKE

Unilateral mistake concerns a mistake by one party which the other party knows or ought to know about. As in the case of mutual mistake, the parties are not in agreement at all. Unlike mutual mistake, however, one party knows of the mistake, or is taken to know of it, as it would have been obvious to a reasonable person.[36] In this category of mistake, one party is prevented from taking advantage of the other's mistake, if it is a mistake which would render the contract void or non-existent under the doctrine of common or mutual mistake.

There are three types of unilateral mistake:

- unilateral mistake as to the terms of the offer or the acceptance;
- unilateral mistake as to the identity of the other party to the contract; and
- unilateral mistake as to the nature of the document signed.

4.1. MISTAKE AS TO THE TERMS OF THE OFFER OR ACCEPTANCE

Where one party has taken advantage of the other's error, the contract will be void for mistake. For example, in *Hartog v Colin & Shields*,[37] the sellers mistakenly offered to sell goods at a given price per pound, when they intended to sell by the piece. All preliminary negotiations were on the basis of a

34 [1913] 3 KB 564.
35 (1871) LR 6 QB 597.
36 *Hartog v Colin & Shields* [1939] 3 All ER 566.
37 [1939] 3 All ER 566.

price per piece. Viewed objectively, the buyers must have realised this mistake, but said nothing. It was held that the contract was void.

If the parties are *ad idem* as to the subject matter and terms of the contract, a clerical mistake by one party will not qualify as an operative mistake. For example, in *Malaita Development Authority v Ganifiri*,[38] the plaintiff claimed to be entitled to be registered as the rightful owner of a parcel of land on the basis of a contract with the Commissioner of Lands. The defendants argued that this contract was void due to the Commissioner using the wrong parcel number in the written agreement. The defendants claimed that a subsequent grant of the same land that had been made to them was valid. The court held that the plaintiff and the Commissioner had reached consensus as to the physical description and identity of the land and therefore the first agreement was valid.

4.2. MISTAKE AS TO IDENTITY

There is a large amount of contradictory case law surrounding mistake as to identity. In order for a contract to be void for mistake as to identity, it must be shown that:

- at the time of the apparent agreement the identity of the other party was material;
- there was an intention to contract, not with the other party, but with a separate entity; and
- this intention was known or ought to have been known to the other party.

It is fairly clear that mistake as to attributes, such as creditworthiness, will not render the contract void, whereas mistake as to identity will. If the parties contracted face to face there is a presumption that they intended to deal with each other, and that the contract is therefore valid. For example, in *Lewis v Averay*,[39] the plaintiff advertised his car for sale. A rogue called round to see it and offered to buy it, claiming to be the actor 'Richard Greene'. He signed a cheque for £450 'RA Green' and asked to take the car away. The plaintiff asked to see proof of his identity and he was showed a Pinewood Studios pass in the name of Richard A Green. The plaintiff, in consequence, allowed him to take the car. The cheque was dishonoured. Meanwhile, the defendant had purchased the car for £200. It was held that the contract with the rogue was voidable only for misrepresentation, not void for mistake.

[38] [2002] SBHC 5.
[39] [1972] 1 QB 198.

By contrast, in the earlier case of *Ingram v Little*,[40] a similar claim succeeded. The plaintiffs were three elderly ladies who advertised their car for sale. A rogue calling himself Hutchinson visited their home and agreed to purchase the car for £717. When he tried to pay by cheque they refused to accept it and to persuade them otherwise he told them what he claimed to be his full name and address and of his local business interests. One of the plaintiffs checked his details in a telephone directory at the local post office, and found them apparently correct. As a result he was allowed to take the car away. The cheque was dishonoured. The defendants bought the car in good faith. It was held that the contract was void for mistake, as the original refusal and the checking of the details showed that identity was of utmost importance. This case was criticised in *Lewis v Avery*[41] and is unlikely to be followed.

More recently, in *Shogun Finance Ltd v Hudson*,[42] it was accepted, obiter, that where contracts are concluded face to face, there is a strong presumption that each party intends to deal with the person before them.

5. DOCUMENTS MISTAKENLY SIGNED

In certain circumstances, the courts recognise a particular kind of mistake concerning written contracts, where one party alleges that the document signed was of a wholly different nature from that which he or she intended to sign.[43] This is known as a plea of *non est factum* (it is not my deed). This plea was referred to in chapter 9, as it is an exception to the rule that a person is bound by the terms of a document once they have signed it.

The plea of *non est factum* was considered in *Maeaniani v Saemala*,[44] where it was made clear that the defence is of limited application. In that case, the defendant signed a document stating that he had received money from the plaintiff as full settlement for his land. He later refused to execute the transfer document and the plaintiff sued for specific performance. The defendant alleged that he had not read the document as he was illiterate and that it had been explained to him as being a document concerning a loan by the plaintiff to the defendant to purchase tools and equipment to build a house on the land as a joint enterprise. Referring to relevant passages from *Gallie v Lee*,[45] Daly CJ distinguished between cases where the signatory was adult and literate and

40 [1961] 1 QB 31.
41 [1972] 1 QB 198.
42 [2004] 1 AC 919.
43 *Colmar v Rose Vanuatu Ltd* [2007] VUCA 18, [30].
44 [1982] SILR 70.
45 [1971] AC 1004. Also known as *Saunders v Anglia Building Society* [1970] 3 All ER 961.

those involving persons who were illiterate, blind or lacking in understanding. In the former case, a successful plea of *non est factum* would be very rare. His Lordship agreed with the view of Lord Wilberforce that:

> The law ought ... to give relief if satisfied that consent was truly lacking but will require of signers even in this class that they act responsibly and carefully according to their circumstances in putting their signature to legal documents.

In this case the plea of *non est factum* was not established. Daly CJ took account of the fact that the defendant was a carpenter and builder, who had lived and worked in the capital for 25 years, before returning to Malaita Island. He operated a number of taxis in the capital, was articulate and intelligent, and could be described in the broader sense as a businessman.[46]

A plea of *non est factum* was also dismissed in *Credit Corporation (Fiji) Ltd v Noodles Bakery Company Ltd*.[47] The court took into account the fact that the applicants were of full age and capacity, they had knowledge of business transactions in Fiji, they had been given the opportunity to obtain legal advice, the document was signed in the presence of a solicitor, and the applicants had also signed an acknowledgement.[48]

Similarly, in *Colmar v Rose Vanuatu Ltd*,[49] the Vanuatu Court of Appeal refused to uphold a plea of *non est factum*, even though neither party had legal advice before signing. In that case, the plaintiff presented an agreement to the defendant's representative whereby the defendant would sell a lease of land to the plaintiff. The agreement was signed, but the transfer of the lease did not go ahead. In an action by the plaintiff for specific performance, the defendant pleaded *non est factum*. The court upheld the contract on the basis that this 'was a contract between two commercially knowledgeable persons. It was their decision whether they wanted their lawyers to approve the contract before they were to be bound by it'.

This can be contrasted with the recent case of *Natonga v Guyenne*,[50] where the plea of *non est factum* succeeded. There, the contract was set aside by the Vanuatu Court of Appeal as the purpose of the contract was not disclosed to the defendant before signing. The contract for the lease of premises was written mainly in Bislama, but partly in English. The defendant did not read English but only Bislama. He was told that the premises were required for a children's playground and snack bar, but in fact the plaintiff intended to establish a nightclub.

46 *Maeaniani v Saemala* [1982] SILR 70, 75.
47 [2015] FJHC 557.
48 Ibid., [4.40].
49 [2007] VUCA 18.
50 [2018] VUSC 45.

The court will not uphold the plea where signatories deliberately remain ignorant of the import of the documents they sign. In *Rigamoto v NBF Asset Management Bank*,[51] the appellants mortgaged their farm to secure loans from the respondent. The appellants later transferred the property to two of their farm hands, who granted a mortgage in favour of the respondent in place of the mortgage given by the appellants. However, the bank advanced no money to the two farm hands, who were not their customers. The Chief Officer of the respondent was a close friend of the appellants. The respondent applied successfully to the High Court to set aside the transfer and the mortgage, on the basis that *non est factum* was made out. The Court of Appeal disagreed with the trial judge's conclusion that the inference from the findings of fact was that the farm hands were acting in connivance with the appellants and had several opportunities to clarify the meaning of the documents, but chose not to. However, they did not disagree with the legal principle expressed, and dismissed the appeal on other grounds.

6. CONSEQUENCES OF MISTAKE

6.1. CONSEQUENCES UNDER COMMON LAW

The general rule is that an operative mistake renders the contract void at common law. The effect of this is that the parties are returned to their original positions. This is a serious consequence as it may result in the rights of innocent third parties who have acquired an interest in the subject matter of the contract being defeated. As mentioned at the outset of this chapter, this explains why the courts are disinclined to expand the doctrine of mistake.

6.2. CONSEQUENCES IN EQUITY

In some circumstances, equity will intervene to ensure that justice prevails between the parties. As can be seen from cases such as *Solle v Butcher*,[52] the common law rules for identifying an operative mistake are very restrictive. Accordingly, the courts have utilised equity to introduce a more flexible approach. In equity, the contract will be voidable, rather than void.

51 [2011] FJCA 42.
52 [1950] 1 KB 671.

6.2.1. *Rescission*

In certain circumstances, equity may be used to rescind a contract on the grounds of a mistake that is insufficient to render the contract void at common law. This might include a mistake as to quality or value of the subject matter. It appears that three conditions must be satisfied before the courts will grant this relief:

- the mistake must be fundamental or, in the case of unilateral mistake, must be known to the other party;[53]
- it must be inequitable for the party seeking to uphold the contract to rely on his strict legal rights; and
- the party seeking to rescind must not be at fault.[54]

In exercising their equitable discretion, the courts have imposed conditions on the grant of rescission. For example, in *Cooper v Phibbs*,[55] the House of Lords set aside a contract for a lease of a fishery to the plaintiff. Both parties believed that the fishery belonged to the defendant, but it transpired that the plaintiff already owned it. The House of Lords ordered that the defendant should have a lien on the property for the cost of improvements to the fishery, as otherwise the plaintiff would have been unjustly enriched by the defendant's mistaken expenditure.

6.2.2. *Rectification*

Equity also permits rectification if there has been a mistake in reducing the contract to writing. Before an order for rectification will be made, it must be shown that:

- the document does not represent the intention of both parties; or
- the document does not represent the intention of one party, and the other party knew of this error.[56]

The fact that the document fails to mention a term which one party, but not the other, intended to be included does not justify rectification.[57] However, rectification may be available where only one party is mistaken, but the other knows this and takes advantage of it.[58]

---

53 *Cooper v Phibbs* (1867) LR 2 HL 149.
54 *Grist v Bailey* [1967] Ch 532.
55 (1867) LR 2 HL 149.
56 *A Roberts & Co Ltd v Leicestershire CC* [1961] Ch 55; *Afolau Construction v SSFA* [2013] WSSC 73.
57 *Riverlate Properties Ltd v Paul* [1975] Ch 133.
58 *Thomas Bates & Sons Ltd v Wyndham's (Lingerie) Ltd* [1981] 1 All ER 1077.

There must be a concluded agreement, but not necessarily a legally enforceable agreement. For example, in *Joscelyne v Nissen*,[59] a father and daughter were negotiating an agreement that the daughter would take over the father's car hire business. At an early stage in negotiations, it was agreed that the father would continue to live on the ground floor of the daughter's house free of rent and that she would pay all household expenses. The written contract did not expressly say that the daughter was to pay the household bills. It was held that the document could be rectified to include this term, as the written agreement failed to reflect the common intention of the parties.

In *Kadir v Native Land Trust Board*,[60] the Fiji Court of Appeal relied on the summary of the principle in *Chitty on Contracts*:[61]

> It has long been the established rule of equity that where a contract has by reason of a mistake common to the contracting parties been drawn up so as to militate against the intentions of both as revealed in their previous oral understanding, the court will rectify the contract so as to carry out such intentions so long as there is no issue between the parties as to their legal rights inter se.

The court was of the view that such a mistake was easier to infer when the contract was in a printed form, but in all cases the court must be satisfied that it is the intent of both parties which has been mistakenly recorded. In this case, although satisfied that the intent of the defendant was not correctly recorded, the court was not convinced that this was the case in respect of the plaintiff.

In *Curry v Tiafau Hotels Ltd*,[62] the plaintiffs sought rectification of a conveyance that transferred several pieces of land to the Government of Nauru. The plaintiffs alleged that it had never been the intention of the parties that all of parcel 219 was to be sold, as this had their driveway on it. Only that part of the land which housed the hotel kitchen and freezers was to be transferred. The court held that the terms of the document signed did not accurately represent the mutual intention of the parties and that in such a case the court was entitled to order rectification.[63]

6.2.3. Refusal of Equitable Remedies

The remedy is discretionary, and may be lost in the case of:

- affirmation;
- lapse of time;

---

59 [1970] 2 QB 86.
60 Unreported, Court of Appeal, Fiji, Speight VP, O'Shea and Holland JJA, 18 July 1986.
61 Ibid., citing J. Chitty, *Chitty on Contracts*, 24th ed., Sweet & Maxwell, London 1977, para. 310.
62 [1980–93] WSLR 532.
63 See *Joscelyne v Nissen* [1970] 2 QB 86, discussed above in the text at n. 59.

- impossibility of restitution; or
- intervention of third party rights.

More generally, if a mistake has been made that falls short of an operative mistake at common law, the court may refuse to grant an equitable remedy if this would be unfair to the defendant. For example, in *Webster v Cecil*,[64] the defendant, having previously refused the plaintiff's offer of £2,000 for certain land which he had put up for sale, wrote to the plaintiff offering to sell the land for £1,250 (instead of £2,250, which he intended). The plaintiff accepted, although, in the light of the previous dealings, he must have known that there had been a mistake. The plaintiff brought an action for specific performance. Whilst acknowledging that the contract might be enforceable at law, the court refused to grant specific performance.

64 (1861) 54 ER 812.

CHAPTER 15
ILLEGALITY

1. INTRODUCTION

Agreements that are illegal are void, even if they comply with all the requirements of a binding contract. The case law dealing with illegality is conflicting. However, there appears to be a presumption in favour of legality.[1] This may be due to efforts by the courts to avoid the consequence of a finding of illegality in circumstances where this would allow a guilty party to avoid liability. Illegal contracts can be subdivided into two categories:

- contracts contrary to law; and
- contracts contrary to public policy.

2. CONTRACTS CONTRARY TO LAW

Contracts will be contrary to law if they contravene a law from any source.

2.1. AGREEMENTS CONTRARY TO COMMON LAW

The courts will not enforce a contract entered into for the purpose of committing a criminal offence or a civil wrong. So, for example, a conspiracy to murder a third party would be illegal. In *Allen v Rescous*,[2] an agreement to commit an assault was held to be void. Similarly, an agreement by promoters of a company to defraud prospective shareholders has been held to be illegal.[3]

In *ALCC Brown Enterprises Ltd v Savaiinaea*,[4] it was accepted that an agreement which improperly sought to influence voters in an election was illegal at common law. In that case, the plaintiff's managing director was running

1 *Deo v Narayan* (1971) 17 FLR 162.
2 (1677) 2 Lev 174.
3 *Begbie v Phosphate Sewage Co Ltd* (1875) LR 10 QB 491.
4 [2009] WSSC 2, [42], applying *Allen v Hearn* (1785) 1 Term Rep 56.

for parliament. The defendants, who were the pastor and secretary of the Methodist Church, agreed orally with the plaintiff that he would build a new church with materials supplied by the Church. When the Church ran out of funds, the plaintiff supplied the materials. After the election, a written agreement was signed. When the plaintiff sued for the outstanding amount, the pre-election oral contract was held to be illegal. However, as it had been replaced by the post-election contract, the plaintiff was entitled to judgment in accordance with the written terms.

2.2. AGREEMENTS CONTRARY TO STATUTE

Care must be taken to distinguish contracts that are contrary to statute when they are created and contracts that are only illegal as performed. Some contracts may be both.[5] The distinction is recognised in the definition of 'illegal contract' in the Illegal Contracts Act 1987 of Cook Islands.[6] This states that an 'illegal contract means any contract that is illegal at law or in equity, whether the illegality arises from the creation or performance of the contract'.

2.2.1. Contracts Illegal in Creation

Where the parties have agreed to something that is contrary to a statute, the contract is void in creation for illegality. Reprehensible conduct is not enough. If the conduct falls short of an offence under the statute in question, this will not be enough to constitute illegality.[7]

An example of an agreement contrary to statute can be found in *Sharma v Singh*.[8] The parties entered into a deed whereby the defendant sold a taxi to the plaintiff together with a taxi permit. The Traffic (Taxis and Rental Cars) Regulations 1967 forbade the transfer of a permit. The agreement was held to be illegal and therefore void.

Another regional example can be found in *Knight v Attorney-General*.[9] In that case, the plaintiff was convicted of purchasing gold from an unlicensed vendor, contrary to provisions of the Mines and Minerals Act.[10] The plaintiff argued that a portion of the gold seized was hers as she had purchased it under a valid contract. The court held that the gold sold to the plaintiff had been extracted by villagers who did not possess an alluvial mining or a gold

5 *Sharma v Singh* (1973) 19 FLR 164, 168.
6 Section 7.
7 *Ram v Pal* (1963) 9 FLR 141, 143.
8 (1973) 19 FLR 164.
9 [2005] SBHC 6.
10 Cap 42 (SI).

dealer's licence. Being contrary to statute, the transaction was illegal and unenforceable. This case was cited with approval in *Malaita Maasina Forum Trust Board Inc v Attorney-General*,[11] where the court found a contract for the sale of bêche-de-mere to be invalid as harvesting of this resource was illegal.

In *Griffiths v Indian Pacific Fisheries Ltd*,[12] it was held that the provision in the Labour Act[13] that dealt with work permits was intended to 'prohibit completely' a contract of employment with an immigrant or non-indigenous worker. The plaintiff's claim for unpaid wages was dismissed, on the basis that no permit was in force. This case draws no distinction between agreements that are illegal as created and those that are illegal in performance. This decision poses a practical difficulty in that, taken broadly, it prevents parties from negotiating, or at least finalising, an employment agreement prior to obtaining a permit. Neither party would want to expend time and money making such an application unless the terms of employment have been agreed on and the employment likely to proceed. As Lyons J put it in *Nair v Public Trustee of Fiji*,[14] in relation to dealings in land requiring consent, to interpret an Act to say the mere reducing to writing of the terms of the agreement is sufficient to transgress the Act is to 'create a mischief'; 'a statute should not be interpreted so as to create a nuisance'. *Griffiths v Indian Pacific Fisheries Ltd* can be contrasted with those cases discussed below, where failures to obtain a permit or consent have been regarded as contracts illegal in performance but not in their initial creation. However, as the plaintiff in this case had rendered some performance, the ratio of the case should be confined to situations where the parties have embarked on performance.

It should also be noted that the position will be different if the statute expressly requires the consent, permit or licence to be obtained prior to entry into a contract. This is the case, for example, under Fiji's Land Sales Act, which provides that no non-resident of Fiji 'shall without the prior consent in writing of the Minister responsible for land matters make any contract to purchase or to take on lease any land: prior to the consent'.[15] In the case of such express prohibition, the contract will be void on creation.

The various Companies Acts in force within the region prohibit a company from purchasing its own shares. Accordingly, an agreement by a company to borrow money to purchase its own shares would be illegal.[16]

---

11 [2014] SBHC 12.

12 [1997] SBHC 51.

13 Cap 73 (SI).

14 Unreported, High Court, Fiji, Lyons J, 8 March 1996, 30.

15 Land Sales Act Cap 137 (Fiji), s 6(1). See *Hunter v Apga* [1989] 35 FLR 180; *Sakashita v Concave Investment Ltd* [1999] FJHC 3; *Gonzalez v Akhtar* [2004] FJSC 2; *Narayan v Narayan* [2009] FJHC 26. Cf. *Port Denarau Marina Ltd v Tokomaru Ltd* [2006] FLR 462.

16 See dicta in *Banque Privee de Credit Moderne v Jet Service Ltd* [1992] VU Law Reports 2, 3.

Illegality may also consist of failure to comply with the process required by statute for the formation of the contract. In *Rolland v Director General of Finance*,[17] it was held that entry into a consultancy contract without obtaining three quotations and without the involvement of the proper officer, as required by regulations made under the Finance Act of Vanuatu[18] was illegal. Similarly, in *Fly River Provincial Government v Pioneer Health Services Ltd*,[19] a contract entered into without advertising for tenders, in a case where this was a statutory requirement,[20] was held to be illegal.

Another example can be found in *Government v Atoa*,[21] where it was held that if an Act[22] requires a contract to be made in a particular way, for example with the consent of and subject to the direction of the High Commissioner, the contract will be illegal if these requirements are not complied with.

2.2.2. *Contracts Illegal in Performance*

In some instances, a contract that is perfectly lawful may be capable of being performed in an illegal way.[23] In *Sharma v Singh*,[24] referred to above, the court held that not only was the contract illegal in formation as it agreed to the sale of a taxi permit, but it was also illegal in performance. Although the plaintiff had conditionally surrendered the permit that had been illegally transferred and asked for a new one, he commenced to operate the taxi even though the permit had not been issued.

A number of cases have come before the court where the illegality consists of failure to obtain the consent required by statute to the transfer of or dealing in land. It has been made clear that the mere entry into an agreement, subject to the consent of the responsible Minister or Director of Lands is not normally illegal,[25] but if the parties proceed with performance this will be illegal. The matter was discussed in *Nair v Public Trustee of Fiji*.[26] Lyons J pointed out that, where the consent of a government official is required prior to the transfer of land, there is no illegality in entering into a contract for sale or a lease. The illegality only comes in when the contract is performed, for example if the purchaser enters into possession of the land and makes improvements even though consent has

17 Unreported, Magistrates Court, Vanuatu, Civ Cas 25/1998, 2 June 1998.

18 Cap 117.

19 [2003] PGSC 4.

20 Public Finances (Management) Act 1995 (PNG).

21 [1950–59] WSLR 84.

22 In this case, the Public Revenue Ordinance 1948, s 122(2).

23 See e.g. *Re Mahmoud v Ispahani* [1921] 2 KB 716.

24 (1973) 19 FLR 164.

25 This will depend on the wording of the legislation in question. See also *Aerolift International (SI) Ltd v Mahoe Heli-Lift (SI) Ltd* [2003] SBCA 16.

26 Unreported, High Court, Fiji, Lyons J, 8 March 1996.

not been obtained.[27] Lyons J gave the example of a contract for the carriage of goods by sea, which by itself was perfectly lawful. However, it might be performed illegally, as where the ship was overloaded.[28] In the present case, an agreement had been made but had never been performed. Accordingly, the statute requiring the consent of the Director of Lands had not been contravened and there was nothing illegal about the contract. The plaintiff was awarded damages for breach of contract for the sale of land.

This case can be contrasted with *DB Waite (Overseas) Ltd v Wallath*.[29] In that case, the parties had entered into a written agreement to transfer a native lease, which required the approval of the Native Land Trust Board for validity. The purchaser paid deposit monies to the vendor before the agreement was submitted by the vendor to the Native Land Trust Board for approval. The vendor did not submit the agreement for approval or take any further action. When the purchaser claimed the return of this deposit and damages, the vendor claimed the agreement was illegal without the consent of the Native Land Trust Board and that no monies were recoverable. The court found that the damages could not be awarded because this would mean that the agreement had passed some interest in the land, which was not possible without Native Land Trust Board approval. Whilst not illegal per se, the court regarded the agreement as 'inchoate'. However, the lack of illegality permitted the court to order the vendor to refund the deposit monies and interest to the purchaser.

Lyons J attempted to distinguish this decision in *Nair v Public Trustee of Fiji*,[30] on the basis that the conduct of the defendant in this case was not unconscionable. In fact, this reasoning is not convincing, as here the defendant had failed to apply for the necessary consent as agreed, and had sold the land to a third party in contravention of its agreement with the plaintiff.

The position in other cases involving contracts which require a permit or licence to validate performance is similar to that in *Nair v Public Trustee of Fiji*,[31] where consent of a third party was required. In the absence of legislation to the contrary, an agreement may be entered into without a permit or licence, provided that the agreement is not performed. For example, in *HP Kasabia Brothers Ltd v Reddy Construction Ltd*,[32] the Court of Appeal held

---

27 Lyons J took this example from *Chalmers v Pardoe* [1963] 3 All ER 502, in the course of distinguishing that case. Affirmed on this point on appeal in *Public Trustee of Fiji v Nair* [1997] FJCA 55.

28 Lyons J took this example from *St John Shipping Corporation v Joseph Rank Ltd* [1957] 1 QB 267, in the course of distinguishing that case.

29 (1972) 18 Fiji LR 141.

30 Unreported, High Court, Fiji, Lyons J, 8 March 1996.

31 Ibid.

32 (1977) 23 FLR 235.

that there was nothing illegal in a building contract entered into without a building permit. It was an implied term of the agreement that the owner would obtain the building permit within a reasonable time and there was nothing to oblige the builder to commence work without it.

As discussed above, the requirement of a work permit under the Solomon Islands Labour Act has been held to render the creation of a contract of employment illegal from the outset,[33] but this case should be restricted to its facts.

As mentioned, where the parties have gone further than entering into the agreement and have proceeded to perform the contract, it will be illegal. In *Damodar & Ratanji Ltd v Redwood Industries Ltd*,[34] the parties entered into an agreement for the sale of land which required the consent of the Native Land Trust Board. The consent was not obtained, but the plaintiff paid the purchase price and entered and remained in occupation for five years. It was held that the transaction was illegal and void.

In *Pelenato v Vaitusi*,[35] the Supreme Court of Samoa held, obiter, that a sub-lease of government land, without the government consent required by the Lands and Environment Act 1989 would be illegal. In this case, however, the plaintiff's wife was only a licensee and the right she had given to the defendant to occupy the land could not amount to a sub-lease. Accordingly, the defence of illegality, put forward in an action to recover arrears of rent, was unsuccessful. Similarly, a contract for the sale of crops grown on land cannot be argued to be illegal for lack of the written approval for the use of the land for that purpose, as required by statute, as a contract for the sale of goods does not call the use of the land into issue.[36]

Another example can be found in *Ramdin v Singh*,[37] where a written contract was entered into for the transfer of the defendant's Crown lease to the plaintiff. Prior to the consent of the Director of Lands being obtained to the transfer (as required by the Crown Lands Ordinance),[38] the plaintiff loaned the defendant $1,000 and in return was allowed to take possession of the land. At the request of the defendant, the plaintiff later paid $997 to the defendant's bank to discharge the mortgage over the land. The consent of the Director of Lands was not forthcoming and the plaintiff sued for the return of both sums. The defendant pleaded that the claim was based on an illegal transaction, as the consent of the Director had not been obtained. It was held that the delivery of

---

33 *Griffiths v Indian Pacific Fisheries Ltd* [1997] SBHC 51.

34 (1988) Fiji LR 10.

35 [1994] WSSC 38.

36 *Primary Produce Exports Ltd v Titali'ahio* [1999] TOSC 9. The provision in question was Land Act Cap 132 (Tonga), s 13.

37 (1977) 23 FLR 128. See also *Singh v Singh* [1980] 26 FLR 77.

38 Cap 113. See now Crown Lands Act Cap 132 (Fiji Consolidation of Laws 1985 ed).

possession without the Director's consent rendered the agreement for sale void and the loan transaction supporting the delivery was tainted with illegality and also void. Marsack JA quoted with approval the following words from *Chitty on Contracts*:[39]

> No court will lend its aid to a man who founds his cause of action upon an immoral act. If, from the plaintiff's own stating or otherwise, the cause of action appears to arise ex turpi causa, or the transgression of a positive law of this country, there the court says he has no right to be assisted.

Another regional example is *Lan v Sharma*,[40] where the parties entered into an agreement for sale of the defendant's Crown lease to the plaintiff. In applying for the Director of Lands' consent to the sale the parties made a false statement as to the purchase price of the land. This was an offence under s 41 of the Crown Lands Ordinance.[41] The Director refused his consent and the plaintiff sued to recover the purchase price. It was held that the transaction was tainted with illegality due to the false declaration and the court refused to assist the plaintiff in recovering the purchase price.

A contract will not be void for illegality because it is performed in contravention of a statute, unless that was the intention of the parties when the contract was entered into. Thus, in *Deo v Narayan*,[42] the defendant sold his vehicle to the plaintiff. The vehicle was later repossessed under a bill of sale due to non-payment by the defendant of money secured by the vehicle. When sued for repayment of the purchase price, the defendant pleaded illegality. Contrary to s 19 of the Traffic Ordinance,[43] the registration had not been transferred to the plaintiff. Neither had the plaintiff insured the vehicle, as required by s 4(1) of the Motor Vehicles (Insurance) Ordinance.[44] However, it appeared from the evidence that this situation had arisen after the agreement was entered into, when it became impossible for the registration to be transferred or the vehicle insured as the bill of sale was still outstanding. It was held that there was no illegality in performance as it was never a term of the contract that the vehicle would be used in a particular way or for a purpose in breach of the law.

Collateral agreements made in respect of an agreement that contravenes a statute will also be void. For example, in *Kulamma v Manadan*,[45] the plaintiff

39 *Ramdin v Singh* (1977) 23 FLR 128, citing J. Chitty, *Chitty on Contracts*, 23rd ed., Sweet & Maxwell, London 1968, p. 808.

40 (1964) 10 FLR 222.

41 Cap 138 (renumbered as Cap 113 in Fiji Consolidation of Laws 1978 ed). See now Crown Lands Act Cap 132 (Fiji Consolidation of Laws 1985 ed).

42 (1971) 17 FLR 162.

43 Cap 152.

44 Now part of Motor Vehicles (Third Party Insurance) Act Cap 177 (Fiji).

45 (1964) 10 FLR 252.

inherited a lease of native land from her late husband which was subject to a share-farming agreement with her husband's brother, under which the brother was to cultivate the farm and share all proceeds equally. After her husband's death, the parties continued to act on the agreement. In November 1960, the plaintiff assigned to the defendant all crops growing on the farm and all receipts from those crops. After a dispute arose, the plaintiff sought to set aside the assignment on the ground, inter alia, that s 12 of the Native Land Trust Ordinance[46] required the consent of the Native Land Trust Board to be obtained to any dealing in native land. The share-farming agreement was held to be illegal. The collateral assignment was also held to be tainted with illegality:

> Neither party can sue on a contract if both knew that it necessarily involves the commission of an act which, to their knowledge, is legally objectionable, that is illegal, or otherwise against public policy.

This decision was overturned by the Court of Appeal of Fiji on the basis that the share-farming agreement was not an 'alienation' or 'dealing' and therefore did not contravene the Act. The Privy Council agreed with the Court of Appeal, but neither appeal court expressed disagreement with the trial court's conclusion regarding a collateral agreement.

If a contract can be enforced without reference to the illegal part of the transaction, the courts may be prepared to grant relief. For example, in *Ram v Pal*,[47] although the parties had made a false statement in their application to the Director of Lands for consent, the consent was not actually required for the transfer of the tenancy in question. The court held that the transaction was therefore valid. A further example can be found in the recent case of *Kumar v Mani*.[48] The plaintiff paid in advance for a parcel of shares, but the shares were never transferred. The transaction was unlawful because the consent of the Reserve Bank of Fiji had not been obtained, as required by statute. However, the court, taking into account the fact that the defendant would be unjustly enriched, held that the payment was made pursuant to an oral contract and could be enforced without reference to the written, illegal contract.[49]

A respondent cannot set up his own election to perform a lawful contract in an illegal manner as a ground for declaring a contract illegal.[50]

---

46 Cap 104.

47 (1963) 9 FLR 141. See also *Ramdin v Singh* (1977) 23 FLR 128.

48 [2018] FJHC 973.

49 See also *Rainbow Holdings Pty Ltd v Central Province Forest Industries Pty Ltd (Provisional Liquidator Appointed)* [1983] PNGLR 34.

50 *HP Kasabia Brothers Ltd v Reddy Construction Ltd* (1977) 23 FLR 235.

2.3. CONTRACTS CONTRARY TO CUSTOMARY LAW

In all countries of the region other than Fiji, Cook Islands, Niue and Tonga, customary laws are recognised as a source of state law.[51] As contracts are illegal if they contravene a law from any source, it is open to the courts to find a contract that is contrary to a customary law to be illegal. Even in countries where customary laws are not a general source of state law, the common law, including the law of contract, only applies insofar as it accords with local circumstances.[52] As customary laws are a feature of local circumstances, it is arguable that contracts should not be upheld if they violate a customary law. There is added support for this view in countries such as Solomon Islands, where customary law is a superior source of law to common law.[53]

3. CONTRACTS CONTRARY TO PUBLIC POLICY

The courts may refuse to enforce a contract on the grounds that it contravenes public policy, rather than any defined legal principle. There are a number of established heads of public policy under which the issue of enforceability has arisen. Examples of these heads are set out below.

3.1. CONTRACTS TO OUST THE JURISDICTION OF THE COURT

A contract to oust the jurisdiction of the court is void, as it is contrary to public policy.[54] However, there is nothing to prevent the parties inserting an honour clause in their agreement, making it clear that the agreement is not intended to be legally binding.[55] Nor is it contrary to public policy for the parties to agree to submit any dispute to arbitration as a prerequisite to accrual of a cause of action. Such a clause is commonly inserted in contracts and is known as a '*Scott v Avery*' clause, by virtue of the name of the case in which the principle was confirmed.[56]

---

51 See further chapter 2.

52 See further J. Corrin and D. Paterson, *Introduction to South Pacific Law*, Intersentia, Cambridge 2017, p. 33.

53 Constitution of Solomon Islands 1978, s 76, Sch. 3 para. 2(1). See further, J. Corrin Care, 'Cultures in Conflict: The Role of the Common Law in the South Pacific' (2002) 6 *Journal of South Pacific Law* 1.

54 *Czarnikow v Roth Schmidt* [1922] 2 KB 478.

55 See further chapter 4.

56 (1855) 5 HLC 811.

3.2. CONTRACTS TO INDEMNIFY AGAINST CRIMINAL ACTS OR DELIBERATE CIVIL WRONGS

A court will not enforce a contract to indemnify against criminal acts or civil wrongs. For example, in *Gray v Barr*,[57] the defendant was cleared of manslaughter by the criminal courts. The victim's widow subsequently sued him in tort. The defendant admitted liability but claimed that he was covered by his insurance policy, which covered sums which he was liable to pay as damages in respect of injury caused by accidents. The Court of Appeal held that his acts amounted to manslaughter, and that he therefore could not recover under the insurance policy.

3.3. CONTRACTS IN RESTRAINT OF TRADE

Contracts in restraint of trade place restrictions on a party's freedom to carry on a particular trade or business in the future. Such contracts usually fall into one of three categories:

- restraints on former employees;
- restraints on vendors of businesses; and
- solus agreements.[58]

A contract in restraint of trade is prima facie void. However, the court may uphold such a contract if it can be shown that:

- the restraint protects a legitimate interest;
- the restraint is reasonable in the circumstances of the case; and
- the restraint is not contrary to public policy.[59]

Whether or not the restraint is reasonable depends on all the facts, including the geographical area and the length of time covered by the clause. In *WA Flick & Co Pty Ltd v RW Thompson*,[60] the defendant had been employed as a pest controller by the plaintiff. His contract contained a clause prohibiting him from setting up a pest control business within five miles of his place of employment or places where he carried out work for three years following the termination of his employment. Five months after the defendant's contract had concluded, he set

---

57 [1971] 2 QB 554.

58 Agreements restricting a party to dealing with one supplier.

59 *Esso Petroleum v Harpers Garage (Stourport) Ltd* [1968] AC 269.

60 (1976) PNGLR 112.

up a similar business within the same area. It was held that in order to be upheld the restraint clause must be fair from the point of view of both parties and the public. In this case the clause was upheld.

This case can be contrasted with *Taurama Pharmacy Pty Ltd v Sherwen*.[61] In that case, a clause in the defendant's contract of employment with the plaintiff pharmacy company prohibited her from employment in a pharmaceutical business within a 40-kilometre radius of the plaintiff's pharmacies for three years. The court held that the restraint was, 'unreasonable in time and space', taking into account the small size of the profession and the lack of sufficient pharmacists to cater for Papua New Guineans.

The geographical extent of the restraint and its duration are both important factors in considering reasonableness. However, they are not always decisive. In *Nordenfelt v Maxim Nordenfelt Guns & Ammunition Co*,[62] the plaintiff sold his armaments business to the defendant and undertook not to carry on such business anywhere in the world for 25 years, except on behalf of the defendant. The agreement expressly reserved the right for the plaintiff to deal in explosives other than gunpowder. The agreement was held to be valid, because the plaintiff had received a large sum of money and the reservation allowed him scope to trade in at least one area of his skill.

The fact that a party has been paid extra money when entering into a contract in return for agreeing to be bound by a restrictive covenant is a legitimate factor for a court to take into account. However, it does not relieve the party seeking to rely on the covenant from the need to justify the restraint.[63]

Restraint of trade clauses are more likely to be struck down if they appear in a standard form contract, and therefore have not been the subject of negotiation. For example, in *Schroeder Music Publishing Co Ltd v Macauley*,[64] a standard form agreement, where the defendant composer agreed to give the publisher all rights to his songs for five years, was declared void.

In the area of solus agreements, the public interest takes on greater significance as such agreements may create a monopoly.[65] In *Esso Petroleum v Harper's Garage (Southport) Co Pty Ltd*,[66] a solus agreement for four years was held reasonable, but an agreement for 21 years was not and it was therefore declared to be void.

In Fiji, restrictive trade practices are specifically prohibited by the Commerce Commission Decree 2010, Part 6. This Decree prohibits contracts

---

61 [1990] PNGLR 97.
62 [1984] AC 535.
63 *Turner and Others v Commonwealth and British Minerals Ltd* [1999] EWCA Civ 3055.
64 [1974] 1 WLR 1308.
65 *Esso Petroleum Co Ltd v Harper's Garage (Stourport) Co Pty Ltd* [1968] AC 269.
66 Ibid.

restricting competition[67] or other misuse of market power.[68] The Act provides a framework for enforcement and criminal penalties.[69] It also authorises civil action for damages and other remedial orders.[70]

In Marshall Islands, restraint of trade clauses are prohibited by the Unfair Business Practices Act.[71] This Act makes it illegal for individuals or bodies to use capital, skills or acts 'to create or carry out restrictions in trade or commerce'. Contracts creating monopolies or lessening competition are specifically outlawed.[72] The Act imposes a penalty of between $50 and $5,000 on conviction.[73] It also allows for a civil suit by any person 'injured' and damages of three times the damage sustained, and costs may be recovered.[74]

The Illegal Contracts Act 1987[75] governs the effect of restraint of trade clauses in Cook Islands. This is discussed further in section 4.2.1.

3.4. CONTRACTS WHICH PROMOTE IMMORAL CONDUCT

As a matter of public policy, the courts refuse to enforce contracts that promote immoral conduct.[76] This is most often encountered by the courts in the form of contracts which are prejudicial to the status of marriage. In *Gavin v Gavin*,[77] the defendant defended a claim for unpaid maintenance under a separation agreement on the basis that the agreement was illegal as it encouraged adultery. Whilst accepting that contracts which were immoral might be contrary to public policy, the court held that a separation agreement was not such an agreement. Ward J held that it was clearly public policy in Solomon Islands to respect and support the sanctity of marriage. Whilst a separation agreement conflicted with that policy, the common law took a realistic view in cases where the marriage has already broken down.

In *Lyden v Folau*,[78] the plaintiff and defendant had been living together and had a child. The plaintiff promised the defendant that he would marry her as soon as he got a divorce. He brought various items of furniture to their

67 Commerce Commission Decree 2010 (Fiji), s 62.
68 Ibid., s 66.
69 Ibid., Pt. 10.
70 Ibid., ss 145–50.
71 Unfair Business Practices Act 20 MIRC Cap 3 (Marshall Islands).
72 Ibid., s 4.
73 Ibid., s 7(1).
74 Ibid., s 7(2).
75 Section 7.
76 *Upfill v Wright* [1911] 1 KB 506.
77 [1990] SBHC 103.
78 [1946] Tonga LR 39.

joint home. Subsequently, the defendant married another man. The plaintiff sued to recover his furniture, alleging that they were given on condition that the defendant married him. The defendant alleged that the furniture was an absolute gift. On appeal from the magistrates finding in favour of the plaintiff, Thompson CJ held that even if there was a conditional agreement, it was based on immoral consideration and therefore could not be enforced.

In *Kairun v Bidesi*,[79] the court upheld a claim for breach of promise to marry, but added that had the contract been made during the life of the defendant's spouse it would not have founded an action. Tuivaga J commented that, '[t]he policy of the law has been to deprecate adulterous associations and not to lend its aid in a way which might tend to encourage immoral conduct'.[80]

3.5. CONTRACTS PROMOTING CORRUPTION

Contracts promoting corruption in public life will not be enforced by the courts. In *Parkinson v College of Ambulance*,[81] a contract made between the plaintiff and the defendant charity, whereby the plaintiff was to donate £10,000 to the charity in exchange for the defendant arranging for him to receive a knighthood, was held to be illegal on public policy grounds.

3.6. CONTRACTS TENDING TO PERVERT THE COURSE OF JUSTICE

Contracts tending to pervert the course of justice will not be enforced by the courts. In *Kearly v Thompson*,[82] for example, the defendant was a firm of solicitors acting for a person who was taking bankruptcy proceedings against a person named Clarke. The plaintiff, who was a friend of Clarke, paid the defendant money not to continue with the proceedings. The defendant did not attend at the public examination of Clarke and was planning not to take further steps in the proceedings. The plaintiff then changed his mind, and demanded his money back. It was held that although a person who repented and withdrew from an illegal contract before any illegality had occurred could recover money he had paid, once the illegality had been even partly accomplished, he could not recover his money.[83]

---

79 Unreported, Supreme Court, Fiji, Civ Cas 421/1978, 5 October 1979.

80 Ibid., 4.

81 [1925] 2 KB 1.

82 (1890) 24 QBD 742.

83 For an example of an illegal contract which was repudiated before performance see e.g. *Tribe v Tribe* [1996] 1 Ch 107.

3.7. CONTRACTS PREJUDICIAL TO PUBLIC SAFETY

Contracts contrary to public safety will not be enforced for public policy reasons. For example, in *Regazzoni v Sethia*,[84] a contract to export products to a country where they were prohibited was held to be illegal, as it might damage foreign relations with that country.

4. EFFECTS OF ILLEGALITY

4.1. COMMON LAW

Generally, illegality, whether due to contravention of the law or of public policy, renders the contract void ab initio, and therefore any property that has already passed cannot be recovered. This principle was discussed by the Fiji Court of Appeal in *Damodar & Ratanji Ltd v Redwood Industries Ltd.*[85] In that case, the facts of which are set out in section 2.2.2, the court at first instance made a declaration that the contract was void. The court held that, consequently, the purchase price should be refunded, even though it had already been paid and the plaintiff had been in occupation for five years. The Court of Appeal reversed this part of the decision on the basis that the court was thereby lending aid to a party to an illegality. The Court cited with approval the words of MacKinnon LJ in *Harry Parker v Mason*:[86]

> The principle of public policy is this: *ex dolo malo non oritur actio*. No court will lend its aid to a man who founds his cause of action upon an immoral or an illegal act. If from the plaintiff's own stating or otherwise, the cause of action appears to arise *ex turpi causa* or the transgression of a positive law of this country, there the court says he has no right to be assisted. It is upon that ground the court goes; not for the sake of the defendant, but because they will not lend their aid to such a plaintiff. So if the plaintiff and defendant were to change sides, and the defendant was to bring action against the plaintiff, the latter would then have the advantage of it; for where both are equally in fault, *potior est conditio defendentis*.

In accordance with this principle, in *Lan v Sharma*,[87] discussed in section 2.2.2, it was held that, as the transaction was tainted with illegality, the plaintiff was not entitled to assistance in recovering the purchase price. Similarly, in *Ramdin v Singh*,[88] also discussed in section 2.2.2, the plaintiff was not

84 [1958] AC 301.
85 (1988) Fiji LR 10. See above text at n. 34.
86 [1940] 2 KB 590, 601.
87 (1964) 10 FLR 222.
88 (1977) 23 FLR 128.

entitled to recover money loaned to the defendant in return for allowing him to enter into possession of land, as such possession was illegal without the consent of the Director of Lands.

Obviously, this approach to illegal contracts may cause hardship. It may also allow a guilty party to keep property which has not been paid for. The courts have on occasion found ways to avoid the harsh consequences of the common law doctrine. If the plaintiff is able to found a claim without reference to the illegality, the court may assist. In *Sharma v Singh*,[89] the facts of which are discussed in section 2.2.1, the court allowed the plaintiff's alternative claim for conversion, as to do otherwise would have left the defendant without the taxi and the purchase price paid for it. A claim for damages for loss of earnings during the period of wrongful possession was not allowed, as the earnings would have derived from the use of the vehicle as a taxi, which was contrary to law.

In *Sakashita v Concave Investment Ltd*,[90] the High Court of Fiji reviewed the authorities dealing with the circumstances in which the court may interfere with the principle that the loss lies where it falls. In that case, the Court ordered the return of a deposit paid in respect of a contract for the sale of land which was illegal due to contravention of the Land Sales Act,[91] on the basis that the claim was for restitution, rather than a claim on the contract. This decision significantly extends the scope for the court to assist parties to an illegal contract. However, allowing recovery on the basis that the remedy was in restitution rather than contract disregards the fact that the claim is still founded on the illegal contract, and the decision does not appear to have been followed.

In *Paradise Farms Ltd v Bank South Pacific Ltd*,[92] the court granted the plaintiff's claim for reimbursement of the costs of improving a property after the sale agreement was rescinded due to the defendant's inability to discharge the mortgage. The defence based on illegality, in that the plaintiff had not obtained the statutory investment approvals required to purchase the property, was dismissed. The court held that this was not a case where the plaintiff was being tried for breach of the statute and the defendant was estopped from raising the illegality as it would otherwise be unjustly enriched. This case can be contrasted with *Gonzalez v Akhtar*, where it was stated that '[i]t is trite law that the right to rely on illegality is not barred by estoppel'.[93]

Judicial ingenuity can also be observed in the case of *Fakatava v Koloamatangi*.[94] The defendant had built a house on a piece of land owned by

---

89 (1973) 19 FLR 164.

90 [1999] FJHC 3.

91 Cap 137.

92 [2010] PGNC 191.

93 [2004] FLR 156, citing *Brooks v Burns Philp Trustee Co Ltd* (1969) 121 CLR 432; and N.C. Seddon and M.P. Ellinghaus, *Cheshire & Fifoot's Law of Contract*, 8th ed., LexisNexis Butterworths, Chatswood 2002, pp. 841–42.

94 [1974–80] Tonga LR 16.

the plaintiffs pursuant to an agreement that breached s 13 of the Land Act of Tonga.[95] The plaintiffs sued for possession on the grounds of non-payment of rent. The court, having observed that neither party could sue upon an illegal contract, encouraged the parties to enter into a properly drawn and approved lease. The parties reached a settlement on this basis, which was embodied in a court order.

4.2. STATUTORY PROVISIONS

4.2.1. Illegal Contracts Act 1987 (CI)

In Cook Islands, the consequences of illegality are regulated by the Illegal Contracts Act 1987.[96] The Act provides that an illegal contract is of no effect and no person shall be entitled to property under a disposition made pursuant to it. However, a proviso saves dispositions for valuable consideration to a person who is not a party to the illegal contract and who has no notice of the illegality. The Act also allows the court to grant such relief as it thinks just to a party to an illegal contract or a person claiming through them. In considering whether to exercise its discretion, the court must have regard to:

- the conduct of the parties;
- the object of any statute breached and the gravity of penalties provided;
- knowledge of the illegality; and
- any other matters that it thinks proper.[97]

It should be noted that several New Zealand statutes preclude recourse to the Illegal Contracts Act.[98]

4.2.2. Contract Rules 2004 (Tokelau)

The Contract Rules 2004 of Tokelau provide as follows:[99]

> (1) A contract which is illegal is unenforceable.

95 Cap 132.
96 Section 5.
97 Ibid., ss 6(3), (4).
98 See e.g. Development Investment Act 1995–96 (NZ), s 40; Employment Contracts Act 1991 (NZ), ss 25, 178; Fisheries Act 1983 (NZ), s 41(5); and Commerce Act 1986 (NZ), s 89(5). See further *Market Reach Pty Ltd v Henry & Associates Ltd* [2002] CKHC 2.
99 Rule 22.

(2) A contract is illegal when the agreement is –

(i) to do something which is an offence, or is intended to enable something which is an offence; or

(ii) contrary to public policy.

The Rules state that an illegal contract is unenforceable, rather than void ab initio. Accordingly, in certain circumstances, equitable relief may be available.

4.3. SEVERANCE

In some cases, the court may be prepared to sever the illegal parts of the contract so that the remainder can be enforced. This power is rarely exercised, except in contracts in restraint of trade. In such contracts, the objectionable clause will, if possible, be severed completely, or in part to reduce its effect. The courts will only sever part of a clause if it is divisible, rather than a single covenant.[100] However, the court will not redraft clauses by adding, substituting or even rearranging words.[101]

In *Deo v Narayan*,[102] it was recognised, obiter, that if a statement in a contract could be 'blue pencilled' without in any way altering the scope of the agreement, then this part might be cut out of the agreement by the court.

In Cook Islands, the Illegal Contracts Act 1987 provides for severance of a provision that is in restraint of trade.[103] The court may also modify the clause to render it reasonable, and such modification is specifically permitted to go further than the mere deletion of words. However, if the deletion or modification would alter the bargain between the parties to an unreasonable extent, the court must decline to enforce the contract.[104]

Severance was discussed in *Cook Islands National Line Agency Ltd v Cook Islands Shipping Corporation Ltd*.[105] In this case, the plaintiff, as liquidator, sought a declaration as to the validity of an agreement for sale and purchase between the appellants, a number of companies now in liquidation, and the respondent, a new company. It was held that the Illegal Contracts Act 1987 did not apply, as the International Shipping Act 1999 (CI) provided that it has 'no application to any agreement made in contravention of this Act'.[106] One of the central issues between the plaintiff and the appellants was whether the

100 *Attwood v Lamont* [1920] 3 KB 571.
101 *Mason v Provident Clothing & Supply Co Ltd* [1913] AC 724.
102 (1971) 17 FLR 162.
103 Illegal Contracts Act 1987 (CI), s 7.
104 Ibid., s 7(c).
105 [2003] CKCA 9.
106 International Shipping Act 1999 (CI), s 16.

agreement was illegal, as it was alleged to contravene the anti-competitive provisions of the International Shipping Act.[107] Applying the common law, the Court of Appeal held that although there was an understanding and expectation of exclusivity between the parties, this was not part of the contract. The Court went on to state that if, contrary to their findings, the agreement was contrary to the prohibition of anti-competitive provisions in the International Shipping Act,[108] the offending provision might be severed. The Court noted that the International Shipping Act rendered anti-competitive provisions unenforceable, not the contracts, arrangements or understandings of which they formed part.[109] The Court held that under all competition statutes the fundamental policy of freedom of contract was subject to extensive restrictions in respect of anti-competitive practices, but that this did not justify striking down whole contracts. Although the element of exclusivity was an important factor in the arrangements between the parties, there were other elements of consideration which passed between the parties, and accordingly, if it was illegal, the provision for exclusivity in the informal part of an overarching arrangement could be severed from the agreement.[110]

4.4. CIVIL LAW

In Vanuatu, it is still possible to found a claim under French law, although, as mentioned in chapter 1, the circumstances in which this will be permitted are unclear. The attitude of French law to illegal contracts differs from the common law and restitution of goods or property which was transferred may be ordered.[111]

---

107 Ibid., s 7(1).

108 Ibid.

109 *Cook Islands National Line Agency Ltd v Cook Islands Shipping Corporation Ltd* [2003] CKCA 9, [99].

110 Ibid., [102].

111 Civil Code, Art. 1131. See further N. Enonchong, 'Effects of Illegality: A Comparative Study in French and English Law' (1995) 44 *The International and Comparative Law Quarterly* 196.

CHAPTER 16
FRUSTRATION

1. INTRODUCTION

Once a legally binding agreement has been reached between the parties, failure to perform the obligations undertaken will normally result in liability for breach of contract. This may be unfair if failure is not the result of fault on the part of the party seeking to escape liability. Accordingly, most legal systems make provision for the discharge of a contract where a change of circumstances arises subsequent to its formation that is beyond the control of either of the parties and prevents the purpose of the contract being attained. At common law, this situation is provided for by the doctrine of frustration. The onus of proving frustration is on the party alleging it.[1]

There are a number of theories as to the basis of the doctrine of frustration.[2] The two main contenders are:

- *Implied term theory*[3]
  According to this theory, frustration depends on the intention of the parties. In the circumstances of the case the court considers that the parties would have inserted a term discharging the contract if they had anticipated the event which arose. The court infers 'from the nature of the contract and the surrounding circumstances, that a condition which was not expressed was a foundation on which the parties contracted', and asks whether the changed conditions are such that a reasonable person would have said, 'If that happens, of course, it is all over between us'.[4]

- *Termination as a matter of law*[5]
  The more generally accepted view is that the doctrine of frustration is a device developed by the common law to temper the inflexibility of

---

1 *Board of Fire Commissioners of Suva v Fiji Public Service Association* [1994] FJCA 11.
2 See M.P. Furmston, *Cheshire Fifoot and Furmston's Law of Contract*, 17th ed., Oxford University Press, Oxford 2017, pp. 713–715.
3 *Taylor v Caldwell* (1863) 3 B&S 826.
4 *FA Tamplin Steamship Co Ltd v Anglo-Mexican Petroleum Products Ltd* [1916] 2 AC 397, 403–04.
5 *Denny Mott and Dickson Ltd v James Fraser & Co Ltd* [1944] AC 265; *Davis Contractors Ltd v Fareham UDC* [1956] AC 696.

> applying the law of contract in a rigid fashion.[6] According to this theory, the courts intervene as a matter of law, independently of the parties' intention, whenever the circumstances have fundamentally changed the nature of the contract.

These two theories were discussed in *Board of Fire Commissioners of Suva v Fiji Public Service Association.*[7] In that case, the country's economy was in serious trouble following a coup. The Permanent Secretary of the Ministry of Finance and Economic Planning issued a circular to Permanent Secretaries and Heads of Departments informing them of the government's policy that all government employees should have their salaries reduced by 15% and asking ministries to instruct statutory boards to do so. Part of the income of the defendant was in the form of a government grant, which was to be cut by 50% of the amount unpaid, but there was no evidence as to whether the defendant had received less money than expected. The legislation governing the grant had not been altered. The defendant unilaterally reduced its employees' salaries by 15%. The plaintiff union applied to the court for a declaration that this was in breach of the collective employment agreement.[8] The defendant alleged that the issue of the circular had frustrated the contract. The Court of Appeal held that the evidence was insufficient to establish that the defendant was unable to pay the salaries at the agreed rate and that frustration was therefore not established.

The court appears to have agreed with the remarks of Lord Wilberforce in *National Carriers Ltd v Panalpina (Northern) Ltd*[9] that the various theories 'shade into one another and that a choice between them is a choice of what is most appropriate to the particular contract under consideration'.

2. REQUIREMENTS

2.1. THE GENERAL TEST

Frustration occurs whenever the law recognises that a contractual obligation cannot now be performed because of a change in circumstances. The change in circumstances must result in there being a 'radical change in the obligation'.[10]

---

6 *Hirji Mulgi v Cheong Yue Steamship Co Ltd* [1926] AC 497, 510.
7 [1994] FJCA 11.
8 See Trade Disputes Act Cap 97 (Fiji), s 2.
9 [1981] AC 675, 693 (Lord Wilberforce).
10 *Davis Contractors Ltd v Fareham UDC* [1956] AC 696, 729.

In *Emperor Gold Mining Company Ltd v Fiji Industries Ltd*,[11] the Fiji Court of Appeal adopted the definition of frustration laid down in *Davis Contractors Ltd v Fareham Urban District Council*:[12]

> [F]rustration occurs whenever the law recognizes that without default of either party a contractual obligation has become incapable of being performed because the circumstances in which performance is called for would render it a thing radically different from that which was undertaken by the contract … [I]t is not hardship or inconvenience or material loss itself which calls the principle of frustration into play. There must be as well such a change in the significance of the obligation that the thing undertaken would, if performed, be a different thing from that contracted for.[13]

The change must not have been brought about by the conduct of the parties.

2.2. SUBSIDIARY REQUIREMENTS

The doctrine is not to be lightly invoked[14] and a set of subsidiary requirements has emerged which restricts its application.

2.2.1. Increased Difficulty or Expense is Insufficient

There must be something more than the contract becoming more onerous, inconvenient or expensive.[15] In *Hin Man Ngai v Fanneng South Pacific Holdings Ltd*,[16] the plaintiff agreed to sell a piece of land to the defendant. The plaintiff paid the purchase price, but the defendant refused to complete the transaction, claiming the contract was frustrated as the tax on the transaction was higher than expected. The court held that the 'mere fact that performance of a contractual obligation will result in some hardship does not necessarily establish frustration'.[17]

The High Court of Kiribati has taken a different approach. In *Kiribati Supplies Company Ltd v Raiha*,[18] the plaintiff had previously done business with the defendant on the basis that the plaintiff would be responsible for paying customs duties and port charges on goods imported for it by the defendant. Normally the port charges were low, as the plaintiff cleared the cargo immediately. On this occasion the goods were imported by the defendant for another customer, but

11 [2000] 1 FLR 311.
12 [1956] AC 696, 727, 729.
13 This definition was also adopted in *HP Kasabia Brothers Ltd v Reddy Construction Ltd* (1977) 23 FLR 235 and *Prasad v Sharma* [2017] FJHC 295, [25].
14 *Prasad v Sharma* [2017] FJHC 295, [26].
15 *Davis Contractors Ltd v Fareham UDC* [1956] AC 696.
16 [2018] FJHC 706.
17 Ibid., [24].
18 [2010] KIHC 46.

that deal fell through and the goods were not collected. The plaintiff agreed to buy them and paid a deposit of half the purchase price, not knowing that the port charges were already running. The charges had mounted to $10,000 by the date of collection and the plaintiff could not proceed with the purchase. The High Court held that that the 'huge' port charges frustrated the contract and ordered a return of the money paid by the plaintiff.

Similarly, in *Bismark Real Estate v Jant Ltd*,[19] the Papua New Guinea National Court upheld a defence of frustration where the defendant was unable to provide vacant possession of houses that he had agreed to rent to the plaintiff, as the occupants refused to leave. A supplementary agreement gave the defendant a further five months to comply, but the occupants still refused to leave. The court held that the doctrine of frustration 'is part of the common law of contract, which means that it has been adopted as part of the underlying law'. The doctrine applied in this case due to the supervening event constituted by the intransigence of the occupants, which was not contemplated or induced by the parties and made performance of the contract impossible.[20] This decision is difficult to reconcile with other decisions in this area as the defendant had the option to take proceedings to evict the occupants, which it did not do until after the extended date for providing vacant possession had expired.

2.2.2. The Event Must not be Provided for

Where the contract contains an express provision dealing with the event alleged to amount to frustration, there is no frustration. For example, in *HP Kasabia Brothers Ltd v Reddy Construction Ltd*,[21] the defendant sought to establish that the contract had been frustrated by the delay in obtaining a building permit. The contract provided for the extension of time for completion of the building work if the delay was caused by non-availability of permits. It was held that this could not amount to frustration as the parties had made provision for it.

However, the express clause must be clear to be applied. For example, in *Jackson v Union Marine Insurance Co Ltd*,[22] the words 'dangers and accidents of navigation excepted' in a charter agreement were not enough to provide for the situation where the ship ran aground and was not repaired for nearly a year.

2.2.3. The Event Must not have been Foreseen by the Parties

Generally, if the parties foresaw or should have foreseen the event, then the contract will not be frustrated. For example, in *Walton Harvey Ltd v Walker*

---

19 [2013] PGNC 190. See also *PK Investments Ltd v Mobil Oil New Guinea Ltd* [2015] PGSC 50.

20 [2013] PGNC 190, [10].

21 (1977) 23 FLR 235.

22 (1874) LR 10 CP 125.

and Homfrays Ltd,[23] the defendants, knowing that there was some likelihood that their hotel would be compulsorily acquired and demolished, permitted the plaintiff to erect an advertising hoarding on its roof. Part way through the seven-year contract, the building was resumed and the sign removed. The plaintiff sued for damages. The defendants argued that the resumption had frustrated the contract and excused them from further liability. It was held that the contract had not been frustrated as the defendants had been aware of the risk, had entered into the contract despite it, made no provision for it and, consequently, were not excused from liability when it eventuated.

In *Picardie Holdings (NH) Ltd v Waegemenn*,[24] the plaintiff was seeking to enforce an agreement for the sale of land to the defendant. The defendant alleged that the plaintiff no longer owned the land due to statutory changes made to land-holding laws, and that therefore the contract was frustrated. It was held that the contract was not frustrated as the contract clearly indicated that the defendant was aware of the changes to the law. In any event, the law did not prevent the sale of the land, but merely meant that the defendant might have to negotiate with customary landowners thereafter.

However, foresight does not always prevent frustration. As noted in *Hin Man Ngai v Fanneng South Pacific Holdings Ltd*,[25] to restrict the operation of the doctrine of frustration to unforeseen events introduces unwanted complications as it is hard to specify the nature and degree of foresight which would prevent automatic termination on the grounds of frustration. In *Bismark Real Estate v Jant Ltd*,[26] discussed above, it was arguable that, given that the houses were occupied when the contract was entered into, the parties should have foreseen that there might be difficulties with the provision of vacant possession.

It is not necessary for both parties to have foreseen the event. If one party conceals information from which it was possible to foresee the frustrating event, that party cannot later rely on the doctrine of frustration. In *Air Transport Ltd v Island Construction Management Ltd*,[27] the plaintiff and defendant entered into an agreement in May 1995 for the defendant to supply a helicopter for haulage of logs from Mono Island. In July 1995, the defendant was preparing to bring the helicopter to Solomon Islands when it discovered that an interim injunction had been granted against the plaintiff in a land dispute case, preventing it from entering Mono Island. With the agreement of the plaintiff, the defendant re-deployed the helicopter to minimise any loss to the parties. In November, the plaintiff, having obtained permission from the court to bring logs already

23 [1913] 1 Ch 274.
24 (1980–88) 1 VLR 5.
25 [2018] FJHC 706, [26].
26 [2013] PGNC 190.
27 [1999] SBCA 2.

felled out of Mono Island, asked the defendant to start work in December 1995. As the original helicopter was unavailable, the parties agreed to negotiate with a third party for the supply of a larger helicopter. The plaintiff made certain advance payments to the defendant to secure this agreement, but the third party refused to conclude the agreement, and the arrangement was abandoned. On 7 November 1995, the injunction was re-imposed by consent of the plaintiff and the parties to the land dispute case, as the plaintiff had decided to abandon its operations on Mono.

The plaintiff sued the defendant for damages for breach of contract to supply a helicopter and reimbursement of money paid in advance. At first instance, it was held that the agreement was frustrated by the imposition of the injunction in the land dispute case. The defendant was ordered to return the advance payments, plus interest to the plaintiff, pursuant to the Law Reform (Frustrated Contracts) Act 1943 (UK). The defendant appealed. The Court of Appeal allowed the appeal on the basis that frustration did not apply, as the plaintiff knew about the land dispute prior to entry into the contract with the defendant. This special knowledge should have led it to foresee the event which was alleged to amount to frustration. This concealed knowledge prevented the doctrine of frustration from applying. The Court of Appeal also held that in order to establish that a party is prevented from relying on the doctrine of frustration on the basis that the event in question should have been foreseen, it is not necessary to prove fraudulent conduct.

In *Soakai v Kingdom of Tonga*,[28] it was held, obiter, that a plea of frustration based on harsh weather conditions would not succeed in Tonga due to the fact that sudden and very heavy rain was always a possibility.

2.2.4. The Event Must not be Due to the Fault of One of the Parties

A party who is responsible for the event relied upon cannot escape liability by alleging frustration. In *Maritime National Fish Ltd v Ocean Trawlers Ltd*,[29] for example, the appellants chartered a steam trawler from the respondents. It was useless for fishing unless fitted with an otter trawl. To the knowledge of both parties, it was illegal to use an otter trawl except under licence from the Canadian Minister of Fisheries. After entering into the charter agreement, the appellants, who had four other ships of their own, applied for five licences, but were granted only three. In naming the ships to which the licences were to apply, they excluded the chartered trawler. It was held that the failure to secure a licence was the consequence of a conscious election, and thus could not be relied on as a frustrating event.

---

28 [1998] TOSC 5.

29 [1935] AC 524.

2.2.5. *The Doctrine of Frustration cannot be Excluded in the Case of Illegality*

Where the frustrating event also renders the contract illegal, the parties cannot exclude the doctrine of frustration, as this would be contrary to public policy. For example, in *Ertel Bieber & Co v Rio Tinto Co Ltd*,[30] the agreement specifically provided for the contract to be suspended during a war. It was held that this clause was void on the grounds of public policy, as its continuing existence promoted the economic interests of the enemy or prejudiced those of the United Kingdom.

As discussed above, apart from this exception, if the parties foresee and provide for the event in question, this will prevent frustration.

2.2.6. *Normally a Lease cannot be Frustrated*

Normally a lease cannot be frustrated, as it creates not a mere contract, but an estate in land. For example, in *London and Northern Estates Co v Schlesinger*,[31] it was held that the lease of a flat was not terminated by the fact that the lessee became an enemy alien and was thereby prevented from living on the premises.

There is some uncertainty about whether a lease may ever be frustrated. In *Cricklewood Property and Investment Trust v Leightons Investment Trust*,[32] the House of Lords held unanimously that there was no frustration of a long-term building lease by the imposition of building restrictions following the outbreak of war. On the question of whether a lease could ever be frustrated, the court was divided. In *National Carriers Ltd v Panalpina (Northern) Ltd*,[33] whilst holding that there was no arguable case of frustration on the merits, the House of Lords appeared anxious to confirm that there were circumstances in which a lease might be frustrated.

3. EXAMPLES OF CIRCUMSTANCES AMOUNTING TO FRUSTRATION

3.1. SUPERVENING ILLEGALITY

Perhaps the most obvious example of frustration is where a change in the law occurs between the making of the contract and its execution, which renders performance of the contract illegal. For example, in *Fibrosa v Fairbairn*,[34] the

30 [1918] AC 260.
31 [1916] 1 KB 20.
32 [1945] AC 221.
33 [1981] 1 All ER 161.
34 [1943] AC 32.

defendant contracted to supply the plaintiff with a number of textile machines to be delivered to Gdynia, in Poland. Before delivery could be made, war broke out and the Germans occupied Gdynia. The contract was thereby frustrated. Similarly, in *Metropolitan Water Board v Dick, Kerr & Co Ltd*,[35] the defendant agreed to build a reservoir for the plaintiff within six years. After two years, the defendant was required by a wartime statute to cease work and sell its plant. It was held that performance had been prohibited for so long that to maintain a contract would have imposed a contract on the parties fundamentally different from that made.

However, mere delay is not normally enough to frustrate a contract. In *HP Kasabia Brothers Ltd v Reddy Construction Ltd*,[36] the defendant argued that a building contract was frustrated due to the lack of building permit that postponed the work for 20 days, which transmuted the job undertaken into a job of a different kind, outside the contemplation of the parties. It was held that there was nothing to show that the contract had become radically different.

3.2. DESTRUCTION OF SOMETHING ESSENTIAL FOR PERFORMANCE OF THE CONTRACT

The situation where the subject matter of the contract is physically destroyed prior to performance is another obvious example of a frustrating event. For example, in *Taylor v Caldwell*,[37] the defendant agreed to hire out a music hall to the plaintiff on certain specified days for the purpose of holding concerts. The hall was accidentally destroyed by fire six days before the date of the first concert, and the plaintiff claimed damages for failure to make the premises available. It was held that the contract had been discharged by frustration.[38]

3.3. UNAVAILABILITY OF THING OR PERSON ESSENTIAL FOR PERFORMANCE

Where the subject matter of the contract or a specific object essential for performance is not available, this will frustrate the contract. This is illustrated by *Corrie v Captain Cook Hotel Ltd*,[39] where the plaintiff and defendant entered into an oral agreement whereby the plaintiff was allowed to access the electricity supply for his residence from the defendant's power box, provided that the

35 [1918] AC 119.
36 (1977)] 23 FLR 235.
37 (1863) 3 B&S 826.
38 See also *Appleby v Myers* (1867) LR 2 CP 651.
39 [2013] KIHC 39.

plaintiff provided his own connection cable and paid for his consumption. The defendant's main generator broke down and its smaller one did not have the capacity to provide the plaintiff with power. The plaintiff sued for breach of contract. The court held that, as the breakdown was not the defendant's fault, the contract was frustrated when the main generator was no longer available, and the defendant was excused from performance.

Similarly, if a person is unavailable, this will frustrate the contract, provided that the person in question is personally significant to the contract. Obvious examples would be the death of person required to perform a contract for personal services. A less clear case can be found in *Morgan v Manser.*[40] In that case, the defendant appointed the plaintiff as his theatrical manager in 1938 for 10 years, for a percentage of his earnings. In 1940, the plaintiff was called up and was in the forces until 1946. After demobilisation, the defendant did not use the plaintiff's services, and the plaintiff sued for a share of the defendant's earnings. It was held that the contract was frustrated by the conscription, which had meant that the plaintiff was not freely available for a lengthy period of time, as it was envisaged he would be when the contract was made. It is noteworthy that, here, the contract was still capable of performance, that is, it was not impossible for the contract to be performed, as is in the most obvious examples of frustration. Rather, the six-year gap in the middle of the contract gave rise to a radical difference between what was agreed and what resulted from the frustrating event.

In *FC Shepherd & Co v Jerrom*,[41] it was held that a sentence of imprisonment imposed on an employee was capable of frustrating the contract of employment, if the sentence was long enough to render the performance of the contract radically different from that which the parties anticipated when they entered into the contract.

Frustration may also result from the unavailability of a person who is not a party to the contract, but is essential to the performance of the agreement.[42]

3.4. METHOD OF PERFORMANCE IMPOSSIBLE

If the method of performing the contract is stipulated, or if the method is contemplated by both parties in circumstances necessitating that method, the contract will be frustrated if that method becomes impossible to use. For example, in *CBIP (PNG) v Landex Ltd*,[43] the parties entered into a contract

40 [1948] KB 184.
41 [1987] 1 QB 301.
42 *Bank Line Ltd v Arthur Capel & Co* [1919] AC 435.
43 [2016] PGNC 416.

for the defendant to carry out earthworks at a palm oil mill. The site was accessible only by sea. The defendant arranged for the necessary machinery to be shipped, but after it had been loaded for transportation to the mill, a cyclone struck and the barge never set sail. The plaintiff was forced to carry out the work by other means and claimed a refund of the advance payment. The court held that the contract had been frustrated by the cyclone and that it terminated the contract for future performance.

However, if there is an alternative method of performance available, the contract will not be frustrated. In *Tsakiroglou & Co Ltd v Noblee Thorl GmbH*,[44] the defendant agreed to sell and ship Sudanese groundnuts to the plaintiff. After the contract was made, the Suez Canal was closed to traffic. The defendant failed to deliver and the plaintiff sued. The defendant claimed frustration. The House of Lords held that shipment via the Cape of Good Hope would have sufficed, and as the mode of delivery had not been specified, the extra expense and different route required to ship the goods did not render the contract radically different from what was envisaged when it was entered into.

3.5. AN EVENT WHICH RENDERS THE COMMON PURPOSE FRUITLESS

If the purpose of the contract is linked to some specific event which does not happen, the contract will be frustrated. For example, in *Krell v Henry*,[45] the plaintiff agreed to let a room to the defendant for the day of Edward VII's coronation. Both parties understood that the letting was for the purpose of viewing the coronation procession, but this did not appear in the agreement itself. The procession was cancelled owing to the illness of the King. The Court of Appeal held that the procession was the foundation of the contract and that the effect of the cancellation was to discharge the parties from further performance.

4. EFFECTS OF FRUSTRATION

The consequences of frustration depend on whether the position is governed by statute or by the common law. It should also be noted that the common law position in England is different from the position in Australia. Theoretically, in most countries of the region where frustration is still governed by the common law, the English common law prevails. However, as discussed in chapter 1, it is open to a regional country to depart from the English common law and

44 [1962] AC 93.
45 [1903] 2 KB 740.

follow the Australian approach or take a new path, on the basis that the English common law is not suitable for local circumstances.

4.1. COMMON LAW

When the doctrine of frustration applies at common law, the effect is to discharge the contract automatically as to the future.[46] There is no question of election or waiver as there is when a contract is discharged on the basis of breach.[47] Each party is automatically released from further performance of the contract. However, this discharge is not backdated as the contract is not deemed to be void ab initio. Unconditional rights accrued before the frustrating event occurred remain enforceable. This means that money payable and paid under the contract before the frustrating event cannot be recovered, and money due but not paid under the contract before the frustration remains payable.[48] On the other hand, rights not yet accrued at the time of frustration are unenforceable. In other words, obligations due for performance after the frustrating event are discharged. Nevertheless, some clauses may continue to bind the parties, for example arbitration clauses.[49]

However, in *Fibrosa v Fairbairn*,[50] the House of Lords, overruling *Chandler v Webster*,[51] which had held that the loss would lie where it fell, held that if there is a total failure of consideration, money paid might be recoverable in quasi-contract. As mentioned above, in *Fibrosa v Fairbairn* a contract for the supply of machinery was frustrated by the outbreak of war and German occupation of Gdynia, where delivery was to have taken place. However, £1,000 of the total contract price of £4,800 had been paid in advance. The plaintiff's request for the return of the deposit was refused on the ground that 'considerable work' had already been done on the machinery. The House of Lords held that as the plaintiff had received no part of the performance bargained for, it was entitled to recover the deposit.

This approach was followed in *CBIP (PNG) v Landex Ltd*,[52] where the court held that a contract for earthworks was frustrated when the defendant was prevented by a cyclone from bringing the necessary machinery to the site. The plaintiff's claim for a refund of the advance payment was granted on the

46 *Hirji Mulgi v Cheong Yue Steamship Co Ltd* [1926] AC 497.
47 Ibid.
48 *Chandler v Webster* [1904] 1 KB 493.
49 *Codelfa Construction Pty Ltd v State Rail Authority (NSW)* (1982) 149 CLR 337.
50 [1943] AC 32.
51 [1904] 1 KB 493.
52 [2016] PGNC 416.

basis that there had been a total failure of consideration. The court upheld the plaintiff's claim for refund of the money, applying *Fibrosa v Fairbairn*[53] as part of the underlying law of Papua New Guinea.[54]

This case overcame the inflexibility of the law by allowing money paid before the frustrating event to be recovered. However, it did not alleviate injustice where the payee had incurred costs in preparing to perform, as was being argued in *Fibrosa*, as there was no provision for restitution of pre-frustration expenditure. Further, relief was dependent on total failure of consideration. If the payer has received any amount of consideration, the right to recover will be lost. Accordingly, the Law Reform (Frustrated Contracts) Act 1943 (UK) was passed, and this is discussed in the next section.

Before departing from the common law, it should also be noted that payment for work done after the frustrating event may be claimed for on a *quantum meruit* basis,[55] Such claims are discussed in chapter 20.

4.2. STATUTE LAW

In Samoa, the injustice that might arise in the event of frustration at common law has been remedied by the Frustrated Contracts Act 1975. This Act is based on the Law Reform (Frustrated Contracts) Act 1943 (UK). Both Acts contain provisions enabling the court to apportion the loss under a frustrated contract. The English Act probably applies in Nauru, Solomon Islands, Kiribati, Tuvalu, and Vanuatu, as an Act of general application. The Frustrated Contracts Act 1944 (NZ) does not appear to apply in Cook Islands or Niue, as it is not referred to in the Reprint of the Laws 1994. However, it does apply in Tokelau.[56] In countries where the English Act does not apply, other than Samoa and Tokelau, frustration is still governed by the common law.

The Frustrated Contracts Act 1975 (Samoa) and the Law Reform (Frustrated Contracts) Act 1943 (UK) provide as follows:

1. Prima facie money paid to a party in pursuance of the contract before the time when it was discharged is recoverable as money received by that party for the use of the party by whom it was paid, and money payable to a party before such time ceases to be payable.[57]

53 [1943] AC 32.
54 [2016] PGNC 416, [12].
55 *Davis Contractors Ltd v Fareham UDC* [1956] AC 696.
56 Contract Rules 2004 (Tokelau), R 19.
57 Law Reform (Frustrated Contracts) Act 1943 (UK), s 1(2); Frustrated Contracts Act 1975 (Samoa), s 4(2).

This rule allows for the return of deposits and other money paid on account, whether or not there has been a total failure of consideration.

2. However, if the party to whom the money was so paid or payable incurred expenses in performance of the contract before the time of discharge, the court may, if it considers it just to do so having regard to all the circumstances of the case, allow the party to retain or recover the whole or part of the money paid or payable, but only up to the amount of the expense incurred.[58]

This provision gives the court a discretionary power to set off against any sum repayable any expenses the payee incurred in taking steps to perform the contract before the frustrating event. If this provision had been in force when *Fibrosa v Fairbairn*[59] was decided, the court would have been empowered to allow the defendant to retain a part of the deposit equivalent to what it had spent on preparing to perform the contract.

3. Further, if one party has, by reason of anything done by the other in performance of the contract, obtained a valuable benefit other than a payment of money to which (1) applies, before the time of discharge, the court may allow the other party to recover from him or her such sum, not exceeding the value of the benefit, as the court considers just.[60]

This provision was discussed in the English case of *BP Exploration v Hunt.*[61] In that case, the defendant had a licence to explore for oil in Libya. The defendant agreed to assign to the plaintiff a half share in the oil concession and 'reimbursement' oil, calculated according to a formula in the contract. The plaintiff was to carry out exploration at its own expense and to make some initial payments to the defendant. An oil field was discovered and both parties benefited from this for over four years. After a revolution in Libya, both parties' shares were expropriated. The defendant received some compensation from the Libyan government. The plaintiff claimed relief under s 1(3) of the Law Reform (Frustrated Contracts) Act 1943. The court held that that the provision must be applied in two distinct stages. First, the benefit must be identified and valued. Then the court must assess what is a just sum to award, with a ceiling being provided by the value of the benefit.

58 Law Reform (Frustrated Contracts) Act 1943 (UK), proviso to s 1(2); Frustrated Contracts Act 1975 (Samoa), proviso to s 4(2).

59 [1943] AC 32.

60 Law Reform (Frustrated Contracts) Act 1943 (UK), s 1(3); Frustrated Contracts Act 1975 (Samoa), s 4(3).

61 [1982] 1 All ER 925.

The court in *BP Exploration v Hunt*[62] also discussed the meaning of 'valuable benefit', and whether it was to be assessed before or after the frustrating event. It was held at first instance and in the Court of Appeal that 'valuable benefit' referred not to the value of work done – in this case the cost of exploration and extraction of oil – but to the end product of the work, being here the enhanced value of the concession. However, the benefit had to be valued after the frustrating event. In this case, the concession was valueless after the event and the court held this had to be reflected in the value of the benefit. In this case, the plaintiff was still able to recover as, whilst the concession was valueless, there was a valuable benefit received by the defendant as a result of the work, prior to the frustrating event, in the form of the oil already produced and the compensation from the Libyan government. Half of the value of this ($85 million) was held to be the valuable benefit, and therefore the upper limit of any award. The court then determined the just sum as $35 million by taking into account the cost of work done and the value of oil transferred to the defendant less the value of the 'reimbursement oil'.

The view expressed in *BP Exploration v Hunt*[63] is open to criticism, as the wording of s 1(3) of the Law Reform (Frustrated Contracts) Act 1943 refers to a valuable benefit obtained 'before the time of discharge', which suggests that it should be assessed prior to the frustrating event.[64]

Four types of contract are excluded from the provisions of the Acts: voyage charter parties, contracts for the carriage of goods by sea, contracts of insurance, and contracts for the sale of specific goods which perish.[65] Any other contract may specifically exclude the provisions of the Acts from applying.[66]

---

62 Ibid.

63 Ibid.

64 See further E. Peel, *Treitel on the Law of Contract*, 14th ed., Sweet & Maxwell, London 2015, p. 1090.

65 Law Reform (Frustrated Contracts) Act 1943 (UK), s 2(5); Frustrated Contracts Act 1975 (Samoa), s 3(5).

66 Law Reform (Frustrated Contracts) Act 1943 (UK), s 2(3); Frustrated Contracts Act 1975 (Samoa), s 3(3).

CHAPTER 17
DISCHARGE BY AGREEMENT

1. INTRODUCTION

A contract may contain terms specifying when it will come to an end. It is also possible for a contract to endow one of the parties with the right to discharge the agreement.[1] For example, an employment contract may authorise an employer to dismiss an employee if the business goes into liquidation.[2] Such authority is construed strictly by the courts.[3] It must be exercised in accordance with any contractual conditions. For example, an employer may have to give written notice in order to dismiss an employee.[4]

Where the contract is silent as to when the agreement is to come to an end, the parties may subsequently agree on termination.[5] Alternatively, a party may waive the need for the other party to perform or be estopped from insisting on performance. Accordingly, discharge by agreement may be divided into two categories:

- contractual discharge; and
- non-contractual discharge.

2. CONTRACTUAL DISCHARGE

An agreement to extinguish the rights and obligations created by the original contract between the same parties may form a binding contract itself, provided it is either made under seal or supported by consideration.

---

1 *Kumar v Fiji Post & Telecommunication Ltd* [1999] FJHC 72, 4.
2 *Edgar v Lawlor Bros* (1967) 13 FLR 14.
3 *Richard Lang & Co v R* [1930–49] WSLR 52, 58.
4 See e.g. *Edgar v Lawlor Bros* (1967) 13 FLR 14.
5 *Polar Holdings Ltd v Dinh* [2007] VUSC 76.

2.1. BILATERAL DISCHARGE

Where the contract is executory, meaning that there are still obligations to be performed on both sides, consideration is provided by the mutual release by each party of the other from performance of the outstanding obligations. This is sometimes referred to as bilateral (two-party) discharge. Where both parties have some right to surrender because the other has not yet performed or only partly performed their side of the bargain, they may agree to discharge the contract altogether, or to discharge it and replace it with another agreement.

2.2. UNILATERAL DISCHARGE

Where the contract is executed, meaning that one party has already performed their side of the bargain, any agreement to discharge the contract and thereby release the other party from performance must be under seal or be supported by fresh consideration. The legal term given for the purchase of a release from an obligation, whether arising in contract or in tort, by means of giving consideration, rather than by performing the obligation, is 'accord and satisfaction'. The 'accord' is the agreement and 'satisfaction' is the price paid for the agreement.[6]

The fact that parties do not expressly reserve their rights under the original contract will not necessarily mean that a subsequent agreement as to how a breach is to be dealt with will amount to an accord and satisfaction. This is illustrated by the case of *Attorney-General v Pacific Risk Consulting Engineers Ltd*,[7] where the plaintiff and defendant had entered into a contract for the provision of professional engineering consultancy services in respect of upgrading the Maritime Training Institute. The plaintiff was not satisfied with aspects of the work and proposed three options for remedying the defects to the defendant. The defendant chose one of these, which was to undertake remedial work at its own cost. However, they failed to do this and the plaintiff commissioned another firm to carry out the work. The issue was whether there was an accord and satisfaction between the parties, or whether the plaintiff could take action pursuant to the original agreement to obtain reimbursement of the payment made to the other firm. The court defined accord and satisfaction as:

> the means by which a party obtains release from an obligation by an offer of valuable consideration which is different from the obligation from which release is sought. The accord is the agreement to discharge the obligation and satisfaction is the consideration which makes the agreement effective.[8]

---

6 *British Russian Gazette v Associated Newspapers* [1933] 2 KB 616, 643, approved in *Malaita Development Authority v Ganifiri* [2002] SBHC 5.

7 [2012] TVHC 7.

8 Ibid., [13].

It held that, in this case, there was no accord. It was not necessary to expressly preserve the rights under the original agreement. The objective intention of the parties could be ascertained from an assessment of communications between and general conduct of the parties.

An exception to the rule that consideration or a deed is required to discharge an executed contract is to be found in the Bills of Exchange Acts applicable in the region.[9] Where the holder of a bill of exchange or promissory note unconditionally renounces their rights against the acceptor, the bill is discharged. The renunciation must be in writing or the bill must be delivered up to the acceptor.[10]

2.3. VARIATION

In some situations, the parties may choose to vary the contract, rather than to discharge it. Variation consists of amendment or discharge of part of a contract. Rather than discharging the whole agreement, parties may wish to alter or dispense with only some of the clauses in it. For example, one party may agree to extend the time that the other has for performance of outstanding obligations.

A right to vary may be conferred on a party by a term of the contract. This right may also be conferred on a third party. In *Charitra v Marlows Ltd*,[11] for example, an engineer was given the power to vary the contract on certain terms.

In the absence of a term allowing unilateral variation or variation by a third party, it may be mutually agreed.[12] However, as in the case of a discharge by agreement, consideration or a deed will be required to vary the agreement.

2.4. FORMALITIES

A discharge by agreement is not required to be in writing.[13] However, where the original contract was required to be made or evidenced in writing,[14] any variation must also be made or evidenced in writing.[15] Similarly, any new

---

9 Bills of Exchange Act Cap 227 (Fiji); Bills of Exchange Act Cap 108 (Tonga); Bills of Exchange Act 1976 (Samoa); Bills of Exchange Act 1882 (UK); Bills of Exchange Act 1908 (NZ).

10 Bills of Exchange Act Cap 227 (Fiji), s 62(1); Bills of Exchange Act Cap 108 (Tonga), s 61(1); Bills of Exchange Act 1976 (Samoa), s 62(1); Bills of Exchange Act 1882 (UK), s 62(1); Bills of Exchange Act 1908 (NZ), s 62(1).

11 Unreported, Court of Appeal, Fiji, Speight VP, O'Shea and Holland JJA, 2 April 1982, 14–15.

12 *IM Carruthers Ltd v Pereira* [1960–69] WSLR 151.

13 *Kumar v Fiji Post & Telecommunication Ltd* [1999] FJHC 72, 4.

14 As to formalities generally, see further chapter 10.

15 If the contract is not required to be in writing the variation may be oral: *IM Carruthers Ltd v Pereira* [1960–69] WSLR 151, 152.

contract in substitution of the discharged agreement must be made or evidenced in writing if the subject matter so requires. Consequently, the position may arise where the oral agreement discharges the original contract, but the new contract is unenforceable because it is oral, and the agreement is required to be evidenced in writing, for example an agreement for the sale of land.

A variation required to be made or evidenced in writing which fails to fulfil these requirements will be ineffective and the original agreement will stand.[16] However, as stated above, a discharge need not be in writing, and if the new agreement is unenforceable due to lack of formalities, the parties will be left without any operative contract. Accordingly, it is important to decide whether a variation or a discharge was intended. An example of this arose in *Morris v Baron & Co.*[17] The plaintiff agreed to sell goods to the defendant, but delivered only part of the goods. The defendant failed to pay and the plaintiff commenced proceedings for the value of the goods delivered. The defendant counter-claimed for damages for non-delivery of all the goods contracted for. Before the action came to trial, the parties orally compromised the dispute. The action was to be withdrawn and the defendant was to have another three months within which to pay the sum due under the contract. It was also to have the option either to accept or to refuse the undelivered goods and was to be allowed £30 to meet the expenses incurred owing to the plaintiff's failure to complete the delivery. Ten months later, £888 4s was still unpaid and the plaintiff brought a second action to recover this sum. The defendant admitted liability, but again counter-claimed for damages in respect of the undelivered goods. The action failed for two reasons:

1. The plaintiff could not claim under the original contract as it was discharged. Its terms were so fundamentally inconsistent with the terms of the compromise as to justify the inference that the parties intended to replace it by an entirely new contract.
2. No claim could be based on the compromise, which amounted to a sale of goods, because the Sale of Goods Act 1893, at that time, required such an agreement to be in writing.

Whether the parties to a contract intend to discharge or vary the contract by a subsequent agreement depends on their intention, ascertained by reference to the oral agreement. If the oral agreement is inconsistent with the written contract to an extent that goes to its root, the courts will infer that the parties intended to discharge and replace it.[18]

---

16 *Goss v Nugent* (1833) 5 B & Ad 58.

17 [1918] AC 1.

18 *British & Bennington's Ltd v NW Cachar Tea Co* [1923] AC 48, 62.

Another question that arises is whether a contract under seal may be discharged without execution of another deed. The common law rule was that it could not, but equity now prevails to allows oral discharge. In *Berry v Berry*,[19] a written agreement varying a provision in a deed of separation was a good defence to an action brought on the deed.

3. NON-CONTRACTUAL DISCHARGE

Non-contractual discharge may occur through estoppel or waiver.

3.1. ESTOPPEL

As discussed in chapter 7, if a person makes a statement of fact and another person acts on it, the maker will be estopped from denying the truth of the statement in subsequent litigation. In the context of discharge by agreement, if parties conduct themselves in such a way as to induce the other party to believe that the contract is at an end, estoppel may prevent enforcement of the contract. However, estoppel will only arise if the other party has acted in reliance on the promise and suffered detriment.[20]

Where the conduct of a party induces the other party to believe and act on the assumption that the contract is varied, estoppel may also be relied on to enforce the varied agreement.

3.2. WAIVER

In *Burgess v Prasad*,[21] it was said that waiver involves a request by one party for the forbearance of the other and the agreement of the other to that request. As discussed in chapter 7, estoppel is related to the principle of waiver. The main distinction is that estoppel requires the other party to have altered their position on the strength of the promise made. Whereas variation involves a formal alteration to the terms of the original contract, waiver occurs when the terms of the contract are not formally altered, but one party indicates that strict performance of those terms of the contract will not be insisted upon. Waiver does not amount to a variation because it is not a mutually agreed change supported by consideration or under seal. Further, variation involves an alteration of the terms of the original contract, whereas waiver is concerned only

---

19 [1929] 2 KB 316.

20 *Burgess v Prasad* (1974) 20 FLR 49.

21 Ibid.

with forbearance as to the method of performance of the contract. Waiver must be an intentional forbearance and the person waiving his or her rights must have full knowledge of all the facts.

A waiver may be granted either orally, in writing or implied from conduct. An example of a waiver granted in writing can be seen in *Bishop of Melanesia v Maile.*[22] In that case, the parties entered into a lease for 99 years from 1 January 1956. During the first 11 years, arrears of rent accrued. In 1967, the parties then signed a written agreement whereby the lessor waived the right to the outstanding arrears. Subsequently, the lessor purported to appropriate the last payment of rent to a period prior to the 1967 agreement and then invoked the forfeiture clause for non-payment of rent. It was held that as the right to the arrears had been waived, the lessor was not entitled to issue the notice.

An example of waiver implied from conduct can be found in *Edgar v Lawlor Bros.*[23] In that case, the plaintiff was employed by the defendant under a contract which stated that he could be dismissed for good cause provided written notice was given to him by the employer. The plaintiff refused to do some work, as directed by the defendant, and when heated words were exchanged he said, 'Sack me then, sack me'. The defendant dismissed the plaintiff orally and he sued for breach of a term of the contract requiring written notice of dismissal. It was held that the plaintiff had waived the right to written notice by telling the employer to sack him on the spot, and by his action in accepting the dismissal. Accordingly, he could not succeed in claiming that the agreement had not been properly brought to an end.

A regional example of waiver implied from conduct is *Vanualevu Hardware (Fiji) Ltd v Sun Insurance Company Ltd*,[24] where the plaintiff took out an insurance policy with the defendant. After the plaintiff's property was damaged by a cyclone, the defendant refused to pay on the basis that it was a condition precedent to the cyclone cover that the plaintiff would supply a current engineer's certificate. In fact, the plaintiff only obtained the certificate after the cyclone. The court held that the condition precedent had been waived by the defendant's conduct, in that they did not decline cover and accepted premiums for the insured peril for the relevant period. The defendant also wrote to the plaintiff, after he had supplied the certificate making an offer of payment, thus implying that it was prepared to honour the policy.

Waiver is binding not only on the grantor, but also on the person at whose request it was granted. For example, in *Levey & Co v Goldberg*,[25] the defendant agreed to buy a quantity of cloth from the plaintiff, with delivery to be within

22 (1973) 19 FLR 49.
23 (1967) 13 FLR 14. See also *Richard Lang & Co v R* [1930–49] WSLR 52, 56.
24 [2013] FJHC 203.
25 [1922] 1 KB 688.

a stipulated time. He then asked the plaintiff to delay delivery and the plaintiff orally agreed. After the original date for delivery had passed but before delivery actually took place, the defendant repudiated the contract on the basis that the plaintiff had failed to deliver as originally agreed (the alleged 'variation' being invalid for want of writing). It was held that the plaintiff's agreement was not invalid, as it was not a variation, but a waiver of the plaintiff's right to deliver at the originally agreed time. The defendant was therefore bound to accept delivery and was liable for failure to do so.

Mere agreement to negotiate regarding the method of performance of the contract will not be enough to waive a party's rights. For example, in *Banque Privee de Credit Moderne v Jet Service Ltd and Another*,[26] it was held that the plaintiff's willingness to negotiate regarding defaults in repayments of loans, evidenced by words and conduct, was not enough to amount to a waiver.

Waiver may be withdrawn by giving reasonable notice. In *Charles Rickards Ltd v Oppenheim*,[27] the defendant ordered a Rolls Royce chassis from the plaintiff, to be completed by March. It was not completed on time. The defendant continued to press for delivery, thereby implying that the condition was waived. In June, the defendant wrote to say that delivery must be by late July, indicating that otherwise he would not accept at all. Delivery was finally made in October, and the defendant refused to accept. The plaintiff sued. It was held that the plaintiff could not succeed as the original waiver had been revoked, thereby allowing the defendant to reject for non-delivery on time.

26 [1992] VU Law Reports 2, 5.
27 [1950] 1 KB 616.

CHAPTER 18
DISCHARGE BY PERFORMANCE

1. INTRODUCTION

Where parties to a contract have performed their obligations, the contract is completely discharged. A party who performs a contract exactly according to its terms will be discharged from further performance. However, performance of a contract must be precise. A party who only partially performs a contract will not usually be entitled to the contract price. Further, if obligations are not performed, not only will the contract not be discharged, but also the defaulting party will be in breach of contract.

2. PERFORMANCE MUST BE EXACT

Under the common law, only a party who has performed the contract exactly is entitled to treat the contract as discharged. This requirement has statutory force in the case of certain contracts for the sale of goods. Under the Sale of Goods Acts applicable in the region, it is provided that in a contract for the sale of goods by description, there is an implied condition that the goods will correspond exactly with that description.[1] Corresponding provisions have been introduced in relation to hire purchase agreements in Cook Islands by the Hire Purchase Act 1986.[2] Similar provision is made by the Supply of Goods (Implied Terms) Act 1973 (UK), which applies to contracts governed by English law in Vanuatu.[3]

---

1 Sale of Goods Act Cap 230 (Fiji), s 15; Sale of Goods Act 1986 (Marshall Islands), s 15; Sale of Goods Act 1975 (Samoa), s 15; Sale of Goods Act 1979 (UK), s 13 (applying in Tonga); Sale of Goods Act 1893 (UK), s 13 (applying in Solomon Islands, Vanuatu, Tuvalu, Kiribati, Nauru); Sale of Goods Act 1908 (NZ), s 15 (applying in Cook Islands and Niue). The Contract Rules 2004 (Tokelau) state only that the goods must conform to description: R 37(1).

2 Hire Purchase Act 1986 (CI), s 14(2).

3 Supply of Goods (Implied Terms) Act 1973 (UK), s 9. French law may apply to contracts in French or between French parties. See further chapter 1.

In deciding whether or not performance is exact, two questions arise:

1. is the contract entire or divisible or severable, rendering performance of a distinct part or parts capable of separate discharge; and
2. has performance occurred on time?

These questions will now be explored.

2.1. ENTIRE CONTRACTS

There is a general presumption that contracts are entire. In an entire contract, complete and exact performance of the contract is provided to be a condition precedent to payment of the contract price. In particular, in some cases it appears to have been taken as a general rule that lump sum contracts[4] are intended by the parties to be entire.[5] The presumption that a contract is entire may be rebutted if the terms of the contract indicate otherwise, and this is discussed further in section 3. In the case of an entire contract, the contract price cannot be recovered by the plaintiff if performance is defective or only partial.

If the contract is entire, a party cannot demand performance of the other in whole or in part until they themselves have rendered complete performance. A classic example of the hardship caused by this rule is *Cutter v Powell*.[6] Cutter signed on as a second mate on a ship sailing from Jamaica. The contract stipulated that he was to be paid 30 guineas, 'provided he proceeds, continues and does his duty ... to the Port of Liverpool'. About three quarters of the way through the voyage, Cutter died and his widow sued for an equivalent proportion of his wages on a *quantum meruit* basis. The action failed as Cutter's contract was 'entire', that is, it was for the whole journey; he did not become entitled to anything until he had performed as required. Similarly, in *Sumpter v Hedges*,[7] the plaintiff agreed to build two houses and stables for the defendant for a fixed price of £565. He did part of the work to the value of £333 and then abandoned the contract. The defendant completed the buildings himself. The plaintiff was not entitled to recover anything for the work done.

A more recent case example can be found in *Bolton v Mahadeva*.[8] The plaintiff contracted to install a central heating system in the defendant's house

---

4 Lump sum contracts are those where the contract provides for payment of a specific sum upon the completion of specific work.

5 *Appleby v Myers* (1867) LR 2 CP 651; *The Madras* [1898] P 90; *Sumpter v Hedges* [1898] 1 QB 190.

6 (1795) 101 ER 573.

7 [1898] 1 QB 673.

8 [1972] 1 WLR 1009.

for the sum of £800. He did so, but it only worked ineffectively and the defendant refused to pay. The Court of Appeal held that the plaintiff could not recover anything.

The standard of performance required in *uberrimae fidei* contracts (contracts of utmost good faith) is particularly high. For example, in *Rentway Rentals Ltd v National Pacific Insurance Ltd*,[9] when completing a motor vehicle insurance claim form, the plaintiff failed to provide full and complete information to the defendant as to the circumstances of the accident or to provide other essential data, such as the name of the driver at the time of the accident. The plaintiff's claim for payment on the policy was dismissed.[10]

2.2. TIME FOR PERFORMANCE

The parties to a contract often prescribe the time for performance of contractual obligations. If no time is specified, obligations must normally be performed within a reasonable time. The question arises whether failure to perform within a specified time or to perform within a reasonable time, where time for performance is not specified, will prevent the contract being performed exactly, and thus prevent the contract from being discharged.

Originally, law and equity had different answers to this question.[11] The position is now that strict compliance with time limits is not required,[12] except in the following situations:

1. where time is stated to be 'of the essence';[13] however, even if time is stated to be of the essence, this will not apply to any obligation to which a fixed time limit has not been specified;[14]
2. where a party has been guilty of unreasonable delay, and the other party gives notice that time has become of the essence;[15]
3. where the surrounding circumstances or the subject matter make it imperative that the agreed date be precisely observed, for example in sales of short leases or sale of shares which are likely to fluctuate in price;[16] or

---

9 [1980–93] WSLR 327.

10 The court was also influenced by the fact that the plaintiff appeared to have acted fraudulently.

11 The common law position was that time was of the essence. This was altered by the Law of Property Act 1925 (UK). Section 41 brings the common law into line with equity.

12 But see *Tozaka v Hata Enterprises Ltd* [1999] SBHC 123, where Muria CJ stated that time was of the essence unless stated otherwise, except in building contracts.

13 *Burgess v Prasad* (1974) 20 FLR 49; *Harold Wood Brick Co v Ferris* [1935] 2 KB 198 (CA).

14 *Cammick v Soqulu Plantation Ltd* (unreported, Supreme Court, Fiji, Kermode J, 9 July 1996).

15 Ibid.; *Kontos v Dinh* [2010] VUSC 158.

16 See *Hare v Nicoll* [1966] 2 QB 130.

4. where the contract is mercantile, in which case time is generally of the essence. In *Quarter Enterprises Pty Ltd v Allardyce Lumber Company Ltd*,[17] the High Court of Solomon Islands was called on to decide whether time was of the essence in a logging agreement. It held, applying Lord Wilberforce's decision in *Bunge Corp New York v Tradax Export SA*,[18] that time is generally of the essence in mercantile contracts.

3. EXCEPTIONS TO THE GENERAL RULE

To temper the severity of the rule that performance must be precisely as stipulated in the contract, the common law has developed a number of modifications.

3.1. DIVISIBLE OR SEVERABLE CONTRACTS

A divisible or severable contract is a contract which clearly indicates that some performance less than the whole may suffice to confer rights on the performing party. In a divisible contract, the promises are 'independent', as opposed to an entire contract, where the promises of the parties are 'interdependent'. A good example of a divisible contract is a building contract where the work is to take place in stages, and progress payments are due from time to time as performance takes place. Another example is a contract for the sale of goods to be delivered by instalments, where each consignment is to be paid for on delivery.

Where the contract is divisible, a party is entitled to payment for the divisible part of the contract which has been performed, even if the balance of the contract has not been completed.

Whether a contract is divisible or entire depends on the parties' intention.[19] However, as mentioned above, there is a general presumption that contracts are entire, which can be rebutted only if the terms of the contract indicate otherwise.

3.2. SUBSTANTIAL PERFORMANCE

In some circumstances, parties who have not precisely carried out all of their obligations, but have substantially performed them, will be able to obtain payment of the contract price. This will be the case where what has been left undone is so minor as not to justify the innocent party in terminating the

17 [2007] SBHC 118.
18 [1981] 1 WLR 711.
19 *Roberts v Havelock* (1832) 110 ER 145.

contract. However, the innocent party may still claim damages as compensation for the minor matter left undone.

The doctrine of substantial performance is illustrated by *Hoenig v Isaacs.*[20] In that case, the plaintiff was engaged to redecorate and furnish the defendant's flat for £750, to be paid 'as the work proceeds, and balance on completion'. Some work was done and the defendant paid £400. After completion of all the work, the defendant refused to pay the balance on the grounds that the work had been poorly done, and that remedial work was necessary. The plaintiff sued, and the defendant contended that the contract was entire. It was held that, whilst the work was partially defective, the plaintiff had substantially performed that which was required of him; the defects were readily remedied. Accordingly, he was entitled to the contract price less a deduction of £55 for the cost of remedial work.

The doctrine of substantial performance has been used in some cases to avoid the injustice which arises from the inflexible application of the rule that partial performance will not suffice. In particular, it has been used to avoid unfairness in the case of lump sum contracts, which, as mentioned above, are generally taken to be entire. This may result in trivial deficiencies preventing discharge of the contract. In *Hoenig v Isaacs*,[21] Lord Denning said that the courts lean against an interpretation of lump sum contracts which would deprive a contractor of any payment at all, simply because there are some minor defects or omissions. This seems to suggest that, in Lord Denning's view, there is a presumption in an ordinary lump sum contract that the parties intended substantial performance to entitle the contractor to payment. Provided the cost of remedying the defect is trivial compared to the contract price, this would appear to be the fairer approach, as the innocent party will be entitled to damages in relation to the deficiencies. If performance falls short of substantial completion, no payment can be claimed.[22]

3.3. TENDER OF PERFORMANCE

As a general rule, where performance cannot be completed without the concurrence of the other party, tender of performance which is refused is equivalent to actual performance and discharges the party tendering from further obligation and may entitle the innocent party to damages for breach of contract. For example, in *Startup v MacDonald*,[23] the plaintiff contracted to sell to the defendant 10 tons of oil to be delivered 'within the last 14 days of March'. The plaintiff did not attempt delivery until 8.30pm on Saturday 31 March.

---

20 [1952] 2 All ER 176.
21 Ibid., 181.
22 See e.g. *Soakai v Kingdom of Tonga* [1998] TOSC 5.
23 (1843) 134 ER 1029.

The defendant refused to accept the goods because it was so late. The plaintiff sued. It was held that the defendant was liable in damages for non-acceptance. Tender had been valid, and within the time provided for. Attempted delivery was a tender of performance, and equivalent in law to actual delivery.

This case must be read in the light of the provisions of the Sale of Goods Acts applying in the region. These provide that tender must be at a reasonable hour.[24]

Where performance consists of the payment of money, special rules apply. Tender must be in the form of 'legal tender' or such other form as is agreed, for example a cheque. The debtor must seek out the creditor and attempt to pay him or her on the due date.[25] Even if the creditor refuses to accept payment, the debtor must remain ready and willing to pay, and if sued for breach of contract must make payment of the sum tendered into court.[26]

3.4. ACCEPTANCE OF PARTIAL PERFORMANCE

As discussed above, a party who only partially performs a contract will not usually be entitled to the contract price. However, if the other party accepts the partial performance, having had an option to reject, so that a fresh promise to pay can be inferred, a *quantum meruit* can be claimed for the work done, that is, such reasonable amount as the claimant deserves.[27] The defendant must have had a choice of accepting or rejecting the partial performance. This was clearly explained in *Sumpter v Hedges*,[28] the facts of which are set out in section 2.1. Collins LJ said that the defendant had had no option but to accept the building work. The mere taking of the benefit did not raise the inference that the defendant accepted partial performance. He was not bound to keep the building unfinished, as in an incomplete state it would be a nuisance to his land. Similarly, in *Wiluszynski v London Borough of Tower Hamlets*,[29] it was said that a defendant 'is not treated by the law as having chosen to accept that which is forced down his throat despite his objections'.[30]

---

24 Sale of Goods Act Cap 230 (Fiji), s 29(5); Sale of Goods Act 1986 23 MIRC Cap 1 (Marshall Islands), s 130(4); Goods Act Cap 251 (PNG), s 29(6); Sale of Goods Act 1975 (Samoa), s 29(5); Sale of Goods Act 1893 (UK), s 29(4) (applying in Solomon Islands, Vanuatu, Tuvalu, Kiribati, Nauru); Sale of Goods Act 1908 (NZ), s 31(5) (applying in Cook Islands and Niue). The Contract Rules 2004 (Tokelau) state that delivery must be 'within a reasonable time after the conclusion of the contract': R 35(iii).

25 *Walton v Mascall* (1844) 13 M&W 452, 458.

26 High Court (Civil Procedure) Rules 1964, O24 R 1(1), applying in Kiribati and Tuvalu; High Court Rules 1988 (Fiji), O18 R 15; Civil Procedure Rules 1972 O15 R 16 (Nauru); Courts (Civil Procedure) Rules 2007 (SI), R 25.1; Supreme Court Rules 1991, O8 R 2(5) (Tonga).

27 *Baltic Shipping Co v Dillon* (1993) 176 CLR 344.

28 [1898] 1 QB 673.

29 [1989] ICR 493.

30 Ibid., 504.

CHAPTER 19
TERMINATION FOR BREACH

1. INTRODUCTION

A party who fails to perform an agreement according to its terms will be in breach of contract. A breach does not automatically bring the contract to an end. The consequences depend on the seriousness of the breach. If it is sufficiently serious, it will entitle the innocent party to treat the contract as repudiated, and to terminate the contract. Less serious breaches entitle the innocent party to claim damages only.[1]

2. FORMS OF BREACH

Breach of contract occurs where a party fails to perform one or more obligations under the contract or makes it clear that he or she does not intend to perform. These forms of breach can be collectively described as 'repudiation', assuming that the breach is sufficiently serious to entitle the innocent party to treat the contract as at an end. Repudiation may take one of three forms:

- breach of an essential term (a condition);
- breach of an intermediate term, where the breach and its consequences are so grave as to substantially deprive the innocent party of the benefit of the contract;[2] or
- indication by express words or conduct that the party does not intend to fulfil his or her obligations under the contract or a clear indication of inability to perform.

The refusal or inability to perform the contractual obligations must relate to the contract as a whole, or to an essential part of it. Repudiation in this third category must take place before performance is due. If performance is due when the failure occurs, the breach will amount to actual breach and must fall into the

1 See further chapter 9.
2 Conditions and intermediate terms are discussed in chapter 9.

first or second category to amount to repudiation. As repudiation occurs before performance is due, this is known as anticipatory breach.

3. TERMINATION FOR BREACH

As explained above, under the common law, the right to terminate for breach will arise where there has been:

- an actual breach of a condition or a serious breach of an intermediate term;[3] or
- an anticipatory breach of the contract as a whole or an essential part of it.

In *Taubmans Paints (Fiji) Ltd v Faletau*,[4] the Supreme Court of Tonga suggested that the breach must be 'fundamental, going to the root of [the contract]' to bring the contract to an end. The use of the word 'fundamental' is perhaps unfortunate, as it is reminiscent of the doctrine of fundamental breach, which was once thought to prohibit the exclusion of liability for breaches which deprived a party of substantially the whole benefit of the contract.[5] This doctrine has now been rejected.[6] In this case, the expression is no doubt being used in a general way. Provided the term breached is a condition or there has been a serious breach of an intermediate term, the innocent party may treat the contract as at an end.

In *Hong Kong Fir Shipping Co Ltd v Kawasaki Kisen Kaisha Ltd*,[7] which is discussed more fully in chapter 9, it was said that where a term cannot readily be categorised as a condition, it may be regarded as an intermediate term. The innocent party may treat the contract as at an end only if the event which occurs as a result of the default substantially deprives them of the benefit of the contract. This case was approved in *Bunge Corporation New York v Tradax SA*,[8] where the House of Lords held that, in the case of breach of an intermediate term, the court must examine the gravity of the breach and consider the seriousness of the consequences.

Repudiation must be proved by the party alleging it.[9] For example, in *Cammick v Soqulu Plantation Ltd*,[10] the plaintiff failed to establish undue delay in a case where no time was specified for subdivision of the land in question.

---

3 See further chapter 9.
4 [1999] TOSC 2, affirmed in *Taubmans Paints (Fiji) Ltd v Faletau* [1999] TOCA 14.
5 See e.g. *Sze Hai Tong Bank Ltd v Rambler Cycle Co Ltd* [1959] AC 576.
6 *Suisse Atlantique Societe d'Armement SA v NV Rotterdamsche Kolen Centrale* [1967] 1 AC 361.
7 [1962] 2 QB 26.
8 [1981] 1 WLR 711.
9 *Singh v Letama Trading Company* (1987) 33 FLR 158.
10 Unreported, Supreme Court, Fiji, Kermode J, 9 July 1996.

4. FORMS OF REPUDIATION

4.1. ACTUAL BREACH

As discussed above, breach may be actual or anticipatory. A party who fails to perform at the requisite time is in actual breach.

Where a party repudiates a contract in the mistaken belief that this is justified, particular difficulties arise. This may happen in two situations:

1. where a party believes the terms of the contract justify termination, but they are mistaken in fact or law; or
2. where a party believes that the other party has repudiated the contract and elects to treat the contract as at an end.

In either case, the mistaken party may find that they have repudiated the contract. The courts have dealt with this problem by making it clear that repudiation by wrongful termination does not include a case where the wrongful termination is based on an honest mistake.

With regard to the position outlined in point (1), the leading English case is *Woodar Investment Development Ltd v Wimpey Construction (UK) Ltd.*[11] In that case, the plaintiff agreed to sell some land to the defendant. The defendant sought to terminate the contract in the mistaken belief that the Secretary of State for the Environment had commenced a compulsory acquisition procedure in respect of the land. The contract expressly reserved the right to terminate in these circumstances. The defendant's motive in rescinding was to escape the transaction, which had become unprofitable. The plaintiff claimed that the defendant had repudiated the contract. It was held that in order to constitute a repudiation there had to be an intention to abandon the contract. In this case, the defendant was not abandoning the contract, but was, in good faith, relying on its terms as justifying their right to terminate.[12]

An example of the circumstances in which the situation in point (2) may arise is where an employee claims constructive dismissal. If an employer acts in breach of an employment contract in such a way as to repudiate it, the employee may accept the repudiation and sue for damages. However, as was pointed out in *Helu v Koloa*,[13] the employee must be able to show that the employer's conduct justified termination of the contract. The employee must be able to show that

---

[11] [1980] 1 WLR 277.

[12] See also *Orion Finance Ltd v Heritable Finance Ltd* [1997] CLY 986. Compare *Federal Commerce and Navigation Co Ltd v Molena Alpha Inc* [1979] AC 757.

[13] [2000] Tonga LR 299.

there was a repudiatory breach on the basis of the contract terms. Unreasonable conduct in itself is not enough to amount to repudiation, although it may be evidence of this.

4.2. ANTICIPATORY BREACH

As mentioned above, anticipatory breach occurs when contractual obligations are renounced by a party before the time to perform has arrived. Anticipatory breach may be explicit, as where there is an express refusal to perform, or implicit, as where the breach may be implied from the defaulting party's conduct.

4.2.1. Express Refusal to Perform

If a party indicates by express words that they do not intend to fulfil their obligations under the contract, this will clearly amount to an anticipatory breach. This was referred to by the National Court of Papua New Guinea in *Leahy v Otri* as 'renunciation'.[14]

An example can be found in *Hochster v De La Tour*,[15] where the defendant engaged the plaintiff as a courier in April, with work to commence on 1 June. Three weeks before the effective date, the defendant wrote to the plaintiff advising him that, despite their agreement, his services would not be required. The plaintiff sued. It was held that the defendant's express repudiation was a clear case of anticipatory breach entitling the plaintiff to damages.

4.2.2. Implied Refusal to Perform

Where the reasonable inference from a party's conduct is that they no longer intend to perform their side of the agreement, this will amount to an anticipatory breach. In *Leahy v Otri*,[16] the National Court of Papua New Guinea made it clear that renunciation may arise from conduct where a party acts 'in such a way as to lead a reasonable man to conclude that [he] did not intend to fulfill [his] part of the contract'.[17] Makail J went on to quote further from Treitel:

> Whether conduct has this effect 'is to be considered as at the time when it is treated as terminating the contract, in the light of the then existing circumstances'. The court therefore looks to the time of rescission to determine whether the injured party

---

14 [2009] PGNC 314, [69].
15 (1853) 118 ER 922.
16 [2009] PGNC 314.
17 Ibid., [69], citing G.H. Treitel, *The Law of Contract*, 11th ed., Sweet & Maxwell, London 2003, p. 862.

reasonably took the view that the refusal was sufficiently clear and absolute to give him the right to rescind.[18]

A repudiation may arise from silence where, for example, the previous conduct of a party in refusing to perform a related contract gives rise to the inference that the party will refuse to perform the contract in question.[19]

4.2.3. Inability to Perform

Where the action or default of one party makes it impossible to further perform the contract, the innocent party will be discharged. This was referred to in *Leahy v Otri*[20] as 'prospective inability', adding that, '[t]he impossibility may be created at the time when performance is due, or before performance is due, thus constituting an anticipatory breach'.[21]

An obvious example of conduct resulting in inability to perform giving rise to anticipatory breach would be where the subject matter of the contract is sold to someone else.[22] A case example is provided by *Air Transport Ltd v Island Construction Management Ltd*,[23] where the plaintiff and defendant entered into an agreement in May for the defendant to supply a helicopter for haulage of logs from Mono Island. The plaintiff made certain advance payments to the defendant. Prior to deployment of the helicopter, the defendant discovered that an interim injunction had been granted against the plaintiff in a land dispute case, preventing it from carrying on its operations on Mono Island. At the beginning of November, the plaintiff abandoned its operations on Mono and four days later the injunction was re-imposed by consent of all parties to the land dispute case. The plaintiff sued the defendant for damages for breach of contract to supply a helicopter and reimbursement of money paid in advance. At first instance, it was held that the agreement was frustrated by the imposition of the injunction in the land dispute case. On appeal, the Court of Appeal held that the contract was repudiated four days before the re-imposition of the blanket injunction relied on by the plaintiff as a frustrating event. The Court held that repudiation took place when the plaintiff abandoned operations on Mono Island. This conduct was a clear demonstration of an intention not to be bound by the contract.

---

18 Ibid.

19 Ibid., [68].

20 Ibid., [69].

21 Ibid., citing G.H. Treitel, *The Law of Contract*, 11th ed., Sweet & Maxwell, London 2003, pp. 857–58.

22 *Lovelock v Franklyn* (1846) 8 QB 371.

23 [1999] SBCA 2. See further J. Corrin Care, 'Case Note on Air Transport Ltd v Island Construction Management Ltd' (1999) 3 *Journal of South Pacific Law, Case Note 3*.

5. THE EFFECT OF BREACH

Unlike other methods of discharge, breach does not automatically bring a contract to an end.[24] Assuming that the breach is sufficiently serious to entitle the other party to treat the contract as discharged, the consequences of the breach depend on the innocent party's election.[25]

In the case of both anticipatory and actual breach, the innocent party may either:

1. elect to treat the contract as discharged;
2. do nothing and rely on the repudiation as a defence in any action by the party in breach; or
3. elect to affirm the contract.

Before looking at these options in more detail, it is necessary to consider the manner of election.

5.1. THE MANNER OF ELECTION

If the innocent party elects to treat the contract as discharged, he or she must make that decision known to the party in default. In *Kumar v Fiji Post & Telecommunication Ltd*,[26] Shameem J cited the words of Asquith LJ to explain the position, '[a]n unaccepted repudiation is a thing writ in water and of no value to anybody, it confers no legal rights of any sort [or] kind'.[27] Once an election is made, the decision is final and cannot be retracted.[28]

In practice, there may be some cases where it is not necessary for a party to actively 'elect' by choosing between acceptance of repudiation or affirmation, as there is no real choice. In *Banque Indosuez Vanuatu Ltd v Ferrieux*,[29] the Court of Appeal of Vanuatu expressed this point in the following words:

> [T]he authorities tend to refer to the injured party being required to choose between acceptance of the repudiation and affirmation of the contract. We think that terminology unfortunate. Any principle of law has to operate in the real world. In many cases of dismissal it is obvious that the employer is not prepared to have the employee back. It is unreal to say that the employee must choose between acceptance

---

24 *Kumar v Fiji Post & Telecommunication Ltd* [1999] FJHC 72.
25 *Banque Indosuez Vanuatu Ltd v Ferrieux* (1989–94) 2 VLR 490, 493.
26 [1999] FJHC 72.
27 *Howard v Pickford Tool Co Ltd* [1951] KB 417, 421.
28 *Scarf v Jardine* (1882) 7 App Cas 345, 361.
29 (1989–94) 2 Van LR 490, 493.

> and affirmation. In reality he has no choice. But acceptance of the inevitable is still acceptance. The issue is not 'which did he choose?' but 'did he accept the repudiation?' Evidence that he tried to keep the contract alive is merely evidence against such acceptance.

In that case, the plaintiff's notification of impending legal action was held to be sufficient notice of acceptance of repudiation.[30] It can be seen from this that the indication of acceptance may be by conduct if it is sufficiently unequivocal.[31]

5.2. EFFECT OF ELECTION

If the innocent party elects to treat the contract as discharged on the grounds of repudiation, both the party electing to discharge and the party in breach are released from all future obligations under the contract. An example can be found in *Tiome v Westpac Banking Corporation*.[32] In that case, the plaintiff entered into a hire purchase agreement with the bank. The plaintiff alleged that the bank, without notice in writing, terminated the agreement and claimed damages for breach of contract. The court commented that 'repudiation by one party standing alone does not terminate the contract. It takes two to end it by repudiation on the one side, and acceptance of the repudiation on the other'.[33] It found that the bank had given a clear demand, authorised by the agreement, for payment in full of the outstanding debt, and notice that failing that it would repossess the goods. The plaintiff's failure to pay constituted a repudiation of the agreement. This entitled the bank to terminate.

The discharge does not operate retrospectively, and some terms, intended to govern liability for breach, will continue to apply. For example, arbitration clauses, liquidated damages clauses and exclusion clauses will normally remain on foot.[34] Because termination is not retrospective, obligations which have accrued must be compensated for in damages. In the case of anticipatory breach, there is no need for the innocent party to wait for the time for performance to arrive before suing.[35]

To say that a party is released from further performance does not mean that obligations that would have arisen after the discharge are to be totally disregarded. They may be relevant to damages.[36] Although the contract is terminated in the

---

30 See also e.g. *Hochster v De La Tour* (1853) 118 ER 922; *Lovelock v Franklyn* (1846) 8 QB 371.

31 *Vitol SA v Norelf Ltd ('The Santa Clara')* [1994] 4 All ER 109.

32 [2006] VUSC 13.

33 Citing *Heyman v Darwins* [1942] AC 356; *Banque Indosuez Vanuatu v Ferrieux* (1989–94) 2 Van LR 558.

34 *Photo Production Ltd v Securicor Transport Ltd* [1980] AC 827.

35 *Hochster v De La Tour* (1853) 118 ER 922.

36 *The Mihalis Angelos* [1971] 1 QB 164.

sense that the parties are no longer bound to continue with performance, the contract 'or its ghost'[37] survives for the purposes of measuring damages. In the case of anticipatory breach, a party is entitled to recover the true value of what has been lost.

Reliance on a ground of termination that proves untenable does not prevent reliance on a legitimate ground that is discovered later.[38]

5.3. FAILURE TO ELECT

As mentioned above, a repudiation prior to the time of performance is of no effect if no election has been made.[39] An innocent party who has not suffered loss or damage by virtue of the breach may choose to do nothing and to rely on the repudiation as a defence in any action by the party in breach. This may be an appropriate course where the guilty party has partly performed or paid a deposit. The innocent party must be able to show that they were ready and willing to perform if called upon to do so.[40]

Even if loss and damage has been suffered, it is open to the innocent party to do nothing and to wait until the date of completion of the contract and deal with the situation then.[41]

5.4. ELECTION TO AFFIRM THE CONTRACT

If a party does not wish to treat the contract as discharged, for example because damages are not an adequate remedy, the party may affirm the contract. The party may then take one of two courses, depending on the circumstances of the case:

1. sue for specific performance; or
2. ignore the breach or threatened breach and perform the contract.

An action for specific performance is available even if the time for performance has not yet arrived. For example, in *Hasham v Zenab*,[42] the defendant agreed to sell the plaintiff a piece of land in Nairobi. Within minutes of signing, the

---

[37] Ibid.
[38] *British & Bennington's Ltd v NW Cachar Tea Co* [1923] AC 48.
[39] *Kumar v Fiji Post & Telecommunication Ltd* [1999] FJHC 72.
[40] *Fercometal SARL v Mediterranean Shipping Co SA* [1989] AC 788; *Ward v Chandra* [2016] FJSC 30, [51].
[41] *Ward v Chandra* [2016] FJSC 30, [43].
[42] [1960] AC 316.

defendant repudiated the contract on the grounds that she had only intended to sell a quarter of the property. The contract was due to be settled within six months of signature. The plaintiff successfully sued for specific performance before the time had arrived.

In the case of actual or anticipatory breach, the innocent party may choose to ignore the breach or threatened breach and perform the contract. This will be an option only where the assent or cooperation of the other party is not required in order to do this. In *White and Carter (Councils) Ltd v McGregor*,[43] the defendant entered into a contract with the plaintiff whereby the latter would display adverts for the defendant's business on litter bins for three years. The defendant requested that the agreement be cancelled on the grounds that an employee had made a mistake in agreeing to this. The plaintiff refused to discharge the contract and went on to display the advertisements for 156 weeks and claimed the contract price. It was held that the plaintiffs were entitled to the contract price. They were not compelled to accept the repudiation and sue for lost profit as damages.

This is a controversial decision as it could be said to encourage wasted expenditure. The minority (Morton and Keith LJJ) held that the plaintiffs should have mitigated their loss. However, there is a restriction on the right to treat the contract as subsisting. Lord Reid made it clear in *Macgregor's Case* that the contract could not be affirmed by a person who had no legitimate interest, financial or otherwise, in performing the contract, rather than claiming damages. Unfortunately, His Lordship did not explain the meaning of lack of a legitimate interest. It appears that merely acting unreasonably would not be enough. A case example where the plaintiff was not entitled to insist on performance by the defendant is *Clea Shipping Corp v Bulk Oil International Ltd.*[44] After 12 months of a two-year charter of a ship, the vessel broke down, necessitating several months of repairs. The defendant indicated that it would not require the vessel, but the plaintiff proceeded with repairs costing $800,000, which were completed in April 1981. They informed the defendant that the vessel was available for the balance of the contract, that is, until December, and they maintained a full crew ready to sail from April to December. The plaintiff argued that it was free to affirm the contract. It was held that, although in general there was an unfettered right to affirm, the court would exercise its equitable jurisdiction to refuse to allow the injured party to affirm if there was no legitimate interest in performing the contract, rather than claiming damages. In this case, the defendant was liable in damages, but could recover the hire charges. The court regarded the conduct of the plaintiff as wholly unreasonable.

If the innocent party elects to treat the contract as subsisting, it remains enforceable by both parties. Thus, an innocent party who affirms the contract,

---

43 [1962] AC 413.

44 [1984] 1 All ER 129.

but later breaches it, may be liable in damages for that breach. Similarly, if the contract is frustrated after the innocent party affirms it, the right to claim damages may be lost. This was the case in *Avery v Bowden*,[45] where the defendant chartered the plaintiff's ship and agreed to load her within 45 days. The defendant made it clear before the expiry of the period that no cargo would be available. The plaintiff remained in port, hoping for cargo. Before the expiry of the 45 days, war broke out and the contract was frustrated as it was illegal to load cargo at an enemy port. It was held that the shipowners could not recover damages for an anticipatory repudiatory breach in failing to provide a cargo, since the plaintiff had affirmed the contract. If the plaintiff had sailed away on being told that no cargo would be available, he would have had a right to claim damages for the loss caused by the breach. As the contract was frustrated between the date of repudiation and the date fixed for performance, he lost the right to claim damages for the initial breach.

In *Air Transport Ltd v Island Construction Management Ltd*,[46] the facts of which are set out in section 4.2.3, there was no evidence of the defendant having made or communicated its election. This leads to the interesting question of whether the contract was still on foot when the frustrating event occurred four days later. If it was, the supervening event could have been argued as having relieved the plaintiff from liability for the repudiation. It would appear that this argument was not advanced before the Court of Appeal.

Where a term imposing a duty on one party is not performed, the party for whose benefit the clause was inserted may waive the need to perform that duty. Thus a party cannot defend a claim for specific performance on the basis of their own non-fulfilment of a condition in favour of the plaintiff.[47]

---

45 (1855) 5 E&B 714.

46 [1999] SBCA 2.

47 *Lee v Mitlal* (1966) 12 FLR 4.

CHAPTER 20
REMEDIES

1. INTRODUCTION

As discussed in chapter 19, a breach of contract may amount to a repudiation, which justifies the innocent party in treating the contract as at end. An innocent party who has suffered loss may also claim damages by way of compensation for not getting what he or she bargained for. In some cases, the breach will not justify treating the contract as at an end, but may still entitle the innocent party to claim damages in respect of any loss. Equitable remedies may also be available and these may be of particular assistance where damages will not provide adequate compensation. Within certain boundaries, the parties are free to choose between the available remedies. Which remedies will be available in any given case depends on the type of contract and the nature of the breach. It may also depend on the innocent party's conduct, particularly where an equitable remedy is sought.

2. LIMITATION

An important consideration when seeking a remedy is that there is a time limit on the right to sue for breach of contract. It is the policy of the law that there should be an end to litigation and that stale demands should be suppressed. Legislation applying in all jurisdictions in the region lays down the period of time within which actions for breach of contract may be brought. After that time limit has expired, a right of action is said to be statute barred. The applicable legislation is:

- Limitation Act Cap 35 (Fiji)
- Civil Procedure Act 1988 [29 MIRC 1] (Marshall Islands)[1]
- Limitation Act 2017 (Nauru)

1 Section 20.

- Frauds and Limitations Act 1988 (PNG)
- Limitation Act 1975 (Samoa)
- Limitation Act Cap 18 (Solomon Islands)
- Crimes, Procedure and Evidence Rules 2003 (Tokelau)[2]
- Supreme Court Act Cap 10 (Tonga)[3]
- Limitation Act 1991 (Vanuatu)

The Limitation Act 1939 (UK) applies in Kiribati[4] and Tuvalu. In Cook Islands[5] and Niue,[6] the Limitation Act 1950 (NZ)[7] applies.

A defence based on a limitation Act must be specifically pleaded.[8] For example, in *Pacific Commercial Bank Ltd v Nonumalo*,[9] Dillon J commented on the fact that neither the pleadings nor argument raised the Limitation Act 1975 (Samoa) in a claim by the plaintiff bank in 1992 on delinquent accounts dating back to 1983. Consequently, the defence was not considered.

The limitation period in contract is usually six years after the cause of action arose.[10] In Tonga it is five years,[11] and in Tokelau two years.[12] The application of the limitation period is illustrated by *Development Bank of Western Samoa v Suhren*,[13] which involved a contract for a loan of $3,000 made on 18 November 1974. The final advance was made on 8 April 1975. The loan was repayable by instalments of $100 per month, commencing in March 1975 or on demand. The instalments were not paid. Action was commenced on 27 October 1981. It was held that the cause of action arose when the first repayment should have been made and therefore the claim was statute barred.

2 Rule 104(2).
3 Section 16.
4 See e.g. *Tiba v Takabwebwe* [1996] KIHC 153.
5 Cook Islands Act 1915 (NZ), s 641.
6 Niue Act 1966 (NZ), s 706.
7 As amended by the following NZ Acts 1952/51; 1951/52; 1954/76; 1956/61; 1957/87; 1962/112; 1963/38; 1963/96; 1964/27; 1967/53; 1970/78.
8 *Busch v Stevens* [1963] 1 QB 1. This requirement is also laid down in civil procedure rules applying in the region: see e.g. High Court (Civil Procedure) Rules 1964 (UK), O21 R 16, applying in Kiribati, Solomon Islands, Tuvalu and Vanuatu; High Court Rules 1988 (Fiji), O18 R 7.
9 [1980–93] WSLR 529.
10 Limitation Act Cap 35 (Fiji), s 4; Civil Procedure Act 29 MIRC 1 (Marshall Islands), s 20; Limitation Act 2017 (Nauru), s 6; Frauds and Limitations Act 1988 (PNG), s 16(1); Limitation Act 1975 (Samoa), s 6; Limitation Act 1991 (Vanuatu), s 3; Limitation Act Cap 18 (SI), s 5; Limitation Act 1939 (UK), s 2(1)(a); Limitation Act 1950 (NZ), s 4(1).
11 Supreme Court Act Cap 10 (Tonga), s 16(1).
12 Crimes, Procedure and Evidence Rules 2003 (Tokelau), R 104(2).
13 [1980–93] 1 WSLR 83.

Most regional limitation Acts apply a time limit of 12 years to contracts under seal.[14] However, in Nauru, the limit is six years,[15] and in Tokelau it is two years.[16]

As mentioned, the limitation period runs from the date on which the action arose.[17] This has been held to be equivalent to the date when 'every fact which it would be necessary for the plaintiff to prove, if traversed, in order to support his right to the judgment of the Court' is in existence.[18] In relation to contracts, this date is usually fairly easy to ascertain, as it is the date of the breach of contract. Thus, in *Fiji Development Bank v Raqona*,[19] the court held that a defence based on the statute of limitations failed. A guarantee had been executed on 28 September 1977 and the writ was filed on 26 October 1983. However, the fact that this was more than six years later was of no relevance, as the demand for payment on the guarantee had not been made until 12 May 1981. The failure to pay on demand constituting the breach thus occurred only two and a half years before the action was commenced, and therefore the Limitation Act had no application.

All the limitation Acts applying in the region provide for the extension of the limitation period in certain circumstances. These circumstances can be summarised as follows.

2.1. DISABILITY

In the event of disability existing at the date when the cause of action accrued, for example unsound mind or minority, the limitation period is extended. The extension will normally be for a period of six years from the date when the injured party ceases to be under a disability.[20]

---

14 Limitation Act Cap 35 (Fiji), s 4; Civil Procedure Act 29 MIRC 1 (Marshall Islands), s 20; Limitation Act 2017 (Nauru), s 6; Frauds and Limitations Act 1988 (PNG), s 16(3); Limitation Act 1975 (Samoa), s 6(3); Limitation Act Cap 18 (SI), s 30; Supreme Court Act Cap 10 (Tonga), s 16(1); Limitation Act 1991 (Vanuatu), s 3(3); Limitation Act 1939 (UK), s 12; Limitation Act 1950 (NZ), s 4(3). There is no extended period for deeds provided in the Civil Procedure Act 29 MIRC 1 (Marshall Islands), therefore the six-year limit specified in s 20 would appear to apply.

15 Limitation Act 2017 (Nauru), s 12.

16 Crimes, Procedure and Evidence Rules 2003 (Tokelau), s 104(2).

17 See e.g. Civil Procedure Act 29 MIRC 1 (Marshall Islands), s 27; Limitation Act 1975 (Samoa), s 6; Limitation Act Cap 18 (SI), s 17.

18 *Read v Brown* (1889) 22 QBD 128, 131.

19 (1984) 30 FLR 151.

20 Limitation Act Cap 35 (Fiji), s 11; Civil Procedure Act 29 MIRC 1 (Marshall Islands), s 21; Limitation Act 2017 (Nauru), ss 29 (12-year extension), 30, 31 (extension until the age of 21 for claimants who were between 15 and 21 when the cause of action arose); Limitation Act 1975 (Samoa), s 22; Crimes, Procedure and Evidence Rules 2003 (Tokelau), R 104(4) (two-year extension); Limitation Act 1991 (Vanuatu), s 10; Limitation Act Cap 18 (SI), s 30; Limitation Act 1939 (UK), s 31; Limitation Act 1950 (NZ), s 28.

2.2. CAUSE OF ACTION CONCEALED

Where the cause of action is based on or has been concealed by fraud, or is for relief from the consequences of mistake, the period of time before the innocent party discovers (or could with reasonable diligence have discovered) the fraud or mistake is not included in the six-year time period.[21]

2.3. ACKNOWLEDGEMENT OR PART PAYMENT

The limitation period may be extended if a party acknowledges the debt or makes a part payment.[22]

2.4. DISCRETIONARY EXTENSION

In most Acts applying in the region, there is also a general discretion to extend the period if it is equitable to do so.[23]

Most Acts state that the time limits do not apply to actions for specific performance or injunctions.[24] However, generally, they will be applied by analogy by the court by virtue of the exercise of the court's discretion, when it exercises its equitable jurisdiction. The equitable doctrine of *laches* also applies to equitable remedies. This doctrine operates to prevent a plaintiff succeeding if he or she has been dilatory.[25] This is discussed further in section 4.4.4.

3. DAMAGES

3.1. INTRODUCTION

Any breach of contract by one party entitles the other to sue for the common law remedy of damages, except where the obligation is to pay a debt or a specific sum

21 Limitation Act Cap 35 (Fiji), s 15; Civil Procedure Act 29 MIRC 1 (Marshall Islands), s 21; Limitation Act 2017 (Nauru), s 28; Limitation Act 1975 (Samoa), s 26; Limitation Act Cap 18 (SI), s 30; Limitation Act 1991 (Vanuatu), s 14; Limitation Act 1939 (UK), s 26; Limitation Act 1950 (NZ), s 24.

22 Limitation Act Cap 35 (Fiji), s 12; Civil Procedure Act 29 MIRC 1 (Marshall Islands), s 22; Limitation Act 2017 (Nauru), s 47; Limitation Act 1975 (Samoa), s 23; Limitation Act Cap 18 (SI), s 30; Supreme Court Act Cap 10 (Tonga), s 16(1); Limitation Act 1991 (Vanuatu), s 11; Limitation Act 1939 (UK), s 23; Limitation Act 1950 (NZ), s 25.

23 See e.g. Limitation Act Cap 18 (SI), s 39; Limitation Act 2017 (Nauru), s 34.

24 See e.g. Limitation Act 1975 (Samoa), s 6(8).

25 *Ram Narayan v Rishad Shah* (1975) 21 Fiji LR 139.

of money which may only be recovered by a specific action for that sum. This is known as an action for an agreed sum.[26]

3.2. PURPOSE OF DAMAGES

The basic purpose of damages for breach is to compensate the innocent party for the loss suffered, not to punish the wrongdoer.[27] The general principle is that:

> where a party sustains a loss by reason of a breach of contract he is, so far as money can do it, to be placed in the same position with respect to damages, as if the contract had been performed.[28]

This principle was recently restated by the National Court of Papua New Guinea in *Finance Corporation v Department of Community Development*[29] in the following way:

> The general principle [is] that the purpose of an award of damages is to put the innocent party in the same position, as far as money can do, as if the guilty party had not committed a wrongful act.

'Exemplary', 'punitive' or 'aggravated' damages are not normally available in contract.[30]

In *Koroi v Suva City Council*,[31] the plaintiff claimed damages from the defendant for unlawfully terminating his employment. The court refused to award exemplary damages, stating that it 'is well established that such damages have never been and cannot be awarded for breach of any contract'.

In *Barrett v Patterson and Patterson*,[32] D'Imecourt CJ stated 'that damages for breach of contract must remain compensatory for loss and in no way punitive'.

---

26 The explanation for this can be found in the history of the common law. Actions for breach of contract originated in the writ of assumpsit, whereas debt was a separate form of action: F.W. Maitland, *The Forms of Action at Common Law*, Cambridge University Press, Cambridge 1968.

27 *Prasad v NBF Asset Management Bank* [2017] FJHC 611, [16]; *Barrett v Patterson* [1992] VU LR 7.

28 *Robinson v Harman* (1848) 1 Ex 850, 855 (Parke B); *Sofield v Ali* [2017] FJHC 406; *Republic of Vanuatu v Mahit* [2014] VUSC 44.

29 [2018] PGNC 297. See also *Keil v Digicel (Samoa)* [2010] WSSC 93, [28].

30 *Prasad v NBF Asset Management Bank* [2017] FJHC 611, [16]; *Pentecost Pacific Ltd and Pentecost v Hnaloane* (1980–88) 1 Van LR 134, 138 (CA); *Addis v Gramophone Co Ltd* [1909] AC 488; *Banque Indosuez Vanuatu Ltd v Ferrieux* (1989–94) 2 Van LR 490, 496. But see the dicta of Boe M in *Rolland v Director General of Finance* (unreported, Magistrates Court, Vanuatu, 2 June 1998, Civ Cas 25/98) where consideration was given to the award of exemplary damages, although the legal basis of the claim is not stated.

31 [2009] FJHC 370.

32 (1989–94) 2 Van LR 558, 569.

However, more recently, in *Republic of Vanuatu v Mahit*,[33] the Supreme Court of Vanuatu ignored this principle. Exemplary damages were awarded on the basis of the defendant's 'high handed and blatant conduct'. Where the conduct complained of also constitutes a tort, punitive damages may be awarded.[34]

As damages are to compensate for loss sustained by reason of the breach, there are two prerequisites to an award. First, it must be shown that the breach of contract caused the plaintiff's loss (causation). Second, it must be shown that the damage is not too remote (remoteness). These requirements will now be explored.

3.3. CAUSATION

3.3.1. General Test

The test for establishing causation in contract is the 'effective or dominant cause' test. That is, the effective or dominant cause of loss must have been the defendant's breach of contract. This can be contrasted with the 'but for' test applicable in tort.[35]

It is not sufficient that a breach merely provides the plaintiff with the opportunity to sustain loss. In *Galoo Ltd v Bright Grahame Murray*,[36] the defendants were the auditors of the claimants. Their audit suggested that the claimants were profitable and had substantial assets. It was claimed that a competent audit would have revealed that claimant companies were unprofitable and worthless. The claimants claimed they had suffered loss because they continued to trade on the basis of the audit, whereas they would not have done so if they had known the defendants merely provided the opportunity to incur further trading losses. They did not actually cause those losses.

It is also worth noting that contributory negligence is not a defence to actions for breach of contract, but only to actions in tort.[37]

3.3.2. Intervening Causes

Where the chain of causation between the defendant's conduct and the plaintiff's loss has been broken, the defendant will not be liable for the loss. For example,

33 [2014] VUSC 44.
34 *Guaschino v Reimers and Reimers* 2 MILR 49.
35 See e.g. *Cork v Kirby MacLean Ltd* [1952] 2 All ER 402.
36 [1995] 1 All ER 16.
37 See further Law Commission of Great Britain, *Report on Contributory Negligence as a Defence in Contract*, Report No. 219, 1993, para. 2.6; *Astley v Austrust Ltd* (1999) 161 ALR 155. It will be a defence in actions for negligent misrepresentation: *Saville Heaton Company Ltd v United Apparel (MGF) Ltd* (unreported, High Court, Fiji, Scott J, 9 April 1996), 20.

in *Beoco Ltd v Alfa Laval Co Ltd*,[38] the first defendant installed a heat exchanger at the plaintiff's premises. Later a leak was discovered, and the second defendant was engaged to repair it. Without inspecting the repair, which would have revealed a defect in the unit, the plaintiff put it back into use. Subsequently the unit exploded, damaging the plaintiff's plant and causing loss of production. In a claim against the first defendant for loss of profits which would have been suffered if the defective unit had been out of action for repair or replacement, the court held that a loss which was purely hypothetical, because the intervening event had caused greater damage, could not be recovered.[39]

Action by a third party will not break the chain of causation if the defendant's actions are the effective or dominant cause. In *Taubmans Paints (Fiji) Ltd v Faletau*,[40] the defendant was successful in a counter-claim for loss of profits caused by the plaintiff's wrongful repudiation of a sole agency contract, even though a third party had taken out an injunction prohibiting the defendant from access to the first consignment of paint sent by the plaintiff.

Further, when the intervening event is foreseeable by the parties, this will not break the chain of causation. For example, in *Stansbie v Troman*,[41] a painter was engaged to decorate a house. On completion, he left the premises unlocked. The house was burgled. It was held that the painter was liable for the value of the goods stolen, since it was reasonably foreseeable that such loss would arise from his actions.[42]

3.4. REMOTENESS

3.4.1. *The Rule in* Hadley v Baxendale

Even where a loss was caused by the breach, it will only result in an award if the damage is not too remote. This is known as the rule in *Hadley v Baxendale*.[43] In that case, the plaintiff's mill in Gloucester was brought to a standstill by a broken crankshaft. It was sent to the makers at Greenwich as a pattern for a new one. The defendant, a common carrier, promised to deliver it the following day. Owing to his neglect, it was delayed in transit, with the result that the mill remained idle for longer than it would have done had there been no breach of

38 (1994) 4 All ER 464 (CA).
39 It was held that the principles here are the same as those in tort (see e.g. *Jobling v Associated Dairies Ltd* [1981] 2 All ER 752).
40 [1999] TOSC 2, upheld on appeal in *Taubmans Paints (Fiji) Ltd v Faletau* [1999] TOCA 14.
41 [1948] 2 KB 48.
42 Compare *Weld-Blundell v Stephens* [1920] AC 956.
43 (1854) 9 Exch 341.

the contract of carriage. The plaintiffs therefore claimed to recover damages for the loss of profit caused by the delay.

The causation test was obviously fulfilled, but was the damage too remote? The carrier had not been told that a loss of profit might result from delay, but only what the article was, and that the plaintiffs were proprietors of the mill. It was held that it was not reasonable to hold the carrier liable for loss of profit.

The rule has been expressly endorsed as part of the common law in Fiji,[44] Kiribati,[45] Papua New Guinea[46] and Vanuatu.[47]

The rule arising from the ratio of *Hadley v Baxendale* has two limbs. Damages will only be recoverable if they may reasonably be considered as:

- arising naturally according to the normal course of things from the breach; or
- having been contemplated by the parties at the time they made the contract as the probable result of it.

These two criteria merit further examination.

3.4.1.1. Loss Arising Naturally

This limb of the rule is to be applied where normal loss occurs. The question is whether the loss or damage flows as a natural consequence of the breach. If the loss flows naturally, it will be presumed to have been within the parties' reasonable contemplation.

It is only necessary that the type of loss should have been within the parties' reasonable contemplation, not that the extent of it should have been foreseen. For example, in *H Parsons (Livestock) Ltd v Uttley Ingham & Co Ltd*,[48] the plaintiffs were pig farmers. They ordered a bulk food storage hopper for storing pignuts from the defendants. When the defendants installed the hopper, they failed to ensure that the ventilator on the top was open. The pignuts went mouldy, and when the pigs ate them they became ill with a rare intestinal disease and 254 pigs died. It was held that the death of the pigs was not too remote, since the parties might reasonably have contemplated some illness to the pigs resulting from the breach and they did not have to foresee the type and extent of the illness that occurred.

---

44 *Manohan Aluminium & Glass (Fiji) Ltd v Fong Sun Development Ltd* [2018] FJCA 23.

45 *Areta v Kiribati Housing Corporation* [2008] KIHC 6.

46 *Finance Corporation v Department of Community Development* [2018] PGNC 297.

47 *Vanuatu Copra and Cocoa Exporters Ltd v Vanuatu Coconut Product Ltd* [2011] VUCA 29, [13].

48 [1978] 1 QB 791 (CA).

3.4.1.2. Contemplated by the Parties

The second test is to be applied where abnormal damage occurs. Whereas under the first limb knowledge of the type of loss in question is imputed to the defendant on the basis that such loss flows naturally from the breach, liability under the second limb arises from the defendant's actual knowledge. The basis of this is said to be that a defendant, with actual knowledge of special facts, is undertaking to bear a greater loss.[49]

3.4.2. *Developments Since* Hadley v Baxendale

The rule in *Hadley v Baxendale* was restated in *Victoria Laundry (Windsor) Ltd v Newman Industries Ltd.*[50] It was held that recoverable loss will depend on the knowledge of the parties. Such knowledge might be either:

- imputed knowledge; or
- actual knowledge.

It is not necessary that the guilty party should actually have asked themselves what loss would result from the breach, as at the time of contracting parties are more likely to be concentrating on performance than on breach. It suffices that if the question had been asked, the party would, as a reasonable person, have concluded that the loss was likely to result.

The principles of remoteness were further refined in *Koufos v Czarnikow Ltd ('The Heron II').*[51] The House of Lords made it clear that the test is not the same as that for recovery in tort, that is, it is not one of reasonable foreseeability. Unfortunately, the House of Lords did not agree upon a general formulation in place of 'foreseeability'.

Lord Reid said:

> The crucial question is whether, on the information available to the Defendant when the contract was made, he should or the reasonable man in his position would, have realised that such loss was sufficiently likely to result from the breach of contract to make it proper to hold that the loss flowed naturally from the breach or that loss of that kind should have been within his contemplation.

In addition to the standard of being 'sufficiently likely', the phrases 'a real danger' and 'a serious probability' were used by Lords Pearce and Upjohn.

---

49 See e.g. *Koufos v Czarnikow Ltd ('The Heron II')* [1969] 1 AC 350.
50 [1949] 2 KB 528.
51 [1969] 1 AC 350, 358.

The drawing of a distinction between the test to be applied in contract and the test to be applied in tort has been criticised, notably by Scarman LJ in *H Parsons (Livestock) Ltd v Uttley Ingham & Co Ltd*.[52] His Lordship suggested that the tests of foreseeability or reasonable contemplation were essentially the same.

Reasonable foreseeability still appears to be the relevant test in Papua New Guinea where, in *Finance Corporation v Department of Community Development*,[53] the National Court commented that the general principle that the purpose of damages was to put the innocent party in the same position as if the wrongful act had not committed is qualified when assessing damages for breach of contract:

> The qualification is that the innocent party only gets the amount of his actual losses that were reasonably foreseeable at the time the contract was formed. What is taken to have been reasonably foreseeable at the time the contract was formed depends on two things: (a) the sort of knowledge that any reasonable person would be expected to have; and (b) knowledge of special circumstances outside the ordinary course of things.

3.5. ASSESSMENT OF DAMAGES

In some cases, the level of damages is laid down by statute.[54] In other cases, resort must be had to the common law.[55] The general rule is that 'where a party sustains a loss by reason of a breach of contract he is, so far as money can do it, to be placed in the same position with respect to damages, as if the contract had been performed'.[56] As explained in *Vanuatu Copra and Cocoa Exporters Ltd v Vanuatu Coconut Product Ltd*,[57] damages awards may fall under one of two limbs:

> Under the first limb damages awarded are broadly described as 'general' damages, and those awarded under the second limb as 'special' damages. The general damages are those which the law presumes to follow 'naturally' from the breach, whereas special damages are of an exceptional nature and are only recoverable where the defendant had prior knowledge of a likelihood that the loss would be suffered.

52 [1978] 1 QB 791 (CA).

53 [2018] PGNC 297, [48].

54 See e.g. Employment Act Cap 160 (Vanuatu), ss 53(1), 56(4). But see *Banque Indosuez Vanuatu Ltd v Ferrieux* (1989–94) 2 Van LR 490, where the Court of Appeal upheld the common law assessment of damages, and stated that any statutory award must be set off against it.

55 In French law cases in Vanuatu, French decisions may be referred to by way of comparison: *Pentecost Pacific Ltd and Pentecost v Hnaloane* (1980–88) 1 Van LR 134 (CA).

56 *Robinson v Harman* (1848) 1 Ex 850, 855 (Parke B).

57 [2011] VUCA 29, [13].

The award of damages should not include an award in respect of legal costs or expenses. These may be the subject of a separate order for costs against the unsuccessful party.[58] It should also be noted that damages may be reduced if the plaintiff's case is 'tainted with moral turpitude'.[59]

There are two primary methods of assessment to achieve this end:

- calculation of 'expectation loss'; or
- calculation of 'reliance loss'.

Which of these methods is used will depend on the circumstances of the case. The factors involved, and the method of calculating each type of loss will now be examined.

3.5.1. Expectation Loss

Calculation of loss by reference to expectation loss is the traditional basis for assessing damages for breach of contract. This method involves awarding damages for the lost bargain. This entails calculating the value of the expectation that the promise created. As mentioned above, damages for breach of contract are designed to place the injured party, so far as money can do, in the same position as if the contract had been performed. Calculation of expectation loss will normally be the best way to do this.

The method of calculating expectation loss will depend on the nature of the contract. The two main types of expectation loss are:

- difference in value; and
- cost of cure.

3.5.1.1. Difference in Value

Expectation loss is calculated by finding the difference between the value of what the innocent party expected to receive, and the value of what was actually received. For example, where the breach consists of the supply of defective goods, the measure of damages will be the difference in value between the goods as promised, and the goods as actually received. Where the contract is for building work that does not proceed, the recoverable loss will be the difference

---

58 *Pentecost Pacific Ltd and Pentecost v Hnaloane* (1980–88) 1 Van LR 134, 138 (CA). Costs are usually said to 'follow the event': see further J. Corrin, *Courts and Civil Procedures in the South Pacific*, Intersentia, Cambridge 2016, p. 311.

59 *Kairun v Bidesi* (unreported, Supreme Court, Fiji, Civ Cas 421, 5 October 1979), 5.

between the original contract price and the reasonable price of having the work completed by someone else.[60]

Perhaps the best illustration of the measurement of expectation loss in terms of difference in value is the process of assessment of damages for a seller's breach by non-delivery in a contract for the sale of goods. In this situation the market price rule applies.

3.5.1.1.1. The Market Price Rule

Where goods are freely available the measure of damages will be the difference between the contract price and the price of obtaining goods on the open market. The market price rule also applies when the buyer is in breach for non-acceptance of the goods. The measure of damages will be the difference in the price obtained by the seller selling the goods to a new buyer on the open market, and the purchase price that would have been received under the original contract. In *Province Forest Industries v Rainbow Holdings*,[61] the National Court of Papua New Guinea applied the definition of 'available market' in *Thompson (WL) Ltd v Robinson (Gunmakers) Ltd*:[62]

> [A]n available market merely means that the situation in the particular trade in the particular area was such that the particular goods could freely be sold, and that there was a demand sufficient to absorb readily all the goods that were thrust on it, so that if a purchaser defaulted, the goods in question could readily be disposed of.

It should be noted that the market price rule is the measure suggested by the Sale of Goods Acts, which may apply in calculating damages in contracts involving the sale of goods. For example, under ss 50(3) and 51(3) of the Sale of Goods Act of Fiji,[63] prima facie the measure of loss is the difference between the contract price and the market or current price.[64] The same applies under the Goods Act in Papua New Guinea[65] and the Contract Rules 2004 of Tokelau.[66]

Where there is no available market, the court may be prepared to award the difference between the contract price and the price at which the plaintiff sold the goods. In *Province Forest Industries v Rainbow Holdings*,[67] the plaintiff claimed damages, but submitted that the market price rule provided by s 54(3) of the

---

60 *HP Kasabia Brothers Ltd v Reddy Construction Ltd* (1977) 23 FLR 235, 259.
61 [1981] PGNC 39.
62 [1955] Ch 177, 187.
63 Cap 230.
64 See also Sale of Goods Acts 1893 and 1979 (UK), ss 50(3), 51(3), which apply in Tonga.
65 Section 54.
66 Rule 84.
67 [1981] PGNC 39. See also *Harrisons & Crosfield (PNG) Ltd v Pous Trading Company Pty Ltd* [1976] PNGLR 106.

Goods Act should not apply as 'there was no available market for the goods in question, which were logs'. The court accepted this and concluded that the measure of loss was the difference between the contract price and the price at which the plaintiff sold the logs.[68]

3.5.1.1.2. Loss of Profit

A question that arises in assessing expectation loss is whether a sum may also be awarded for loss of profits. In sale of goods contracts, if supply exceeds demand, there will be no available market for a vendor to make an alternative sale. In such cases, although the item in question may eventually be sold at the same price, one less sale has been made, and there has therefore been a loss of profit. The courts have held that this loss of profits is recoverable if there is no available market.[69] For example, in *Thompson (WL) Ltd v Robinson (Gunmakers) Ltd*,[70] there was no available market for a Vanguard car, as supply exceeded demand. It was held that the vendor was entitled to be compensated for one less sale.

On the other hand, if demand exceeds supply, the innocent party has lost nothing as he can readily resell and the loss will be in accordance with the market rule. For example, in *Charter v Sullivan*,[71] the subject matter of the sale was a Hillman Minx, and demand for such cars exceeded supply. Accordingly, the seller could sell as many as he was able to get hold of, and could not succeed in a claim for loss of profit.

Where the goods are unique, it has been held that there is never an available market, and the courts must estimate the value of the goods. If the goods have in fact been sold, then damages will be the difference in the price actually obtained by the seller from the new buyer and the purchase price that would have been received under the original contract.[72] But, just as where demand exceeds supply, loss of profit cannot be recovered.

The plaintiff may also have lost profits where the goods were expected to generate income. For example, in *Victoria Laundry (Windsor) Ltd v Newman Industries Ltd*,[73] the plaintiffs were entitled to damages for loss of profit between the date when a boiler should have been supplied, and the date when it was supplied.

Profits may also be claimed in contracts of hire. In *Tetley v The Administration*,[74] the defendant hired a dumb barge from the plaintiff. The defendant moored the

---

68 Goods Act 1951 (PNG), s 54(2).
69 *Akzo Chemite v Patel & Co* [1979] 25 FLR 6.
70 [1955] Ch 177.
71 [1957] 2 QB 117.
72 *Hooper v Oates* [2014] Ch 287.
73 [1949] 2 KB 528.
74 [1971] PNGLR 65.

barge in the wrong place and it was wrecked. It was held that the plaintiff was entitled to the market value of the barge and to the loss of profit for hire. The court stated that:

> if it appears on the facts that there was a reasonable likelihood or probability that the barge could have been hired after the date of loss then the measure of damages must be taken to include, in addition to the market value of the barge, such loss of hire as was reasonable in the circumstances.

Profits may also be lost in contracts for services. For example, if a builder agreed to build a house for $100,000, which would cost $80,000 to build, the builder would be entitled to recover the amount expected to be gained by performance, that is $20,000, if the other party breached the contract prior to the commencement of building.

Loss of profits may also be recovered in other circumstances, as for example where an agency agreement is wrongfully terminated.[75]

In calculating loss of profits, the expenses incurred in earning the profits must be deducted from the assessed income.[76] The innocent party is not allowed to obtain a share of any profit made by the guilty party through the breach.

3.5.1.2. Cost of Cure

In some circumstances, it may be possible to recover the cost of repairs or restoration. This is the usual way of measuring loss caused by defective or incomplete workmanship. In such cases, the only way that the plaintiff's expectation can be achieved is to have the work put right or completed.[77]

This appears to have been accepted as a proper measure of damages in Samoa. In *Iofi Faafouina Rev v Keil (Bolko)*,[78] the defendant contracted to build a house for the plaintiff. The work done was substandard, and when the plaintiff's representative complained about this, the defendant refused to complete the job. The plaintiff claimed for the difference between WS$22,456 and WS$13,702, which was all that he could account for, and was made up of materials paid for, labour, expenses and a profit margin. This amount was awarded, plus the cost of reinstating the substandard work done. Bremner J pointed out that one would have expected the plaintiff to claim for all expenses incurred in building the

---

75 *Taubmans Paints (Fiji) Ltd v Faletau* [1999] TOSC 2.

76 *Singh v Letama Trading Company* (1987) 33 FLR 158. The Court of Appeal deducted the purchase price of the timber to be resold and the cost of felling and exporting and freight, but allowed the cost of drawing up the contract of purchase. As this was an expense which would have been incurred in earning the profit, this would seem to be erroneous.

77 *Mertens v Home Freeholds Co* [1921] 2 KB 526.

78 [1980–93] WSLR 160.

house, over and above US$50,000. In other words, had the plaintiff claimed costs of cure, the court would have awarded it.

Whilst the preference of the innocent party was relevant, it was not the only factor. The plaintiff will be entitled to insist on cost of cure if it is reasonable to insist on that course. An example of this can be seen in *Ruxley Electronics & Construction Ltd v Forsyth.*[79] There, the defendant employed the plaintiff to build a swimming pool with a maximum depth of 7'6". The finished pool was only 6' deep at the point where people dived in. The only way to remedy the defect was to rebuild, which would have cost £21,650. At first instance it was found that, as the pool was safe for diving as constructed, there was no difference in value between the pool as specified in the contract, and the pool as constructed. £2,500 was awarded for loss of amenity. On appeal, the Court of Appeal awarded the full costs of rebuilding. However, the House of Lords held, unanimously, that damages were not recoverable on a cost of cure basis in these circumstances. Such costs would only be available 'if it is reasonable for the plaintiff to insist on that course'.

3.5.2. *Reliance Loss*

The alternative method of assessing damages is to consider reliance loss. This method is applied in circumstances where calculation of damages by the expectation loss method does not accurately reflect the loss of the plaintiff. It entails claiming reimbursement for money spent by the innocent party in reliance on the promise of the other party, for example money spent investigating title by the purchaser of land. In other words, it is a claim for wasted expenditure, being expenses incurred in reliance on the contract. The object of damages based on reliance loss is to put the innocent party back into the pre-contract position.

As a general rule, damages are recoverable on this basis only where:

- there is no way of quantifying expectation loss; or
- no profit will be made on the contract.

An award of damages calculated on the basis of reliance loss was made in *Anglia Television Ltd v Reed.*[80] The defendant, an actor, contracted with the plaintiffs to play the leading male role in a television play, from 9 September to 11 October. On 3 September, he repudiated. The plaintiffs could not get a substitute and abandoned the production. The defendant argued that the plaintiffs could recover only the expenditure incurred after they made the contract (£854). The Court of Appeal held that since the plaintiffs had elected to claim reliance loss,

[79] [1995] 3 All ER 268.
[80] [1972] 1 QB 60.

they could recover all their wasted expenditure, including pre-contract expenses, provided this was not too remote. The court awarded £2,750.

3.5.3. *Where Damages are Difficult to Assess*

The fact that damages are difficult to assess is no reason for not awarding them. This point is illustrated by *Vaioleti v Cross*.[81] In that case the Board advertised a prize draw for employees. Only those who were not late or absent from work during a specified period were qualified to enter. The prize draw was cancelled by the Board, because it considered that none of its employees qualified. The plaintiff brought proceedings to compel the Board to hold the prize draw, or for damages. It was held that the plaintiff qualified to be included in the draw. Specific performance not being appropriate in the circumstances, it was held that damages had to be calculated on the basis of her chance of winning a prize in the draw.

In *Nair v Public Trustee of Fiji*,[82] discussed in chapter 15, Lyons J was faced with a difficult case in which to assess damages. The approach he took was to make a 'global award'.

There is a difference between difficulty in assessing damages in principle and lack of evidence. In *HP Kasabia Brothers Ltd v Reddy Construction Ltd*,[83] it was suggested that there may be cases where the court will be justified in allowing no damages, on the basis that lack of proof would involve making a 'shot in the dark'. In other cases, the court held that it would do its best on the material before it, allowing wide margins in favour of the party against whom damages were being awarded, to ensure that the party did not suffer by reason of the lack of evidence. In *Nickel v Ah Vui*,[84] as there was no evidence of loss, the court awarded nominal damages.

3.5.4. *Non-Pecuniary Loss*

At one time it was thought that only damages for pecuniary loss could be awarded in contract. Although reluctant to award damages for non-pecuniary loss, the courts have been prepared to make an award in a limited range of cases. Damages may now be recoverable for:

- substantial physical inconvenience or discomfort;[85]
- mental distress, for example injured feelings or disappointment.

---

81 [1990] Tonga LR 108; see also *Chaplin v Hicks* [1911] 2 KB 786.
82 Unreported, High Court, Fiji, Lyons J, 8 March 1996, 36.
83 (1977) 23 FLR 235.
84 [2000] WSSC 37.
85 *Hobbs v London & South Western Railway Company* (1875) LR 10 QB 111.

Traditionally, damages were not recoverable under the second head. However, this rule has gradually been eroded. The first sign of this was in cases where the main object of the contract was provision of comfort, pleasure or relief from discomfort. An obvious example is a contract for a holiday. This was the case in *Jarvis v Swans Tours Ltd*,[86] where the plaintiff booked a winter holiday which the defendant promised in their brochure would be like a 'houseparty', with special entertainment and proper facilities for skiing. The skiing facilities were in fact inadequate, the entertainment far from special, and in the second week the plaintiff was there alone. The Court of Appeal held that the plaintiff was entitled to recover not only the cost of the holiday, but also general damages for disappointment suffered.

In *Jackson v Horizon Holidays*,[87] the court went even further than this and allowed the plaintiff to recover not only for his own discomfort and distress, but also for that of his wife and children, when his holiday was ruined by reason of the breach.[88]

A less obvious example of a contract with the main purpose of providing pleasure is provided by *Ruxley Electronics and Construction Ltd v Forsyth*,[89] discussed above, where the House of Lords awarded the plaintiff £2,500 for loss of pleasure when the defendant failed to build his swimming pool to the agreed depth.

Jarvis and *Jackson* were cited with approval in *Harding v Teperoi Timbers*,[90] where the National Court of Papua New Guinea allowed recovery for non-pecuniary loss in relation to a contract of employment. In that case, the plaintiff's employment contract was wrongfully terminated by the defendant. The plaintiff's claim for general damages included an item for 'distress, loss of reputation and embarrassment'. The court allowed a sum under this head on the basis that:

> in employment contracts there cannot be any doubt that it is in the contemplation of the parties that if the employee is dismissed in breach of contract it is foreseeable that the effect would be to cause him/her to suffer some degree of mental distress, frustration or upset.

This approach to employment contracts has also been taken in Tonga. In *Helu v Koloa*,[91] the Court of Appeal upheld the decision of the Supreme Court awarding

86 [1973] QB 233.
87 [1975] 3 All ER 92. See also *Peninsular and Oriental Steam Navigation Co v Yowell* [1997] Times LR 184.
88 It should be noted that the rules of privity should have applied to prevent damages being recovered on behalf of others. See further chapter 8.
89 1995] 3 All ER 268.
90 [1988] PNGLR 128.
91 [2000] Tonga LR 299.

damages to the defendant for humiliation and distress suffered as a result of his dismissal. It has also found favour in Vanuatu. In *Tari v Republic of Vanuatu*,[92] the plaintiff was engaged by the Ministry of Internal Affairs as a consultant/ senior manager for a company He was abruptly dismissed, apparently over questions of managerial control in a project, and he sued for outstanding wages, severance allowance and common law damages. The court acknowledged that it was 'not just the dismissal and the financial difficulties that this caused but the damage he also suffered to his reputation' with government departments. The plaintiff was unable to find work after dismissal, which had a continuing financial effect on him and his family. The court awarded damages for hurt, humiliation and distress. Similarly, in *Melcoffee Sawmill Ltd v George*,[93] where an employee was abused and sworn at before being sacked on the spot, the Court of Appeal awarded damages for emotional pain and distress arising out of the manner of termination, which the court categorised as 'peremptory, insulting, harsh and overbearing'. More recently, the Vanuatu Supreme Court awarded damages for 'the unnecessary humiliation and suffering caused to the claimant by the manner of his dismissal', after the employee was dismissed without notice by a letter hand-delivered outside office hours in front of his friends.[94]

The Tuvalu High Court has also indicated, obiter, that it might be prepared to allow damages for injury to reputation arising out of breach of contract of employment. In *Paeniu v Tuvalu National Council of Women*,[95] the plaintiff claimed damages when her employer was unable to pay her and she was forced to resign. Whilst the court refused to allow an amount for the adverse effect on the plaintiff's reputation, it appears that the reason for this was lack of proof. Ward CJ stated:

> I appreciate that, in a society as small and close as Funafuti, inaccurate rumours arise frequently and may have a very profound effect but, without evidence of any such rumour and of its effect, this ground cannot succeed and it is refused.

However, these cases can be contrasted with the Samoan case of *Tovio v SV Mackenzie & Co Ltd*,[96] where the plaintiff claimed for wrongful dismissal after he had been summarily dismissed by the defendant. The plaintiff's claim was dismissed and the court stated that damages are not 'available to compensate an employee for distress, anxiety or injured feelings resulting from the dismissal'.[97] Similarly, in the Tongan case of *Leiola Group Ltd v Moengangongo*,[98] it was held

92 [2012] VUSC 23.
93 [2003] VUCA 24.
94 *Mann v Air Vanuatu Ltd* [2010] VUSC 168.
95 [2005] TVHC 11.
96 [2004] WSSC 22.
97 Cf. *Maimoaga v Vaai* [1988] WSSC 1.
98 [2010] TOCA 10.

that the plaintiff was not entitled to damages for loss of reputation and hardship, because this would have amounted to double compensation as she was already receiving damages for loss of the income she would have earned if she had not been dismissed. These cases are in line with the earlier English authority of *Addis v Gramophone Co Ltd*,[99] where the defendant was dismissed in a particularly abrupt way, but damages for non-pecuniary loss were not allowed.

In wrongful dismissal cases, damages are not available for difficulty in obtaining new employment or loss of career prospects.[100]

Non-pecuniary damages have also been refused in other types of claim. In *Lapon v Dobel Farming & Trading Pty Ltd*,[101] the plaintiff hired his truck to the defendant. The defendant made no payments for a whole year and the plaintiff sued for breach of contract. The plaintiff's claim included compensation for frustration. The court allowed the claim for the hire fees owing, but refused to award any amount for frustration, noting Kidu CJ's remark in *Harding v Teperoi Timbers*[102] that 'it is not for every breach of contract that damages can be recovered for mental distress' and that this case was a 'purely business arrangement for the hire of a truck'. However, in *Nickel v Ah Vui*,[103] the court's acknowledgment that the plaintiff suffered inconvenience, anger and disappointment when the defendant failed to repair his vehicle on time suggests that it might have been prepared to make an award under this head. However, as no claim had been made under this head, the court did not need to decide the point.

A regional example of a broad approach to non-pecuniary loss can be found in *Areta v Kiribati Housing Corporation*.[104] The plaintiff was a government employee who rented a house from the defendant on a three-year lease. Rent was deducted from her salary. She and her family went abroad for the purpose of her studies. The plaintiff's relatives occupied the house for some of the time she was away and, after they moved out, they visited the house from time to time check on it. One of the defendant's property officers found the house unoccupied, with some damage to the front and back door. Consequently, the plaintiff's possessions were all removed and the house was let to another tenant. The plaintiff sued for breach of the tenancy agreement. The court found in favour of the plaintiff and awarded damages under several heads, including damages for 'loss, upset and inconvenience' because the family was split up when the plaintiff's husband had to go back to Tarawa to find alternative accommodation.

---

99 [1909] AC 488.

100 *Banque Indosuez Vanuatu Ltd v Ferrieux* (1989–94) 2 Van LR 490, 496.

101 [1992] PNGLR 215.

102 [1988] PNGLR 128.

103 [2000] WSSC 37.

104 [2008] KIHC 6. See also *Compass Rose Enterprises v Iuta* (unreported, High Court, Kiribati, 14 May 1982), where the court stated, obiter, that damages for mental distress might be awarded under the head of general damages in a contract for the sale of company assets.

Further exceptions have been made within the region. For example, in *Beti v Aufiu*,[105] the High Court of Solomon Islands awarded damages for frustration and disappointment after breach of a contract for sale of a residence. Similarly, in *Sofield v Ali*,[106] whilst acknowledging that non-pecuniary losses were generally not recoverable, the Fiji High Court held that, 'in some circumstances a modest sum may be awarded for disappointment suffered through not receiving the promised performance'. In that case, the vendor of real property who had resold the property for the same price after the purchaser refused to complete the transaction was awarded a small sum on this basis.

3.6. MITIGATION

3.6.1. *The General Principle*

The general rule is that plaintiffs must mitigate their loss.[107] Plaintiffs are not entitled to claim for loss which they could have avoided by taking reasonable steps.[108] The onus of proving that the plaintiff has acted unreasonably is on the defendant.[109]

Reasonableness is a question of fact, and will depend on the individual circumstances of the case. For example, in a claim for wrongful dismissal, dismissed employees must take reasonable steps to minimise their loss by seeking and accepting any reasonable offer of alternative employment.[110]

3.6.2. *Limitations on the Mitigation Principle*

A plaintiff is not required to resort to steps that are costly or extravagant, but need only take those steps that are reasonable to mitigate the loss suffered. For example, in *Pilkington v Wood*,[111] the plaintiff instructed the defendant solicitor to act for him in the purchase of a house. The defendant negligently advised that the vendor's title was good, while, in fact, the vendor held as a trustee. The

105 [1991] SBHC 1. See further K. Shah, 'Case Note on *Donley Beti v Peter Aufiu*' (2001) 5 *Journal of South Pacific Law*.

106 [2017] FJHC 406.

107 *Kaiea v Attorney-General iro Ministry of Linnix* [2005] KIHC 72.

108 *HP Kasabia Brothers Ltd v Reddy Construction Ltd* (1977) 23 FLR 235, 244.

109 Ibid. See also *Cox v Fielder Industries (SI) Ltd* [1990] SBHC 121. But see *Primary Produce Exports Ltd v Titali'ahio* [1999] TOSC 9, where Finnegan J took into account the plaintiff's failure to explain why it had done nothing to mitigate its loss in finding that it had not discharged the burden of proof upon it. To this extent, it is respectfully suggested that the decision is wrong.

110 *Cox v Fielder Industries (SI) Ltd* [1990] SBHC 121.

111 [1953] Ch 770.

defendant argued that the plaintiff should have mitigated his loss by bringing proceedings against the vendor for having conveyed a defective title. It was held that there was no duty to embark on a complicated and difficult piece of litigation in order to protect the defendant from the consequences of his own carelessness.

The duty to mitigate does not apply unless the plaintiff's claim is for damages, as distinct from an action for a debt or liquidated sum. An example of this is *White and Carter (Councils) Ltd v McGregor*.[112] In that case, the defendant entered into a contract with the plaintiff whereby the latter would display adverts for the defendant's business on litter bins for three years. The defendant requested the cancellation of the agreement on the grounds that an employee had made a mistake in agreeing to this. The plaintiffs refused to discharge the contract and went on to display the advertisements for 156 weeks, and claimed the contract price. It was held that there was no obligation to mitigate loss, as it was an action for an agreed sum. The plaintiffs were entitled to the contract price. They were not compelled to accept the repudiation and sue for lost profit as damages.

If the defendant's conduct prevents the plaintiff from mitigating the loss, then the defendant cannot complain.[113]

3.7. DATE OF ASSESSMENT OF DAMAGES

Generally, damages will be assessed at the time of the breach, which will usually be when the time for performance is due. For example, the time for assessing the buyer's damages for the seller's non-delivery of the goods is the time when the goods ought to be delivered. The application of the market price rule will involve finding out the cost to buy replacement goods on that day. This rule is given statutory force in countries where sale of goods legislation applies. For example, s 51(3) of the Sale of Goods Act (Fiji)[114] provides that where there is an available market damages are calculated by finding the difference between the contract price and the market price at the 'time or times when they ought to have delivered or, if no time was fixed, then at the time of the refusal to deliver'. The Contract Rules of Tokelau refer to the 'current price at the time of avoidance'.[115]

In cases where there is no specific date for performance, the court may fix a date by reference to the events which occurred. Thus, in *Singh v Letama Trading Company*,[116] where the defendant wrongfully repudiated a contract allowing the

112 [1962] AC 413.
113 See *Nair v Public Trustee of Fiji* (unreported, High Court, Fiji, Lyons J, 8 March 1996), 35, 37.
114 Cap 230. See also e.g. Sale of Goods Act 23 MIRC 1 (Marshall Islands), s 51(3); Sale of Goods Act 1975 (Samoa).
115 Contract Rules 2004 (Tokelau), R 84(2).
116 (1987) 33 FLR 158.

plaintiff to fell and purchase sandalwood, the market price was fixed at the date of issue of a licence to fell and remove the trees.

In contracts for building work, the time for the assessment of damages has been held to be the time when the plaintiff first became aware that the defendant did not intend to proceed with the work.[117]

3.8. AGREED DAMAGES CLAUSES

The parties may agree on the sum to be payable in the event of a breach. If this sum is a genuine pre-estimate of loss, it will be accepted by the court and awarded as 'liquidated damages'. It will not be accepted by the court if it amounts to a penalty (an amount fixed at random to prevent or penalise a breach). In *National Capital District Commission v Yama Security Services Ltd*,[118] the Supreme Court focused on construction of the clause and whether its principal purpose was compensatory or deterrent.

If it is a genuine pre-estimate, and thus enforceable, it can be recovered without being proved. If it is a penalty, the injured party can recover only the actual loss, which must be proved in the normal way.

Whether a clause is a liquidated damages clause or a penalty clause depends on the intention of the parties. The express intention in the contract is not conclusive, but it will fix the burden of proof.

In *Dunlop Pneumatic Tyre Co Ltd v New Garage Ltd*,[119] the court provided the following rules for guidance in determining where a clause amounts to a penalty:

1. If the stipulated sum is excessive as compared with the greatest possible loss from a breach, it will be a penalty.[120]
2. If the breach is failure to pay money, and the stipulated sum is a greater amount, it will be a penalty.
3. If the sum is payable on the occurrence of one of a list of events, which would have varying amounts of loss, some serious, some trifling, it will be presumed to be a penalty.
4. It is no obstacle to the stipulated sum being liquidated damages that the consequences of a breach are such as to make precise estimation of damage impossible.[121]

---

117 *HP Kasabia Brothers Ltd v Reddy Construction Ltd* (1977) 23 FLR 235, 260.
118 [2017] PGSC 34.
119 [1915] AC 79.
120 See e.g. *Burgess & Others v Prasad* (1974) 20 FLR 49, 53.
121 Ibid., 86, 87.

This case has been cited with approval in the region in cases including *Tozaka v Hata Enterprises Ltd*[122] and *National Capital District Commission v Yama Security Services Ltd.*[123]

A party is not entitled to assessed damages in addition to liquidated damages.[124]

4. SPECIFIC PERFORMANCE AND INJUNCTIONS

4.1. INTRODUCTION

Where a contract contains a promise to do a specified act, it may sometimes be enforced by an order for specific performance. A promise not to do an act may be enforced by an injunction. These are both equitable remedies and are therefore discretionary. They will not normally be granted if hardship would be caused to the defendant or if the common law remedy of damages is adequate in the circumstances.[125]

4.2. SPECIFIC PERFORMANCE

Specific performance is an order of the court requiring the party in breach to perform his primary obligations under the contract. It cannot assist in perfecting an otherwise incomplete agreement. As stated by Connolly P in *Solomon Islands Housing Authority v Onio*:[126]

> the remedy of specific performance exists to enforce a contract made between the parties. It is not a remedy in which the Court is free to invent a contract or to vary the terms of the contract of the parties in order to do what it thinks to be just.

However, the mere fact that there are formalities to be completed will not prevent the court from awarding specific performance.[127] In relation to the sale of goods, the remedy has been put in statutory form. For example, s 52 of the Sale of Goods Acts of Fiji, Marshall Islands, Papua New Guinea, Samoa and the

---

122 [1999] SBHC 123.

123 [2017] PGSC 34.

124 *Tozaka v Hata Enterprises Ltd* [1999] SBHC 123.

125 *Port Workers & Seafarers Union of Fiji v Ports Terminal Ltd* [1998] FJHC 210.

126 [1989] SBCA 1.

127 *Daba Hisiuna v Turner and Davey Electrical* [1974] PNGLR 164.

United Kingdom[128] gives the court discretion to order specific performance in any action for breach of contract to deliver specific or ascertained goods.[129]

In *Lee v Mitlal*,[130] Marsack VP said:

> [b]efore specific performance of any contract will be granted by the courts it is necessary ... that the agreement must be certain, fair and just in all its parts. If any of those ingredients were wanting the court would not decree specific performance.

A party will also lose the right to claim specific performance if there is a delay in applying for it. This was the case in *Vaioleti v Cross*,[131] where 18 months had elapsed since the scheduled date of a prize draw, which the plaintiff was claiming the defendant should be ordered to hold.

4.3. INJUNCTIONS

In applying for an injunction, a plaintiff is seeking to prevent the defendant from breaching a negative stipulation in a contract. For example, application may be made to prevent a defendant from breaching a restraint of trade stipulation.

4.4. RESTRICTIONS ON THE RIGHT TO SPECIFIC PERFORMANCE AND INJUNCTIONS

Although specific performance and injunctions are completely separate remedies, they have several things in common, due to the fact that they both originate in equity. Both remedies are subject to the following constraints.

4.4.1. Damages an Adequate Remedy

If damages are an adequate remedy, neither specific performance nor an injunction is available. Accordingly, these remedies will not usually be available in contracts for the payment of money. However, there are certain cases where equity's assistance will be required. A good example is *Beswick v Beswick*.[132] In that case, Peter Beswick ran a coal merchant's business. When he retired, he transferred the business to his nephew, the defendant, in return for a promise by

---

128 Sale of Goods Act Cap 230 (Fiji); Sale of Goods Act 23 MIRC 1 (Marshall Islands); Goods Act 1951 (PNG); Sale of Goods Act 1975 (Samoa); Sale of Goods Act 1979 (UK).

129 That is, goods identified and agreed upon at the time of contracting or subsequently.

130 (1966) 12 FLR 4.

131 [1990] Tonga LR 108.

132 [1968] AC 58.

the defendant to employ him as a 'consultant' during his lifetime and after his death to pay an annuity of £5 per week to his widow. On Peter Beswick's death, the defendant failed to pay the widow. She brought an action against him in her personal capacity as the person entitled to benefit under the contract and also in her capacity as administratrix of her deceased husband's estate. It was held that the plaintiff could not succeed in her own right, as she was not a party to the contract, but she could succeed as administratrix. The estate could not recover substantial damages as it was the widow who had suffered loss, not the estate. However, the estate was entitled to specific performance of the contract, as damages were an inadequate remedy.

Damages will not be an adequate remedy where the subject matter of the contract is unique, and this includes all contracts for the sale of land. For example, in *Kumar v Nasinu Land Company Ltd*,[133] the court ordered specific performance of a contract for the sale of land which had been paid for by instalments over a number of years.[134] Another example is *Shankar v Suva City Council*,[135] where the defendant entered into a contract with Suva Bowling Club to sub-lease to it some of the land for a term of 80 years. Later the defendant decided not to proceed with the sub-lease, and said it would prefer to pay damages, as it wanted to use the land itself. The Supreme Court of Fiji held that a contract to sell or lease land was the type of contract in which an order for specific performance was normally granted if a party failed to proceed, because damages were not an adequate remedy. This was especially so in this case, because the Club did not have enough greens to cater for its existing members, and it was likely that membership would increase in the future and still more greens would be required. In this case, damages were an inadequate remedy. Accordingly, an order for specific performance was made directing the defendant to prepare and sign a sub-lease of the land, as it had agreed to do.

Other examples are *Maeaniani v Saemala*[136] from Solomon Islands and *Leahy v Otri*[137] from Papua New Guinea. In both cases, the plaintiff obtained an order for specific performance of a contract to purchase the defendant's land.

In most sale of goods contracts, damages will be an adequate remedy, as replacement goods can be purchased. However, if the contract is for a unique item such as an antique, then specific performance may be available.

4.4.2. *Supervision*

Specific performance will not normally be ordered where the contract extends over a period of time, because of the difficulty of supervising the contract.

133 [2016] FJHC 318.
134 See also *Vision Properties Ltd v Northern Projects Fiji Ltd* [2011] FJHC 204.
135 (1982) 28 FLR 148.
136 [1982] SILR 70.
137 [2009] PGNC 314.

For example, in the English case of *Ryan v Mutual Tontine Westminster Chambers*,[138] the lessor of flats contracted to provide a porter to be in constant attendance. In fact, he employed a chef as porter, and the chef was away for several hours a day, during which time his duties were performed by a variety of other persons. A tenant sued for specific performance. It was held that this was not a suitable case for an order of specific performance as the court could not oversee compliance. The court awarded damages instead.

4.4.3. Contracts for Personal Services

Generally, a court will not order specific performance of a contract requiring personal services. This restriction could be regarded as a specific example of the courts' reluctance to order specific performance of a contract which would requires supervision. The courts' reluctance also stems from the fact of the personal relationship between the parties. Accordingly, it is not an appropriate remedy for unfair dismissal. In *Keil v Polynesian Airlines Ltd*,[139] the plaintiff's contract of employment was terminated by the defendant by notice, giving two months salary in lieu of notice. The plaintiff's claim for specific performance and what was taken by the court to be an alternative claim for damages was dismissed on the basis that the termination was within the express terms of the contract. The court also took the opportunity to make some general observations. Bathgate J said:

> The Court will not decree specific performance of contracts of personal services even though there may be a wrongful termination by the employer. ... The reason for this is that the Court cannot practically supervise the terms of a personal contract or require, effectively, the personal relationship of an employer and an employee to continue when one of the parties is clear that it does not wish to continue with the personal relationship.

Where there is a negative stipulation in the contract, for example whereby one party must render exclusive services to the other and promises not to work for anyone else, the court will not grant an injunction to restrain the breach of the latter promise if it would have the same effect as specific performance and compel the person to work for another. For example, in *Page One Records Ltd v Britton*,[140] the plaintiff was the manager of a band called 'the Troggs'. The management contract stated that the Troggs would not engage 'any other person firm or corporation as [their] managers or agents or act themselves in such capacity'. The plaintiffs sought an injunction to restrain them from engaging new managers. It was held that such an injunction would be tantamount to an order

138 [1893] 1 Ch 116.
139 [1980–93] WSLR 222.
140 [1967] 3 All ER 822.

of specific performance, as the band could not continue to operate successfully without a manager. Accordingly, this relief was denied.

In Vanuatu, it has been held that there is an exception to this rule. The principles do not prevent the granting of an injunction to prevent the removal of a managing director in contravention of his contract of employment, if there is no evidence that this removal has the support of the majority of shareholders.[141]

Further, equity does not take a rigid approach. If negative obligations may be enforced without compelling the defendant to perform a personal employment contract or enforcing any other contract which cannot be specifically enforced, an injunction may be granted. For example, in *Lumley v Wagner*,[142] the defendant agreed that she would sing at the plaintiff's theatre in London for three months from 1 April and that she would not sing elsewhere during that period. An injunction was granted to prevent her singing elsewhere than at the plaintiff's theatre. An injunction would not have been available to prevent the defendant from working in any capacity elsewhere, as this would have had the same effect as specific performance.

Similarly, in *Warner Bros v Nelson*,[143] the defendant agreed to work exclusively for the plaintiff as an actress for one year. In breach she then accepted a role for another company. The plaintiff sued. An injunction was granted on the basis that the defendant was not being forced to work for the plaintiff; she could work for anyone she liked, provided she did not work as an actress. Branson J summed up the position as follows:

> The conclusion to be drawn from the authorities is that, where a contract of personal services contains negative covenants the enforcement of which will not amount either to a decree of specific performance of the positive covenants of the contract or to the giving of a decree under which the defendant must either remain idle or perform those positive covenants, the court will enforce those negative covenants; but this is subject to a further consideration. An injunction is a discretionary remedy, and the court in granting it may limit it to what the court considers reasonable in al the circumstances of the case.

4.4.4. *Improper Behaviour by the Plaintiff*

The remedies are available only where the plaintiff has not behaved improperly. If the plaintiff's actions are tainted by illegality, then equity will not assist. For example, in *Murray Cockburn v Bilo Ltd*,[144] the Court of Appeal of Fiji set aside a decree of specific performance of lease agreement as the plaintiff had not obtained the statutory consents.

---

141 *Virelala v Air Vanuatu (Operations) Ltd* [1999] VUSC 15.
142 (1852) EWHC J96.
143 [1937] 1 KB 209.
144 Unreported, Court of Appeal, Fiji, 24 November 1984.

Similarly, a plaintiff who has made a false representation, a plaintiff who is not ready willing and able to perform, or a plaintiff who has delayed in bringing action will not be assisted by equity. A regional case example of such delay is *Narayan v Shah.*[145] In 1968, the defendant contracted to purchase the plaintiff's farm. In 1970, the plaintiff told the defendant he did not intend to go ahead with the sale, but it was not until September 1973 that the defendant started court proceedings for an order for specific performance. The Court of Appeal refused to grant specific performance because the defendant had waited too long before starting court proceedings.

In *Nair v Public Trustee of Fiji,*[146] the action had taken many years and it was held that 'due to such delay specific performance would neither be a just nor a suitable remedy'.

4.4.5. *Where Specific Performance is Impossible*

One of the equitable 'maxims' is that 'equity will do nothing in vain'. Accordingly, specific performance and injunctions will not be ordered in circumstances where it would serve no purpose, for example if a third party has acquired rights in property which the defendant had contracted to sell to the plaintiff. This was the position in the Solomon Islands case of *Beti v Aufiu,*[147] where the plaintiff succeeded in an action for breach of contract against the defendant, who had sold the land for a higher price after contracting to sell it to the plaintiff. The High Court was prevented from granting specific performance by the sale to an innocent third party, but awarded damages instead.

Another situation where specific performance will not be possible is where property is sold by a person who is not the owner. The common law rule, expressed in Latin as *nemo dat quod non habet,* is that a person who does not own property or goods does not have the ability to transfer ownership to a third party. This principle has been embodied in sale of goods legislation.[148]

An order for specific performance will also be refused if the terms of the contract are uncertain. A regional example of this is *Sherani v Jagroop.*[149] In that case, the third defendant – the executor of the deceased's will and legatee of one undivided half share of the residuary estate – granted the plaintiff an option to purchase his one undivided half share of all land comprised in a particular

145 (1975) 21 Fiji LR 139.

146 Unreported, High Court, Fiji, Lyons J, 8 March 1996, 34. This case was partly overturned on appeal, but not on this point: *Public Trustee of Fiji v Nair* [1997] FJCA 55.

147 [1991] SBHC 45.

148 Sale of Goods Act Cap 230 (Fiji), s 23(1); Sale of Goods Act 1908 (NZ), s 23(1); Sale of Goods Act 1975 (Samoa), s 22(1); Sale of Goods Act Cap 40.60 (Tuvalu), s 22(1); Sale of Goods Act 1893 (UK), s 21(1), applying in common law cases in Vanuatu (see *ANZ v Marchand* [2001] VUCA 2).

149 (1973) 19 FLR 85.

certificate of title. The court refused to grant specific performance, inter alia on the ground that it was unenforceable for lack of certainty as it was impossible to ascertain and identify the area and nature of the land that the third defendant had purported to lease.

5. RESTITUTION

5.1. INTRODUCTION

Restitution is based on unjust enrichment, which has been received in the region as one of the principles of equity.[150] For example, in *Mariango v Nalau*,[151] the Court of Appeal of Vanuatu said, '[t]he equitable principles that have application to this case including … unjust enrichment … are incorporated into the law of Vanuatu.'[152] Similarly, in *Detabene v Ronphos*,[153] whilst ultimately concluding that there was no evidence of unjust enrichment, the court dismissed the defendants' submission that the doctrine formed no part of English law, and therefore had not been received as part of the law in Nauru.

As the name 'restitution' suggests, the remedy is concerned with restoring. The remedy compels a party to return money, or pay for the benefit of work done, goods supplied, or services rendered, when it would be unjust to allow those benefits to be retained.

In the recent case of *Manohan Aluminium & Glass (Fiji) Ltd v Fong Sun Development Ltd*,[154] the Court of Appeal of Fiji relied on two definitions of unjust enrichment, stating:

> Unjust enrichment has been described as follows:
>
> 'Unjust enrichment arises in a situation in which the defendant is enriched at the expense of the claimant and there is in addition a reason, not being a, manifestation of consent or a wrong, why that enrichment should be given up to the claimant' (Peter Berks, Unjust Enrichment, second ed. 2005).[155]
>
> Unjust enrichment has also been described as follows:
>
> 'The principle of unjust enrichment requires first, that the defendant has been enriched by the receipt of a benefit, secondly that this enrichment is at the expense of the claimant, and that the retention of the enrichment be unjust and finally that there

150 See further chapter 1.
151 [2007] VUCA 15.
152 See further Constitution of Vanuatu 1980, Art. 95(2).
153 [2011] NRSC 9.
154 [2018] FJCA 23, [34]–[43].
155 Ibid., [33].

> is no defence or bar to the claim'. (Chitty on Contracts, Vol 1, para 29-018, Sweet & Maxwell, 2004).[156]

Whilst these remarks were obiter, they were cited with approval in *Kumar v Mani.*[157]

From these definitions it is clear that there are three requirements for a finding of unjust enrichment:

(a) the defendant has been enriched by the receipt of a benefit;
(b) the defendant has been enriched at the expense of the plaintiff; and
(c) it would be unjust to allow the defendant to retain that benefit.[158]

Unjust enrichment differs from other remedies, as it does not depend on there being a breach of contract; in fact it can apply even where the parties are not in a contractual relationship. For this reason, restitution is sometimes known as 'quasi-contract'.[159] This was explained by Lord Wright in the English case of *Fibrosa v Fairbairn*[160] in the following words:

> It is clear that any civilised system of law is bound to provide remedies for what has been called unjust enrichment, that is, to prevent a man from retaining the money of, or some benefit derived from, another which it is against his conscience he should keep. Such remedies in English law are generically different from remedies in contract or in tort, and are now recognised to fall within a third category of the common law which has been called quasi-contract or restitution.

Similarly, in *ANZ Banking Corp Ltd v Ale*,[161] Ryan CJ dismissed the argument that civil disputes must fall into either contract or tort. He referred to the United States approach, which recognises restitution as a legitimate category under which to grant relief irrespective of the origin of the claim. The Chief Justice considered this to be more realistic than the English approach prevailing at that time and expressed the view that, 'the courts in Western Samoa should not be bogged down by academic niceties which have little relevance to real life'.[162]

As the law of restitution exists separately from the law of contract and can be sought as a remedy where no contractual arrangements exist, it is not explored

156 Ibid., [34].
157 [2018] FJHC 973.
158 *ANZ Banking Corp Ltd v Ale* [1980–93] 2 WSLR 468, 469.
159 *Reid v Fiso* [2001] WSCA 4.
160 [1943] AC 32, 61. See also *Moses v MacFerlan* (1760) 97 ER 676, 681 (Lord Mansfield).
161 [1980–93] 2 WSLR 468.
162 Ibid., 469.

in detail here. This section examines only those restitutionary claims that are most relevant to contract law.

5.2. RECOVERY OF MONEY PAID

Money and other benefits received by the defendant from the plaintiff may be recovered under the doctrine of restitution in the following circumstances.

5.2.1. Total Failure of Consideration

The injured party is entitled to recover money paid where there has been a total failure of consideration, that is, the injured party has received no part of the contractual performance. If the failure to perform amounts to breach of contract, restitution may be an alternative to a claim for damages. On the other hand, where the cause of the failure is not the fault of the other party, for example where the contract has been frustrated, restitution will be the only remedy available. Most claims for total failure of consideration will not arise out of a breach.[163]

A case example of a contract where the failure to perform was due to frustration is *Fibrosa v Fairbairn*.[164] In that case, the respondents, an English company, agreed in July 1939 to sell and deliver certain machinery to a Polish company in Gdynia within three or four months. The contract price was £4,800.00, of which £1,600 was payable in advance. Great Britain declared war on Germany on 3 September, and on 23 September the Germans occupied Gdynia. The contract was thereby frustrated. On 7 September, the London agent of the appellant requested the return of £1,000 which had been paid in July to the respondents. The request was refused on the ground that considerable work had already been done on the machinery. The House of Lords held, overruling *Chandler v Webster*,[165] that where there is a total failure of consideration, money paid may be recovered in quasi-contract.

In *Oceania Islands Ltd v Poy Loy Pty Ltd*,[166] the plaintiff and defendant entered into a joint venture arrangement whereby the plaintiff's ship would be used to carry on a fisheries business in Solomon Islands. The plaintiff advanced money to the defendant pursuant to a signed memorandum of agreement, but the joint venture did not go ahead. The court held the memorandum to be too uncertain to constitute a binding contract. The plaintiff sued to recover the money paid and was allowed to recover in quasi-contract.

---

163 See e.g. *Rowland v Divall* [1923] KB 500.

164 [1943] AC 32, 61. See also *Moses v MacFerlan* (1760) 97 ER 676, 681 (Lord Mansfield).

165 [1904] 1 KB 493.

166 [2018] SBHC 26.

5.2.2. *Money Paid under a Mistake of Fact*

Money paid under a mistake of fact may be recovered if the mistake is as to a fact which, if true, would have legally or morally obliged the payer to pay.[167]

A regional case example is *ANZ Banking Corp Ltd v Ale.*[168] In that case, Linda Ale purchased a bank draft for AUD$800 from one of the plaintiff's Australian branches in favour of her father, the defendant. The amount of the draft should have been WST$1,496, but in fact it was made out for WST$17,506. The defendant presented the draft to the Bank of Western Samoa and received WST$17,506, which he spent. In an action by the plaintiff for money had and received, the court dismissed as 'esoteric' the debate as to whether civil claims should be categorised in contract or in tort. Instead the court preferred to concentrate on the simple issue of whether the defendant had been unjustly enriched.[169] Ryan CJ had no doubt that the facts fulfilled the three conditions required for a finding of unjust enrichment, and judgment was entered for the plaintiff for the difference between the amount that the draft should have been made out for and the amount paid to the defendant.

There are three circumstances in which recovery is not possible under this head:

1. where the payer intends or is deemed by law to have intended that the payee should have the money in any event;
2. where the payment is made for good consideration, for example the discharge of a debt from the payer to payee; or
3. where the payee has or is deemed to have changed their position in good faith as a result of the payment.[170]

5.2.3. *Money Paid under a Void Contract*

If the plaintiff pays money under a void contract, the money may be recovered in an action for restitution. Examples are:

- contracts void for mistake, for example where, unknown to the parties, the subject matter of the contract ceased to exist prior to the making of the contract;[171]
- contracts void because they are contrary to public policy;[172] and

---

167 *Aiken v Short* (1856) 1 H&N 210, 215.
168 [1980–93] 2 WSLR 468.
169 See the quotation from this judgment in chapter 1, section 2.1.
170 *Barclays Bank v Simms & Cooke* [1980] QB 677.
171 See further chapter 14.
172 See further chapter 15.

- contracts which are void because they are ultra vires, for example contracts made with a minor.[173]

Restitution is not normally available in respect of void contracts where the invalidity is the result of illegality. In the case of illegality consisting of contravention of a statute, whether or not restitution will be an available remedy depends on the wording of the statute in question.[174] However, the court may order restitution in favour of the person for whose protection the law making the contract illegal has been imposed.[175] The court may also order restitution where the action can be framed without reliance on the contract. For example, in *Sharma v Singh*,[176] the parties entered into a deed whereby the defendant sold a taxi to the plaintiff together with a taxi permit. The Traffic (Taxis and Rental Cars) Regulations 1967 forbade the transfer of a permit. The agreement was held to be illegal and therefore void and the court refused to enforce any part of it. However, the court ordered restitution of the vehicle on the basis of the plaintiff's alternative claim for conversion, as to do otherwise would have left the defendant with the taxi and the purchase price paid for it. A claim for damages for loss of earnings during the period of wrongful possession was not allowed, as the earnings would have been earned from the use of the vehicle as a taxi, which was contrary to law.

In *Sakashita v Concave Investment Ltd*,[177] the High Court of Fiji ordered the return of a deposit paid in respect of a contract for the sale of land which was illegal due to contravention of the Land Sales Act,[178] on the basis that the claim was for 'money had and received' or restitution, rather than a claim on the contract. This decision significantly extends the availability of restitution in the case of illegality, but is unlikely to be followed, as it appears to confuse the claim, which was founded on the illegal contract, with the remedy sought, which was restitution.

A further example can be found in the recent case of *Kumar v Mani*.[179] The plaintiff claimed for the return of money advanced for the purchase of shares in the defendant company. The money was paid but no shares were transferred in return. The transaction was unlawful, because the consent of the Reserve Bank of Fiji had not been obtained, as required by statute, However, the court also held that the second defendant would be unjustly enriched and that the payment

173 See further chapter 11.
174 *Storage & Export Trading Co Ltd v Tu'ipulotu* [1990] Tonga LR 174, citing *Orakpo v Manson Investments* [1977] 3 All ER 1 (HL).
175 Ibid.
176 (1973) 19 FLR 164.
177 [1999] FJHC 3.
178 Cap 137.
179 [2018] FJHC 973.

was made pursuant to an oral contract and the claim could therefore be enforced without reference to the written, illegal contract.

Just as restitution is not normally available where the contract is illegal, in some circumstances, it may be refused if the law renders the contract unenforceable. For example, in *Storage & Export Trading Co Ltd v Tu'ipulotu*,[180] the Supreme Court of Tonga held, obiter, that restitution was not available in respect of a contract for the sale of goods which was unenforceable by virtue of the Contracts Act[181] (since repealed).[182]

5.2.4. *Money Paid to a Third Party*

Money paid by the plaintiff to a third party for the defendant's benefit is recoverable in an action for restitution, provided that the payment was compulsory rather than voluntary.[183]

5.2.5. *Unreasonable Deposits*

A court will not usually intervene to return a deposit to a purchaser.[184] Unlike a part payment in advance, a deposit is regarded as a guarantee of performance by the purchaser. However, where the vendor's conduct is unconscionable, the court may order the return of the deposit.[185] In particular, if the sum paid is a penalty, rather than a deposit, the court may order its return on the basis that it is unjust for the vendor to keep it. It has been held that a deposit in excess of 10% will be regarded as a penalty, unless the vendor can show 'special circumstances'.[186]

The rule that a deposit is not repayable applies to deposits in contracts for the sale of land as well as sale of goods contracts. For example, in *Brown v Bank of Western Samoa*,[187] a clause in a contract for the sale of land provided that if the purchaser defaulted in performance the vendor was entitled to rescind the contract and thereupon the deposits and any instalment payments (up to a maximum of 10% of the purchase price) would be forfeited to the vendor. On default by the purchaser, the vendor enforced this clause and this was upheld by the Supreme Court.

180 [1990] Tonga LR 174.
181 Cap 26.
182 Contracts (Repeal) Act 1990 (Tonga).
183 *Brook's Wharf & Bull Wharf v Goodman* [1937] 1 KB 534.
184 But see *Sakashita v Concave Investment Ltd* [1999] FJHC 3.
185 *Fifita v Bailiff Officers* [1999] TOCA 19.
186 *Workers Trust Bank Ltd v Dojap Ltd* [1993] AC 573.
187 [1980–93] WSLR 174.

5.2.6. *Bars to Recovery of Money Paid*

Restitution cannot normally be awarded in the following circumstances:

- where the payee has changed their position as a result of the payment; or
- where there has been partial performance.

The reason why the courts are reluctant to order restitution where there has been partial performance is that they will not embark on the task of apportioning the value of performance in relation to the money paid.[188] However, there are three exceptions to the rule that restitution cannot be ordered where there has been partial performance.

5.2.6.1. Where Performance is Divisible

As discussed in chapter 18, contracts are presumed to be entire. However, where the presumption is rebutted and the contract is proved to be divisible, restitution may be ordered in respect of payments made for those parts where performance has not been rendered.[189]

5.2.6.2. Return of the Partial Benefit

The return may be voluntary, or by compulsion of law.

5.2.6.3. Sale of Goods

In the case of sale of goods, the courts may be prepared to find that there has been a total failure of consideration, even where the goods have been used by the plaintiff for some time. This is because the essential thing being sold is deemed to be the title to the goods. For example, in *Rowland v Divall*,[190] the plaintiff bought a car from the defendant and used it for several months. He then discovered that the defendant had never had any title to the car, and the plaintiff was compelled to restore it to the true owner. The plaintiff succeeded in an action to recover the full purchase price.

Where the claim is for payment in a contract for services partly performed, there is no bar to a claim for recovery. To the contrary, as demonstrated by the Supreme Court of Papua New Guinea's decision in *Fly River Provincial*

---

188 See *Whincup v Hughes* (1871) LR 6 CP 78, which explains the difficulties that apportionment would involve.

189 *Ebrahim Dawood Ltd v Heath* [1961] 2 Lloyd's Rep 512.

190 [1923] 2 KB 500.

Government v Pioneer Health Services Ltd,[191] the fact that the contract had been partly performed will be a good reason for restitution to be awarded. In that case, the parties entered into a contract for the supply of medical and consultancy services. When sued for arrears of payments, the appellant argued that the contract was void for illegality. The court upheld that claim, but held that the respondent was still entitled to a remedy in restitution under the doctrine of part performance, provided that it could demonstrate that it was an innocent party to the illegal contract.

5.3. RECOVERY FOR SERVICES RENDERED

There are a number of situations in which a party may seek compensation for services rendered which are not recoverable in an action founded in contract. The claim will be in quasi-contract, on the basis of *quantum meruit* ('as much as he has earned'), which is the basis of payment where one party has conferred a benefit on another in circumstances where there is no contractual right to payment. The principle types of cases where such claims may be made are set out below.

5.3.1. Where Work is Accepted

5.3.1.1. Partial Performance

As discussed in chapter 18, a party who only partially performs a contract will not usually be entitled to the contract price. However, if the other party accepts the partial performance, having had an option to reject it, an obligation to pay for the reasonable value of the work done arises on the basis of unjust enrichment.[192] In *Turik v Gubag*,[193] the plaintiff had agreed to act as the defendant's sales agent for the purpose of selling a piece of land in return for 10% commission upon sale. He informed the defendant that he had found a potential buyer and began negotiating. The defendant then began negotiating directly with the buyer and sold him the land. The defendant refused to pay the commission. The court held that there was no enforceable contract, but that the plaintiff could recover on a *quantum meruit* basis in quasi-contract, having fulfilled the three required elements, which were:

- the plaintiff has done something of benefit to the defendant;
- the thing done by the plaintiff relates to an arrangement of some sort (which might but is not necessarily a contract);

191 [2003] PGSC 4.
192 *Christy v Row* (1808) 1 Taunt 300. See also *Baltic Shipping Co v Dillon* (1993) 176 CLR 344.
193 [2013] PGNC 299.

- it would be unjust to allow the defendant to obtain the benefit without some remuneration or reward for the plaintiff.[194]

The requirement of an opportunity to reject partial performance was clearly explained in *Sumpter v Hedges*,[195] where the plaintiff agreed to build two houses and stables for the defendant for a fixed price of £565. He did part of the work to the value of £333 and then abandoned the contract. The defendant completed the buildings himself. The plaintiff was not entitled to recover anything for the work done. Collins LJ said that the defendant had had no option but to accept the building work. The mere taking of the benefit did not raise the inference that the defendant accepted partial performance. He was not bound to keep the building unfinished as in an incomplete state it would be a nuisance to his land. Similarly, in a more recent case, it was said that a defendant 'is not treated by the law as having chosen to accept that which is forced down his throat despite his objections'.[196]

5.3.1.2. Where Agreement is not Reached

If a party does work at the request of another during the course of negotiations and that work is freely accepted, the fact that agreement does not eventuate does not prevent a claim for payment on a *quantum meruit* basis.[197] A regional case example can be found in *Sun Islands Inc v Fewtrell*.[198] In that case, an employment agreement was to commence 'upon final paperworks needed'. As the paperwork was never completed, it was held that the agreement had never commenced. However, the defendant was entitled to recover $2,500 for the value of work done. Another example can be found in *Keboki Business Group (Inc) v State*,[199] where the agreement for the plaintiff to provide sanitary waste and garbage removal services in a provincial area was outside the competency of the defendant and had not been duly executed. It was held that the plaintiff was entitled to be paid on a *quantum meruit* basis for the first three months' services, but not subsequently, as it had been informed by the defendant that it would not receive any further payment.

---

194 Ibid., [14].
195 [1898] 1 QB 673.
196 *Wilusznski v London Borough of Tower Hamlets* [1989] ICR 493.
197 *British Steel Corporation v Cleveland Bridge Engineering Co* [1984] 1 All ER 504.
198 [1991] Tonga LR 8.
199 [1984] PNGLR 281. See also *Ifunaoa v Howell Enterprises Ltd* (unreported, High Court, Solomon Islands, 26 September 1984); *Island Enterprises Ltd v Adamasia Hire Transport* (unreported, High Court, Solomon Islands, 24 September 1984).

5.3.2. *Void or Unenforceable Contracts*

Where a contract turns out to be void or unenforceable, for example due to illegality, the plaintiff may be able to recover on a *quantum meruit* basis. In *Craven-Ellis v Canons Ltd*,[200] the plaintiff was appointed as managing director of a company under an agreement under seal. The company's articles required all directors to obtain certain shares within two months of appointment. In fact, none of the directors had complied with this requirement. It was held that the management contract was void, but the plaintiff was allowed to claim for the work he had done on a *quantum meruit* basis.

The principles in this case have also been applied to the situation where work is done at the other party's request, but a contract does not eventuate, rather than where it is found to be void.[201]

5.3.3. *Frustrated Contracts*

In the case of a frustrated contract, where work is done after the frustrating event occurs, a claim may be made for the value of the work done on a *quantum meruit* basis.[202]

5.3.4. *Where Performance is Prevented by the Defendant*

Where the plaintiff is prevented from performing by the actions of the defendant, a claim for *quantum meruit* may succeed. For example, in *Planche v Colburn*,[203] the plaintiff had agreed to write a book on costume and ancient armour for 'The Juvenile Library', a series published by the defendant. The plaintiff was to receive £100 for this on completion of the book. He wrote part of the book, and then the defendant abandoned the series. There were negotiations for publishing the book as a separate work but these fell through, because the plaintiff felt he had written especially for children, and to publish as an independent work would ruin his reputation. It was held that the original contract had been discharged and the plaintiff was entitled to recover 50 guineas on a *quantum meruit* basis.

A regional example can be found in *Bohn v Vanuatu Maritime Authority*.[204] In that case. the parties entered into a contractual agreement on 31 May 1999 for the salvage of two ships. The total remuneration was agreed to be VT27 million, with half to be paid in advance. The work was to be completed

---

[200] [1936] 2 KB 403.
[201] *William Lacey v Davis* [1957] 1 WLR 932.
[202] *Davis Contractors Ltd v Fareham UDC* [1956] AC 696.
[203] (1831) 131 ER 305.
[204] [2003] VUSC 137.

within 30 days. However, the plaintiff encountered problems finding qualified personnel and equipment and sought an extension, but the defendant failed to reply. The plaintiff continued to work, despite the fact that the defendant behaved in an obstructive manner. Eventually, one vessel was completely salvaged and the other was 90% salvaged. The defendant then terminated the contract on the basis of the plaintiff's failure to comply with the time limit. It was held that '[t]he defendant cannot be allowed to obstruct the plaintiff's ability to complete the final phase of the contract work and then retain half of the moneys provided for by the contract, that would be unjust and unconscionable'. Accordingly, the plaintiff was awarded payment of the work done on a *quantum meruit* basis.

INDEX

ABOUT THE AUTHOR

Professor Jennifer Corrin is Director of Comparative Law in the Centre for Public, International and Comparative Law at the TC Beirne School of Law, The University of Queensland. Before joining the University, Jennifer spent five years at the University of the South Pacific, having joined the Faculty after nine years in her own legal firm in Solomon Islands. Her research focusses on law reform and development in plural legal regimes. Jennifer retains strong links with the profession and is admitted as a legal practitioner in Fiji, Solomon Islands, England and Wales, and Queensland.

www.ingramcontent.com/pod-product-compliance
Ingram Content Group UK Ltd.
Pitfield, Milton Keynes, MK11 3LW, UK
UKHW051919100926
8556IPUK00021B/1255

9 781780 687865